Baseball and
the Blame Game

Baseball and the Blame Game

Scapegoating in the Major Leagues

JOHN BILLHEIMER

McFarland & Company, Inc., Publishers
Jefferson, North Carolina, and London

LIBRARY OF CONGRESS CATALOGUING-IN-PUBLICATION DATA

Billheimer, John W.
Baseball and the blame game : scapegoating in the major leagues /
John Billheimer.
p.   cm.
Includes bibliographical references and index.

ISBN-13: 978-0-7864-2906-6
softcover : 50# alkaline paper ∞

1. Baseball — Unted States — History.   2. Baseball players —
United States — Case studies.   I. Title.
GV863.A1B565   2007   796.3570973 — dc22   2007017160

British Library cataloguing data are available

©2007 John Billheimer. All rights reserved

*No part of this book may be reproduced or transmitted in any form
or by any means, electronic or mechanical, including photocopying
or recording, or by any information storage and retrieval system,
without permission in writing from the publisher.*

On the cover: (top, left to right) Mike Donlin (Library of Congress),
Fred Merkle and Max Flack (National Baseball Hall of Fame Library,
Cooperstown, N.Y.); (background) the crowd streams onto
the field following the September 23, 1908, game at
the Polo Grounds (Brown Brothers)

Manufactured in the United States of America

*McFarland & Company, Inc., Publishers
Box 611, Jefferson, North Carolina 28640
www.mcfarlandpub.com*

For anyone who ever dropped a lazy fly ball,
watched an easy grounder skitter under their glove,
or raged in silence against the inequity of an umpire's
blown call: roughly half the population, I should guess

Acknowledgments

This book could not have been written without the resources and help of the National Baseball Hall of Fame Library, the Society for American Baseball Research, and the Library of Congress. Pat Kelly of the Hall of Fame Library was particularly helpful in guiding me through the thicket of photo rights, and Mark Coggins helped to turn the photographic images into illustrations suitable for publication. In addition, Sheila York applied her copy-editing skills and love of baseball to the task of proofreading the manuscript.

As always, any blame for misstatements or misinterpretation of the research materials rests with the author. In the interest of spreading the blame, however, I wish to acknowledge the contributions of the Wednesday Night Wine Tasting and Literary Advancement Society, whose ranks include

>   Harriotte Aaron   Anne Cheilek
>   Sheila Scobba Banning   Mark Coggins
>   Bob Brownstein   Ann Hillesland

Although the members of this quasi-elite group had signed on to share fellowship and fiction writing, they generously came to grips with my nonfiction accounts of baseball games, even though several had only a nodding acquaintance with the intricacies of the infield fly rule. They set deadlines, shared insights, rooted out excess verbiage, and offered opprobrium. Without them, this book would have been later, longer, and loaded down with jargon.

Courage is grace under pressure. — Ernest Hemingway

Yes, *courage* is a fancy word that gives us all a brace,
And yellow is another term we splash about the place.
But there are things behind the scenes that none of us can see,
An edict from the gods of chance, whoever they may be,
Who set the score — and laugh aloud at our philosophy.
    — Grantland Rice, "It Can Happen This Way"

Table of Contents

Acknowledgments — vii
Preface — 1
Introduction: Disgrace Under Pressure — 3

ONE ♦ He Who Hesitates — 11
  Scapegoat: Johnny Pesky, 1946 Red Sox — 11
    The Legend: Pesky Hesitates — 11
    What Really Happened — 12
  Escaped Goats — 15
    Dick Bartell: Everybody Was Yelling "Home! Home!" — 15
    Why Pesky and Not Bartell? — 17
    Johnny Evers: "Pulled a boner which he usually works on the other fella" — 17
  What's Remembered and What's Forgotten — 20

TWO ♦ Baserunning Gaffes — 21
  Scapegoat: The Merkle Incident — 21
    The Dress Rehearsal — 21
    The Merkle Game — 23
    The Play-off Game — 25
    Afterthoughts — 26
  Escaped Goats — 29
    Eric Byrnes and Miguel Tejada: Three Stooges Baseball — 29
    Babe Ruth's "Only Dumb Play" — 33
    Stand-up Guys — 34

THREE ♦ Muffed Fly Balls — 39
  Scapegoat: Fred Snodgrass and the $30,000 Muff — 39
  Escaped Goats — 42
    Max Flack: The War-Shortened Season — 42
    Bob Meusel and the Heroics of Pete Alexander — 43
    Bobby Tolan and Riverside Stadium's Center-Field Fence — 45
    Hack Wilson: "The Most Spectacular Rally in the History of Sport" — 45
    Willie Davis: The Laurel and Hardy School of Outfielding — 47
  Summing Up — 49

Four ♦ Dropped Foul Pop-Ups — 50
Scapegoat: Hank Gowdy and the $50,000 Muff — 50
Escaped Goats — 52
    The Mathewson-Merkle-Meyers Mix-Up — 52
    Jack Clark's Royal Screw-Up — 54
    Yogi Berra and the Reynolds No-Hitter — 55
    Bob Boone and the Rose Rescue — 56

Five ♦ Botched Grounders — 58
Scapegoats — 58
    Bill Buckner and the Curse of the Bambino — 58
    Roger Peckinpaugh and the Record — 62
Escaped Goats — 65
    Honus Wagner: The Pre-Peckinpaugh Record — 65
    Tony Fernandez and the Curse of Rocky Colavito — 66
    Mike Andrews and Charley O. — 68
    Leon Durham and the Cub Curse — 69
The Role of the Press — 71

Six ♦ Gopher Balls I — 72
Scapegoats — 72
    Ralph Branca and the Shot Heard 'Round the World — 72
    Mitch Williams: The Ditch Mitch Movement — 78
    Donnie Moore: In Memoriam — 80

Seven ♦ Gopher Balls II — 85
Escaped Goats: Two Pitchers Who Shed Goat Horns — 85
    Ralph Terry: Redemption — 85
    Dennis Eckersley and Gimpy Gibby — 89
A Few Who Were Never Crowned — 93
    Bob Lemon and the Long and Short of It — 93
    The Ordeal of Byung-Hyun Kim — 96
    Other Walk-off Home Runs — 98
Keys to the Goat Pen — 99

Eight ♦ Errant Throws — 101
Scapegoat: Zimmerman and the Chase — 101
Escaped Goats — 103
    Buck Herzog, Art Fletcher, and the Series Error Record — 103
    Vern Stephens' Brown-out — 105
    Al Kaline's Near-Perfect Throw — 107
Summing Up — 109

Nine ♦ Weak-Fielding Pitchers — 111
The Bungled Bunt Defense — 111
Designated Fielders?: Escaped Goats — 112
    Bullet Joe Bush's "Whimsical Throw" — 112

Nelson Potter's Double Dip	113
Calvin Schiraldi: One Throw Away	114
Dave Stewart and the Defunct Dynasty	115
Mariano Rivera: No Relief from the Best Reliever Ever	117

TEN ♦ Passed Balls — 119
Scapegoat: Mickey Owen and the Dodger Debacle — 119
Escaped Goats — 123
    Boss Schmidt and the Gathering Darkness — 123
    Jimmie Wilson, the "Almost Goat" — 125
Passed Balls from 1903 to the Present — 126

ELEVEN ♦ Wild Pitches — 129
Scapegoat: Jack Chesbro and His "Revolutionary" Pitch — 129
Escaped Goats — 132
    John Miljus vs. the 1927 Yankees — 132
    Bob Moose and the Bad Bounce — 134
Wild Pitches from 1903 to the Present — 136

TWELVE ♦ Asleep at the Switch — 139
Scapegoat: Ernie Lombardi and the Schnozz's Snooze — 139
Escaped Goats — 142
Jack Lapp and Larry Doyle's Fadeaway Slide — 142
    Art Wilson and the Greatest Game Ever Pitched — 144

THIRTEEN ♦ Misjudgments and Miscommunication — 148
Escaped Goats — 148
    Turkey Mike Donlin: 1908 (the Merkle Game) — 148
    Christy Mathewson and Cy Seymour: 1908 (the Play-off Game) — 149
    Art Fletcher: 1912 (the Snodgrass Game) — 149
    Mark Koenig and Bob Meusel: 1926 (the Meusel Muff) — 150
    Charlie Dressen and Gil Hodges: 1951 (the Shot Heard Round the World) — 151
    Willie Davis and Ron Fairly: 1966 (the Davis Drops) — 151
    Curt Flood: 1968 (Brock's Stand-up Play) — 152
    Marty Barrett and Bob Stanley: 1986 (the Buckner Boot) — 153
Defensive Misplays — 154

FOURTEEN ♦ Managerial Misfires — 155
Scapegoats: Grady Little and Pedro Martinez — 156
Escaped Goats — 157
    Personnel Moves That Backfired — 157
    Defensive Oversights — 162
    Strategic Second-Guessing — 164
Decisions and Outcomes — 167

FIFTEEN ♦ Fan Interference — 169
Historical Perspective — 169
The Primal Urge — 170

Scapegoat: Cub Fan Needs Witness Protection Program — 171
Escaped Goat: Yankee Fan Lends a Hand — 175

SIXTEEN ♦ Blown Calls — 178
Scapegoat: Don Denkinger's Death Threats — 178
Escaped Goats — 180
    Doug Eddings and the Not-Yet-Out Call — 180
    Ken Burkhart's Behind-the-Back Call — 182
    Bill Stewart and the Timed Pickoff — 185
    Art Passarella and the Six-Column Photograph — 186
    Other Calls and Consequences — 187

SEVENTEEN ♦ Errors, Scapegoats, and Escaped Goats — 191
Errors in Season and Series — 191
Characteristics of Scapegoats and Escaped Goats — 193
    Lost Games and/or Lost Championships — 193
    Superstar Immunity — 197
    Late-Inning Prerequisite — 197
    East Coast Press — 198
    Turning Victory into Defeat — 199
    Mental Errors — 199

EPILOGUE ♦ Injustice, Failure, and Redemption — 200
Baseball and Life — 200
Failure and Redemption — 203

Bibliography — 205
Index — 211

Preface

Most baseball fans can tell what links the names of Fred Merkle, Fred Snodgrass, Mickey Owen, Bill Buckner, and Johnny Pesky. It's a pantheon of public failures. One's baserunning gaffe cost his team the pennant. One muffed a fly to help lose a World Series. One dropped a third strike to cost his club a crucial Series game. One botched a grounder that contributed to a World Series loss. One held the ball too long while the winning World Series run crossed the plate.

Even the most rabid fans would be harder put to say what links the names Eric Byrnes, Max Flack, Boss Schmidt, Tony Fernandez, and Dick Bartell. These players made exactly the same misplays as those in the first list, yet their names haven't become permanent benchmarks for failure.

In this book, I try to determine what elements combine to condemn one player to a life sentence while another gets a wrist slap for the same offense. Each chapter reviews the history of players who were marked for life because they failed, or were judged to have failed, on a grand scale, as well as many others who survived similar misplays without earning eternal goat horns. The difference between a lower-case *e* in a forgotten box score and a lifetime of opprobrium can hinge on a number of factors, including timing, geography, reputation, misunderstanding, media bias, and just plain bad luck.

Many of the scapegoats dotting baseball history were largely innocent of the misplays that earned them their horns. Pesky didn't hesitate, Lombardi didn't snooze, and Merkle was just following the custom of the day. Some players, like Fred Snodgrass and Bill Buckner, were saddled with blame that should logically have been shared with several other teammates. Baseball is a team game, and it is rare that a player manages to lose a game, let alone a World Series, all by himself. There is an *e* in *team*.

In an effort to determine why the failures of certain players have achieved legendary status while other equally damaging misplays have been lost in the dusty files of defunct newspapers, I have read the news accounts of the day, reviewed oral histories, and examined baseball statistics to address a number of questions:

- ♦ Are specific errors more likely to occur in the glare of postseason play?
- ♦ Are certain types of players more likely to be branded as scapegoats?
  - hitters vs. pitchers?
  - rookies vs. veterans?
  - superstars vs. journeymen?
  - batters vs. fielders?
- ♦ Are the fans and press in certain cities more likely to demand sacrificial goats than those in other locales? and
- ♦ Are certain types of failure more likely to earn a player lasting opprobrium?

In many cases, a few inches or innings can determine the difference between a scapegoat and an escaped goat. Or it can be a matter of miles and media malice. Would Bill Buckner still be remembered if he hadn't played for Boston? Maybe not, but then he might not have been in the World Series, either.

Introduction: Disgrace Under Pressure

> Maybe Buckner could have missed a ground ball for another team in the World Series, and it wouldn't have mattered as much. But he missed one for the Red Sox in that World Series and in that game. Red Sox fans couldn't forget that.
>   Mike Sowell, *One Pitch Away*

♦ ♦ ♦ ♦

Baseball is the first thing most men fail at. It can happen as early as age eight in Little League with a muffed fly ball or a crucial strike out. Or later, with a failure to make the high school or college team. Even those who excel in high school or college and sign professional contracts are likely to wash out before making the major leagues.

And for those talented few who do make it to the majors, failure is a familiar teammate. It's axiomatic that even the best hitters fail 70 percent of the time. And the pitcher with the best winning percentage since 1900, Whitey Ford, lost 31 percent of his decisions.

For a few big leaguers, failure proved to be more than a temporary teammate. A single misplay at a critical moment branded them with a stigma that lingered long after they left the game, followed them to their graves, and was featured in their funeral notices.

The list of players stigmatized for life by baseball blunders includes "Bonehead" Fred Merkle, whose baserunning gaffe cost the Giants the 1908 pennant; another Giant, Fred Snodgrass, whose dropped fly ball put the tying run on base in the tenth inning of the final game of the 1912 World Series; Ernie "Schnozz" Lombardi, the Cincinnati catcher who appeared to be snoozing at home plate while Joe DiMaggio scored the final run of the 1939 World Series; another catcher, Mickey Owen, who dropped the third strike that allowed Tommy Henrich to reach first base and ultimately cost the Dodgers the fourth game of the 1941 Series; Johnny Pesky of the Red Sox, who allegedly held the ball while Enos Slaughter scored the winning run of the 1946 Series; and the Red Sox's Bill Buckner, who watched Mookie Wilson's grounder roll through his legs as Ray Knight scored the winning run of the sixth game of the 1986 World Series.

Pitchers, too, have been permanently stigmatized, usually for pitches that hitters parked in the bleachers at a crucial time. The Dodgers' Ralph Branca is indelibly marked by the high inside fastball that the Giants' Bobby Thomson turned into the "Shot Heard 'Round the World" in 1951. Irate Philadelphia fans broke the windows in Mitch "Wild Thing" Williams' home after Joe Carter launched Williams' knee-high slider into the seats to cap a come-from-behind Toronto victory in the 1993 World Series. And Donnie Moore shot himself within three years of the day he gave up a go-ahead home run to Dave Henderson of the Red Sox with Moore's Anaheim Angels one strike away from winning the 1986 American League Championship.

Unlike Moore, many of the players branded by fate, a misplay, or a bad pitch came to terms with their failure when their playing days ended. After a nine-year career with the Giants, Fred Snodgrass went on to become a successful banker and rancher and the mayor of Oxnard, California. Yet when he died in 1974, the *New York Times* headline for his obituary read:

Fred Snodgrass, 86, Dead
Ball Player Muffed 1912 Fly

Nearly every player in the history of baseball has muffed a fly, butchered a grounder, or struck out at a crucial moment. Yet relatively few have wound up wearing goat horns to their grave. The name of Max Flack is not nearly so well known as that of Fred Snodgrass. In the final game of the 1918 World Series, Flack dropped a fly ball that allowed the only two Red Sox runs of the game to score and sent his Chicago Cubs down to a 2–1 defeat. Even though Flack's muff was arguably more costly than that of Snodgrass, since it allowed two runs to score while Snodgrass' merely allowed the tying run to reach base, the *New York Times* didn't bother to note Flack's passing with an obituary, let alone chide him for missing an "easy fly."

What elements combine to condemn one player to a life sentence while another gets a wrist-slap for the same offense? What is it that enables one player to survive a misplay with a lower-case *e* in the box score and a single sentence in the next day's newspaper while another makes the same error and becomes a permanent benchmark for failure? How is it that some players are blamed endlessly for mistakes they never made? The answers include timing, fan expectations, mischance, misunderstanding, media bias, reputation, image, and just plain bad luck.

Fred Snodgrass, who was stigmatized when he dropped the fly ball that would have been the first out in the tenth inning of Game Seven of the 1912 World Series. The runner who reached base eventually scored the tying run, and when the Red Sox came from behind to beat the Giants, Snodgrass' error was immortalized as the "$30,000 muff" and headlined his obituary sixty-two years later (Library of Congress, Prints and Photographs Division).

Timing

In baseball as in life, timing is everything. It goes without saying that if you muff a fly ball, bobble a grounder, or drop a third strike in the seventh game of a 162-game season, nobody will remember your gaffe, even if your team finishes one game out of first place. Make the same mistake in the late innings of the seventh and deciding game of the World Series, though, and you can qualify for permanent disgrace.

Timing is a relative matter. It's obvious that it takes a national stage and a crucial game to convene the jury that awards goat horns. It's less obvious, though, that the error must not only be decisive, but must also occur near the end of the game. A key difference between Snodgrass' 1912 error, which has been immortalized, and Flack's in 1918, which has been all but forgotten, is that Snodgrass dropped his fly ball in the tenth inning, while Flack muffed his in the bottom of the third, leaving his Cubs six innings to make up for his misplay. They never came close, managing only five base runners and one run, scored by Flack himself, over that span.

Timing helped to burnish Snodgrass' image as a failure in another way. His error marked the first time that the World Series had been decided by an unearned run. Since that time, unearned runs have accounted for the margin of defeat in the final games of twelve other World Series. These games have branded several other players (i.e., Heinie Zimmerman, Roger Peckinpaugh, Ernie Lombardi) for life, but Snodgrass' dropped fly remains the base reference.

Bobby Thomson's "Shot Heard 'Round the World" provided baseball with another first in 1951. His blast into the left-field stands against the Dodgers marked the first time that a league championship play-off or a World Series had been decided by a home run in the bottom of the ninth inning. Just as Thomson's triumphant leap onto home plate into a mob of happy teammates has achieved a special place in the minds of baseball fans, so the pitcher who gave up this first-time shot, Ralph Branca, has become a poster boy for the lonely walk to the clubhouse while the opponents celebrate. Other pitchers since Branca have given up Series-deciding home runs (notably Ralph Terry in 1960 and Mitch Williams in 1993), but the Brooklyn right-hander remains the benchmark.

The Defense Never Rests

Goat horns aren't made to fit batting helmets. They are reserved for pitchers, fielders, and base runners. Except for the Mighty Casey, the goat of Ernest L. Thayer's poetic fiction, no batter has ever been stigmatized for life because he struck out or popped up at a crucial moment. The first World Series ended with Honus Wagner, arguably the greatest player of that era, striking out. No one suggested he live with the label "Hitless Honus" or "Worthless Wags." In the first hundred World Series since the interleague competition began in 1903, eleven other hitters have struck out to end the final game. The list of victimized batters includes two other Hall of Famers, Goose Goslin and Jackie Robinson, but neither fans nor the media suggested these players carry their failures over to the next season, much less to their graves.

The implicit assumption is that the team in the field will do its job and keep the team at bat from scoring. This is hardly an ill-founded assumption. In the first hundred World Series, only eleven have ended with the team at bat scoring the winning run. The other eighty-nine times, pitching and defense have prevailed, and the teams in the field have held their leads to win the championship. Those few times when the hitting team has come from behind or broken a tie to win the Series have often left a losing pitcher (i.e., Mitch Williams in 1993) or a hapless fielder (i.e., Fred Snodgrass in 1912) vilified for life.

It's more than just the expectation that the defense is likely to prevail that causes fans and sportswriters to stigmatize fielding failures rather than a hitter's untimely outs. Every sandlot player and Little Leaguer has caught a looping fly ball or gobbled up a bouncing grounder. They may even have memories of running catches and back-hand stabs that robbed batters of sure hits. So when a Fred Snodgrass muffs an easy fly or a Bill Buckner watches a grounder bounce between his legs, the fan's internal calculus says, "I could have caught that ball." The thought may never surface, but the belief that they could have made the play is ingrained. On the other hand, fans who haven't played professional baseball can never be sure that they could turn on a big-league fastball or hit a slider on the outside corner. Hitting a ball thrown by a big-league pitcher is one of the toughest jobs in professional sports, and fans and sportswriters tend to cut a little more slack for the batter who fails to connect than they do for the fielder who muffs an easy chance.

Media Spin

The spin the media puts on a story can make or unmake heroes or goats. In the seventh and deciding game of the 1926 World Series, the St. Louis Cardinals scored three unearned runs in the fourth inning that stood up for a 3–2 victory over one of the strongest Yankee teams ever. The first Cardinal run scored when Yankee left fielder Bob Meusel dropped an easy fly with the bases loaded as he tried to position himself to make a strong throw home. Meusel was spared the disdain of the media, however, when the story of the game became the performance of Grover Cleveland Alexander, in the twilight of a Hall of Fame career. After pitching a complete-game win over the Yankees one day earlier in Game Six, Alexander was called on to pitch in relief in the bottom of the seventh inning of Game Seven with the bases loaded, two outs, and Yankee rookie Tony Lazzeri at the plate. Alexander struck out Lazzeri to end the threat and went on to set the Yankees down in the eighth and ninth innings to preserve the win for the Cardinals. The next day's *New York Times* headlined, ALEXANDER AGAIN THE HERO, and other newspapers followed suit, so that the story of "Alexander the Great" overshadowed Meusel's misplay.

The media has proven to be just as adept at awarding goat horns to the undeserving as it has at withholding them from the deserving. Johnny Pesky didn't hold the ball *or* hesitate as Slaughter hustled home; Ernie Lombardi wasn't felled by a home-plate collision, and he wasn't snoozing when DiMaggio scored what turned out to be an inconsequential run; and the Giants' Heinie Zimmerman, who was vilified by the press for not throwing the ball and chasing Eddie Collins across the plate with what turned out to be the decisive run of the 1917 World Series, actually had no one to throw the ball to.

There Is an e in Team

The three examples of misplaced media blame cited above can also serve to illustrate the importance of team play in crucial situations. Pesky had to contend with a lobbed throw from a replacement center fielder, Leon Culberson; a similar late throw from Cincinnati right fielder Ival Goodman, who had kicked around DiMaggio's single, short-hopped Lombardi's protective cup and left him stunned and virtually helpless, since pitcher Bucky Walters had neglected to back up the play; and the Giants' first baseman and pitcher both failed to cover home as Collins jockeyed between Zimmerman and catcher Bill Rariden, leaving Zimmerman no choice but to turn the aborted rundown play into a futile run-after play.

Instances in which a single play or player will lose a game for a team are rare. After Snodgrass muffed a fly to lead off the bottom of the tenth inning in 1912, Christy Mathewson gave up a long smash to center that Snodgrass ran down, a walk, and a double to Tris Speaker that came after Matty himself had misdirected traffic around a foul pop-up that dropped safely but should have ended Speaker's at-bat. After Mickey Owen's passed ball put Tommy Henrich on first base in 1941, Dodger pitcher Hugh Casey gave up a single, a walk, and two doubles that turned a one-run lead over the Yankees into a three-run deficit. For all the attention it has received, Bill Buckner's error came after two Red Sox pitchers had already surrendered a two-run lead and even then didn't cost the Sox the Series—they lost that the next day in the decisive seventh game.

The media has a tendency to single-mindedly single out a convenient scapegoat for what is usually a team failure. Commenting on this in the case of Fred Snodgrass, Bill James wrote in his *Historical Abstract*, "Snodgrass wound up with goat horns, although he had done no more to earn them than a dozen other players; The music simply stopped when he didn't have a chair."

Baseball history is replete with examples of would-be goats who escaped lasting vilification when their teams rebounded to win a key game or the World Series itself. Johnny Evers held the ball while a crucial run scored in the tenth inning of Game Three of the 1914 World Series, but was bailed out when his teammates came from behind to tie the score and win the game later in the twelfth. Diamondback reliever Byung-Hyun Kim gave up game-tying two-run home runs to the Yankees in the ninth inning of two consecutive World Series games in 2001. The Yankees won both games in extra innings to go up three games to two in the Series, but Kim, whom the press labeled "Ralph Branca times two" for his unprecedented breakdowns, was spared eternal goatdom when Arizona rallied to salvage the final two games and win the Series. It's become a maxim of the game that championship teams must play at a high enough level to overcome the ever-threatening bad calls, bloop hits, mental miscues, and botched plays that can sink lesser teams.

Hero Worship

Quick to vilify the errors of everyday players, the media plays as many favorites as your third-grade teacher and often ignores the mistakes of diamond legends. Honus Wagner of Pittsburgh struck out to end the first World Series in 1903. He also made six errors, including two that aided a six-run onslaught in the sixth inning of the fifth game that turned the Series around for Boston. His six errors stood as a Series record until Roger Peckinpaugh of the Senators made eight miscues in the 1925 Series against the Pirates. While Peckinpaugh was saddled with goat horns for his 1925 errors, no one ever suggested that Wagner be branded as a goat for his performance in 1903. For one thing, Wagner played the Series while limping on a badly injured right leg. For another, he was the premier player of that day and is generally recognized to be one of the four or five greatest players of all time.

The player most judge to be the greatest of all time, Babe Ruth, was given a free pass by the media for what baseball historians generally consider a bonehead play, a failed attempt to steal second base that produced the last out of the 1926 World Series. The *New York Times* gave Ruth the benefit of the doubt and characterized the final out as a failed hit-and-run play. Actually, Ruth decided to run on his own in a straight steal attempt. Baseball historians to the contrary, Ruth's gamble wasn't necessarily a bad one. When the gamble failed, however, it took the bats out of the hands of cleanup hitter Bob Meusel and the on-deck hitter, Lou Gehrig. If a lesser player had been thrown out at second to end the Series, it's likely he would have been crucified by the unforgiving New York press.

Whether or not one believes Ruth's gamble was justified, it hardly makes sense to try to hang goat horns on a man who reached base safely in all five of his plate appearances that day, walking four times and homering, and whose performance in the 1926 fall classic set ten new World Series records, including the records for most home runs (4) and most walks (11) in a single Series.

Past performance and reputation also kept the media from awarding goat horns to Yankee reliever Mariano Rivera, who failed to protect a 2–1 lead in the ninth inning of the seventh game of the 2001 World Series. Luis Gonzalez's soft single over a drawn-in infield to win the game for the Arizona Diamondbacks ordinarily wouldn't have been enough to make a goat of Rivera, but the Yankees' stellar reliever had helped to seal his team's doom by misplaying a sacrifice bunt to put the tying and winning runs on second and first with nobody out. The blown save was the first in a World Series game for Rivera, who holds the record for the most saves in Series history.

The Hometown Disadvantage

Hometown reporters have generally been less forgiving and quicker to award instant infamy to players making key errors than writers representing the teams benefiting from those errors. While the *New York Times* was excoriating the Giants' Fred Snodgrass for his "$30,000 muff" ($30,000 being the difference between the winning and losing team's share of Series receipts), the *Boston Globe*, whose Red Sox were the beneficiaries of the muff, was much more magnanimous. In the early days of the century, it was common for big-league stars to have newspaper columns written under their bylines, a forerunner of today's post-game interviews. In his *Globe* column the day after the Snodgrass muff helped the Red Sox win the Series, Sox centerfielder Tris Speaker wrote

> I sympathize with Snodgrass, whose error in the 10th gave Boston its chance. Nine hundred and ninety-nine times out of a thousand, Snodgrass would make the catch, but he failed this time on the easy chance and his error certainly proved costly for his team....
>
> It ought to be remembered, however, that in a previous game, he made an almost impossible catch and saved his team from defeat thereby. That great play is probably forgotten in view of his slip up in this last game.

East Coast Media Malice

List the names of players who have worn goat horns to their graves and a few similarities begin to jump out at you. "Bonehead" Fred Merkle, Fred Snodgrass of the $30,000 muff, Mickey Owen, who dropped Tommy Henrich's third strike, Ralph Branca, who gave up the "Shot Heard 'Round the World," and Heinie Zimmerman, who chased Eddie Collins across home plate in the deciding game of the 1917 World Series, all played for teams representing one of the five boroughs of New York City. Because permanent goatdom requires a national stage in a crucial game, and because the Yankees, Brooklyn Dodgers, New York Giants, and, more recently, the New York Mets have been overrepresented in World Series contests, accounting for 67 of 200 team appearances in the first hundred Series, it is difficult to know whether this predominance of New York players among the ranks of permanent goats reflects the law of averages or a particularly vicious trait of the New York media.

Still, if you add to the New York names Bill Buckner and Johnny Pesky of the Red Sox, Roger Peckinpaugh of the Washington Senators, who set a record for Series errors in 1925, and Mitch Williams of the Phillies, who gave up Joe Carter's walk-off homer in 1993, a geographic pattern of Eastern Seaboard cities emerges. Because modern major league baseball began with half of its teams along the Eastern Seaboard, this still may not mean much. Baseball started expanding westward in 1953, when the Braves left Boston for Milwaukee, and made the big jump to the West Coast in 1958, when the Dodgers and Giants relocated to Los Angeles and San Francisco. Even so, the West Coast and Middle America have contributed relatively few names to baseball's roster of infamy. On the West Coast, only Donnie Moore of the Angels stands out as a tragic scapegoat, while Ernie Lombardi of the Cincinnati Reds is one of the few players to qualify as a heartland anti-hero.

East Coast fans and media simply appear to expect more and be more unforgiving in defeat than fans in the Midwest. It's the flip side of the claim, "If you can make it there, you'll make it anywhere," made in the lyrics of "New York, New York." Whereas teams along the Eastern Seaboard from Washington to Boston have accounted for half of the World Series appearances, they have produced at least three-quarters of the all-time Series goats.

The East Coast press is particularly virulent in its treatment of scapegoats, perhaps because its cities have historically had so many newspapers vying for the attention of readers. In his book *The Curse of the Bambino*, veteran *Boston Globe* reporter Dan Shaughnessy described the situation in Boston as follows:

> Media coverage of the Red Sox is enormous and would certainly border on excessive were it not for the thousands of thirsty fans who want more.... There are simply too many reporters with too many questions, and it's a point of unending distraction and annoyance for the Red Sox ball players.

The need to root out and broadcast blame is not too surprising in an area that gave rise to the Shibe Park boo birds, the House Un-American Activities Committee, and the Salem Witch Trials.

Bill Buckner, who broke the hearts of Red Sox fans when Mookie Wilson's grounder skittered through his legs as the Mets scored the winning run in Game Six of the 1986 World Series. Two Red Sox pitchers had already blown a two-run lead in the bottom of the tenth, but it was Buckner who became the lightning rod for media criticism (National Baseball Hall of Fame Library, Cooperstown, N.Y.)

Coping with Instant Infamy

Some players have coped with their public failure better than others. Fred Snodgrass, of the $30,000 muff, reported in Lawrence Ritter's 1966 book, *The Glory of Their Times*:

> Well, life has been good to me since I left baseball... In contrast, my years in baseball had their ups and downs, their strife and torment. But the years I look back on most fondly, and those I'd most like to live over, are the years when I was playing center field for the New York Giants.

Ralph Branca credited his faith in the Lord with helping him survive the Bobby Thomson home run. In an interview for a TV special in 2003, he said, "I wasn't going to crawl under a rock and stay there... It's just a ball game. I've got nothing to be ashamed of. I'm happy with my life."

Other players branded by the media didn't fare nearly so well as Snodgrass and Branca when they left baseball. Ernie Lombardi tried to commit suicide by slitting his throat with a razor while being taken to a sanitarium to undergo treatments for severe depression. A month after being released by the Kansas City Royals minor-league affiliate in Omaha, Donnie Moore fired five shots at his estranged wife and then shot and killed himself.

Whether or not the players crowned with goat horns learned to cope with their burden, I'm guessing their misplays were never far from their thoughts. Interviewed in 1966, Fred Snodgrass reported that:

> For over half a century I've had to live with the fact that I dropped a ball in a World Series. "Oh you, you're the guy that dropped that fly ball, aren't you?"—and for years and years, whenever I'd be introduced to somebody, they'd start to say something and then stop, you know, afraid of hurting my feelings.

While it's impossible to know what goes on in another's mind, a little personal history, or anecdotal "mother-in-law research," may help provide some insight. The summer after my freshman year in college, I worked with the Corps of Engineers in my hometown of Huntington, West Virginia. I played first base for the Corps team in the local fast-pitch softball league, and we finished the season tied for first place with another team. The one-game play-off to decide the championship occurred over forty years ago, so that I don't remember the name of the opposing team, but I'll never forget the game's last inning.

The game was played after work on one of the few diamonds in the city with overhead lights, and the only fans in attendance were the wives or girlfriends of three or four players. We went into the final inning of the seven-inning game tied 4–4 and failed to score in our turn at bat. In the bottom of the seventh, a leadoff single followed by a double put men on second and third for the opposition with nobody out. Both the third baseman and myself pinched in toward the plate, and when they tried a squeeze bunt I was close enough to home to field the ball, beat the runner to the plate, and start a rundown that left them with one out and runners on first and third and a left-handed hitter at bat.

I held the runner on first base until the pitcher delivered the ball and then took a couple of steps toward home plate. The batter hit an easy bouncer straight at me. I could see the runner heading for the plate and bent to take the high hop and throw home. The ball bounced twice on the ground and then a third time off the tip of my glove and landed at my feet. I picked it up and threw home too late to keep the winning run from scoring.

If I'd fielded the ball cleanly, we had an easy out at home plate. I couldn't tell you, now or then, whether I took my eye off the ball at the last minute, reached out too eagerly to grab it before it arrived, was the victim of a bad hop, or just choked under pressure. I do clearly remember the look of disgust on our catcher's face as he picked up his mask after watching the winning run score. Forty years later, I can't recall the exact location of the diamond or the names of any of my teammates except that catcher, Robby Miller, who had curly blond hair and a broad smudge of mask-deposited dust on his forehead that darkened his glare before he looked away.

My misplay didn't make the local papers, and the fans in the stands were outnumbered by the players on the field, but the details of that play have stuck with me for over forty years. I can't imagine what images must haunt the mind of Bill Buckner, who muffed a ground ball in front of fifty-five thousand screaming fans and millions of TV viewers and whose name is invoked whenever the Red Sox's recently broken string of championship-free seasons is discussed. Or what it must be like for Cleveland's Tony Fernandez, who escaped Buckner-like opprobrium even though he booted an eleventh-inning grounder that helped to cost the Indians the final game of the 1997 Series. Or for dozens of other players, some forgotten, some still vilified, whose errors have cost their teams crucial games.

This book reviews the history of players who were marked for life because they failed, or were judged to fail, on a grand scale, as well as others who survived similar misplays without earning eternal goat horns, and tries to sort through the reasons for the disparate treatment of scapegoats and escaped goats.

CHAPTER ONE

He Who Hesitates

> I'm the goat. It's my fault. I'm to blame ... I had the ball in my hand. I hesitated and gave Slaughter six steps. When I saw him, I couldn't have thrown him out with a .22.
>
> Johnny Pesky, quoted in the *Boston Globe*
> October 16, 1946 — The day after the final game of the 1946 World Series

> But I didn't hesitate. I dropped my hands and to some it looked like I cradled the ball and held it. Really, I was just trying to get ready to throw as I tried to see where the hell he (Slaughter) was. If anything, I might have saved motion, but I'll never convince the baseball world of that.
>
> Johnny Pesky, quoted by Mike Blake
> in his 1994 oral history, *Baseball Chronicles*

♦ ♦ ♦ ♦

Scapegoat: Johnny Pesky's Phantom Pause

The Legend: Pesky Hesitates

The decisive play of the 1946 World Series between the St. Louis Cardinals and the Boston Red Sox is one of the most memorable in Series history. With the score tied 3–3 in the seventh game, Enos "Country" Slaughter opened the home half of the eighth inning for the Cardinals with a single to center. A botched sacrifice attempt and a fly to center field left the Redbirds with two outs, Slaughter still on first, and Harry Walker, who was hitting .375 for the Series and would lead the National League in batting the next year, at the plate.

On a two-and-one count, Slaughter got a good jump on the pitch to Walker, took off for second, and appeared to have the base stolen when Walker lofted the ball safely to left center. With the play in front of him, Slaughter rounded second running hard and headed for third intending to try for home.

The center fielder, Leon Culberson, a late-inning replacement for the injured Dominic DiMaggio, fielded the ball and threw it to the Red Sox shortstop, Johnny Pesky, on the lip of the outfield grass. The legend tells us that Pesky hesitated with his back to the infield, not realizing that Slaughter was thundering around third and tearing for the plate. When he finally became aware of Slaughter's mad dash, the shortstop's hurried throw home pulled the catcher up the third-base line as the hustling Slaughter slid home safely with what proved to be the winning run.

The next day's newspapers and subsequent reports gave different accounts of Pesky's hesitation. Jerry Nason of the *Boston Daily Globe* wrote that Pesky "'froze' momentarily with the ball in his hand." Pesky himself was quoted in the *Globe* as saying, "I hesitated and gave Slaughter six steps." Red Smith of the *New York Herald Tribune* wrote that Pesky "stood morosely studying Ford Frick's signature on the ball.... At length, he turned dreamily, gave a small start of astonishment, and threw in sudden panic."

The Cardinals' Harry Walker claimed that he wanted to stretch his hit into a double to distract Pesky from the play at the plate and cause him to turn to his right for a possible play at second base. Quoted by John B. Holway in *The Ol' Ball Game*, Walker said, "Because I came into second ... that's what made Pesky look. The whole play balanced around that. He probably would have thrown him out if he'd gone the other way."

Years later, a piece in the 1961 *World Series Encyclopedia* embellished the tale by reporting that "Shortstop Johnny Pesky took the relay, wheeled around and, instead of throwing immediately to the plate, began to run toward home, the ball in his hand. When he did throw, it was too late and too wide."

Whether Pesky froze momentarily, counted the ball's stitches, turned toward second, or ran toward home plate, the gist of the legend is clear. The shortstop's hesitation allowed Slaughter's gamble to pay off with the Series-winning run.

What Really Happened

The World Series of 1946 was not televised, and even if it had been there would have been no instant replays to help sort out the action. However, a few black-and-white films survive. One film, shot from the lower stands, shows the play in its entirety. A portion of the play is hard to follow because the outfield was overexposed by sunlight while the infield grass was in shadows, but the key details are there for anyone to see. The film shows Pesky start toward second to cover Slaughter's attempted steal, then turn and run to the lip of the outfield grass as Walker's hit flew into center field. The center fielder Culberson retrieved the ball and looped a throw in to Pesky, who caught it at his waist just after Slaughter rounded third. He then wheeled and threw home.

He didn't hold the ball, turn toward second, study Ford Frick's signature, run toward home, hesitate, or freeze. He wheeled and threw home. "Catch to throw took less than a second," wrote Glen Stout and Richard Johnson, who also studied the film while writing their book, *The Red Sox Century*. "He does not pause or freeze with the ball, although his body language exhibits surprise."

To the list of things Pesky did not do, add one crucial factor. He did not make a very good throw home. His looped toss pulled catcher Ray Partee about six feet up the third-base line and another foot out toward the pitcher's mound. The film shows Partee catching the throw just as Slaughter starts his slide immediately behind him. It's likely, therefore, that a perfect throw might have nailed Slaughter. Pesky's throw was far from perfect, and Slaughter won his gamble and slid into immortality.

The odds that Slaughter's eighth-inning dash would succeed were improved considerably by a play that occurred in the top half of the inning. With two outs, Red Sox center fielder Dom DiMaggio doubled off the wall in right-center field to drive in two runs and tie the score. DiMaggio hobbled into second with a pulled hamstring, however, and had to be replaced by Leon Culberson. Whereas Dominic DiMaggio may not have been the best center fielder in baseball with his surname, he and his brother Joe were easily the two best defensive center fielders in the American League. Culberson, on the other hand, was a journeyman, a wartime fill-in whose career did not last long once major league stars returned from their World War II service.

Culberson's presence in center field weakened the Red Sox in a number of ways. He was slower and less aggressive than DiMaggio, had an inferior throwing arm, was less familiar with the Cardinal hitters and less comfortable in the rough and bumpy outfield of Sportsman's Park,

Enos Slaughter of the Cardinals slides home with the go-ahead run in the final game of the 1946 World Series as catcher Ray Partee of the Red Sox fields an up-the-line throw from Johnny Pesky (National Baseball Hall of Fame Library, Cooperstown, N.Y.).

which was characterized by Red Sox second baseman Bobby Doerr as "brutal." All of these considerations hurt Boston when Slaughter started his "mad dash" and Harry Walker lofted his hit to left center. Culberson initially played Walker in straightaway center field, but moved a few steps toward left center on signals from DiMaggio (but not nearly far enough, DiMaggio told David Halberstam years later).

When Walker's hit landed in the left-center field gap, Culberson was a little slow in getting to it. Slower, it can be assumed, than DiMaggio would have been. Once he'd retrieved the ball, the kindest thing that can be said about his throw was that it lacked urgency. The film shows that the center fielder lobbed the ball to Pesky, who had to bend his knees to catch it waist-high on its downward arc, not exactly the best position for starting a quick relay.

Slaughter said many times afterward that he wouldn't have gambled on a try for home if DiMaggio had been in the outfield. Quoted by John B. Holway in *The Ol' Ball Game*, he said, "You know DiMaggio had a great arm, but Culberson didn't have too good an arm, and he wasn't as quick as DiMaggio. DiMaggio would have gotten rid of it a lot quicker. I don't think I would have even tried (for home)."

A minor myth that has persisted regarding Slaughter's "mad dash" is that he ran through a stop sign held up by the Cardinals' third-base coach Mike Gonzalez. Several accounts perpetuate this myth, and Slaughter's teammate Stan Musial, recounting the play with obvious relish in a filmed 1992 interview, said: "Enos kept running and took everybody by surprise, because we all thought Mike Gonzalez had his hands up to stop him. Enos kept running and that was the winning run. It was a great play."

Slaughter himself was ambivalent on the subject of the third-base coach's signal, at times saying, "Mike told me to keep going," while at other times claiming that he ran through the coach's red light. In a TV interview in 2000, Slaughter said, "I never saw Mike Gonzalez, the third-base coach. Whether he tried to stop me or not, I don't know. I never looked up."

Gonzalez heatedly denied trying to stop Slaughter, saying that with two out and the bottom of the order coming up, he was down the line waving his arms like a windmill. His account was corroborated by several reporters, and the game film shows the coach pointing enthusiastically toward home plate as Slaughter rounds third.

As a practical matter, it probably wouldn't have made any difference what sort of a signal the third-base coach put up. Slaughter was a hell-for-leather player who had read the situation and made up his mind to try for the plate. As a result of a play in the first game of the Series, moreover, Slaughter had the go-ahead from his manager to try to score if he thought he could, regardless of the sign from the third-base coach. As Slaughter tells it:

> In the first game, I tripled and Mike Gonzalez stopped me at third on a bad relay and we lost the ball game. So Eddie Dyer, the manager, he says, "From now on with two men out, if you think you've got a chance to score, you go ahead and gamble, and I'll be responsible." And that was on my mind on the play.

None of the players on the field that day blamed Pesky for his part in Slaughter's score. Quoted by Joseph L. Reichler in *The World Series*, Slaughter himself said:

> Pesky got hit with a bum rap.... Because of the steal sign, I already had a pretty good jump on the pitcher when Walker hit this little floater into center field. The play was in front of me, so I could easily see that nobody was going to catch the ball. In fact, the ball was still in the air when I came into second base. I knew that third base was a cinch and I began to think I might make it all the way, especially since I knew Culberson was not a strong thrower.

Ted Williams, who was in left field when Culberson picked up the ball, said in *My Turn at Bat*, "Nobody yelled to him.... Not Doerr, or Higgins, or anybody. So you can't blame Pesky." Bobby Doerr, Pesky's longtime friend and keystone partner at second base, told David Halberstam in an interview for his 2003 book, *Teammates*:

> All these years later, people are still talking about that play.... And they ask "Why didn't someone yell out to John?" Well, I was there, and you couldn't hear a thing. They say John held the ball. He didn't.... If Dominic is out there in center, Slaughter stays on third base. Period.

The myth that Pesky held the ball while Slaughter scored has persisted for over half a century. It's worth asking how the myth got started in the first place. What caused seventeen sportswriters representing twelve different papers to report something that never happened? Pesky himself, in the locker room after the game, bought into the myth of his hesitation.

Part of the explanation undoubtedly lies in the writers' expectations. Slaughter was on first, and no one expected him to score on what appeared to be a medium-deep flare to left center. The fact that Slaughter broke with the pitch, was at second before the ball landed, read the play and the players perfectly, and was the kind of head-down dirty-shirt hustler who could take advantage of the situation, wasn't immediately apparent. There was no instant replay to help the writers analyze all the diverse elements. They could watch the ball or watch Slaughter, but not both at once. Slaughter had started out on first and had scored on a flare that wasn't much more than a single (although it was scored a double when Walker wound up on second following Pesky's relay). There must have been a slip-up somewhere.

John B. Holway, writing in "The Myth of Pesky's Throw," puts forth a plausible but unprovable explanation for the writers' perception that Pesky held the ball. Many of the same writers had been in the press box at the seventh game of the 1940 World Series, when shortstop Dick Bartell of the Tigers had held the ball on a relay long enough to let the Cincinnati runner, Frank

McCormick, score the run that tied a game Cincinnati went on to win. The situations were not entirely similar, since McCormick was a lumbering runner starting from second while Slaughter was running flat out from first, but they both involved a shortstop relay. It's possible that someone in the press box in 1946, influenced by the memory of the 1940 play, thought he saw Pesky hold the ball before throwing it. If he shared his perception after the play was over ("Did you see that, Pesky held the ball!"), those writers who were watching Slaughter rather than the ball were likely to buy into this observation, since it explained how Slaughter was able to survive what J. Roy Stockton of the *St. Louis Post Dispatch* characterized as a "run to certain death."

Writing in the *Boston Globe* the next day, Harold Kaese made the analogy explicit, saying, "It was like Cincinnati scoring the winning run [sic] in the seventh game of the 1940 World Series, as Dick Bartell held the ball with Frank McCormick going home reluctantly."

Whatever the source of the misperception, for over fifty-five years Johnny Pesky has been "the guy that held the ball while Enos Slaughter scored the winning run in 1946." Having had a chance to watch the game film over and over ("hundreds of times" by his own estimate), Pesky is aware of the injustice of this version of history, but accepts it stoically. "What are you going to do?" Pesky says, quoted by John B. Holway:

> Things have happened to better ballplayers than me. They're looking for the good guy and the bad guy. Some people want to blame me, but that's OK.... Baseball is a game of mistakes, and you make one, you're going to hear about it. I've been called a bum many times. But deep down in my own heart, I know I didn't do anything wrong.

The most succinct eyewitness summary of Pesky's phantom pause and Slaughter's "mad dash" is probably that offered by Bobby Doerr to David Halberstam. "They say John held the ball. He didn't. He ... made a normal play. Slaughter made a great play."

Escaped Goats

Dick Bartell:
Everybody Was Yelling "Home! Home!"

If it was indeed Dick Bartell's 1940 freeze-up that caused sportswriters to perceive a non-existent delay in Johnny Pesky's relay, then it's doubly ironic, because Bartell's actual blunder is all but forgotten today, while Pesky has been branded for life for his phantom pause.

In the 1940 World Series, the underdog Detroit Tigers were leading Cincinnati 1–0 in the seventh inning of the seventh game at Cincinnati's Crosley Field. Bobo Newsom, who had won two Series games and at that point had held the Reds to two earned runs in twenty-four innings was pitching for the Tigers with just one day of rest.

National League MVP Frank McCormick began the seventh with a double off the left-field fence. The next batter, Jimmy Ripple, lofted a long fly that eluded the outstretched glove of Tiger outfielder Bruce Campbell and bounced off the right-field screen for a double. Because of the chance that Campbell might make the catch, McCormick held up between second and third until he saw the ball clear the right-fielder's glove. Campbell retrieved the ball and threw it to shortstop Dick Bartell as McCormick, a gangly first baseman, ambled around third and headed home.

Bartell took Campbell's throw with his back to home plate and, assuming that McCormick must have scored, held onto the ball. Actually, the slow-footed McCormick was still forty feet from the plate when Bartell took the throw. The catcher, Billy Sullivan, was waving his arms and yelling for the ball, and the third baseman, Pinky Higgins, who had gone to back up the play, was also shouting, "Home! Home!" In the words of H. G. Salsinger, writing for the *Detroit News*, though,

Frank McCormick scores the tying run of the final game of the 1940 World Series as Detroit catcher Billy Sullivan waves his arms and yells for Dick Bartell to throw the ball home (National Baseball Hall of Fame Library, Cooperstown, N.Y.).

> In the roar of the crowd the yells of Sullivan and Higgins were lost. When Bartell, who took it for granted that McCormick had scored, finally turned to the plate, it was too late for a play. There is no question that if Bartell, who has one of the best "infield" arms in the game, had thrown to Sullivan, the ball would have beaten McCormick to the plate.

Bartell never did throw the ball. The picture accompanying Salsinger's *Detroit News* column tells the whole story. It shows catcher Billy Sullivan still standing in front of the plate and waving his arms, yelling for the ball as McCormick scores standing up.

The next Cincinnati hitter, 40-year-old coach Jimmy Wilson, pressed into service because of a sprained ankle sustained by regular catcher Ernie Lombardi, bunted Ripple over to third, where he scored what proved to be the Series-winning run on a sacrifice fly hit by shortstop Billy Meyers.

In his autobiography, written in 1987 with Norman L. Macht, Bartell recalls,

> Everybody says they were all yelling, "Home! Home!" at me. Gehringer, Newhouser out in the bullpen. The crowd was screaming — we're in Cincinnati, remember — and I don't hear any of them. I'm standing with my back to the infield with the ball in my hand for what I guess must have seemed like a day and a half to everybody else.... By the time I did turn around McCormick still hadn't scored. He must have gone by way of left field or stopped in the dugout for a drink on the way or something. But it was clearly too late to get him by then.

A few Detroit players tried to deflect the blame from their shortstop by noting that second baseman Charley Gehringer should have been the cutoff and relay man for Campbell's throw rather than Bartell. Commenting on the play in the 1993 book *Cobb Would Have Caught It*, Gehringer himself said:

Bartell thought, "Gee, with that double, McCormick must have scored," but McCormick had waited to see whether it was going to be caught. So McCormick, who was no speed demon, was just rounding third when Bartell got the ball. I kept yelling, "Home, home, home!" Gee whiz, with Bartell's arm, he's a dead pigeon. But he never did throw the ball. Even after he looked and still had a chance, he didn't throw. And to this day I don't know why.

Why Pesky and Not Bartell?

When Bartell died in 1995, the *New York Times* didn't mention his gaffe, saying only that he played in three World Series and the first All-Star game. Two modern histories of the World Series, Josh Leventhal's 2001 *Illustrated Encyclopedia* and Eric Enders' 2003 book, *100 Years of the World Series*, say only that the Reds tied the game on consecutive doubles by McCormick and Ripple, entirely ignoring Bartell's contribution. It's impossible to imagine that any historian will ever summarize the conclusion of the 1946 Series by saying only that Slaughter, who had singled, scored the winning run on a double off the bat of Walker.

What is it that has caused Pesky's "pause" to live in infamy while Bartell's blunder is all but forgotten? It certainly can't be attributed to the personalities of the players. Pesky was a cheerful, popular player who spent eight of his ten major league years with the Red Sox, losing three prime years to the Navy and compiling a lifetime average of .307. Bartell, on the other hand, was a firebrand, a volatile player who jumped from team to team over eighteen years, playing for the Pirates, Phillies, Giants, Cubs, and Tigers. Nicknamed "Rowdy Richard," he was an excellent fielder with a .284 lifetime average, but his loud mouth caused him to wear out his welcome with teammates and fans alike. Through the second half of his career, writes Bill James in his classic *Historical Baseball Abstract*, Bartell was "routinely booed in almost every city."

One common element in both Pesky's and Bartell's play was third baseman Pinky Higgins, who was evidently unable to make his voice heard over the din of the hometown crowd either time. The run scored by McCormick while Bartell stood and watched only tied the game, while Slaughter's dash ahead of Pesky's relay provided the winning run. The judgment that Bartell could have thrown Mc-

"Rowdy Richard" Bartell, who held the ball with his back to the plate as the Cincinnati Reds scored the tying run in the final game of the 1940 World Series (National Baseball Hall of Fame Library, Cooperstown, N.Y.).

Cormick out is purely speculative. If Bartell had been able to nail McCormick, however, it's likely that Detroit's 1–0 lead would have held up.

The 1940 Series didn't end with Bartell's blunder, and Slaughter's dash didn't close out the 1946 Series. The Tigers had two innings to overcome the one-run deficit, but Cincinnati's Paul Derringer shut them down in the eighth and ninth innings. The Red Sox mounted a threat in the top of their ninth inning on leadoff singles by Rudy York and Bobby Doerr, but Harry Brecheen got the final three outs for his third win of the Series.

It does seem that the East Coast is a more fertile breeding ground for goats than the Midwest, whose fans are somewhat more forgiving, and it's certainly true that at the time of their respective losses Boston was more accustomed to winning World Series than Detroit. The 1946 Series marked the first loss for Boston against five wins, while the 1940 Series marked the fifth loss for the Tigers against one win. None of this speculation adequately explains why Pesky's phantom pause has become a fixed part of diamond history while Bartell's botched relay is all but forgotten. It's likely that the explanation rests with the runners rather than the fielders. The image of Slaughter's daring dash makes a much more attractive addition to baseball lore than the image of a slow-footed McCormick laboring to score from second base on a double.

Johnny Evers:
"Pulled a boner which he usually works on the other fella"

Another case of a held ball that did not earn goat horns for the holder involved the peppery Hall of Fame second baseman Johnny Evers. Evers escaped goat horns because his team, the Boston Braves, erased his gaffe by coming from behind to win the third game of the 1914 World Series and going on to engineer the first four-game Series sweep, closing out the Philadelphia Athletics.

The case is of interest primarily because it involves Evers, who was known for taking advantage of the bonehead plays of others, and because it illustrates the different perspectives brought to the game by hometown reporters.

Evers was a high-strung pepper pot who fought his way through eighteen years as a second baseman, alienating both his own teammates and opposing players. His extensive knowledge of the rule book led him to exploit the Merkle mistake that cost the Giants the pennant and made his Chicago Cubs the National League Champions in 1908 (see Chapter Two). He was the kind of player appreciated by hometown fans and roundly hated by opponents, as can be seen in the reporting of a gaffe of his own that nearly cost his Braves the third game of the 1914 World Series.

With the score tied 2–2 in the top of the tenth inning, the Philadelphia A's loaded the bases, and Frank "Home Run" Baker hit a hard smash toward right field that Evers knocked down, but couldn't retrieve in time to get a force at home or first, so that the runner on third scored. Reporter Jim Nasium (a pseudonym for Edgar Forrest Wolfe) provides the *Philadelphia Inquirer*'s view of what happened next:

> While Evers was venting his displeasure over the event by tossing the ball idly in his hands, Eddie Murphy caught Johnny asleep and stole home without drawing a throw, putting the Athletics two runs to the good.

A second Philadelphia correspondent felt that "Evers was lucky to get near the ball at all," and wrote that "While Evers was prancing around second with the ball in his hands, Murphy, who had reached third, just took a sneak home."

The Boston reporters, basking in the glow of victory, viewed Evers' transgression much less harshly. An anonymous *Boston Globe* reporter wrote that "Baker smashed a fierce grounder

Johnny Evers of the Boston Braves, who held the ball as the Athletics scored a crucial run in the top of the tenth inning of Game Three of the 1914 World Series. Evers escaped goatdom when the Braves came back to tie the game in the bottom of the tenth and win it in the thirteenth (photograph from the National Baseball Hall of Fame Library, Cooperstown, N.Y.; 1914 cartoon by Wallace Goldsmith of the *Boston Globe*).

that Evers blocked, but could not get his man at first, Schang scoring. Evers was evidently injured, as he made no effort to act as Murphy ran on home."

And George Stallings, the Braves' manager, observed in a *Globe* column:

> Don't let our Boston Friends get the wrong impression of Johnny Evers in the tenth inning. Johnny's fighting spirit was paralyzed when Baker's hard hit ball got away from him and his lapse of thoughtfulness is the only one I have ever seen since I have known Johnny.

Hall of Fame shortstop Rabbit Maranville, Evers' teammate in 1914, added a player's perspective to the incident in a subsequent interview in *Sport Magazine*.

> Evers, for some reason or other, failed to relay the ball back to the infield after he picked it up in short right field. Instead, he walked slowly back to the infield, tapping the ball in his glove. I looked over and yelled, "Johnny, watch the plate." He didn't seem to hear me.
> Just at that time, Murphy made a break for home. And by the time Evers recovered, Murphy had scored easily. The inning ended 4–2 in favor of the A's.
> Well, when Evers returned to the dugout, he was crying like a baby.

Evers was spared permanent goat horns when Boston came back in the bottom of the tenth to tie the score on a home run by Hank Gowdy, a walk, a single by Evers himself, and another single by left fielder Joe Connelly. Boston then won the game in the bottom of the twelfth when

Philadelphia pitcher Joe Bush threw wildly to third in an attempt to get a force out after fielding a sacrifice bunt.

The disparate treatment by the different hometown papers serves to emphasize an observation of Evers himself, who said, "A ballplayer has two reputations, one with the other players and one with the fans. The first is based on ability. The second the newspapers give him."

What's Remembered and What's Forgotten

Of the three cases of indecision reported here, only one, Pesky's presumed hesitation, has lived on in baseball lore. Ironically, it is the only one of the three where the alleged perpetrator was virtually blameless. The legend has Pesky hesitating as a counterbalance to Slaughter's now-heroic dash. Bartell's blunder is lost to history, presumably because most onlookers, including Bartell, expected McCormick to score from second on a double anyway and, possibly, because Detroit fans were more forgiving than Boston rooters. Evers' pause is forgotten and forgiven because his teammates bailed him out by coming back to win the game. Over the years, dozens of potential goats have had their date with destiny cancelled by a late-inning comeback. Give the Red Sox one more hit in the top of the ninth inning in 1946 and Pesky's phantom pause would be forgotten as well.

CHAPTER TWO

Baserunning Gaffes

**BLUNDER COSTS
GIANTS VICTORY**
Merkle Rushes Off Base Line
Before Winning Run is Scored,
And is Declared Out

Censurable stupidity on the part of player Merkle in yesterday's game
at the Polo Grounds between the Giants and Chicago placed the New
York team's chances of winning the pennant in jeopardy.

New York Times headline
September 24, 1908

♦ ♦ ♦ ♦

Scapegoat: The Merkle Incident

Before Bill Buckner, before Johnny Pesky, even before Fred Snodgrass and his $30,000 muff, there was Fred Merkle. A nineteen-year-old part-time player for the New York Giants, Merkle was branded for life as a bonehead for failing to touch second base in what has since become one of the most famous games in baseball history. It was the game that helped decide the tight three-way 1908 pennant race in the National League between the Giants, Pirates, and Cubs.

Several books have been written about Merkle's blunder and the historic pennant race. The blunder has taken on all the trappings of a legend, with a colorful cast of characters, a public dress rehearsal, a dramatic climax, and a tragic denouement.

The Dress Rehearsal

The dress rehearsal for Merkle's downfall took place on September 4, 1908, in a game in Pittsburg between the Chicago Cubs and the Pittsburg Pirates, two of the three clubs battling for the pennant. Merkle was in Philadelphia that day, where the Giants won handily to retain a slim grip on first place, and his role in the rehearsal was taken by stand-in Warren Gill, a Pittsburg first baseman playing his first month in the major leagues. At the time, Pittsburg and Chicago were in a virtual tie for second place, one game behind the Giants, and the tightness of the race was reflected in the tightness of the game. Neither team had scored after nine innings. In the bottom of the tenth, however, Pittsburg put runners on first and third with only one man out. The Chicago pitcher, Mordecai "Three-finger" Brown, hit the rookie Gill with a pitch, loading the bases.

The next hitter struck out, bringing another rookie, outfielder Chief Wilson, to the plate.

Wilson singled sharply past Cub second baseman Johnny Evers, bringing Pittsburg player-manager Fred Clarke home with the winning run. Seeing Clarke cross the plate, Gill followed what was reportedly a common practice of the time and veered from the base path to head for the clubhouse without touching second base. This practice was born out of self-preservation, since fans typically poured onto the field in game-ending situations, and there was little security to protect players and umpires.

Even with the fans streaming onto the field, several of the Cubs held their ground and didn't run for the clubhouse. Seeing Gill veer from the base path, second baseman Johnny Evers called for outfielder Jimmy Slagle to throw him the ball. Evers caught the ball, touched second, and went off to inform the lone umpire, Hank O'Day, that Gill had been forced out, nullifying Clarke's run.

Unfortunately, umpire O'Day was one of those who broke and headed for cover as soon as Clarke crossed the plate. The *Chicago Tribune* reported that O'Day had turned his back on the diamond to get a drink of water, had not seen Evers' follow-up play, and simply remarked, "Clarke was over the plate, so his run scored anyway," a strange comment from a veteran umpire.

The *Tribune* account goes on to present a biased but fairly accurate analysis of the situation.

> If O'Day had watched the finish of that base hit and had seen what really came off, he could not have decided otherwise than in Chicago's favor, ruling out Clarke's run and leaving the score tied at 0 to 0. Everyone knows no run can count if the third out is made before the batsman reaches first, or if the third man out is forced out....
>
> That was what happened to Gill in the tenth when he failed to touch second base. In fact, he hasn't touched it yet, and according to all rules and precedent the play which Evers pulled off had exactly the same status and the same effect on the game as if Johnny had knocked down Wilson's hit and tossed the ball to Tinker on second base before Gill got there. No man could think for a minute that Clarke's run could score under the latter circumstances. No more could Clarke's run count as the play came up today but for the fact O'Day took it for granted the game was over when Wilson's hit landed safe, just as Gill did.

The specific rule in question was Rule 59, since updated to Rule 4.09 (a), which stated:

> One run shall be scored every time a baserunner, after having legally traveled the first three bases, shall legally touch the home base before three men are put out; provided however, that if he reach home on or during a play in which the third man be forced out or be put out before reaching first base, a run shall not count.

Credit for interpreting the rule to the Cubs' advantage in the face of the traditional practice of vacating the field as quickly as possible is generally given to Chicago's second baseman, Johnny Evers. A high-strung player nicknamed the "Crab," Evers was a keen student of the game and had a history of alienating both teammates and opposing players. One-third of the celebrated double-play combination of Tinker, Evers, and Chance, he went for several years without speaking to shortstop Joe Tinker because of an imagined slight, and first baseman Frank Chance, quoted in Bill James' *Historical Baseball Abstract*, said that Evers was a great player, but, "I wish he had been an outfielder so I wouldn't have to listen to him."

The fact that Evers and his teammates remained on the field argues strongly that they had planned in advance to claim a force-out on a departing runner as soon as the occasion presented itself. The only flaw in their plan was umpire O'Day, who claimed that since he didn't see the play and couldn't rule on it, the winning run could not be nullified.

Chicago protested the outcome formally, claiming that Gill should have touched second base before he ran to the dugout, and produced several affidavits saying that he failed to reach the base. *The Pittsburg Post* quoted Cubs president Charles W. Murphy as saying, "I do not expect the protest will be allowed, but it is certainly just and should prove a strong argument in favor of the double umpire system." (For several years in the early twentieth century, Pittsburgh was spelled without the "h.")

The president of the National League, Harry Clay Pulliam, disallowed the Cubs' protest on September 9, backing umpire O'Day and ruling that the question of the force play rested "solely with the umpire" and could not be established by evidence presented by players and/or spectators.

In their Sunday newspaper following the controversial contest, the *Pittsburg Post* observed, "That final play of Friday's game between the Cubs and Pirates is one that does not come often, but next time it happens it is safe to predict that none who took part in the game will overlook the importance of touching the next base." While this observation was certainly true for the Cubs and Pirates players and umpire Hank O'Day, it evidently didn't register beyond those two cities and the office of the league president. In today's world of coast-to-coast sports coverage, the Chicago protest and its outcome would have been headline news, fodder for nighttime viewing on ESPN, and hotly debated in the sports weeklies. In 1908, however, local newspapers were the chief source of baseball information. While both the Chicago and Pittsburg papers covered the Cubs–Pirates game in some detail, only one New York newspaper, the *Globe*, mentioned the protest at all, and then only to note that Chicago's claim had been denied. None of the details that might have alerted Giant players to the need to touch second base before running to the dugout made the New York papers, setting the stage for the blunder that cost the Giants the 1908 pennant and left Fred Merkle permanently disgraced.

The Merkle Game

Wednesday, September 23, 1908, began with the Giants scant percentage points ahead of the Cubs in the battle for first place in the National League and Pittsburg one game behind the two leaders. The first eight innings of the game at New York's Polo Grounds between the Giants and Cubs did nothing to help decide ownership of first place. The two teams were tied 1–1, with the premier pitcher of the day, the Giants' Christy Mathewson, going against Cub left-hander Jack Pfiester. When Mathewson set the Cubs down one-two-three in the top of the ninth inning, the curtains opened on Fred Merkle's life-altering performance.

Merkle, who started the game at first base in place of the ailing regular Fred Tenney, came up in the bottom of the ninth with two men out and a runner, Moose McCormick, on first base. Merkle hit a long single to right field, advancing McCormick to third base. With runners on first and third, the next batter, Al Bridwell, hit the first pitch he saw on a line past second baseman Johnny Evers into right-center field for a clean single.

McCormick scored easily on the hit, opening the floodgates for the crowds spilling onto the field. Seeing McCormick score, Merkle followed the reported tradition of the day (and the lead of Pittsburg's Warren Gill three weeks earlier) and sprinted for the clubhouse without touching second base. As he had in the earlier Pittsburg game, the Cubs' Johnny Evers held his ground and called for the ball. Center fielder "Circus" Solly Hofman retrieved the ball before the crowd got to him, but threw it wildly past Evers and past Evers' back-up, shortstop Tinker.

At this point, the Giants' third-base coach, "Iron Man" Joe McGinnity, realized what the Cubs were up to and intervened by retrieving the ball himself. McGinnity was immediately set upon by Cubs players, but he pulled free long enough to hurl the ball into the stands. At least two Cubs followed the game ball into the crowd and in due course the ball, or a reasonable facsimile, found its way into Evers' glove. According to the *New York Herald*, "Evers stood proudly on second base, holding the ball aloft," and calling for the base umpire, Bob Emslie, to declare a force-out on Merkle.

Emslie, who had fallen to the earth to avoid being hit by Bridwell's line drive, claimed that he did not see the play and called for help from the home-plate umpire. As luck would have it, the home-plate umpire was Hank O'Day, who had been on the field in Pittsburg three weeks

The crowd at New York's Polo Grounds streams onto the field following the "Merkle Game" on September 23, 1908. The presence of fans on the field was one of the factors that caused players to bolt for the locker rooms as soon as the last out was recorded (or, in Merkle's case, a little before the last out was recorded) (Brown Brothers).

earlier. Primed by his experience in the Gill dress rehearsal, O'Day had advanced to the pitcher's mound during the final play to observe the action at second base.

With the crowd swirling around them, Cubs manager and first baseman Frank Chance argued with O'Day, claiming not only that McCormick's run should not count, but also that the breakdown in security on the part of the home team meant that the game could not continue and should be forfeited to the visiting Cubs. The mood of the crowd, who believed the hometown Giants had won the game, turned ugly. O'Day and Chance were shoved and struck, and a police escort had to be formed to lead the umpire back to the safety of the clubhouse. When the crowd had thinned and some semblance of order had been restored, O'Day emerged in his street clothes to announce that Merkle never reached second, McCormick's run did not count, and the game ended in a tie.

The New York club and their fans left the Polo Grounds believing they had won the game by a score of 2–1. When O'Day's decision became widely known, the Giants protested to the league office, arguing that they should not be penalized for Merkle's failure to touch second, since such failures had become traditional when the home team scored the winning run. The Cubs first argued that they should have won by forfeit when the rampaging crowd made it impossible to continue, but subsequently demanded that the game be replayed as part of a double-header the next day when the Chicago team was still in New York.

As he had in the Pittsburg incident, League President Pulliam backed umpire O'Day and declared the game a tie. Because his ruling came too late to allow the double-header demanded by the Cubs, it was subsequently decided that the game would be replayed after the scheduled season ended only if it had a bearing on the outcome of the pennant race.

The New York newspapers showed no mercy in their treatment of the nineteen-year-old first baseman. The *New York Times* cited "censurable stupidity on the part of player Merkle," and when Manager John McGraw returned Fred Tenney to the lineup the next day, the *New York Evening Mail* reported that

> Fred Tenney is playing solely on his nerve. His feet are in very bad shape and his back is lame. Every time he stoops it is pain. But McGraw had enough of Merkle the day before and called on Tenney for his brains. A one-legged man with a noodle is better than a bonehead.

The appellation "bonehead" followed Merkle throughout his baseball career. Out-of-town newspapers piled on as well. In their account of the game, the *Chicago Tribune* referred to "the fatheaded Merkle," and when the youngster made his next appearance in a game, substituting for Tenney, the *Cincinnati Enquirer* observed, "Fred Tenney is quite lame, and he gave way to Merkle in the fourth inning of the second game yesterday. No plays came up in which Merkle had to think, so he got by."

Fred Merkle of the Giants, reportedly one of the smartest players of his day, was known as "bonehead" during and after his sixteen-year career for his failure to touch second base in the late stages of the 1908 National League pennant race. His failure cost the Giants a key game against their rival Cubs, and ultimately the National League Pennant as well (National Baseball Hall of Fame Library, Cooperstown, N.Y.).

The Play-off Game

Chance, in the form of fate and the Chicago manager, conspired to force a season-ending tie between the Giants and the Cubs and a replay of the Merkle game. The Cubs and the Pirates ended their respective seasons with a game in Chicago on October 4. A win by Pittsburg would make them champions and effectively eliminate both the Cubs and the Giants. A Cubs win would eliminate the Pirates and leave Chicago a game and a half ahead of the Giants, who still had three games to play against Boston.

With Chicago ahead 4–2 in the top of the eighth, the *New York American* reported:

> Leach hit a fierce drive straight over first, and it looked like a sure double until Chance, with a running jump, shoved out one hand, turned backwards and clung to the ball. Against that kind of defensive work, Pittsburg had no chance.

The Cubs eventually won the game 5–2, eliminating Pittsburg. When the Giants won three straight games against Boston, both Chicago and New York had identical records, 98 wins against 55 losses, setting up a one-game replay of the Merkle game for the National League championship.

The deciding game, played on October 8 at the Polo Grounds, is well described in one of the best first-hand accounts of a baseball game ever printed, Christy Mathewson's *Pitching in a Pinch*. By the time of the play-off game, Mathewson reports, "Merkle had lost twenty pounds, and his eyes were hollow and his cheeks sunken."

The same two pitchers that started the Merkle game started the play-off, Mathewson for the Giants and Pfiester for the Cubs. When the Giants scored one run quickly in the bottom of the first, Chance yanked Pfiester and replaced him with Three-finger Brown. As the Giants took their early lead, Mathewson reports, "For the first time in almost a month, Merkle smiled. He was drawn up in the corner of the bench, pulling away from the rest of us as if he had some contagious disease and was quarantined."

The Giants' early lead didn't last. Mathewson tells us that his arm felt "dead" after four days of unaccustomed rest, and Chicago scored four runs in the top of the third, which began with a triple by Tinker that was misjudged by center fielder Cy Seymour and ended with an off-field double by Chance that drove in two runs. As the Giants came off the field after the Cubs took the lead, Mathewson reports:

> None of the players spoke to one another as they went to the bench. Even McGraw was silent. We knew it was gone. Merkle was drawn up behind the water cooler. Once he said: "It was my fault, boys." No one answered him.

Neither team scored again until the seventh, when the Giants loaded the bases with no one out. McGraw sent up Larry Doyle to bat for Mathewson, and Doyle lifted a weak pop-up behind the plate. Mathewson's description of the obstacles faced by Cub catcher Johnny Kling as he circled under the pop-up emphasizes the difference between today's game and baseball as it was played in 1908.

> Kling went back for it, and someone threw a pop bottle which narrowly missed him, and another scaled a cushion. But Kling kept on and got what he went after, which was the ball. He had a habit of doing that.

After Kling dodged flying debris to catch Doyle's pop-up, the Giants tallied one run on a sacrifice fly. But there was no more scoring and the Cubs won the game and the pennant, 4–2. The hooliganism of the fans wasn't limited to the throwing of pop bottles. The winning Cub pitcher, Three-finger Brown, described the eruption of post-game emotions in *My Greatest Day in Baseball*,

> As the ninth ended with the Giants going out one-two-three, we all ran for our lives, straight for the clubhouse with the pack at our heels. Some of our boys got caught by the mob and beaten up some. Tinker, Howard, and Sheckard were struck. Chance was hurt most of all. A Giant fan hit him in the throat and Husk's voice was gone for a day or two in the World Series that followed. Pfiester got slashed on the shoulder by a knife.

In the light of Brown's description, it's easy to see why the players of the day headed for the clubhouse as quickly as possible as soon as their game ended.

Afterthoughts

While accounts of the day suggest that it was not uncommon for a runner on first to head for the dugout as soon as the winning run scored, there is no way of knowing how common this practice really was. Obviously, the practice was abandoned in the wake of the Merkle incident. Even in 1908, though, the opportunity for a misplay like Merkle's was relatively rare. In the 154 games of the 1908 season, there were only three games in which the Chicago Cubs and Johnny Evers were on the field when the home team scored the winning run in their final at bat with a runner on first base. In two of those three games, the Gill game and the Merkle game,

Johnny Evers of the Cubs, who snapped the trap on the Giants' Fred Merkle, and called for the ball when Merkle headed for the dugout instead of touching second base. Evers had failed to pull off the same play a month earlier against the Pirates, when the home-plate umpire, Hank O'Day, claimed not to have seen the transgression (Library of Congress Prints and Photographs Division).

the runner on first, a relatively inexperienced player, headed for the dugout and failed to touch second base. The first game occurred early in the season, when St. Louis beat Chicago 4–3 on May 29, following an eleventh-inning single with the bases loaded. The run was not challenged by Chicago, but there is no way of knowing whether or not the runner on first went on to touch second. If he didn't, it's possible that Evers observed the omission and filed the knowledge away for future use.

Several accounts of the 1908 season depict Evers as a scholarly player who spent his evenings poring over a baseball rule book, seeking ways to turn the regulations to his advantage. The rules of baseball tend to be learned by observation and experience, so the image of any player in the early 1900s immersing himself in the rule book doesn't quite ring true. Evers was a brainy, excitable player, and it's more likely that he watched a runner celebrating victory by heading for the clubhouse instead of second base and asked himself "What if?" To his credit, he was the first player to turn this reportedly common practice to his advantage, and his alert play stole the 1908 pennant for the Cubs. Ogden Nash celebrated the "Crab's" all-out approach to the game with the poem,

> E is for Evers
> His jaw in advance
> Never afraid
> To Tinker with Chance.

The eagerness of the press to saddle the hapless Fred Merkle with goat horns has overshadowed the alert play of Evers and the Cubs in recognizing the opportunity and springing the trap.

In retrospect, it's difficult to fault Merkle, a young, second-year player, for following the custom of the day and heading for the clubhouse. Still, someone on the Giants should have recognized the trap and taken steps to avoid it. Even though the New York press didn't cover the dress rehearsal in Pittsburg when the rookie Warren Gill failed to touch second, Pittsburg played New York in the three weeks between that incident and the Merkle game, and it's hard to believe that word of Evers' attempt to take advantage of Gill's lapse didn't reach the ears of the Giants' players. It's fair to infer that Giant pitcher–coach Joe McGinnity knew of the earlier incident. After Merkle had headed for the dugout and Evers called for the ball, McGinnity intercepted the throw from the outfield as if he knew Evers' intent and what was at stake. And Christy Mathewson was quoted in the *New York Evening Mail* the next day as saying, "I had started for the clubhouse when I heard Chance call to Hofman to throw the ball to second. I remembered the trick they had tried to play on Pittsburg and caught Merkle by the arm and told him to go to second." If Mathewson knew of the Pittsburg incident, and McGinnity presumably knew, then manager John McGraw must certainly have known. It's fair to ask why McGraw, one of the savviest and most successful managers of his day, didn't warn his players to be on the lookout for the Cub stratagem and why McGraw's first-base coach didn't remind Merkle to be sure to touch second in the event of a Bridwell hit.

Neither McGraw nor his players ever blamed Merkle for the loss of the 1908 pennant. The Giants lost six of the seventeen games they played following the Merkle game, including the play-off. A win in any one of those six games would have given them the championship. McGraw himself gave Merkle a $500 raise following the season and constantly reaffirmed his faith in the youngster, who went on to play eight more years with the Giants, taking over as their regular first baseman in 1910. He finished a sixteen-year career with a respectable .273 batting average and was on the losing side in six World Series. Not surprisingly, his worst year at the plate was 1909, the year after his baserunning gaffe, when he batted only .191.

The Merkle game has been one of the most discussed in baseball history, affecting many lives and remaining controversial to this day. A sampling of the post-game fallout and controversy appears below:

- ♦ Upset over the controversy and pressures visited upon him by the Merkle decision and its aftermath, National League President Harry Pulliam committed suicide in July, 1909.
- ♦ In a 1951 interview with *Collier's* magazine, Hall of Fame umpire Bill Klem, who was behind the plate for the Cubs–Giants play-off game (and reportedly refused a bribe to tilt the game in the Giants' favor), called O'Day's decision in the Merkle case "The worst decision in the history of baseball," because O'Day "was accepting a technicality and ignoring perhaps half a century of custom, usage, tradition, and the intent of the rule."
- ♦ In the second edition of his *Historical Baseball Abstract*, published in 2001, Bill James wrote, "Giant fans always claimed that what Merkle did ... was common practice at the time. If, in fact, it was common practice, then the umpire used poor judgment in deciding to commence enforcement of the rule at that particular moment, when the pennant was on the line."

Wherever one stands on the wisdom of the decisions of O'Day and Pulliam, the one thing everyone seems to agree on is that Merkle was virtually blameless. Yet he had to bear the nickname "bonehead" throughout his baseball career and at one point, according to *The Baseball Hall of Shame*, lamented near the end of his life, "When I die, I guess they'll put on my tombstone, 'Here Lies Bonehead Merkle.'"

While it never made his tombstone, his mistake wasn't overlooked in his obituary notices.

Members on the National Baseball Commission (January 1909). From left to right, Harry Pulliam, August Herrmann, Ban Johnson, and L. E. Bruce. National League President Pulliam upheld the Cubs' claim that Merkle was out for failing to touch second (after disallowing a similar claim by the Cubs in a Pittsburg game earlier in the month). The pressures of his decisions were thought to contribute to his subsequent suicide in July 1909 (Library of Congress, Prints and Photographs Division).

In observing his passing in 1956, nearly 48 years after the "Incident" that bears his name, the *New York Times* headlined:

> FRED MERKLE, 67,
> BALL PLAYER, DIES
> Giant First Baseman's Boner
> In Failing to Touch 2nd Led
> To Loss of '08 Pennant.

Escaped Goats

Eric Byrnes and Miguel Tejada: Three Stooges Baseball

It would be difficult to imagine a baserunning error as damaging to a team's pennant chances as Fred Merkle's failure to touch second base. But in the 2003 American League Division Series, Oakland A's players managed to make two equally costly mistakes in a single inning. Even though their successive baserunning gaffes cost the A's the chance to advance in the playoff series that year, neither player was branded for life, or even for the remainder of the postseason, with a devastating nickname like "bonehead."

In the first round of the American League's 2003 play-offs, the Oakland A's, champions of the League's Western Division, won the first two games of a best-three-out-of-five series against the wild card team, the Boston Red Sox. The A's traveled to Fenway Park needing to win only one more game to advance to the League Championship Series. On Saturday, October 4, they played a game that A's third baseman Eric Chavez called "the ugliest game I've ever been a part

Jason Varitek of the Red Sox tags out Eric Byrnes of the Athletics after Byrnes failed to touch home plate in the first round of the American League play-offs in 2003. Byrnes' failure cost the A's a crucial run in a game they lost in extra innings. A win for the A's, who were up two games to none at the time, would have taken them to the League Championship Series. Instead, they lost the next two games to Boston and were eliminated from the play-offs (AP Photo/James Rogash).

of" and that Bay Area columnist Mark Purdy said "captured the vital essence and athletic techniques of all Three Stooges."

The ugliness first manifested itself in the second inning, when Boston scored a run on an infield hit and three Oakland errors, but did not come into full flower until Oakland came to bat in the top of the sixth inning, trailing by the single gift run their misplays had awarded Boston. The first batter up for Oakland was outfielder Eric Byrnes, who singled off pitcher Derek Lowe, stole second, and advanced to third on a groundout. When designated hitter Erubiel Durazo walked, the A's had runners on first and third with only one out.

The next batter, shortstop Miguel Tejada, squibbed a grounder toward third. The pitcher Lowe left the mound, fielded the ball and, off-balance, flung it toward the catcher, Jason Varitek, who was blocking home plate in an attempt to keep Byrnes from scoring. Charging home, Byrnes tripped over Varitek and missed home plate entirely.

Thinking he'd been thrown out, Byrnes stood up, shoved catcher Varitek in disgust, and limped around the general vicinity of home plate without ever touching it, ignoring both the shouts of his teammates and one of the first rules of baseball—keep trying to score until the umpire calls you out. The noise of the crowd may have made it impossible for him to hear the shouts of his teammates, but he didn't hear the umpire's out call because the umpire hadn't called him out—yet. The throw from Lowe had skipped by the catcher, who had time to retrieve the ball, return to home plate, and tag out Byrnes before the A's center fielder thought to direct his wanderings toward a useful target.

In the words of sportswriter Bruce Jenkins of the *San Francisco Chronicle*,

> Byrnes blew his main assignment—to touch the plate just in case. He could have crawled there. He could have reached it with a broken leg. Of all people, Byrnes, the ultimate hustler, gave up on a play. What did it cost the team? Merely the first Division Series title of the Billy Beane [the A's general manager] era.

Unhappily for A's fans, the worst was yet to come. While Byrnes was perambulating in the vicinity of home plate, Durazo went to third, and the batter, Tejada, proceeded to second. After Eric Chavez was walked intentionally to load the bases, catcher Ramon Hernandez hit a bouncer that eluded the glove of Boston shortstop Nomar Garciaparra for an error. Durazo scored on the misplay and Tejada ran to third, where he slammed into third baseman Bill Mueller. As the third base umpire charged Mueller with obstruction, Tejada disentangled himself and headed for the plate. Instead of going all-out to score, however, he stopped halfway home and pointed back at Mueller like a tattletale accusing a schoolyard bully.

Left fielder Manny Ramirez fielded the ball and loosed a wild throw toward home plate that Tejada could have beaten easily if he'd just kept running. Instead, he stood with his finger pointing back at third base as the catcher ranged wide of the plate to take the throw and tag him out, ending the inning. As the home-plate umpire raised his thumb to give the out signal, Ken Macha, the A's manager, stormed out of the dugout. The third-base umpire had signaled obstruction, he argued. How could Tejada be called out?

While Macha argued, the umpires huddled for over five minutes and the television commentators debated the call, which they clearly did not understand. The one person in the park not wearing blue who did understand the ruling was Umpire Supervisor Steve Palermo, who happened to be attending the game. Palermo explained that the umpires were applying Rule 7.06 (b), which states that the runner advances at his own peril following an obstruction call if no play was being made on him at the time of the obstruction.

An arcane, little understood, and seldom applied regulation, Rule 7.06(b) states:

> When obstruction occurs, the umpire shall call or signal "Obstruction." If no play is being made on the obstructed runner, the play shall proceed until no further action is possible. The umpire shall then call "Time" and impose such penalties, if any, as in his judgment will nullify the act of obstruc-

tion. Under 7.06 (b) when the ball is not dead on obstruction and an obstructed runner advances beyond the base which, in the umpire's judgment, he would have been awarded because of being obstructed, he does so at his own peril and may be tagged out. This is a judgment call.

In the umpire's judgment, if Tejada had not stopped, but had simply continued to try to score, he would have been awarded home plate even if the Ramirez throw had been true and beaten him by a step or two. When the A's shortstop pulled up short in the base paths, however, the play, and the protection of the obstruction call, stopped. In the eyes of A's fans, the umpire's judgment call showed extremely poor judgment. Mueller's obstruction was blatant, and Tejada clearly would have scored if the third baseman hadn't interfered with his progress. Ironically, he would probably have scored anyhow, if he'd just kept running. Like Byrnes, he had violated one of baseball's primary rules: never stop the action in anticipation of an umpire's call. Keep on playing and let the umpires sort it out when the dust has settled.

The irony of the situation was multiplied by the fact that Boston's second-inning run had scored on an obstruction call when A's third baseman Eric Chavez blocked the path of Red Sox catcher Jason Varitek, who was caught in a run-down between third and home. Because Varitek was trying to outrun a throw to Tejada, who was covering third at the time, the umpire stopped play and awarded Varitek home plate. This earlier play may have been on Tejada's mind when he stopped midway between third and home in the sixth inning. That is, he may have expected the umpires to award him home plate as they had Varitek, even though no play was being made on Tejada at the time Mueller interfered with his progress. We'll never really know what was on Tejada's mind, because he refused to discuss the play after the game. Usually an affable, outgoing interviewee, he told reporters only, "You saw what happened. I (messed) up. Put that in the paper."

Neither team scored in the seventh, eighth, or ninth inning, and the game went into extra innings with the score tied 1–1. Boston won in the bottom of the eleventh on a home run by Trot Nixon. If either Byrnes or Tejada had scored in the sixth, the A's could have expected to win the game and the series in the regulation nine innings. Since both players were called out, moreover, if either had kept their focus on home plate and scored, the A's would have one more out and at least one more opportunity to bring home the runners left on the bases.

Boston went on to win the remaining two games, taking the best-three-of-five series, so the unscored runs cost Oakland the series win and the chance to advance to the League Championship play-offs.

Both the nature and impact of the Oakland players' gaffes were close to Merkle's blunder. In both cases, poor baserunning cost their teams a crucial, but not decisive, game. Oakland went on to lose two more games to Boston, and the 1908 Giants lost six more times after the Merkle incident. Wins in any one of these subsequent games would have nullified the impact of the baserunning mistakes. Merkle, Byrnes, and Tejada each failed to go all-out to reach the next base. Both the A's players were confused: Byrnes by what he thought the umpire had called, and Tejada by what the umpire actually called.

Both the A's players were seemingly more culpable than Merkle, who was just following the custom of the day. Yet neither Byrnes nor Tejada was roasted by the media or saddled with a sobriquet like "bonehead." One reason for this unequal treatment may lie in the previous reputations of the principals. Both Byrnes and Tejada were popular players: Byrnes, a local Bay Area native, was known for his hustle, while Tejada, the league MVP in 2002, was one of the most popular players ever to wear an A's uniform. Even though he left Oakland to sign with Baltimore as a free agent following the 2003 season, A's fans welcomed him back with a standing ovation the first time he returned to Oakland in an Orioles uniform. As a part-time player in 1908, the young Merkle did not have much time to make an impression on the fans or the press before his fateful blunder, and nothing he did afterward would ever erase the image supplied by the New York press in the days that followed.

Babe Ruth's "Only Dumb Play"

Another example of a player's reputation overcoming the media's hunt for scapegoats occurred when Babe Ruth made the final out of the 1926 World Series on a failed attempt to steal second base. Modern baseball historians have questioned the wisdom of this strategy, with Nash and Zullo in the *Baseball Hall of Shame* calling it the "biggest boneheaded play" of Ruth's career, claiming that the "overweight Ruth ... took off for second with all the speed of a sedated elephant." Yankee owner Ed Barrow shared this view of Ruth's attempted steal, calling it the Babe's "only dumb play."

The media of the day were much kinder to Ruth. The *New York Times* gave the baseball legend the benefit of the doubt and characterized the final out as a failed hit-and-run play. Actually Ruth, who had walked with two men out on a close 3–2 pitch from Grover Cleveland Alexander, decided on his own to try to steal on Alexander's second pitch to Yankee cleanup hitter Bob Meusel. Cardinal catcher Bob O'Farrell gunned down the Babe with a throw to second baseman Rogers Hornsby to end the game and the Series.

Modern-day second-guessers generally consider Ruth's dash to have been ill-advised, since it took the bats out of the hands of cleanup hitter Meusel and the on-deck batter, Lou Gehrig. A closer look at the season records of Meusel and Gehrig, however, suggests that Ruth's

Rogers Hornsby tags Babe Ruth for the last out of the 1926 World Series. With two outs in the top of the ninth, Ruth tried to steal second to put himself in scoring position. Although the play was not necessarily a bad gamble, it failed and has been called "Ruth's Biggest Blunder" (National Baseball Hall of Fame Library, Cooperstown, N.Y.).

gamble wasn't necessarily a bad one. Using their season records to predict the likely performance of Meusel, Gehrig, and the next hitter, Tony Lazzeri, a consideration of conditional probabilities shows that Ruth needed to have only a 50-50 or better chance of stealing successfully in order to improve the Yankees' chances of tying the game. During the 1926 season, Ruth had stolen eleven bases in twenty tries, a success rate of 55 percent. Not a particularly good success rate, but better than the 50 percent rate necessary to improve the Yankees' chances.

The way Pete Alexander was pitching, moreover, it wasn't likely that Meusel and Gehrig would be able to perform nearly as well as they had during the season. After pitching a complete-game win over the Yankees one day earlier in Game Six, Alexander came in as a reliever in the bottom of the seventh with two out and the bases loaded to strike out Yankee rookie Tony Lazzeri. He went on to set the Yankees down one-two-three in the eighth and got the first two outs in the ninth before walking Ruth.

From what we know of Ruth, he wasn't standing on first base calculating conditional probabilities. He felt Alexander wasn't paying much attention to him and thought he had a good chance of reaching second, where he could score on a single. He'd already stolen one base during the Series, the only Yankee to do so. One of the Babe's biographers, Marshall Smelser, in *The Life that Ruth Built*, quotes Ruth's probability-free analysis of the situation: "I wasn't doing any fucking good on first base."

Claiming in the 1986 edition of the *Baseball Hall of Shame* that Ruth had moved with the grace of a "sedated elephant" does a disservice both to Ruth and to history. While he was obviously not known for his base stealing, Ruth did amass 123 steals over his career and was successful in 52 percent of his attempts during the regular season. He also had two successful steals in the 1922 World Series, including a steal of home.

None of the papers of the day vilified Ruth for his failed attempt to steal second. Newspaper coverage of the final game focused on the flawless pitching of the Cards' Alexander, so that the story of "Alexander the Great" overshadowed both Ruth's final out and an earlier muffed fly by center fielder Meusel that gave St. Louis the runs that were their margin of victory. By 1926, Ruth's reputation and image were secure in the public mind, and his performance at the plate in the final Series game, when he walked four times and homered, enhanced that image and more than made up for his failed steal attempt.

Stand-up Guys

At least two players have been criticized in the press for failing to slide into home plate at crucial moments in post-season play. The two players, Lou Brock and Jeremy Giambi, are polar opposites, and their subsequent treatment by the media reflected their reputations and achievements.

Lou Brock. One of the best base runners of his day, Hall of Famer Lou Brock had three banner World Series while playing for the St. Louis Cardinals in 1964, 1967, and 1968. In the 1968 Series, St. Louis was up three games to one on the Detroit Tigers and led 3–2 in the fifth inning of the fifth game when Brock doubled off Detroit pitcher Mickey Lolich. The next hitter, Julian Javier, singled to left, sending Brock sprinting around third toward home.

The left fielder, Willie Horton, fielded the ball cleanly and threw it on one hop to catcher Bill Freehan, who was straddling home plate. Brock elected not to slide, slammed into Freehan standing up, and was called out when the catcher took Horton's throw waist high and applied the tag. The consensus of the TV commentators and the next day's newspapers was that Brock would have scored if he'd only hit the dirt. The Cardinals failed to register any more runs, and lost 5–3 when Detroit scored three runs in the bottom of the seventh. Detroit went on to take the next two games as well, winning the championship, and the run Brock didn't score has often been cited as the turning point in the Series.

Lou Brock of the Cardinals tries to score standing up and is tagged out by Bill Freehan of the Tigers in the fifth inning of Game Five of the 1968 World Series. The bang-bang play could have gone either way and has been cited as the turning point in the Series, which the Tigers won after coming back from a three-games-to-one deficit (National Baseball Hall of Fame Library, Cooperstown, N.Y.).

As in the case of Babe Ruth in 1926, it proved difficult to hang goat horns on Lou Brock. He hit .464 over the seven games and set or tied records for the most hits and stolen bases in a single Series and for most stolen bases in a Series career. His decision not to slide may have been a bad one, but as a player with 938 stolen bases in his career, he had more experience making those decisions than the TV commentators and newspaper reporters who second-guessed him.

A review of the play on the World Series DVD produced by Major League Baseball, which reiterates the claim that Brock's failure to slide was the turning point of the 1968 Series, brings several things into perspective. The throw from Horton was perfect, but it came from left field, over Brock's shoulder, so that he couldn't see it. In close plays at the plate, it's the job of the on-deck hitter to give the runner the signal to slide or stand up. The film of the play shows on-deck hitter Curt Flood approaching the plate, bat in hand, but it doesn't show him giving Brock the traditional palms-down signal to slide. In any case, Brock's view of Flood was obscured by the catcher Freehan.

A review of the play in stop-action reveals another surprising fact. The umpire may have blown the call. It's very close, but Brock's foot seems to land on home plate between Freehan's legs an instant before the catcher swings his glove into the runner's midsection. In the heat of the moment, the TV announcer first called Brock safe, then reversed his opinion when he saw the umpire's upraised thumb. In all fairness, the umpire, Doug Harvey, would have had a clearer view of the play if Brock had chosen to slide. By coming into home standing up, Brock's body shielded the umpire from the actual tag.

It's likely that Brock would have been called safe if he'd slid, but he got no help from his teammate Flood or the umpire Harvey. Even so, his out only cost the Cardinals one run, while the Tigers' winning margin was two runs. The out may have been an emotional turning point, and fodder for second-guessers, but it's hard to see that it cost the Cards the game, let alone the Series.

Jeremy Giambi. Jeremy Giambi was no match for Lou Brock as a base runner. Well below average in both speed and baserunning savvy, the only thing he had in common with the fleet Cardinal was that they both stood accused of the same mistake, a failure to slide in a crucial situation.

Giambi's baserunning gaffe occurred on October 13, 2001, in the third game of the American League Division Series. Giambi's team, the Oakland A's, had won the first two games of the best-three-out-of-five series against the New York Yankees in Yankee Stadium, and returned home to Oakland needing only one win to advance to the League Championship Series.

With two out in the bottom of the seventh and the A's behind 1–0, Giambi reached first base on a single. Terence Long followed Giambi with a double into the right-field corner. Giambi rounded third and headed for home as Yankee right fielder Shane Spencer, usually a left fielder, retrieved the ball and heaved it toward the cutoff man, second baseman Alfonso Soriano. The ball missed Soriano by a wide margin, skipped past first baseman Tino Martinez, and looked as if it would miss catcher Jorge Posada as well as it rolled wide of the first-base line.

Yankee shortstop Derek Jeter raced across the infield, scooped up the off-target throw, and, in a single fluid motion, redirected the ball to the catcher Posada just as Giambi, running upright, was about to cross home plate. His failure to slide cost him and the A's dearly, as Posada's sweeping glove caught his right calf just before he touched the plate.

Giambi had evidently decided not to slide when he saw Spencer's poor throw miss the cutoff man and bounce erratically down the first-base line. His reaction to Jeter's heads-up, athletic play must have been the same as that of the fans and the TV announcers: "Whoa — where did he come from?" Unfortunately for the A's, Giambi didn't react at all to the palms-down slide signal given by his teammate, the on-deck hitter Ramon Hernandez.

The A's failed to score in the eighth and ninth, lost the game 1–0, and went on to lose the next two games and the series. Giambi's baserunning gaffe foreshadowed the home-plate blunders of the A's Byrnes and Tejada against Boston two years later. In both cases the A's led the Division Series by two games and lost three in a row to be eliminated from championship contention.

While the A's rooters readily forgave the 2003 blunders of Byrnes and Tejada, they were less willing to forget Giambi's 2001 gaffe. When the outfielder came to bat for the first time in the 2002 season, the Oakland fans shouted "Slide! Slide!" and the news reporters and television commentators made a point of recalling Giambi's failure to get down and dirty when the A's traded him to Philadelphia in May of 2002.

Fan reaction to the contrary, it can be argued that Giambi was not nearly so culpable as Byrnes and Tejada. Giambi was the victim of an extraordinary play by an all-star shortstop, while Byrnes and Tejada had no one to blame but themselves. There is no guarantee that a sliding Giambi would have been safe, and the decision to remain upright on close plays at the plate

Catcher Jorge Posada of the Yankees has just tagged out Jeremy Giambi of the Athletics, who tried to score standing up as shortstop Derek Jeter crossed into foul territory to rescue an off-target throw from rightfielder Shane Spencer and redirect it to Posada. The Yankees, who trailed the A's two games to none in the best-of-five 2001 Division Championship Series, won the game 1–0 and went on to take two more games from Oakland and advance to the American League Championship Series (photograph courtesy of Nick Lammers of the *Oakland Tribune*).

is not an uncommon one. Sliding can slow a player's progress somewhat, and an upright runner may be able to jar the ball loose from the catcher's grasp.

Even though Giambi may have been less culpable than Byrnes or Tejada, it's likely that his gaffe will live longer and loom larger in baseball lore, partly because it was the flip side of a storied defensive play by Jeter. Tapes of Jeter's play are shown frequently (a photo appeared on an action baseball card the following year), and Giambi's failure to slide makes an easier story to tell than, for example, Tejada's failure to understand the intricacies of an obscure obstruction rule. Furthermore, both Byrnes and Tejada were popular players with well-formed positive images that didn't readily accommodate goat horns. Giambi, on the other hand, was more of a cipher, a part-time player known primarily as the younger brother of Jason Giambi, the American League's Most Valuable Player in 2001. While Jeremy Giambi's burden will never approach the calumny heaped on poor Fred Merkle, he'll always be remembered as "the guy who didn't slide into home."

Of the baserunning gaffes chronicled in this chapter, the player with the least to answer for, Fred Merkle, bore the greatest amount of ridicule for the longest time. Even though it may have been common practice, his failure to touch second brought the term *bonehead* into popular use, and it remains associated with his name to this day.

Chapter Three

Muffed Fly Balls

> Snodgrass dropped it. Maybe once a year a man would drop a ball like that. I'd seen it happen to Speaker, to Hooper, to all of them. No reason. It just happens. The ball hits your glove and falls out and that's all there is to it. If it happens in the middle of the season it's forgotten the next day. But in a World Series, and in particular *that* kind of situation, well, here we are, sixty-six years later, still talking about it.
>
> Smoky Joe Wood
> Interviewed by Donald Honig in 1978

♦ ♦ ♦ ♦

Fielding is one of the most difficult baseball skills to quantify and evaluate. Batting averages can help to separate a good hitting team from a poor one, and a low earned-run average may be the hallmark of a good pitching staff, but a fielding average tells very little about a team's fielding capabilities. Good teams and bad teams alike will record twenty-seven outs in winning most games, and even the worst fielders sport fielding averages in excess of .900 — that is, they make errors on less than 10 percent of their chances. Moreover, the process of assigning errors itself can be misleading. No penalty is assigned to a slow, poorly positioned outfielder who fails to get anywhere close to a batted ball, while a faster, surer outfielder who is able to run down the same ball, only to see it glance off his glove, may be charged with an error.

Baseball fans tend to judge good fielding the way courts judge pornography — they know it when they see it. A spectacular diving catch will always bring the crowd to its feet. And a glove-clanking error on a fly ball at the wrong time can lose a game and ruin a reputation.

Scapegoat: Fred Snodgrass and the $30,000 Muff

The most famous dropped fly in baseball history is undoubtedly the $30,000 muff committed by the Giants' Fred Snodgrass in the final game of the 1912 World Series. With the Series knotted at three wins apiece, the Giants and Red Sox completed nine innings of the decisive game tied 1–1. In the top of the tenth, however, the Giants scored once on doubles by Red Murray and the much-maligned Fred Merkle.

With their ace Christy Mathewson pitching, the Giants went into the bottom of the tenth confident that they would shut down the Red Sox and get the three outs needed to make them world champions. The first batter up for the Red Sox was Clyde Engle, who was pinch-hitting for the pitcher, Smokey Joe Wood. As Snodgrass recounted the event to Lawrence Ritter in *The Glory of Their Times*, Engle

> ... hit a great big, lazy, high fly ball halfway between Red Murray in left field and me. Murray called for it first, but as center fielder I had preference over left and right, so there'd never be a collision. I yelled that I'd take it and waved Murray off and — well — I dropped the darn thing. It was so high that Engle was sitting on second base before I could get it back to the infield.

The Giants expected the next batter, Harry Hooper, to try to bunt Engle over to third, and moved their infield defense in toward the plate. Snodgrass remembers pulling in and playing close behind second, "figuring that if Matty threw to second and the ball got by second in any way, I could still keep Engle from going to third."

After fouling off one bunt attempt, Hooper swung away and smashed the ball over Snodgrass' head in deep left center. Sprinting after it, Snodgrass made what he called "one of the greatest plays of my life," catching the ball over his shoulder on a dead run. Engle was so sure the ball would sail over the head of Snodgrass and drop safely that he had passed third when the ball was caught and barely made it back to second ahead of the center fielder's throw.

"Nobody ever mentions that catch to me," Snodgrass said years later. "All they talk about is the muff."

Mathewson pitched carefully to the next batter, Steve Yerkes, and walked him, bringing up Boston's most dangerous hitter, future Hall of Famer Tris Speaker. Speaker swung lustily at the first pitch, a fadeaway, and lofted a high foul pop-up just off the first-base line that sportswriter Fred Lieb said, "any high school player could have caught." Unfortunately for the Giants, no high school players were on the field. Mathewson, first baseman Fred Merkle, and catcher Chief Meyers all congregated and watched as the ball dropped to earth untouched by any hands, professional or amateur.

Red Sox players Harry Hooper and Smokey Joe Wood, who watched the pop-up drop from the vantage point of the first-base dugout, subsequently reported that Mathewson called for Chief Meyers to catch the ball. Mathewson, who Snodgrass observed could have caught the ball "in his hip pocket himself," later said he had called for Merkle to catch it. Whatever the cause of the mix-up, the missed pop-up clearly unnerved Mathewson. Given a new life, Speaker ripped Matty's next pitch over Merkle's head for a single. Engle scored the tying run and drew a throw from the right fielder that put runners on second and third. After Mathewson walked Duffy Lewis to load the bases, Larry Gardner lofted a sacrifice fly to right field that scored Yerkes with the run that gave the Red Sox the championship.

The 1912 World Series was the first to be decided in the final inning by a home-team comeback, and the first to be decided by an unearned run. Seeking a goat to blame for the Giants' last-minute loss, the New York press settled on Snodgrass, whose muffed fly allowed the tying run to reach base. The *New York Times* coverage was typical. Under the headline

SOX CHAMPIONS
ON MUFFED FLY
Snodgrass Drops Easy Ball
Costing Teammates $29,514
Boston Winning 3–2.

The *Times* lead paragraph read:

Write in the pages of world series baseball history the name of Snodgrass. Write it large and black. Not as a hero, truly not. Put him rather with Merkle, who was in such a hurry that he gave away a National League championship. Snodgrass was in such a hurry that he gave away a world championship. It was because of Snodgrass's generous muff of an easy fly in the tenth inning that the decisive game in the world's series went to the Boston Red Sox this afternoon by a score of 3 to 2, instead of the New York Giants by a score of 2 to 1.

In the second edition of his *Historical Baseball Abstract*, Bill James commented on the seemingly arbitrary nature of this blame game. "Snodgrass wound up with goat horns, although he had done no more to earn them than a dozen other players; the music simply stopped when he didn't have a chair."

In looking back over the years, however, the selection of Snodgrass as a goat seems far from arbitrary. Sportswriters and fans, who have never faced big league pitching or tried to retire

Left: Fred Snodgrass, who dropped the fly ball that put a Red Sox runner on second to lead off the tenth inning of the final game of the 1912 World Series. Snodgrass wasn't the only Giant to contribute to Boston's come-from-behind win, but as the caption at right shows the press put the brunt of the blame on him, and his error came to be known as "the $30,000 Muff," reflecting the difference between the winners' and losers' Series shares (Card image: Library of Congress, Prints and Photographs Division; 1912 cartoon by Wallace Goldsmith of the *Boston Globe*).

big-league hitters, have all caught fly balls. When a major leaguer drops an easy fly, therefore, the unspoken reaction is, "I could have caught that — why couldn't he?"

Other candidates for goatdom included Mathewson, who stood by with Merkle and Meyers as Speaker's foul fly dropped to earth untouched and subsequently gave up both Speaker's double and Gardner's game-winning sacrifice fly. But it is difficult to cast Mathewson, one of the most popular pitchers of his day, in the role of goat when he held Boston to one run over nine innings and his defense made five errors behind him. As for Merkle and Meyers, tradition demands only one goat per series, and it was difficult to apportion blame for the untouched foul fly that gave Speaker an extra life at the plate.

The entire Series was marred by errors, with a total of thirty-one by both teams (one short of a Series record) and seventeen of those by the Giants. New York shortstop Art Fletcher was at least as guilty as Snodgrass, pulling up short in the seventh inning and failing to catch a bloop double by Red Sox manager Jake Stahl. Stahl subsequently scored the only run Mathewson allowed in the regulation nine innings. In searching for a scapegoat, however, Snodgrass' tenth inning muff, which bounced off his glove, easily overshadowed Fletcher's earlier transgression, which wasn't scored as an error because the shortstop never caught up with the ball.

In retrospect, it's easy to see why the press singled out Snodgrass to blame for the Series loss. The choice was logical, but it was also unfair. As Snodgrass observed to Lawrence Ritter fifty years later,

> according to the newspapers, Fred Snodgrass lost the World Series. I did drop that fly ball, and that did put what turned out to be the tying run on base, but that's a long way from "losing a World Series." However, the facts don't seem to matter.

While the New York press flayed Snodgrass for his error, the Boston papers, whose Red

Sox were the beneficiaries of the "$30,000 muff," were much more magnanimous. The *Boston Globe*'s headlines trumpeted **BOSTON NOW SUPREME IN BASEBALL WORLD** and focused on the heroics of their hometown heroes, reducing Snodgrass' error to regular type as just one element in their play-by-play description of the final inning.

In his *Globe* column the day after the Boston win, Sox hero Tris Speaker sympathized with his fellow center fielder, noting that Snodgrass would make that catch "nine-hundred and ninety-nine times out of a thousand" and recalling that "in a previous game, he made an almost impossible catch and saved his team from defeat thereby." Speaker went on to note, "That great play is probably forgotten in view of his slip up in this last game." Viewed from today's perspective, Snodgrass' entire nine-year baseball career has essentially been forgotten in the light of that one slip-up.

Certainly the New York press never let Snodgrass forget his error. He was branded for life by his misplay, and when he died in 1974, after a life as a successful banker, rancher, and politician, the *New York Times* headline on his obituary read:

FRED SNODGRASS, 86, DEAD
BALL PLAYER MUFFED 1912 FLY.

Escaped Goats

Max Flack: The War-Shortened Season

Max Flack of the Cubs, whose dropped fly ball in the third inning of the final World Series game of 1918 allowed two Red Sox runs to cross the plate and paved the way for a 2–1 Boston win and their last World Championship for eighty-six years (National Baseball Hall of Fame Library, Cooperstown, N.Y.).

The 1918 major-league season was shortened by the war in Europe. With baseball designated as a nonessential industry, the federal government decreed that both leagues would complete their regular seasons by Labor Day. The Chicago Cubs met the Boston Red Sox in the World Series, which featured tightly pitched, low-scoring contests.

After five games, the Cubs were down three games to two, losing two games to a 23-year-old Babe Ruth and one to the underhand pitching of Carl Mays. Mays was on the mound for the Red Sox in Game Six, facing Lefty Tyler of the Cubs. Neither team scored until the third, when Tyler walked two batters. A groundout put runners on second and third when the hitter, George Whiteman, a thirty-two-year-old rookie purchased from Toronto to help fill out Boston's war-depleted roster, hit a sinking line drive to right field. The right fielder, Max Flack, got his glove on the ball but couldn't hold it, and both runners scored on the error.

The two runs that scored on Flack's muff were all that Boston would record for the day. But they were enough, as Mays held the Cubs to a single run, so that the Red Sox won the game 2–1 and the World Series, four games to two.

The newspapers of the day were much kinder to Flack than they had been to Fred Snodgrass in

1912. The *Boston Globe*, for example, apportioned the blame equally between Flack, whose error allowed the winning runs to score, and the pitcher Tyler, who issued free passes to put the runners on base, headlining its lead story,

**RED SOX WIN SIXTH
GAME AND THE TITLE**
Beat Cubs 2–1, Tyler's Wildness and Flack's
Muff Accounting for Victory.

One reason that Flack's muff has been all but forgotten today is that the nation had bigger fish to fry in September 1918. The Red Sox Series win was only the third lead on the front page of the *Boston Globe* on September 12, giving way to a banner headline:

MANPOWER OF NATION POURS OUT TODAY,

announcing a massive nationwide draft registration, and a second lead,

GERMANS PREPARE FOR BIG RETREAT,

announcing Berlin's abandonment of their forward line in France.

The New York press did not have a horse in this particular Boston/Chicago race, and the war and draft news moved the Series result entirely off the front page of the *New York Times*. Inside the paper, the headlines on the *Times* sports page announced that

**SOX GIVE CUBS
COUP DE GRACE
IN SIXTH GAME**

and

**BATTLE IS CLOSE
BUT NOT EXCITING.**

Smaller type noted that **FLACK'S MUFF TELLS TALE**, and the *Times* correspondent described Flack's error in sarcastic detail.

> Whiteman lifted a line drive to right field and Flack came running in to make an easy catch. He caught up to the rapidly descending ball and had it entirely surrounded by his hands. Tyler was offering thanksgiving for crawling out of a bad hole when the ball squeezed its way through Flack's buttered digits.

With the future of baseball as a nonessential business in doubt, the *Times* went on to note:

> It may be a long time before there is another world's series, and the finish, which hinged on a life-sized laughable muff, closes a topsy-turvy season in much the same way as the famous $30,000 muff of Fred Snodgrass ended the series of 1912 when the hopes of the New York Giants trickled through his hands in centre field on the same Fenway meadow.

Writing six years after the 1912 World Series, the *Times* correspondent had already elevated the Snodgrass muff to mythic proportions, overstating its importance by claiming it "ended the series of 1912" when all it did was allow the tying run to reach base. Even though Flack's error, which allowed two decisive runs to score, was arguably more costly than that of Snodgrass, the Cub outfielder's muff never achieved the same mythic status. When Flack died in 1975, the *New York Times* didn't bother to note his passing with an obituary, let alone chide him for missing an "easy fly."

Bob Meusel and the Heroics of Pete Alexander

A muffed fly ball helped to decide one of the most famous World Series games of all time, the seventh game of the 1926 series between the New York Yankees and St. Louis Cardinals, the game in which 39-year-old Grover Cleveland Alexander came in from the bullpen in the bottom of the seventh inning to strike out Tony Lazzeri with the bases loaded and preserve the Cardinals' 3–2 lead. Alexander pitched flawlessly for the next two innings, allowing only one runner to reach base. That runner was Babe Ruth, who walked and was thrown out trying to steal second to end the game and install the Cardinals as World Champions.

Alexander's heroics overshadowed the fact that all three of the Redbirds' runs in their 3–2 victory were unearned, coming in the fourth inning courtesy of two Yankee errors. With one out in the fourth, Yankee pitcher Waite Hoyt gave up a single to Cardinal first baseman Jim Bottomley. The next batter, Lester Bell, hit a grounder to short that appeared to be tailor-made for a double play, but the young shortstop Mark Koenig fumbled it, putting runners on first and second. The next hitter, Chick Hafey, fisted a short fly to left center that barely fell safely between the shortstop Koenig and the left fielder, Bob Meusel, loading the bases and setting the stage for disaster.

With two strikes on him, Bob O'Farrell lifted a high fly ball to left center that could have been caught by either left fielder Meusel or center fielder Earle Combs. Meusel, who possessed one of the strongest throwing arms in the league, anticipated that Bottomley would try to score after the catch and called for the ball so that he could make the throw home.

Meusel stepped in front of Combs and was evidently so intent on making a strong throw home that he neglected to catch the ball. In the words of the *New York Times*, "The white pill hit his outstretched hands and popped out again, like a rabbit from the magician's hat." Bottomley scored easily from third on the error, and the bases remained loaded. The next batter, Tommy Thevenow, unloaded them with a two-strike single that scored two runs. As a result of the errors by Koenig and Meusel, all three of the Cardinals' fourth-inning runs were unearned. They were the only runs scored off Hoyt, who pitched brilliantly, and, thanks to Alexander's relief pitching, the unearned runs held up for a 3–2 Cardinal win.

For most newspapers, the story of the game was the heroic relief pitching of "Pete" Alexander, in the twilight of his Hall of Fame career. His performance in striking out Lazzeri with the bases loaded and setting down the

Bob Meusel of the Yankees, whose dropped fly ball provided the margin of victory for the Cardinals in the seventh game of the 1926 World Series. Meusel's fourth-inning muff was overshadowed by the relief heroics of the Cards' Grover Cleveland Alexander, who struck out Tony Lazzeri with the bases loaded to end the seventh inning, and held the Yankees hitless for the next two innings to seal the St. Louis victory (Library of Congress, Prints and Photographs Division).

strong Yankee batting order in the eighth and ninth was all the more remarkable because it came just one day after he had pitched a complete-game victory in Game Six. The next day's *New York Times* headlined **ALEXANDER AGAIN THE HERO**, and most other newspapers followed suit.

One newspaper correspondent chose to call attention to Meusel's misplay. That correspondent was New York Giant manager John McGraw, who headlined his column on page 20 of the *St. Louis Post-Dispatch* with the statement,

> Meusel's Muff Caused Downfall of Yanks — McGraw

> This is the second time in my recollection that a world's series has been lost by an outfielder muffing a fly ball. Nobody knows better than I how much the other one cost. It was made by Snodgrass in Boston in 1912 when my team lost.

Given McGraw's history, it's understandable that he would draw a direct line between Meusel's muff in 1926 and that of Snodgrass in 1912. Since he counts Meusel's muff as only the second one of its kind, Flack's 1918 error had evidently already passed from public memory. McGraw's column goes on to echo the perspective of most other sportswriters, saying that the "... sight of Old Pete Alexander, 39 years old, turning back the foe and winning the championship, can never be forgotten." For every columnist and writer except McGraw, the story of "Alexander the Great" easily overshadowed Meusel's misplay.

Bobby Tolan and Riverside Stadium's Center-Field Fence

Cincinnati center fielder Bobby Tolan was a key cog in the Big Red Machine that won the National League pennant in 1970, when he batted .316 and led the league in stolen bases. After tearing his Achilles tendon playing basketball in the off-season, he sat out the entire 1971 season, and never quite regained his pre–1971 form afterward. Still, he performed well enough to help the Reds reach the World Series against the Oakland Athletics in 1972. The Reds and A's split the first six games of the Series, and in the first inning of the seventh and deciding game, Tolan misjudged a fly off the bat of A's center fielder Angel Mangual. Tolan first charged the hit, then realized the ball was sailing over his head and leapt for it at the last minute. The ball glanced off his glove for an error and rolled to the fence as Mangual hustled around to third. He scored when cleanup hitter Gene Tenace hit a sharp grounder that struck the lip of the Astroturf carpet and bounced over the third baseman's head.

The Reds tied the game in the bottom of the fifth, but Oakland went ahead for good in the top of the sixth when Tenace doubled in Campy Campaneris and Sal Bando followed with a blast to the center-field fence. Tolan fell at the warning track chasing Bando's hit, and it landed untouched for a run-scoring double. Reporting on the contest, Roger Angell said, "Extraordinarily, most of this game seemed to be played at the foot of that center-field fence, 404 feet away." The Reds tallied once more to make the final score 3–2 in favor of the Athletics, so that the unearned run scored on Tolan's error proved to be the margin of victory. Because his error occurred in the first inning, however, and the Reds subsequently tied the score, Tolan was never fitted for goat horns. In fact, none of the World Series histories published in 2003 to commemorate 100 years of the interleague rivalry mentioned Tolan's error at all.

Hack Wilson: "The Most Spectacular Rally in the History of Sport"

The 1929 World Series between the Philadelphia Athletics and the Chicago Cubs featured the greatest single-game comeback in Series history. In *The Story of the World Series*, Frederick

G. Lieb called it "Perhaps the most spectacular rally in the history of sport." The rally was fueled by two sun-drenched fly balls misplayed by Cub center fielder Hack Wilson.

Wilson, a squat, fireplug of a man who stood 5'6" tall and weighed 190 pounds, was voted into the Hall of Fame on the strength of his hitting prowess. It was his play in the outfield, however, that contributed to the Cubs' downfall in the fourth game of the 1929 Series.

Connie Mack's Athletics had won two of the first three games, but Chicago seemed on the verge of evening the Series at two games apiece as they took an 8–0 lead into the bottom of the seventh inning of the fourth game, played at Philadelphia's Shibe Park.

The Cubs' lead appeared particularly safe in the hands of pitcher Charlie Root, who had limited the Athletics to three hits over the first six innings. When the first A's batter, Al Simmons, led off with a home run onto the left-field roof to end the shutout, therefore, there was no cause for alarm in the Chicago dugout. After the next hitter, Jimmy Foxx, singled, Bing Miller lofted a short fly to center field that Wilson lost in the sun. The ball fell safely for a single, putting runners on first and second. Still, seemingly no cause for great worry on the part of the Cubs. Three singles and a pop-out later, however, the Cubs lead had been halved to 8–4 and manager Joe McCarthy was concerned enough to replace Root with a relief pitcher, veteran left-hander Art Nehf.

The first batter to face Nehf was Mule Haas, who came to the plate with Joe Boley on third and Max Bishop on first. Haas hit a long drive to deep center, and, in the words of John Drebinger of the *New York Times*,

The squat Hack Wilson, Cub centerfielder, wheeled about and ran at top speed, his short stubby legs leaving nothing but a blur as they carried him over the ground. He got under the ball in time to make the catch, but as it came down it crossed the glaring sun. Hack lost sight of it. The ball almost struck him as it landed at his feet, and as it rolled away Boley and Bishop scampered wildly over the plate and Haas, too, completed the circuit for a home run.

Haas' inside-the-park homer made the score 8–7. The Athletics scored three more times to set a Series record that still stands for most runs in a single inning. That brought the score to 10–8, where it stood at the end of the game. The A's ended the Series the next day, defeating the shell-shocked Cubs 3–2 by coming back from a 2–0 deficit and scoring three runs in the bottom of the ninth.

Even though the fourth game and the Series turned on the A's seventh-inning rally and the fly balls that Wilson lost in the sun, there was no attempt to summon up the ghost of Fred Snodgrass and hang permanent goat horns on the stocky center fielder. The horns would have been a poor fit, since Wilson led all hitters on both teams with a .471 average, and actually caught more flies

Hack Wilson, Cub centerfielder, chases a fly ball with his sunglasses on. The glasses were no help in Game Four of the 1929 World Series, when Wilson lost two balls in the sun to help the Philadelphia A's stage the greatest single-inning comeback in Series history, as they scored ten runs to overcome an 8–0 Cub lead and win the game (National Baseball Hall of Fame Library, Cooperstown, N.Y.).

than any other player in the Series. Moreover, writers in the press box understood the impact of the afternoon sun in Philadelphia's home park.

As Wilson, quoted by Joseph L. Reichler in *The World Series, a 75th Anniversary*, said afterward:

> The sun shining over the roof of the Shibe Park stands from in back of home plate was blinding. It was so bad that Art Nehf was having a hard time catching Zach Taylor's throws back to the pitcher's box. I couldn't see the ball at all after it left Haas' bat until it was almost to the ground. I started after it, but it was too late. Remember, that didn't lose the game. It helped, but we were still ahead even after it happened.

Anyone who has played baseball has had the frustrating, helpless experience of losing track of a fly ball as it passes in front of the sun and watching it thud to earth untouched. For this reason, writers generally grant a dispensation to fielders victimized by glare, and official scorers are circumspect in assigning errors when fly balls are lost in the sun.

Willie Davis: The Laurel and Hardy School of Outfielding

In the 1966 World Series, the sun played a major role in undoing another center fielder, Willie Davis of the Los Angeles Dodgers. After the Dodgers lost the first game of the Series to the Baltimore Orioles, future Hall of Fame pitchers Sandy Koufax and Jim Palmer both pitched shutout ball for the first four innings of the second game.

In the top of the fifth, with Oriole Boog Powell on first base and one out, Paul Blair lifted a fairly deep fly to left center that Davis lost in the sun. In the words of the *Los Angeles Times*, "Willie staggered around a bit as the ball was coming down. It bounced out of his glove and by the time he could get it back to the infield, Powell was on third and Blair was on second."

If the ball had fallen untouched, tradition dictates that no error would have been assigned on the play. Because Davis got close enough to touch the ball, however, the official scorer awarded him his first error of the inning. He doubled that total on the very next play.

The next batter, Andy Etchebarren, hit a fly to shallow left-center. Davis got under it easily and started to position himself for the throw home when he lost the ball again. He gestured helplessly with his arms, made a late stab at the ball, and saw it plop out of his glove for his second error.

In the words of Roger Angell in *The Summer Game*, "Still suffering under the weight of so many footcandles, Davis now pounced on the ball and made his first really unforgivable play—an angry Little League heave into the Dodger dugout that scored the second run."

Two sun-basted fly balls and a wild throw added up to three errors in one inning, still a Series record for a single player. In fact, the Series record for most errors by a player in a single *game* is three. But Willie Davis bunched his errors in a single inning on two successive batted balls. As *LA Times* columnist Jim Murray noted, "Willie's record was not only for center fielders. It was an all time record for any position for errors—including sailors on leave, bank presidents who bet on horses, and guys who get married by mail."

Los Angeles made three more errors in the game, for a total of six, and lost, 6–0. They went on to lose the Series in four straight games. It's difficult to argue that Davis' misplays affected the Series outcome, since the Dodgers failed to score a single run in the last three games.

After the second game, Davis at first lost his composure with reporters, but then calmed down quickly and answered a long series of questions touching on the exacerbating impact of LA smog, which creates a glare along the rim of the Coliseum, and the obvious fact that the sun had affected his play.

Dodger center fielder Willie Davis — who had lost the previous batter's fly in the sun — does a repeat performance as he loses the pop fly of Baltimore's Andy Etchebarren in the fifth inning of World Series Game Three in 1966. Davis picked up the ball and threw wildly to third for his third error of the inning — a new World Series record (AP/Wide World Photos).

> I lost both balls. I could see them both until they got in the sun at a certain point on their way down. You've always got a chance if you stab at a ball, even if you don't see it. So I did. I don't think they were errors. I didn't see the balls. If I can see them I can catch them. But I suppose they have to give you an error if you touch the ball.

The columnists of the day had a lot of fun at Davis' expense following the second game. Jim Murray of the *Los Angeles Times* wrote, "Willie looked as if he got his basic training from Laurel and Hardy. You could almost hear the announcer on nationwide television saying 'there's a high fly ball to Davis in center and Willie makes a routine drop.'"

And Arthur Daley of the *New York Times* closed his column with the following joke: "'I'm willing to give odds,' said one embittered spectator, 'that when the Dodgers leave for Baltimore tonight, Willie doesn't even catch the plane.'"

But Davis had many defenders. Roger Angell reported that in the visiting team's dressing room, Oriole manager Hank Bauer, himself a former outfielder, "closed the accident report on Davis when he said, 'If the Dodgers don't want him, I'll take him.'"

New York Times writer Leonard Koppett called up the memory of Fred Snodgrass, inflating his error from a $30,000 muff to a $100,000 muff, but concluded that Davis wasn't likely to endure the same fate as the Giant center fielder. Koppett began his column by observing, "How values and reactions have shifted over the years, in baseball and in life, was demonstrated today by the case of William Henry Davis, resident center fielder of the Los Angeles Dodgers."

Koppett then went on to compare the errors of Snodgrass and Davis, noting that a half a century after "Fred Snodgrass's $100,000 (sic) muff became a part of baseball lore, ... baseball fans who know nothing else about Snodgrass recognize this phrase as the epitome of costly error."

In spite of the fact that Willie Davis had just set a series record by making three errors in one inning, however, Koppett did not consider him a "prime candidate for long-lived 'goathood,'" since the reaction in the world of 1966 to his performance appeared to be, "Sympathy, understanding, and a pervasive sense of proportion about the whole business, on all sides."

> "All I can say is I feel sorry for him," said Manager Walter Alston. "He can't catch what he can't see. If I didn't have Willie Davis playing center for me all year and if he hadn't hit a homer with two men on last Sunday, we might not be playing in the series at all."

Koppett also invoked the recent experience of the greatest center fielder of the day, Willie Mays, saying, "It happened to Willie Mays here on Labor Day, a little later in the day when the sun was lower and almost touching the rim, and it cost the San Francisco Giants an important loss to the Dodgers." Koppett ended his comparison by concluding that Davis would avoid the fate of Snodgrass.

> In short, the chances are that Davis will live down his terrible inning, and he is not the sort to be bothered by such things anyhow. He is 26 years old, cool to the point of indifference, the fastest runner in major league baseball.... The boos he heard today are not likely to rankle him, nor to be continued long by the basically worshipful Los Angeles fans. Because times have changed.

The *New York Times* columnist was right about Davis and the LA fans living down the impact of his ignominious inning. He went on to play seven more years with the Dodgers and four years beyond that with four different teams, ending an eighteen-year career with a batting average of .279 in an era when pitchers were dominant, and retired with no stigma attached to his name. While no one has equaled his record of three errors in a single World Series inning, other players have made three errors in a single game. The last player to accomplish this dubious feat was the Red Sox Bill Mueller in the 2004 World Series, and when he did it, none of the announcers or writers invoked the name of Willie Davis.

While Koppett was right in predicting that Willie Davis wouldn't suffer "long-lived 'goathood'" for his misplays, he was wrong in asserting that times had changed enough to eliminate the prospect of long-lasting blame. Times might have changed on the West Coast, but not on the other side of the country. Twenty years after Koppett's column appeared, Bill Buckner suffered every bit as much condemnation for botching a grounder in 1986 as Fred Snodgrass had for muffing a fly in 1912.

Summing Up

Today, over ninety years after he dropped a fly ball struck by the leadoff hitter in the tenth inning of the deciding 1912 World Series game, Fred Snodgrass remains the base reference for muffed flies. Timing, geography, and fate have conspired to keep his name at the head of the list. His error marked the first time that the World Series had been decided by an unearned run, and it has been invoked whenever a subsequent Series has turned on a muffed fly or botched grounder. He was a young player, with no established image, and he wore the uniform of the New York Giants, whose home town press could be particularly vicious. He waited until the tenth inning to muff his fly, unlike such now-forgotten players as Max Flack and Bobby Tolan, whose equally costly errors came earlier in decisive games. He didn't misjudge the ball, or lose it in the sun, but had it in his hands for what looked to everyone like an easy catch. A catch, Tris Speaker said, Snodgrass would make nine hundred and ninety-nine times out of a thousand. A catch your Aunt Minnie could have made. Except your Aunt Minnie never suited up for the New York Giants in front of 17,000 screaming Fenway fans with $30,000 at stake.

CHAPTER FOUR

Dropped Foul Pop-Ups

> What baseball means to me is standing as a child on third base of our local softball field and praying that no ball would be hit my way....
>
> My admiration for the men who play this game has been intensified by this early revelation of the courage it takes. The courage, too, to stand alone, surrounded by green space, and have your mistakes show in full view of the stadium.
>
> John Updike
"What Baseball Means to Me"

◆ ◆ ◆ ◆

An outfielder who muffs a fly ball in fair territory puts his team in immediate jeopardy. A batter who should have been put out reaches base, any base runners advance, and crucial runs may score. When fielders drop catchable pop-ups in foul territory, though, there is no immediate impact. A batter who should have been retired is given another chance to hit. If he fails to capitalize on the opportunity, the dropped pop-up is all but forgotten, at most a footnote in the next day's box score if the botched catch was egregious enough to be ruled an error by the official scorer.

There are times, though, when the batter uses his newfound life to break a game open or keep a rally going with a key hit. Batters operating on borrowed time have helped to decide several crucial postseason games or tight pennant races. In the wake of these Lazarus-like heroics, the enablers who extended the hitters' lives by botching foul pop-ups have seldom received the same opprobrium as fielders who have misplayed fly balls in fair territory.

Scapegoat: Hank Gowdy and the $50,000 Muff

Hank Gowdy was a tall, skinny redhead, a shy, gangly man who didn't look anything like the image of a big-league catcher. Too slow to play most positions in the field, he was pressed into service behind the plate by the Boston Braves in 1914 and became the hero of the 1914 World Series, batting .565 and leading both teams in doubles, triples, and home runs as the Braves swept the Philadelphia Athletics in four games. Midway through the 1917 season, he became the first major leaguer to enlist in the armed forces, serving in the trenches of World War I and emerging with the rank of sergeant. After a seventeen-year career that ended in 1929, however, he is best known for a pop-up he misplayed in the final game of the 1924 World Series.

The 1924 World Series between the Washington Senators, led by first-year manager and shortstop Bucky Harris, and John McGraw's New York Giants was memorable for a number of reasons, not the least of which was the remarkable seventh game. It was the first Series appearance for the Senators and their Hall of Fame pitcher Walter Johnson, who was nearing the end of his 21-year career. Until 1924, the line on the Washington club was that it was "first in war, first in peace, and last in the American League." Generally regarded as the greatest pitcher of all time, Walter Johnson was 37 years old in 1924 and, even though he had an exemplary season (winning 23 games against 7 losses with a league-leading 2.72 ERA), he blew his two Series starts against the Giants, losing Game One 4–3 in twelve innings and dropping Game Five 6–3.

Down three games to two after Johnson's Game Five loss, the Senators tied the Series at three-all with a 2–1 win in Washington, forcing a seventh game for only the second time in Series history. New York led the seventh game 3–1 in the bottom of the eighth when the Senators loaded the bases with two outs and the Fates gave the Giants a preview of coming distractions. Washington manager Bucky Harris hit a weak grounder toward third baseman Fred Lindstrom that appeared to be the final out of the inning until the ball hit a pebble and bounced high over Lindstrom's head, bringing in the tying runs.

With the scored tied in the ninth inning, Harris brought in his ace pitcher, Johnson, who was operating with only one day of rest. Pitching in and out of trouble, Johnson held the Giants scoreless from the ninth through the twelfth innings, when the Fates delivered on their promise. With one out in the bottom of the twelfth, Senator catcher Muddy Ruel lifted a high fly toward the grandstand behind home plate. In the words of third baseman Lindstrom,

> Hank Gowdy, our catcher, threw his mask aside and went after the ball. It looked like an easy out. But then the wind began carrying the ball back toward the plate and Hank moved with it. It still looked like an easy out. But then one of those fluke things happened. As he moved under the ball with his glove up to make the catch, Hank stepped right onto that mask, lost his balance, slipped and fell, and the ball came down on the grass alongside of him.

Hank Gowdy pursues a foul pop-up during the regular season, having thrown his mask out of harm's way (**National Baseball Hall of Fame Library, Cooperstown, N.Y.**).

Up until that time, Ruel had managed only one hit in the entire Series, a single in the Senators' eighth-inning comeback. Given a new life by Gowdy's clog dance with his mask, Ruel doubled sharply into left field. The next batter, Walter Johnson, hit a grounder that the shortstop Travis Jackson fumbled, putting runners on first and second with one out. That brought a rookie, Earl McNeely, to the plate. McNeely lashed a hard bouncer down the third-base line. Improbably, the Fates stepped in again.

"Well, it happened again," Lindstrom told Donald Honig in 1978, "the ball hit a pebble — maybe the same darned pebble that Harris' ball had hit — and took a big kangaroo hop over my head." As the ball bounced untouched over Lindstrom's head, Muddy Ruel rounded third and came home with the Series-winning run.

Thus, the Senators manufactured the winning run from a pop-up dropped by a catcher who developed a sudden case of foot-in-mask disease, a grounder fumbled by a usually sure-handed shortstop, and a bad-hop bouncer that looked suspiciously familiar. Losing pitcher Jack Bentley summed up the proceedings by observing, "Walter Johnson is such a loveable character that the Good Lord didn't want to see him get beat again."

While the headlines in the next day's papers focused on the popular Johnson's first World Series victory, most stories found space to draw a parallel between Gowdy's error and Snodgrass's $30,000 muff twelve years earlier. Both misplays occurred in extra innings in the seventh Series game (the only seventh games to date), and both helped to deny John McGraw's Giants the world championship. By 1924, though, the difference between the winning and losing Series shares was $50,000, so that the cost of Gowdy's error was inflated accordingly. In the words of the *New York Times*,

> Gowdy made a $50,000 muff of a foul pop off Muddy Ruel's bat when he stumbled over his mask and let the ball get away from him. It was baseball history repeating itself. McGraw and Christy Mathewson lost the 1912 championship when Fred Snodgrass dropped a fly ball in the twelfth (sic).

"I've been in baseball thirty years and that's the first time I ever saw a catcher step into his own mask," said Christy Mathewson. "Everything bad seems to happen to Giant teams in the World Series." Gowdy's glitch did have one positive result. Ever since the 1924 Series, instruction books have cautioned beginning catchers pursuing foul balls to "locate the pop-up and throw your mask as far as possible from the path of the ball's descent."

Escaped Goats

The Mathewson-Merkle-Meyers Mix-Up

One of the most costly dropped pop-ups in baseball history occurred in the final game of the 1912 World Series and has already been mentioned in connection with the $30,000 muff of Giant center fielder Fred Snodgrass. With one out and the Giants ahead 2–1 in the bottom of the tenth inning, the Red Sox had Clyde Engle on second as a result of Snodgrass' error and Steve Yerkes on first as a result of an uncharacteristic walk from Christy Mathewson. Red Sox captain Tris Speaker lofted a pop-up just off the first-base line that could have been handled easily by Mathewson or first baseman Fred Merkle. It was a tougher play for the catcher Chief Meyers, who chased the ball down the line and arrived in time to see it drop untouched near the first-base coach's box as each Giant waited for someone else to make the play. Given a new lease on life, Speaker singled on Mathewson's next pitch, driving home Engle with the tying run and moving Yerkes to third, where he tagged up and scored the winning run on a sacrifice fly off the bat of Larry Gardner.

The newspapers of the day awarded goat horns to Snodgrass for the error that put Engle on second base to start the inning. The misplayed pop-up was written off as an ancillary screw-up, either the result of poor communication or another blunder by "bonehead" Fred Merkle, whose first-base position was closest to the ball's final resting place. One reporter wrote that Merkle "appeared to be in a trance," and Hugh Fullerton of the *New York Times* was particularly hard on the hapless first baseman. Fullerton wrote of the foul pop-up:

> Anyone could have caught it. I could have jumped out of the press box and caught it behind my back. But Merkle quit. Yes, Merkle quit cold. He didn't start for the ball. He seemed to be suffering from financial paralysis. Perhaps he was calculating the difference between the winner's and loser's end. He didn't start. Mathewson saw the ball going down. Meyers saw it would fall safe and they raced toward it, too late, and the ball dented the turf a few feet from first.

In later years, Red Sox players Harry Hooper and Smokey Joe Wood, who viewed the mix-up from the vantage point of the first-base dugout, offered an explanation for Merkle's inactivity. Mathewson, they said, had called for Meyers to make the catch. Wood, who was the winning pitcher in the game, told Donald Honig in the author's 1979 compilation of interviews, *October Heroes*,

> The first baseman, Fred Merkle, had the best shot at it. But instead of calling for Merkle to take it, Mathewson came down off the mound calling for Chief Meyers, the catcher. Merkle could have caught it easily, but Mathewson kept calling for Meyers. I'll never know why. You see, Merkle was coming in on the ball and the Chief was going with it. It's a much easier play for Merkle. But there was Matty, yelling for the Chief. I can hear him to this day. But Meyers never could get to it. The ball dropped. It just clunked down into the grass in foul ground and lay there. We couldn't believe it. Neither could Mathewson. You never saw a man as mad as he was when that ball hit the ground. But the way we saw it, it was his own fault. He called for the wrong man. That's what we always felt won the Series for us. The write-ups in the papers never stressed that as much as they did Snodgrass dropping the ball in center field.

In later years, Mathewson claimed he called for Merkle, not Meyers, to take the pop-up. Meyers himself, interviewed by Lawrence Ritter in *The Glory of Their Times*, doesn't mention hearing any Giant call for the catch, but suggested that the Red Sox may have contributed to the confusion by calling off Merkle.

Center: 1912 cartoon by *Boston Globe* reporter Wallace Goldsmith depicting the Mathewson–Merkle–Meyers mix-up that preceded Tris Speaker's game-tying RBI in the tenth inning of the "Snodgrass" game. Baseball cards at left, top and right show Meyers, Mathewson, and Merkle (baseball cards from the Library of Congress Prints and Photographs Collection).

I gave that pop-up the old college try, but it was too far away for me to get. Matty came over, too, but waited for Merkle to take it, and it fell between all of us. I think the Red Sox dugout coached Merkle off it. The Boston bench called for Matty to take it, and called for me to take it, and I think that confused Fred. He was afraid of a collision. You see, the Red Sox bench was right there, near where the ball fell, and they just coached them off it. Well, that's all right. It's all part of the game.

It's also been suggested that Speaker himself, running down the first-base line, called for Meyers, the least likely suspect, to make the catch. Given his actions, Merkle must have heard someone call him off the ball, most likely his teammate Mathewson, whose job it was to direct traffic in such cases. Whatever the cause of the confusion, the botched play clearly unnerved Mathewson, who, the *Times* notes, returned to the mound arguing with Merkle and Meyers and "saying things which he emphasized with angry gestures." He gave up the game-tying single to Speaker on his very next pitch, and the misplayed pop-up proved to be at least as costly to the Giants as the Snodgrass error that received most of the press attention.

Jack Clark's Royal Screw-Up

In the 1985 World Series between the St. Louis Cardinals and the Kansas City Royals, dubbed the I-70 Series in honor of the Interstate linking the two Missouri cities, the Cards were up three games to two and seemed about to close out the Series when they broke a scoreless tie in the eighth inning of the sixth game and took a 1–0 lead into the bottom of the ninth. At that point, fortune seemed to favor the Cardinals. In the entire regular season and postseason, they had never lost a game when they led going into the ninth inning; their relief pitcher, rookie Todd Worrell, had never lost a major-league game; and just one day earlier in Game Five, Worrell had struck out all six of the Royal hitters he'd faced.

Fortune didn't wait long to turn her back on the Cards. The first Royals batter, pinch hitter Jorge Orta, squibbed a bouncer that Card first baseman Jack Clark fielded and threw to Worrell covering first. The ball and Worrell appeared to have beaten Orta to the bag, but American League umpire Don Denkinger spread his palms in the safe sign. Clark, Worrell, and Cardinal manager Whitey Herzog argued their case heatedly without moving Denkinger. The instant TV replay showed that the runner was clearly out, but the replay was not admissible evidence in Denkinger's court of appeals and Orta remained on first.

The next batter, Steve Balboni, lifted a high fly near the first-base dugout. Jack Clark drifted over, called for the ball, realized he'd misjudged it, glanced warily at the dugout steps, backtracked hastily, and lunged

Jack Clark, who came to the majors as an outfielder and shifted to first base late in his career after age had weakened his defensive skills, misplayed a foul pop-up in the crucial sixth game of the 1985 World Series between the Cardinals and Royals (National Baseball Hall of Fame Library Cooperstown, N.Y.).

for the ball as it dropped just beyond his reach and bounced high off the top step of the dugout.

Given another chance, Balboni singled, putting runners on first and second. A failed sacrifice attempt forced the lead runner, Orta, at third and left runners on first and second with one out. The runners advanced to second and third on a passed ball, and scored the tying and winning runs on a bloop single by pinch-hitter Dane Iorg.

Feeling they'd been robbed of a Game Six victory by Denkinger's blown decision, the disheartened Cardinals were overmatched by Royals pitcher Bret Saberhagen the next day and lost Game Seven and the Series 11–0. While the umpire's miscall has been cited as the turning point in the Series, the muffed pop-up and the passed ball that followed were just as costly. After the call went against them, Card manager Whitey Herzog recalled, "Guys did things they hadn't done all year. Darrell Porter, my catcher, missed a pitch for a passed ball. Clark misjudged a pop foul. We just fell apart."

Jack Clark had started his professional career as a third baseman, but his strong throwing arm proved inaccurate, and after leading the minor leagues in errors for two seasons, he was shifted to the outfield and eventually to first base. Sandwiched between Denkinger's bad call and Porter's passed ball, his muffed pop-up has been relegated to a footnote in the history of the 1985 World Series. Baseball historians and St. Louis fans tend to blame Denkinger for the turnaround that led to the Cards' downfall. In reporting on the I-70 Series for the *New Yorker*, however, Roger Angell took a more measured view.

> I can sympathize with the indignation of Cardinal fans and players who may still believe that ... they were jobbed out of a World Championship, even though I don't agree. Baseball luck is an inescapable part of the game, and how a team responds to a sudden, unfair shock very often turns out to be what matters in the end.

Yogi Berra and the Reynolds No-Hitter

Few dropped foul pop-ups lead to the dire consequences experienced by Hank Gowdy, Jack Clark, and the combination of Merkle, Meyers, and Mathewson. In fact, the majority of dropped fouls leave no ill after-effects. Two which caused only temporary heartburn involved a pair of premier catchers, Yogi Berra and Bob Boone.

In late September 1951, the Yankees were playing the Red Sox. A Yankee win would cinch the pennant, and Yankee pitcher Allie Reynolds was working on a no-hitter through the first eight innings. The Yankees led 8–0, so a victory was hardly in doubt, but Reynolds' no-hitter would be his second of the year, a feat accomplished only one other time in the history of the major leagues.

Reynolds retired the first two hitters he faced in the ninth, so that the only person standing between him and the record was Ted Williams, still one of the most feared hitters in baseball. Reynolds got Williams to lift a high pop-up behind home plate. John Drebinger of the *New York Times* gave this account of the pop-up's flight.

> Yogi Berra, usually sure on these, scampered under it, but in the next agonizing minute the ball squirmed out of his glove and the Yanks chunky backstop went sprawling on his face. It meant Williams would have to be pitched to some more. But Reynolds, an amazingly good-natured competitor under the most trying circumstances, said, "Don't worry, Yogi, we'll get him again."

Sure enough, Reynolds induced Williams to hit another foul pop-up. This one drifted toward the Yankee bench, a tougher chance than the first, but Berra pursued it doggedly and captured it in his glove directly in front of the dugout. The dugout emptied as the entire Yankee team piled happily on top of him. "For a moment," Drebinger wrote, "it looked as if Berra, not Reynolds, was the hero of the occasion."

Standing fans watch Yogi Berra misplay the foul pop-up that would have ended Allie Reynolds' second 1951 no-hitter. Berra was spared embarrassment when, moments later, he caught a second pop-up off the bat of the dangerous Ted Williams (©Bettmann/Corbis).

Bob Boone and the Rose Rescue

The Philadelphia Phillies, in pursuit of their first-ever World Championship, led the Kansas City Royals three games to two in the sixth game of the 1980 World Series. Ahead 4–0 in the top of the eighth inning, they brought in reliever Tug McGraw to close out the game. McGraw, a fastballing left-hander with a disconcerting screwball, believed in giving the fans their money's worth. In the previous game, he'd won a tight 4–3 contest for the Phillies, but only after walking the bases full in the bottom of the ninth before striking out Royals right fielder Jose Cardinal to get the win.

Called in to relieve in the eighth inning of the sixth game, McGraw allowed a runner inherited from starter Steve Carlton to score and loaded the bases again before getting the third out. Having hit on a successful, if somewhat harrowing, formula, he loaded the bases once more with one out in the ninth. Royals batter Frank White, representing the tying run, lifted a high pop foul off the first-base line. Catcher Bob Boone and first baseman Pete Rose both converged on the pop-up and Boone called for the catch. The ball landed in Boone's glove and bounced out, but the alert Rose managed to catch it before it hit the ground. McGraw then fanned Willie Wilson for the third out and the championship.

Phillies catcher Bob Boone juggles a foul pop-up with the bases loaded in the ninth inning of the final 1980 World Series game as teammate Pete Rose moves in to make the catch (Associated Press).

Of the pop-up droppers chronicled in this chapter, only Hank Gowdy was measured for goat horns by the media. Berra and Boone were rescued by the perseverance of their respective teammates, Allie Reynolds and Pete Rose. The Alphonse-Gaston-and-Friend act put on by Merkle, Meyers, and Mathewson in 1912 was not scored as an error and was overshadowed by the $30,000 muff of Fred Snodgrass. In a similar fashion, Jack Clark's misplay was overlooked by fans furious with the blown call by umpire Don Denkinger. Only Gowdy, stumbling in front of 32,000 fans like a bear with his foot caught in a trap, was charged with an error by the official scorer and charged with the $50,000 difference between the winners' and losers' shares by the baseball press.

CHAPTER FIVE

Botched Grounders

"It was bouncing, bouncing, bouncing ... and it went under," Buckner said, facing the glare of what seemed like every camera in America. "I hadn't missed a ground ball in two months. What a hell of a one to miss."

Bill Buckner
Boston Sunday Globe
October 26, 1986

◆ ◆ ◆ ◆

Scapegoats

Bill Buckner and the Curse of the Bambino

When the Red Sox came back from a 3-games-to-none deficit in the American League Championship Series of 2004 to defeat their arch-rival Yankees and went on to sweep the St. Louis Cardinals in the World Series, nearly every sportswriter covering their remarkable comeback had something to say about the Curse of the Bambino. According to (fairly recent) legend, the curse was levied in January 1920 when Red Sox owner Harry Frazee sold the greatest player of all time, Babe Ruth, to the New York Yankees for a $300,000 loan and $100,000 in cash which he invested in a Broadway play.

By way of validating the curse, the legend asserts that from the day of the sale onward (until October 2004, at least) the fortunes of the Red Sox plummeted, while those of the Yankees soared. Prior to the sale of Ruth, Boston had appeared in five of the fifteen World Series played to that point and won all five. The Yankees, on the other hand, had never appeared in a Series before Ruth joined them. Between 1920 and 2003, however, the Red Sox appeared in only four World Series, losing all four in seven games, while the New York club appeared in thirty-nine fall classics and won twenty-six, easily the most imposing victory record of any club in baseball. The Yankees' nearest competitor for Series wins, the St. Louis Cardinals, appeared in fifteen World Series over that span and won nine.

The notion of a Bambino Curse is a relatively recent journalistic invention. There was no talk of a curse in the 1920s when the Ruth-led Yankees were pummeling the competition and the Red Sox slipped to seven last-place finishes in ten years. This was the period when the sale of Ruth, along with the ill-advised trades of such stellar players as Carl Mays, Waite Hoyt, Herb Pennock, Sam Jones, Bullet Joe Bush, and Everett Scott from Boston to New York had a direct impact on the fortunes of both teams.

There was no talk of a curse in 1946 when the Red Sox appeared in their first World Series since 1918 and lost to the Cardinals in a seventh game that featured Enos Slaughter's mad dash home and Johnny Pesky's phantom pause. There was no talk of a curse in 1978, when light-hitting Yankee shortstop Bucky Dent lofted a three-run home run over Fenway Park's Green Monster to erase a 2–0 Red Sox lead and key a 5–4 New York victory in the one-game play-off that decided the American League championship.

The Curse of the Bambino, with its attendant myths, did not become common baseball parlance until Red Sox first baseman Bill Buckner let a ground ball skip through his legs while the New York Mets scored the winning run in the sixth game of the 1986 World Series. After that, with the help of a column by George Vecsey of the *New York Times* and a 1990 book by Dan Shaughnessy of the *Boston Globe*, the curse and its supporting iconography became an established part of baseball lore and Bill Buckner was its poster boy.

Bill Buckner was an above-average player, a lean line-drive hitter who spent 22 years in the majors and amassed a batting average of .289 with over 2,700 hits. He came up to the majors as a fleet outfielder with the Dodgers in 1970, but injured his left ankle sliding in 1975 and was traded to the Chicago Cubs in January 1977. Robbed of his speed by his ankle injury, he shifted to first base with the Cubs and spent seven productive years in Chicago, winning the National League batting championship in 1980, before being traded to Boston early in the 1984 season for pitcher Dennis Eckersley.

By 1986, Buckner had been in the majors for seventeen years, and time had taken its toll on his legs and ankles. He tore his Achilles tendon in a late–September game, and spent over an hour before each post-season game icing and taping his hobbled ankles. He also ordered and wore special high-topped shoes to protect his aching ankles during the Series.

Describing Buckner's pre-game ritual, Roger Angell observed that the first baseman was playing "only on courage and pain killers." In particular, Angell described Billy Buck's painful and comical hobbling gallop around third base and down the line to home plate in the third inning of Game Five, when, "he looked like Walter Brennan coming home—all elbows and splayed-out achy feet, with his mouth gaping open with the effort and his head thrown back in pain and hope."

In his *Washington Post* column the morning before the crucial Game Six of the World Series, Thomas Boswell wrote that Buckner was "both amusing and inspiring. He's very kind of blood n' guts. He's the willingness to endure any amount of pain and any potential for embarrassment or failure just so he can say he played the game." Boswell then asked the rhetorical questions, "Is he playing hurt? Or is he hurting the team?" and made the prescient observation, "It is unlikely that any man so hurt—at least so conspicuously hurt—ever has played a major role in a Series. Or been so determined not to get off the stage, no matter what the cost to himself. Or to his team."

Because of Buckner's painful lack of mobility, Red Sox manager John McNamara often replaced him in late innings with light-hitting Dave Stapleton, who offered sounder footwork around the first-base bag. McNamara neglected to make this move to improve his team's defense in the final innings of Game Six, however, to the dismay of Boston fans and the delight of second-guessers everywhere.

Boston entered Game Six at Shea Stadium leading the New York Mets three games to two and needed only one more win to cinch the Series. The game started well for the Red Sox. Roger Clemens allowed only four hits and left after seven innings and 135 pitches with a 3–2 lead and a blister on his pitching hand. His replacement, Calvin Schiraldi, gave up the tying run in the eighth on a single, his own errant throw to second, a sacrifice, and a sacrifice fly.

Neither team scored in the ninth, and the game went into extra innings tied at three all. The Red Sox untied it in the top of the tenth by scoring twice on a home run by Dave Henderson and back-to-back hits by Wade Boggs and Marty Barrett.

The Red Sox took the field in the bottom of the tenth needing only three outs to cinch their first World Championship since 1918, when Babe Ruth pitched two of Boston's four wins. The first two outs came quickly on fly balls to the outfield. In the Red Sox clubhouse, attendants brought in the championship trophy, wheeled in buckets of champagne, and taped protective plastic sheets over the lockers as the NBC Television Crew, led by Bob Costas, set up shop to interview the apparent winners. At the same time, someone in the Shea Stadium control booth punched the wrong button and the scoreboard lit up with the message CONGRATULATIONS, BOSTON RED SOX, WORLD CHAMPIONS. The scoreboard message was quickly erased, and the clubhouse preparations proved premature as well.

Catcher Gary Carter came to the plate carrying the Mets' last hopes on his bat and singled to left field on a 2-and-1 fastball. Pinch hitter Kevin Mitchell, called back to the field from the locker room where he'd had to retrieve the uniform he'd already discarded, lined Schiraldi's second pitch, a hanging slider, into center for another single. With Mets runners on first and second, Schiraldi was beginning to show signs of strain, and Red Sox pitching coach Bill Fischer visited the mound to try to settle him down. After the visit, Schiraldi got two quick strikes on the next Met batter, Ray Knight, and the Red Sox were one strike away from their first championship in 68 years. Then Knight looped a broken-bat single over the head of the second baseman, scoring Carter and sending Mitchell to third base.

At that point, McNamara replaced Schiraldi with native New Englander Bob Stanley, who had saved 124 games in ten years with the Red Sox, including the second game of the World Series. Mookie Wilson, the next Met batter, swung at and missed an outside pitch from Stanley, took two balls, and then fouled off a pitch, running the count to two-and-two and taking the Mets down to their last strike one more time. Mookie fouled off two more sinkers on the outside of the plate, and catcher Rich Gedman set his glove as a target on the outer half of the plate for the next pitch.

Stanley's next pitch was a fastball off the inside corner. Expecting another outside pitch, Wilson jackknifed to get out of the way of the pitch. Gedman couldn't get his glove over in time, and the ball squirted off it and rolled to the backstop while Mitchell scored the tying run from third and Knight advanced to second base.

The official scorers saddled Stanley with a wild pitch on the play, although many observers felt that the pitch was close enough to the plate for Gedman to handle and that the catcher should have been charged with a passed ball. Gedman himself said that he could have caught the pitch. Regardless of how the played was scored, the Mets had tied the game at 5–5, and Mookie Wilson was still at bat with a runner on second and a count of three balls and two strikes. The TV crews cleared out of the Red Sox clubhouse, and the champagne and trophy disappeared.

Wilson fouled off two more pitches before pulling the tenth pitch thrown by Stanley down the first-base line. Buckner, who had been playing deep, sidestepped quickly over to the line. The ball bounced once, bounced twice, and then skipped under Buckner's glove and rolled between his legs as he bent to catch it. Buckner straightened, took two quick steps after the ball as it trickled down the left-field foul line, then stopped and stood watching dejectedly as Knight crossed the plate and the Mets scoreboard flashed WE WIN! in gigantic red letters.

Contrary to popular lore, Bill Buckner did not single-handedly cost the Red Sox the World championship in 1986. Calvin Schiraldi and the Stanley/Gedman misfire had already done most of the damage by the time Wilson's grounder squeezed under Buckner's glove and through his aching wickets. Even if Buckner had caught the ball and he or Stanley had beaten Wilson to the bag, the Mets had already tied the score. The game would have gone into the eleventh inning, and there is certainly no guarantee that the Red Sox would have won it. Moreover, the loss of Game Six did not hand the Series to the Mets. It just pushed the decisive contest off to an anticlimactic Game Seven, which the Mets won 8–5.

Never in baseball history had a team come so close to winning the championship without taking home the trophy. A two-run lead in the bottom of the tenth with two out and nobody on presents an almost insurmountable obstacle to the home team. A maker of board games reportedly calculated that the odds of a successful Mets comeback in that situation were 279 to 1. Add to that the fact that the Mets were down to their last strike more than once during their comeback. Hall of Fame pitcher Tom Seaver, who finished his career with the Red Sox and was on their roster in 1986, was quoted by *Sports Illustrated* as saying, "When you get within one strike and don't win, you don't deserve to win." In Game Six, Red Sox hurlers had the Mets down to their last strike on four separate pitches and failed to close out the contest.

Game Six of the 1986 World Series, and Buckner's role in it, have since taken on mythic proportions. The ball that rolled through Buckner's legs, autographed by Mookie Wilson, was auctioned off six years later to actor Charlie Sheen for a bid of $85,000, plus a ten percent commission to the auction house. In their special Baseball Issue ushering in the 1987 season, *Sports Illustrated* devoted fourteen pages to a dissection of the game by Peter Gammons, in which he declared that "Game Six has now taken its place with the other great World Series Contests," including Game Eight in 1912 (the Snodgrass Muff), Game Four in 1947 (Blevens' near no-hitter), Game Seven in 1960 (Mazeroski's home run), and Game Six in 1975 (Fisk's reverse–English homer), and concluded that "it stands alone as the greatest 'bad' game in Series history." Accordingly, Bill Buckner has been enshrined alongside such lifetime goats as Fred Snodgrass, Mickey Owen, and Fred Merkle.

Mookie Wilson's grounder eludes Bill Buckner as the Mets score the winning run in game Six of the 1986 World Series and introduce "The Curse of the Bambino" into baseball lore (*Boston Globe* photograph by Stan Grossfeld).

As in the case of Snodgrass, Owen, Merkle, and other miscreants, the relative importance of Buckner's error has been amplified over time. In a perceptive article entitled "Jim Bowie's Letter and Bill Buckner's Legs," anthropologist Stephen Jay Gould observes that "humans tend to construct their stories along a limited number of pathways," and force facts to fit these pre-set pathways. Gould notes that within a year of Buckner's boot, reports of the actual event had been subtly altered to fit a familiar but false canonical version — "the claim that, but for Buckner's legs, the Sox would have won the Series, forgetting the inconvenient complexity of a tied score at Buckner's ignominious moment, and sometimes even forgetting that the Series still had another game to run."

Red Sox fans greeted Buckner with a mixture of boos and cheers in his first at-bat in Fenway Park the following year. When the team fell out of contention early in the 1987 pennant race, it released Billy Bucks midway through the season. He continued to play for three more years, migrating to Anaheim and Kansas City before returning to Boston as a part-time player and earning his final release in June, 1990. In 1993, he moved from his Massachusetts home to a ranch in Idaho, at least partially to escape harassment over the botched grounder. "They keep beating a dead horse," he told baseball historian Mike Sowell in 1995. "It kind of gets old after a while." Asked about the fans in Boston, he said, "They're tough. They're like New York. If you're going good, they're great. If you're not, then it gets a little tough."

The bitterness of Boston fans toward Buckner is exemplified by a blog I came across while trying to track down a quote he ostensibly gave to a reporter following the suicide of former Angel pitcher Donnie Moore, who surrendered the home run that allowed Boston to beat California and make its way to the 1986 World Series. A friend told me he remembered reading that, when asked if, like Moore, he had ever considered suicide after his landmark error, Buckner had replied, "What for? It's only a game." I was able to document that the question had been posed by an Associated Press reporter, but Buckner's answer was lost, overridden by reports of his wife's outrage at the insensitivity of the question. In searching for the answer, however, I came across an even more insensitive observation in a Web site created by two New Hampshire brothers, where a correspondent had posted the following quote in 2004: "Moore subsequently committed suicide, something that Bill Buckner never had the grace to do although all of New England devoutly wished it."

In this era of videotape and wall-to-wall sports coverage, Buckner's error has achieved an immediacy unmatched by, for example, Merkle's boner or Snodgrass' muffed fly. There are no videotapes of Merkle missing second or the ball bouncing out of Snodgrass' glove. Whenever the Red Sox find themselves in a tight pennant race, however, journalists resurrect the "Curse of the Bambino" and TV viewers are treated to the image of Buckner bending over and watching Wilson's grounder bounce between his aching legs.

Finally in 2004, when the Red Sox improbably overcame a 3–0 deficit in games to wrest the American League championship from the Yankees and went on to sweep the Cardinals and bring Boston their first championship since 1918, the national media boldly pronounced that the CURSE HAS BEEN REVERSED. In the wake of the Red Sox victory, pundits suggested it was time to "forgive and forget" Buckner's error. Forgiveness is problematic, but it's unlikely that the memory of the error will be erased by a single World Championship. The New York Giants went on to win four World Championships after their failures in 1908 and 1912, but Merkle is still remembered as "bonehead" and Snodgrass' muffed fly headlined his 1974 obituary.

Roger Peckinpaugh and the Record

Roger Peckinpaugh, shortstop of the 1924 World Champion Washington Senators, had an extraordinary season to help the Senators defend their title in 1925. He batted .294, fielded his position well, and was voted the American League's Most Valuable Player. In the World Series against the Pittsburgh Pirates, however, he put on one of the worst fielding exhibitions in Series history, making eight errors in seven games. His eight miscues set a Series record that still stands, eclipsing the previous mark of six set by Hall of Fame shortstop Honus Wagner in the first World Series ever played, the 1903 matchup between Wagner's Pittsburg Pirates and the Boston Pilgrims. (In 1903 the Red Sox were called the Pilgrims and Pittsburgh was spelled Pittsburg. Go figure.)

"I told people I broke Honus' record," Peckinpaugh was quoted as saying, "but I didn't tell them which one." Though he never threatened any of Wagner's other records, Peckinpaugh's physical makeup and approach to the game resembled that of the Hall of Fame shortstop. *The Biographical Encyclopedia of Baseball* tells us that Peckinpaugh, like Wagner, was "broad-shouldered, big chested, and bow legged. Seldom slick and never graceful, he nonetheless covered ground and got the job done." He was also a cerebral player, so much so that in 1914, when he was 23, the New York Yankees made him the youngest person ever to manage a big-league team.

Almost every one of Peckinpaugh's errors in the 1925 Series came at a crucial time. In the eighth inning of the second game, he fumbled a grounder that put a runner on base ahead of a Kiki Cuyler home run, contributing to a 3–2 Senator defeat. It was the only Pirate win in the first four games, and Pittsburgh entered Game Five down three games to one. At the time, no team had ever come back from such a deficit, but the Pirates took Game Five 6–3 to keep their hopes alive. It was the only game in which Peckinpaugh didn't record an error. His failure to field a made-to-order double-play grounder led to the Senators' downfall in Game Six, as both the runner and batter spared by his error scored to key another 3–2 win for the Pirates and force a deciding seventh game.

The seventh game of the 1925 World Series was played under deplorable weather conditions. It rained before and during the contest, but Commissioner Landis, who was present, decreed that the game should go on if at all possible. In a column in the *Washington Post*, Ring Lardner wrote that "the game was played in semi-darkness and on a field that resembled nothing so much as chicken à la king." Low-lying clouds so hindered visibility that infielders often couldn't see outfielders, umpires couldn't make out the foul lines, and spectators couldn't follow the flight of the ball. In the *New York Times*, James Harrison wrote that the game was

> the wettest, weirdest, and wildest game that 50 years of baseball has ever seen. Water, mud, fog, mist, sawdust, fumbles, muffs, wild throws, wild pitches, one near fistfight, impossible rallies — these were mixed up to make the best and the worst game of baseball ever played in this country. Players wallowing ankle deep in mud, pitchers slipping as they delivered the ball to the plate, athletes skidding and sloshing, falling full length, dropping soaked baseballs — there you have part of the picture that was unveiled at Forbes Field this dripping afternoon. It was a great day for water polo.

Walter Johnson, the hero of the 1924 Series, started the game for the Senators. He had already beaten the Pirates twice, winning Game One 4–1, and shutting out the opposition 4–0 in Game Four. It looked as if Washington might have an easy time of it when the Senators staked Johnson to a 4–0 lead in the top of the first, but the renowned pitcher couldn't duplicate the mastery he exhibited in the drier climate of the earlier games. The Pirates tied the game at six-all in the seventh inning when Peckinpaugh slipped going after Eddie Moore's pop-up and dropped it for a two-base error. (The *Washington Post* called it Peck's daily error.) Max Carey followed with a long double to left that Goose Goslin, Washington's left fielder, claimed was foul but was called fair by the umpires, whose view of the left-field foul line was suspect. The mist-shrouded double scored Moore, and Pie Traynor followed with a triple that scored Carey with the tying run.

Peckinpaugh redeemed his seventh-inning error with a home run in the top of the eighth that put the Senators ahead 7–6. Unfortunately, his redemption was short-lived. By the bottom of the eighth, Fred Lieb writes in his *Story of the World Series*, "the mist over the field had thickened and the outfielders looked like ghoulish figures in a tragedy on the Scottish moor." Johnson got two quick outs, but then gave up back-to-back doubles that tied the score and walked Eddie Moore.

The rally appeared over when the next batter, Max Carey, hit a ground ball that Peckinpaugh caught cleanly. Lieb's tragedy of the moors continued, however, as the sportswriter tells us, "Roger picked up the ball, but the unhappy shortstop stumbled in the mud and dropped the slippery pill as he was running over to touch second for a force play on Moore." A last-ditch attempt to shovel the ball to the second baseman went wide, and the Pirates had the bases loaded. After Johnson called for a load of sawdust to stabilize the muddy footing on the pitcher's mound, Kiki Cuyler unloaded the bases with a long drive that disappeared into the mists in right field. Cuyler's hit at first appeared to be a home run, but the umpires convened, determined that the ball had lodged under a tarpaulin, and limited the damage to a ground-rule double that put the Pirates ahead 9–7. That proved to be the winning margin when the Senators went down one-two-three in the top of the ninth.

At least one of Peckinpaugh's errors in Game Seven can be blamed on the sloppy field conditions, but if it hadn't been for his earlier errors in Games Two and Six, Johnson and the

Roger Peckinpaugh of the Senators, who set a Series record by making eight errors in the 1925 World Series, including a bobble in the eighth inning of Game Seven that set up the winning runs for the World Champion Pirates (National Baseball Hall of Fame Library, Cooperstown, N.Y.).

Senators might never have had to endure the travesty and tragedy of Game Seven. It represented a significant fall from grace for the man who had been voted the American League's Most Valuable Player (MVP).

In his *Historical Baseball Abstract*, Bill James adds an interesting footnote to Peckinpaugh's record-breaking World Series performance. Up until 1925, the MVP award for each league had been announced prior to the start of the World Series. Peckinpaugh's dismal performance in the 1925 World Series changed this procedure. In the light of his generosity toward the Pirates, one reporter commented that "Peckinpaugh was not only the MVP of the American League, but of the National League as well." James notes that "There was a feeling that announcing the MVP Award before the series had (a) put pressure on Peckinpaugh, and (b) detracted from the award. The policy of holding off the MVP announcement until after the series was played began the next season."

Another footnote to Peckinpaugh's porous performance is provided by J. G. Taylor Spink in his book *Judge Landis and 25 Years of Baseball*. In 1925, baseball was still reeling from the Black Sox scandal of 1919, and Judge Kenesaw Mountain Landis was in his first term as the Commissioner hired to restore and safeguard the image of the sport. Landis was aware that professional gamblers had wagered large sums of money on Pittsburgh to win the 1925 World Series. When Peckinpaugh's errors kept Pittsburgh in the Series, Landis arranged to have the shortstop followed by a private detective. According to Spink, "there never was any question that Peckinpaugh, an honest, conscientious player wasn't trying his best." In view of the large sums bet on the games, though, "If there was to be any unpleasant aftermath, or any innuendo against Peckinpaugh, (Landis) wanted to be in a position to clear the great shortstop."

Peckinpaugh himself was haunted by the memory of his performance for the rest of his days as a player and manager. Joseph Wallace in his *World Series: 100 Years, an Opinionated Chronicle* quotes the following tirade from the shortstop's later years.

> Why do you want to know about that goddamn record? I played in three World Series. I was the most valuable player and I was a major leaguer for eighteen years when there were only sixteen major league teams in the world. And all you want to know about is that goddamn record for errors.

Escaped Goats

Several players have botched grounders in crucial post-season situations without earning the lasting opprobrium heaped upon Bill Buckner and Roger Peckinpaugh. The list of infielders whose misplays proved less costly to their reputations includes Honus Wagner, Tony Fernandez, Mike Andrews, and Leon Durham.

Honus Wagner: The Pre-Peckinpaugh Record

The 1903 World Series was the first ever, so the batting, pitching, and fielding marks established in that contest stood as Series records for at least two years until the second Series was played in 1905. Honus Wagner's 1903 mark of six errors lasted much longer, standing unchallenged as the Series record for twenty-two years before Roger Peckinpaugh was charged with eight miscues in 1925. While Peckinpaugh was saddled with goat horns for his 1925 errors, which figured in three Senator losses, including the seventh game that gave Pittsburgh the World Championship, no one ever suggested that Wagner be branded as a goat for his 1903 performance, when his errors contributed to at least one key Pirate loss.

For the most part, Wagner's errors rarely led to decisive Boston runs. Moreover, the Pittsburgh shortstop earned the sympathy of the press by playing every game while limping on a badly

Playing on an injured right leg, Hall of Fame immortal Honus Wagner made six errors in the inaugural World Series of 1903, setting a record that stood until Roger Peckinpaugh surpassed it in 1925 (Library of Congress, Prints and Photographs Division).

injured right leg. More to the point, Wagner was widely admired as the premier player of his day and is generally recognized to be one of the two or three greatest players of all time. Even in the face of a sub-par series performance — in addition to his errors, he batted only .222 and struck out to end the final game — no sportswriter was likely to suggest that the "Flying Dutchman" be fitted for goat horns.

Given Wagner's skills and reputation, it was obvious to all that even at eighty percent efficiency he was better than anyone else Pittsburg could put on the field. This wasn't the case with Bill Buckner, which was why the Red Sox were criticized for keeping him in the lineup. Buckner at eighty percent was a better hitter than Dave Stapleton, which was why he was playing. But he wasn't a better baserunner, and a 32-year-old Buckner, even at 100 percent, wasn't a better fielder than Stapleton.

Tony Fernandez and the Curse of Rocky Colavito

Ever since 1960, the Cleveland Indians have been said to be laboring under the Curse of Rocky Colavito, a minor hex that is to the Curse of the Bambino as Rocky Colavito was to Babe Ruth. A popular right fielder who led the American League in home runs in 1959, Colavito was traded to Detroit in April of 1960 by General Manager Frank Lane, who considered any day without a trade as a day lost. In return for Colavito, the Indians got American League batting champion Harvey Kuenn, a singles hitter who was three years older than Colavito, and thirty-plus years of mismanagement and bad luck. This bad luck, documented in a book by sportswriter Terry Pluto, included thirty-two years of finishes lower than third place, the loss of all-star players and promising rookies to alcoholism (Sam McDowell), a nervous breakdown (Tony Horton), the pro golf tour (Ken Harrelson), a home-plate collision with Pete Rose (Ray Fosse), a wife's affair with a teammate (Dennis Eckersley), and death in a boating accident (Steve Olin and Tim Crews).

By the mid–1990s, the Indians appeared to have dispelled this curse by acquiring a number of solid veterans like Omar Vizquel, Tony Fernandez, and Orel Hershiser and signing a group of promising young players to long-term contracts. These young players, who included Albert Belle, Sandy Alomar, Kenny Lofton, Manny Ramirez, and Charles Nagy, returned the Tribe to postseason playoffs and led them to the World Series in 1995 and 1997.

Tony Fernandez was a four-time all-star who won four gold gloves as an American League shortstop and spent seventeen years in the big leagues with six different clubs, including four separate stints totaling twelve years with the Toronto Blue Jays. In 1997, his travels took him to Cleveland, where he played second base alongside shortstop Omar Vizquel, and propelled the Indians into the World Series against the Florida Marlins with a game-winning home run against Baltimore in Game Six of the American League Championship Series.

A little personal history may be in order here. I'm a lifelong Cleveland Indians fan. This covered the long dry spell that started with their four-game World Series loss to the Giants in 1954, spanned the period covered by the Curse of Rocky Colavito, and saw their re-emergence as a force to be reckoned with in 1995. When the Indians made it to the seventh game of the World Series against the Florida Marlins in 1997, I interrupted a vacation trip to make my way to Joe Robbie Stadium in South Florida and paid scalper prices for a seat thirty rows behind the third base dugout, where I sat beside a Cleveland dentist who had taken the day off and flown in to do business with the same scalper.

The game was tight and exciting, and Cleveland made two third-inning runs driven in by Tony Fernandez hold up for a 2–1 lead going into the bottom of the ninth. The Indians brought in their closer, Jose Mesa, to finish off the Marlins. At least one Indian, Omar Vizquel, had reservations about the move to Mesa. As he recounted in his biography, *Omar!*:

> All we had to do was get three outs and we'd win the ultimate title. The eyes of the world were focused on every move we made. Unfortunately, Jose's own eyes were vacant. Completely empty. Nobody home. You could almost see right through him.

From where we sat behind third base, my dentist companion and I couldn't see through Mesa. I remember that we both laughed when our reliever bounced his first pitch five feet short of the plate, but it was nervous laughter. We weren't laughing when Mesa gave up two singles to put runners on first and third with one out, and we were dead silent in the midst of screaming hometown fans when Craig Counsell drove in the tying run with a sacrifice fly.

The game was still tied in the bottom of the eleventh when Florida put a runner on first with one man out. Craig Counsell hit what looked like a double-play grounder to second baseman Fernandez, but the ball ticked off his glove into right field, putting runners on first and third. Slumped forward in our seats, the dentist and I exchanged shrugs and glances as we felt the game start to drain away. After an intentional walk and a force-out at home, Counsell scored the winning run on a soft line drive up the middle of the diamond off the end of the bat of Marlin shortstop Edgar Renteria.

I remember accepting the condolences of the Marlin fans around us and shaking hands with the Cleveland dentist as we left our seats. Neither he nor I felt like demonizing reliever Mesa or second baseman Fernandez. We were happy to have seen our team play well in the seventh game of the World Series.

It appeared that both the Cleveland media and hometown fans felt the same way. Press accounts in both the Cleveland and Miami papers covered the error in play-by-play accounts, but there were no headlines proclaiming goatdom for Fernandez or comparing him to the likes of Bill Buckner and Fred Merkle. Rather, local newspapers featured stories of the hometown heroes, with the *Miami Herald* lauding Craig Counsell, who drove in the tying run and scored the winning run, Edgar Renteria, who drove in the winning run, and reliever Rob Nen, who shut the door on the Indians in the ninth and tenth innings, while the Cleveland writers focused on the performance of rookie pitcher Jaret Wright, who held the Marlins scoreless for six innings and left in the seventh with a 2–1 lead.

In post-game interviews with Fernandez, both Cleveland and Miami newspapers emphasized the second baseman's role in getting Cleveland into the World Series and driving in both Tribe runs in the seventh game. About his error in the eleventh inning that set up the winning run, Fernandez said,

> I won't make an excuse. I just missed the ball. I wanted to get the lead runner. I think that was a mistake, but I knew Bobby (Bonilla) wasn't running well, and that's why I wanted to get the lead runner.

Fernandez, who would retire from baseball after the 2001 season and become an ordained minister of the Pentecostal faith, was philosophical in dealing with the post-game questions.

Second baseman Tony Fernandez of the Indians misplays a potential double-play grounder in the eleventh inning of Game Seven of the 1997 World Series. The Florida Marlins capitalized on the error to score the unearned run that made them World Champions (AP Photo/Mike Levy, *Cleveland Plain Dealer*).

"Like anything else in life, this also shall pass," he told reporters. Regarding both his ALCS home run and his eleventh-inning error, he said, "I did my best. I made a great effort. I don't think people will remember that. It's just a part of baseball."

While Fernandez himself may never forget the error, it isn't likely to appear in his obituary notices and hasn't become a part of the baseball folklore linking unlucky players like Merkle, Snodgrass, and Buckner. Cleveland fans remember, but they also remember he drove in the two runs that gave their team the lead in the first place.

Mike Andrews and Charley O.

Mike Andrews, a steady but unspectacular second baseman for the Red Sox and White Sox in the late sixties and early seventies, was nearing the end of his eight-year career in the majors, playing as a utility infielder for the Oakland A's when lightning struck in the twelfth inning of the second game of the 1973 World Series. Andrews, the third A's player to staff second base in the game, made two errors on successive grounders in the top of the twelfth to allow three runs to score and pave the way for a 10–7 Mets win over Oakland.

The A's went on to win the Series in seven games, so Andrews never really qualified as a goat in the eyes of Oakland fans. He belongs in this discussion because his performance was unforgivable in the eyes of one spectator, the A's autocratic and meddling owner, Charles O. Finley. Finley was so incensed by Andrews' errors that he forced the second baseman to sign a false affidavit that he had injured his shoulder so that Finley could remove him from the Series roster and replace him with another player. In his book *Five Seasons*, Roger Angell noted that "The vindictiveness of this maneuver exceeded several low marks previously held by the excessive Mr. Finley, and this time his troops came to the very edge of mutiny."

Finley's high-handed move so angered the Oakland players and manager that they threatened to boycott the next Series game if Andrews wasn't returned to the roster. Fortunately, Baseball Commissioner Bowie Kuhn saw through Finley's maneuver, fined the Oakland owner, and ordered him to reinstate the second baseman. Andrews made one other appearance in the Series, as a pinch hitter in Game Four. It was his last at-bat in a major league uniform.

The fallout from Finley's move didn't end with Andrews' reinstatement. Weary of the owner's meddling, Oakland manager Dick Williams held a team meeting in which he vented his frustration and announced his intention to leave the A's organization voluntarily at the end of the season. Roger Angell had this to say about Williams' announcement:

> This may seem a curious form of encouragement for a team in the very midst of a World Series, but it should be understood that the vivid, what-the-hell morale of the A's has always been built out of a shared abhorrence of the man at the top. They display the utter unity of a pack of ragged and sequestered Dickensian schoolboys, and Charley Finley is their Gradgrind.

Leon Durham and the Cub Curse

The history of baseball frustration logged by the Chicago Cubs makes the Red Sox Curse of the Bambino look like a fortune cookie bromide. Before 2004, Red Sox fans lamented that they hadn't won a World Series since 1918. At that time, the Cubs' winless Series record stretched back to 1908. Moreover, the Red Sox had been in five World Series since the Cubs' last Series appearance in 1945.

In 1984, it looked as if the Cubs were finally ready to put an end to their years of frustration and defeat. They won the National League East crown, finishing six-and-a-half games ahead of the New York Mets, and quickly went up two games to none against the West Champion San Diego Padres in the best-of-five League Championship Series. They'd begun to make believers out of even the most hardened Cub fans when the team left the friendly confines of Wrigley Field and flew to San Diego needing only one win in the final three games to advance to the World Series for the first time in 39 years.

The win never came. Padre pitcher Ed Whitson shut the Cubs down in the first game at San Diego, winning 7–1, and Steve Garvey hit a two-run home run in the bottom of the ninth of the next game to break a 5–5 tie and even the Championship Series at two games apiece. Still, the Cubs had their best pitcher, Rick Sutcliffe, available to pitch the decisive fifth game. Sutcliffe was 16-and-1 on the season, and had shut out San Diego over seven innings in the opening game in Chicago.

Sutcliffe continued his mastery of the Padres over the first five innings of the fifth game, shutting them out while the Cubs built a 3–0 lead on home runs by first baseman Leon Durham and catcher Jody Davis. The Padres scored twice in the sixth inning to draw within one run, and got their leadoff hitter in the seventh inning, Carmello Martinez, on base via a four-pitch walk. After a sacrifice put Martinez on second, pinch hitter Tim Flannery hit a routine five-hop grounder at first baseman Durham. Thomas Boswell described what happened next in the following day's *Washington Post*.

Durham did everything but lie down in the ball's path. "Every grounder bounces," explained Garvey. "You never keep your glove *all the way* down. Well, that ball never came up one inch."

There was just room between Durham's big leg, his big knee and his big glove for a baseball to pass. And that's where it went.

The crowd gasped in disbelief, then exploded in cheers as the white streak skittered into right field and Martinez dashed home. The Cubs' lead was gone. And so was their heart.

It took a ton to break the Cub spirit, but that did it.

After Durham's error, the Padres piled on. A bloop single by Alan Wiggins, a slashing double by Tony Gwynn that took a bad hop over second baseman Ryne Sandberg's head, and a single through the box by Garvey built the Padre lead to 6–3. Reliever Goose Gossage then pitched two scoreless innings to seal the Cubs' fate.

Leon Durham was a powerful, speedy player, whose nickname of "Bull" echoed a brand of chewing tobacco but could just as easily have reflected his aggressive approach to the game. After starting his career as an outfielder, the Cubs shifted him to first base in 1984, following a time-honored tradition of moving power hitters with questionable defensive skills to a position generally thought to be less demanding. Ironically, the Cub first baseman that Durham replaced was Bill Buckner, who'd been traded to the Red Sox for Dennis Eckersley at the start of the season.

Leon Durham of the Cubs, whose seventh-inning error in the decisive game of the 1984 National League Championship Series allowed the San Diego Padres to tie the score and opened the door to a four-run rally that kept Chicago from their first World Series appearance since 1945 (National Baseball Hall of Fame Library, Cooperstown, N.Y.).

Durham's error never achieved the notoriety of his predecessor's 1986 bobble. Even if Durham had made the play successfully, the Cubs would not have been out of the inning. While his misplay allowed the tying run to score, it was followed by legitimate base hits that built a commanding three-run Padre lead. Since Durham's error occurred in the seventh inning, moreover, it didn't have the finality of Buckner's boot. The Cubs still had two innings to try to come back. (Of course, the 1986 Red Sox had the entire seventh game to redeem themselves, but this inconvenient fact never seemed to bother the myth-makers blaming Buckner.)

Durham also benefited from a kinder, gentler press treatment. No headlines linked his failure to the Cubs' defeat, and press reports generally mentioned his offensive contributions along with his defensive lapse. Boswell's *Washington Post* coverage is typical.

"I have nothing to be ashamed of," said Durham, who had 420-foot two-run homers in each of the last two games. "That was my first error with the glove all year.... I'm not going to think about it, but it'll stay on my mind."

Durham went on to play first base for the Cubs for three more years, before being traded to Cincinnati early in the 1988 season. He spent a good part of that season undergoing drug rehabilitation, and ended his career in 1989, when he was once again suspended for drug use.

The Role of the Press

In the final analysis, Bill Buckner stands head and shoulders above the competition as the poster boy for botched grounders. Bad timing, the Curse of the Bambino, the last-strike drama and unlikely nature of the Mets comeback, and an unforgiving press combined with Billy Buck's aching back and legs to raise his misplay to epic proportions.

The nature of the Boston press goes a long way to explaining why Buckner's name is known nationally while, for example, the names of Fernandez and Durham are remembered only by die-hard fans in Cleveland and Chicago. In *The Curse of the Bambino*, veteran *Boston Globe* reporter Dan Shaughnessy describes the competitive and sometimes antagonistic nature of the Red Sox press coverage

> Media coverage of the Red Sox is enormous and would certainly border on excessive were it not for the thousands of thirsty fans who want more.... You can let the Metro section slip a little and use wire services for national and international news, but you can't leave the Red Sox alone for a minute.... The glut of microphone-waving, notebook-wielding reporters creates intense competition among members of the press, which results in inevitable friction between the team and the press. There are simply too many reporters with too many questions, and it's a point of unending distraction and annoyance for the Red Sox ball players. It is, however, great for the Boston fans, who are more knowledgeable than those anywhere in the land.

In his book on the 1986 season, *One Pitch Away*, baseball historian Mike Sowell elaborates on the impact of Boston reporters and fans on the Buckner legend.

> Maybe Buckner could have missed a ground ball for another team in the World Series, and it wouldn't have mattered as much. But he missed one for the Red Sox in that World Series and in that game. Red Sox fans couldn't forget that.

Six months after the Series had ended, Peter Gammons foresaw the unrelenting reaction of Red Sox fans and the lasting imprint Buckner's error would make on baseball lore in his 1987 *Sports Illustrated* article deconstructing Game Six.

> Forget it? New Englanders haven't let .307 lifetime hitter Johnny Pesky forget he held the ball in the '46 Series—and he wasn't even at fault. Forget it? When the Today Show observed Fred Merkle Day a while back it wasn't because "Bonehead" had a good rookie year in 1908. Forget it? At the New York Baseball Writers Dinner last January, Ralph Branca was introduced to Clemens as "the guy who gave up Bobby Thomson's homer." That happened only 36 years ago. There are just some things you never forget.

Chapter Six

Gopher Balls I

"If it hadn't been for that homer, who would remember Ralph Branca?"
Ralph Branca
Quoted in *Baseball's 50 Greatest Games*
Selected by *The Sporting News*
Written by Lowell Reidenbaugh

♦ ♦ ♦ ♦

Scapegoats

The etymology of the term *gopher ball*, a pitch destined to go for, or "go fer" a home run, is somewhat cloudy. The *1955 Baseball Almanac* reports that it was coined by Yankee pitcher Lefty Gomez in the early thirties as a play on the words "go far." Other schools of thought have suggested that the ball hit into the stands vanishes as quickly as a gopher retreating into his hole, or that the expression reflects a pitcher's feelings that he'd like to crawl into a hole as he watches his offering disappear over the fence.

While botched grounders and dropped fly balls reflect misplays on the part of fielders, a gopher ball is not necessarily the result of a pitcher's poor execution. True, a home run may land in the stands because a pitcher hangs a curve ball, loses a little speed off his fastball, or leaves his slider over the heart of the plate. It's also possible, however, that a batter's skill, guesswork, or blind luck may turn a hurler's premier pitch into a gopher ball. And a pitcher who gives up a decisive home run in a crucial game can be measured for goat horns even if he throws the best pitch in his arsenal to the exact location called for by his catcher.

Ralph Branca and the Shot Heard 'Round the World

Compendiums of the "Greatest Baseball Games Ever Played" invariably put the final 1951 National League play-off game between the Brooklyn Dodgers and the New York Giants at or near the top of the list. That was the game that ended when Giant third baseman Bobby Thomson hit the "Shot Heard 'Round the World," a three-run home run in the bottom of the ninth to give the Giants a 5–4 victory over their arch-rival Dodgers and win the National League pennant. Thomson's heroics came at the expense of the Brooklyn pitcher whose fastball wound up in the left-field stands of the Polo Grounds, Ralph Branca.

The names of Branca and Thomson are forever linked in baseball lore. Thomson, nicknamed the "Flying Scot" because of his birthplace in Glasgow, Scotland, hit thirty home runs during the regular season in 1951. A starting Giant outfielder since 1947, he'd been moved from center field to third base midway through the '51 season to make room for rookie Willie Mays.

Branca, the fifteenth of seventeen children born to John and Katherine Branca in Mount Vernon, New York, won 21 games for Brooklyn at age 21 in 1947 and had averaged nearly fourteen wins a season since becoming a regular starter.

The saga of Branca and Thomson is part and parcel of the intense hostilities between the Giants and Dodgers, a bitter rivalry that stretched back to the earliest days of the National League, when they became the only two franchises in baseball history to represent the same city and compete in the same league. In 1951, the Giants found themselves thirteen and a half games behind the league-leading Dodgers as late as August 11, when the New York club launched a sixteen-game winning streak. The Giants continued to win regularly after their streak ended, while the Dodgers, whose lineup included future Hall of Famers Roy Campanella, Duke Snider, Pee Wee Reese, and Jackie Robinson, and featured the fabled "boys of summer," found their bats going unaccountably cold. The Giants caught up with the Dodgers, and the two teams finished the regular season with identical records, forcing a best-two-out-of-three play-off for only the second time in league history.

The Dodgers won the coin toss for the right to select the sequence of home parks and elected to open the series at Brooklyn's Ebbets Field and move up to the Polo Grounds for Game Two and the third game, if necessary. Ralph Branca started the first game for the Dodgers and lost, 3–1, to the Giants' Jim Hearn. "I scattered four hits," Branca notes in "Bums," the oral history of the Dodgers, "two inside the park and two outside." One of the two hits that left the park was struck by Bobby Thomson, the other by Monte Irvin. Clem Labine of the Dodgers won the second play-off game 10–0 to even the series and force a deciding third game.

The Game. Starting pitchers in the third game were Sal Maglie for the Giants and Don Newcombe for the Dodgers. Both performed well, and the game went into the eighth inning tied 1–1. Thomson, the eventual hero of the contest, came perilously close to being the goat. In the bottom of the second inning, the Flying Scott lined what looked to be an extra-base hit down the left-field line with a runner, Whitey Lockman, on first. Thomson was so sure he could turn his drive into a double that he put his head down, shifted his long-legged stride into high gear, and headed for second base. Unfortunately, the runner ahead of him, Lockman, decided not to risk taking third, so that when Thomson steamed into second he found his teammate there waiting for him. Embarrassed, he began to backtrack toward first, but was tagged out easily by Dodger second baseman Jackie Robinson.

Thomson followed his baserunning lapse in the second inning with two less-than-stellar fielding plays in the top of the eighth inning. With Dodger runners on first and third and one man out, Maglie broke off a curve that sailed wide of the catcher and rolled to the backstop, allowing Pee Wee Reese to score from third and advancing Duke Snider to second base. After Jackie Robinson was walked intentionally, the next batter, Andy Pafko, hit a tricky bouncer that glanced off Thomson's glove into left field as he tried to backhand it and rolled beyond third while Snider scored and Robinson took second. After Maglie fanned Gil Hodges for the second out, Billy Cox smoked a hard shot toward third that Thomson was unable to field, and Robinson scored the third run of the inning, giving the dodgers a 4–1 lead. Both of the balls hit to Thomson were playable, but hard enough to field so that the official scorer ruled they were hits when the converted outfielder couldn't come up with either of them.

Although he reportedly complained that he was beginning to tire, Newcombe, who had shut out the Phillies on the previous Saturday and had pitched five innings of tough relief in the Dodgers' final game the next day to keep them tied with the Giants, had enough left to set New York down one-two-three in the bottom of the eighth. When relief pitcher Larry Jansen did the same for the Dodgers in the top of the ninth, the Giants came to bat in the bottom of the ninth down 4–1 with their pennant hopes fading.

The first batter up for the Giants, Alvin Dark, stroked a seeing-eye single that ticked off the glove of first baseman Hodges and rolled between him and Jackie Robinson into right field. As the next hitter, Don Mueller, came to bat, Hodges, presumably in response to instructions from Manager Charley Dressen, chose to guard the line and hold Dark close to the base, creating a wide gap between himself and the second baseman. Mueller, a slap hitter with good bat control, took advantage of the opening by guiding a single through the gap between Hodges and Robinson. The hit sent Dark to third and brought up the Giants' clean up hitter, Monte Irvin.

Overanxious, Irvin tried to pull an outside slider from Newcombe and popped out to Hodges at first. With the Dodgers only two outs away from the pennant, it was announced in the press box that "World Series credentials for Ebbets Field can be picked up tonight after six o'clock at the Biltmore Hotel." No one thought the announcement was premature, even though the Giants still had runners on first and third with only one out and Whitey Lockman coming to the plate.

Lockman, a left-handed hitter, went with an outside pitch from Newcombe and hit it solidly to left field for a double, scoring Dark and sending Mueller to third, where he jammed his foot against the bag, twisted his ankle, and had to be replaced by a pinch runner. With the potential tying run on second base, Dodger manager Dressen had seen enough of Newcombe. Ever since the burly fastballer appeared to be tiring, Dressen had been making anxious calls to the bullpen asking coach Clyde Sukeforth about the readiness of the two pitchers he had warming up, Carl Erskine and Ralph Branca. While the Giant trainers attended to the injured Mueller, Dressen made one final call, and Sukeforth reported that Branca was throwing well, but Erskine had bounced a curve in the dirt. Dressen went out to the mound and gave the fateful signal to bring Branca into the game.

When Branca arrived at the mound from the bullpen, Dressen flipped him the ball and said, "Here, get an out." That was all. A single, terse command from a manager who would usually linger on the mound with detailed instructions for incoming pitchers. At least one Dodger, center fielder Duke Snider, took the manager's quick departure as a bad signal that Dressen was no longer in full control.

Branca later said Dressen's lack of instructions struck him as strange, but his immediate problem was the batter at the plate, Bobby Thomson. Branca's first pitch was a tempting fastball that caught a lot of the plate, but Thomson took it for strike one. Ahead in the count, Branca and catcher Rube Walker decided to waste the second pitch high and inside to set Thomson up for a curve low and away. Branca threw the setup fastball high and tight, out of the strike zone, but Thomson turned on it, caught it squarely, and sent it into the left-field stands 315 feet from home plate.

In the WMGM radio booth above the field, Giant broadcaster Russ Hodges followed the flight of the ball and screamed the litany that would immortalize the moment. "There's a long fly ... it's gonna be ... I believe ... The Giants win the pennant! The Giants win the pennant! The Giants win the pennant!"

As Thomson leapt around the bases, jumped on home plate, and was carried off by his delirious teammates, the stunned Dodgers left the field and headed for the center-field clubhouse. Once there, Ralph Branca stretched out face down on the short flight of six concrete steps that bisected the dressing area and buried his face in his hands. Don Newcombe, who had been in the shower when Thomson's home run left the park, emerged to find Branca sitting on the steps with his head down between his legs, crying.

"That image really affected me," Newcombe said later in a book co-authored by Thomson, Lee Heiman and Bill Gutman, "I was just 22 years old and at the time it didn't seem that these things should be so important. So you lost the championship. No big deal. You win another one the next year. But as long as I live I'll never forget Ralph Branca sitting there,

Jackie Robinson (42) watches as the happy Giants welcome Bobby Thomson to home plate and Ralph Branca leaves the mound for the clubhouse (National Baseball Hall of Fame Library, Cooperstown, N.Y).

sitting there and crying like a baby. I said to myself, 'goddamn, is this what baseball does to people?'"

Press Coverage. The next day's newspapers were lavish in their praise of the game itself. Tommy Holmes of the *Brooklyn Eagle* called it "one of the greatest ball games ever played," and Red Smith led off his column, titled the "Miracle of Coogan's Bluff," by writing, "Now it is done, now the story ends. And there is no way to tell it. The art of fiction is dead. Reality has strangled invention."

Still, most reporters found a way to tell the story. And the story they told had clearly defined roles, as spelled out in the headline of the *New York Daily News*: THOMSON THE HERO, BRANCA THE GOAT IN BIG PLAYOFF. A few newspapers hung goat horns on manager Dressen as well. The *Brooklyn Eagle's* headlines trumpeted FANS PUT BLAME ON DRESSEN AND BRANCA, and announced that Dressen had been hung in effigy from a lamp post at 75th Street and 3rd Avenue and depicted as a corpse in several bars and shop windows around the borough. *The LA Times* reflected this reaction by labeling its box score of the contest UN-DRESSEN.

Second Guessing. The manager's decision to bring in Branca was second-guessed mercilessly. Why not leave Newcombe in? (He was out of gas.) With first base open, why not walk Thomson to get at the next batter, rookie Willie Mays? (Thomson represented the winning run, and baseball lore frowns on putting the winning run on base.) Why Branca? Why not Erskine, or anybody else? (Bullpen coach Sukeforth said Branca was pitching better than Erskine, and no one else was ready.)

Dressen's responses to second-guessers were all defensible, and could be filed under the heading, "good decision, rotten outcome." No one asked about his decision to position Hodges close to the line against Don Mueller, a much less defensible choice which cost the Dodgers at least one out and a possible double play. Dressen also deserves censure for overworking his pitching staff during the stretch run, relying on a limited number of starters and leaving a few pitchers sore-armed and worn out.

Dressen had the reputation of being a smart manager, but his reputation reportedly went to his head and he had certain blind spots. In a generally unflattering portrait of the manager in *The Boys of Summer*, a look back at the 1950s Dodgers twenty years later, author Roger Kahn reports that Dressen believed and preached that oral sex weakened pitchers in warm weather, since it made them sweat. And Branca himself, interviewed for an HBO special on the fiftieth anniversary of the "Shot Heard 'Round the World," said of his manager, "He knew absolutely nothing about pitching. Absolutely nothing. What he knew about pitching you could put on the head of a pin and still have room for the Constitution on it."

Another decision, presumably made by Dressen, also affected the outcome of the play-offs, although there was no way of anticipating its impact in advance. After winning the coin flip, the Dodgers chose to hold the first play-off game in Ebbets Field, with the remaining games to be played in the Polo Grounds. The oval-shaped Polo Grounds offered unique dimensions to hitters, with short measurements to the fences down the foul lines and the most distant center-field fence in baseball. The ball that Thomson hit for a home run in the first game, which barely carried over the Ebbets Field fence in left-center field, would have been caught for an out in the Polo Grounds, while the "Shot Heard 'Round the World," which cleared the Polo Grounds fence near the short left-field line at the 315 foot mark, might have been caught in Ebbets Field, where the left-field fence was 343 feet from home plate.

Sign Stealing. Nearly fifty years after Thomson hit his home run, information came to light that fueled additional speculation regarding the outcome of the Dodger–Giant play-off. The *Wall Street Journal* published evidence that during the second half of the 1951 season, the Giants had been stealing the signs of the opposing catcher using a high-powered telescope hidden in manager Leo Durocher's office above the center-field fence in the Polo Grounds. The intercepted signs were sent electronically to the Giants' bullpen, where they were relayed to the batter by third-string catcher Sal Yvars. Yvars would toss a ball in the air to indicate a breaking pitch was on its way. No toss meant a fastball was coming.

The Giants protested that they didn't use the illegal setup to steal signs during the play-off games, and Thomson vehemently denies knowing in advance that Branca's ill-fated second pitch was to be a fastball. On the face of the evidence, it's difficult to believe the New York team had any extracurricular help in their home play-off games. After winning the first game in Ebbets Field, they were shut out in the Polo Grounds in the second game by Clem Labine, and managed only one run in eight innings off Don Newcombe in the third game. It's even difficult to attribute the Giants' late-season surge to sign stealing. During the second half of the season, the team batting average actually fell by seven points in home games and rose by seventeen points on the road. It's more likely that the surge was fueled by improved pitching. After July 20, the Giants' staff ERA dropped by a full run. Still the Giant hitters, including Thomson, admitted that they received stolen signals during the second half of the season, and, as Branca points out in the HBO Special, "All you have to do is get one hit, some place, somehow, knowing the signs, and that's all you need to win one (more) game." If even one win could be attributed to sign stealing, which seems likely, then the Dodger claim that the Giants stole the pennant has some validity.

The Aftermath. Over fifty years later, Branca is still introduced as the man who gave up the Thomson home run. His brief biographies in baseball references all begin with some version of the theme, "Ralph Branca is remembered as the man who threw the pitch that Bobby Thomson hit for the 'Shot Heard 'Round the World.'" One of the most famous home runs in baseball history, Thomson's shot marked the first time that a league championship play-off or a World Series had been decided by a home run in the bottom of the ninth inning. Just as Thomson's triumphant leap onto home plate into a mob of happy teammates has achieved a special place in the minds of baseball fans, so Ralph Branca has become the poster boy for the lonely walk to the clubhouse while the opponents celebrate.

Through it all, Branca has borne his role with grace and good humor. The day after he gave up the home run, still insisting he had "made a good pitch," he appeared at the opening game of the World Series between the Yankees and Giants and posed in his overcoat pretending to strangle his nemesis, Thomson. In the off-season, both he and Thomson appeared on the *Ed Sullivan Show*. Standing in front of an outsized portrait of Branca, Thomson sang lyrics crafted from the then-popular song, "Because of You."

Thomson's version of the song went,

> Because of you, there's a song in my heart.
> Because of you, my technique is an art.
> Because of you, a fastball high,
> Became a dinky, chinky fly.
> Now Leo and me-o won't part.
> My fame is sure, thanks to your Sunday pitch,
> Up high or low, I don't know which is which.
> But come next spring, keep throwing me that thing,
> And I will swing, because of you.

Branca followed, singing in a clear baritone to a portrait of Thomson,

> Because of you, I should never have been born.
> Because of you, Dodger fans are forlorn.
> Because of you, they yell drop dead,
> And several millions want my head.
> To sever, forever, in scorn.

His rendition brought down the house.

The following year, Branca injured his back in spring training and never regained the form or fastball that had made him an all-star at age 21. While he averaged nearly 14 wins a season between 1947 and 1951, he never won more than four a season in subsequent years. The Dodgers traded him to Detroit in the middle of the 1953 season, and he retired in 1956 after a short stint with the Yankees and a return visit to Brooklyn.

After retiring from baseball, Branca became a successful insurance underwriter. Over the years, he and Thomson have appeared together at old-timers' games, reunions, card shows, and TV specials, and have become friends. In the mid eighties, Branca was named the first president of the Baseball Assistance Team (BAT), an organization that provides help to former baseball players and umpires who have fallen on hard times.

Branca credits his faith in the Lord with helping him survive the notoriety of the "Shot Heard 'Round the World." At times, however, he has expressed a certain ambivalence toward that notoriety. "You know, if you kill somebody, they sentence you to life," he told Ray Robinson in the author's book on the 1951 pennant race. "You serve twenty years and you get paroled. I've never been paroled." On balance, however, Branca has few complaints. In an interview for the HBO Special that aired in 2002, he said, "I wasn't going to crawl under a rock and stay there.... It's just a ball game. I've got nothing to be ashamed of. I'm happy with my life."

Mitch Williams and the Ditch Mitch Movement

"I pitch like my hair's on fire," Mitch Williams once said. Since his long shaggy hair featured a mullet cut during his prime pitching years, the mental image conjured up by that quote is a raging conflagration. The image fit the player. Nicknamed "Wild Thing" after the character played by Charlie Sheen in the 1989 movie *Major League*, Williams did his best to live up to his reputation. A left-handed reliever wearing No. 99, he entered games to the tune "Wild Thing" made popular by the sixties rock group the Troggs. Plagued by wildness throughout his career, he gave up more walks than hits, and his lifetime record of 544 walks in 641 innings (7.6 walks in a nine-inning game) represents the worst control ratio ever recorded by a pitcher with a significant number of appearances.

Despite his wildness, he had several successful years as a closer, averaging over 30 saves a season from 1989 to 1993. His best year was 1993, when his 43 saves helped lead the Philadelphia Phillies to the National League pennant. Even then, his saves were not easy for faint-hearted fans to watch. One-two-three innings were rare. More common were innings in which he mingled walks and hits, putting runners in scoring position before closing out the opposition to preserve the Phillies' lead and earn his save.

Williams' claim to infamy came in the 1993 post-season. He began to implode during the National League Championship series against the favored Atlanta Braves. Although he had a hand in all four victories recorded by the underdog Phillies, saving two games and winning two, his two wins came after he had blown saves, losing one-run leads in the ninth inning, only to be bailed out by Phillies' bats in the tenth. In both instances, the starting pitcher who handed his one-run lead over to Williams was Curt Schilling. Television shots of Schilling during Williams' relief stints showed the retired starter with a towel draped over his head, staring at the dugout floor, unable to watch the reliever's erratic performance.

The 1993 World Series matched the Phillies against the defending champion Toronto Blue Jays. The two teams were a study in contrasts. The Blue Jays represented white-collar efficiency with established, no-nonsense players and a payroll of over $50 million. The Phillies, on the other hand, were definitely a working-class, dirty shirt group, with a payroll roughly half of that paid to their opponents. Seven players on the Jays team made more than the highest paid Phillie, Williams, who earned $3.5 million that year.

The Phillies gloried in their scruffy image and their reputation for "winning ugly." In addition to Williams, their blue-collar entourage included John Kruk, whose autobiography was entitled, *I Ain't an Athlete, Lady*, and who was characterized by one writer as looking like "a third helping of mashed potatoes," and Lenny "Nails" Dykstra, a tobacco-chewing throwback whose uniform was perpetually dirty. Prior to the Series, the *Toronto Sun* sponsored a contest in which they challenged their readers to describe the ugliness of the Phillies. The winning entry read, "The Phillies are so ugly the turf spits back."

The Phillies and Blue Jays split the first two games in Toronto, with Williams gaining a save in Game Two. After Toronto won Game Three to go up two games to one, things really began to unravel for the Phillies. The next game was a pitcher's nightmare, a high-scoring brawl in which both starters went to the showers early and the Jays led 7–6 after three innings. In writing about the game, Thomas Boswell of the *Washington Post* observed that the scoring was helped along by the plate umpire, "Charlie Williams, of whom Whitey Herzog once said, 'It's a good thing he only has two guesses.'" The Phillies came back to lead 12–7 after five innings, and seemed well on their way to evening the series at two games apiece when they turned the ball over to their closer Williams with a four-run lead, one out, and two runners on in the eighth. Williams entered the game with the score 14–10 Phillies and five outs to get to preserve the win. He only managed to get two of them. By the time he left the mound, the Jays were up 15–14 in what proved to be the highest-scoring series game ever (Boswell noted that the 29 runs by both teams eclipsed the previous record of 22 by one touchdown) and eventually won by that count.

Philadelphia Phillies fans are not known for their forbearance. Legend has it that they've been known to boo Santa Claus. Thomas Boswell elaborated on this legend by writing that they not only booed St. Nicholas, but also "... booed the Easter Bunny, and even booed the toddler sons of Phillies' players during parent-child games." After the Phillies' heartbreaking Game Four loss, Boswell wondered, "what special ring of hell will be reserved for No. 99?" But boos were the least of Williams' worries. He also received three separate death threats. And things were going to get worse.

Down three games to one, Curt Schilling pitched Game Five and shut out the Jays 2–0, going all nine innings so as not to tempt fate with another faulty relief performance. In Game Six back in Toronto, the Blue Jays appeared ready to cash their corporate Series checks when they led 5–1 after six innings. But then a three-run Dykstra homer cut the lead to 5–4 and the Phillies sent ten men to the plate in the seventh to take a 6–5 lead. The Jays fought back, loading the bases in the eighth against reliever Larry Andersen. At this point, Toronto fans began chanting "We want Mitch," but Andersen stayed the course and retired the side without allowing the tying run to score.

Toronto fans got their wish in the ninth inning, when manager Jim Fregosi sent Mitch Williams in to protect the Phillies' 6–5 lead. "Say one thing for Jim Fregosi," Boswell wrote with the benefit of hindsight in the *Washington Post*, "he's got more faith than the Pope. The current population of the United States is 252,686,000. Only Fregosi would have brought in Wild Thing to protect a one-run lead in the ninth." In truth, Fregosi's move was more a matter of hidebound tradition than faith. Most major league managers will bring in their currently anointed closer to close out a game, regardless of his recent performance.

Because Andersen had faced so many Blue Jay batters in the eighth, the Toronto lineup had turned over and Williams had to face the top of the order — no easy task. Wild Thing walked Rickey Henderson on four pitches, got Devon White to fly out, and gave up a single to Paul Molitor. That brought cleanup hitter Joe Carter to the plate with the potential tying and winning runs on base. "When I saw him (Williams) come in," Carter said later in the *Philadelphia Inquirer*, "I knew something good was going to happen."

The count ran to two and two on Carter. Then Williams shook off catcher Darren Daulton's signal for a fastball. "The shakeoff was a decoy," Williams explained later to reporters, "he puts down the same sign. Fastball. I got it inside. I wanted it outside. If he swung and missed, it (still) would have been a bad pitch."

Williams' fastball tailed down and in, to Carter's strength. Carter didn't swing and miss. He swung, connected, and sent the ball into the left-field stands to win the game and the series for the Blue Jays. It was the only time in Series history that a team had come from behind to win the final game with a home run.

Williams sat patiently talking to reporters in the locker room after the game, holding a can of Labatt's Blue, the arms of his red T-shirt rolled up to show the words "Wild Thing" tattooed on the upper part of his throwing arm. "There are no excuses," he said. "I didn't get the job done ... I threw the pitch that cost us the World Series. That's tough to deal with, but I'll deal with it.... I'm not going to commit suicide."

True to form, the fans and press of Philadelphia weren't kind to Williams. He returned to his Pennsylvania home to find all the windows broken, and the next day, the *Inquirer's* World Series Sports Extra ran a front-page column headlined PHILLIES MUST TRADE WILLIAMS. "There is no way around this other then to say: Ditch Mitch," wrote columnist Bill Lyon. " Mitch Williams has outlived his usefulness in Philadelphia. His act has worn thin and tiresome." Staff Writer Jayson Stark prophesied, "This pitch, this gopher ball, this World Series, is going to hang over him like a thundercloud as long as he remains on earth."

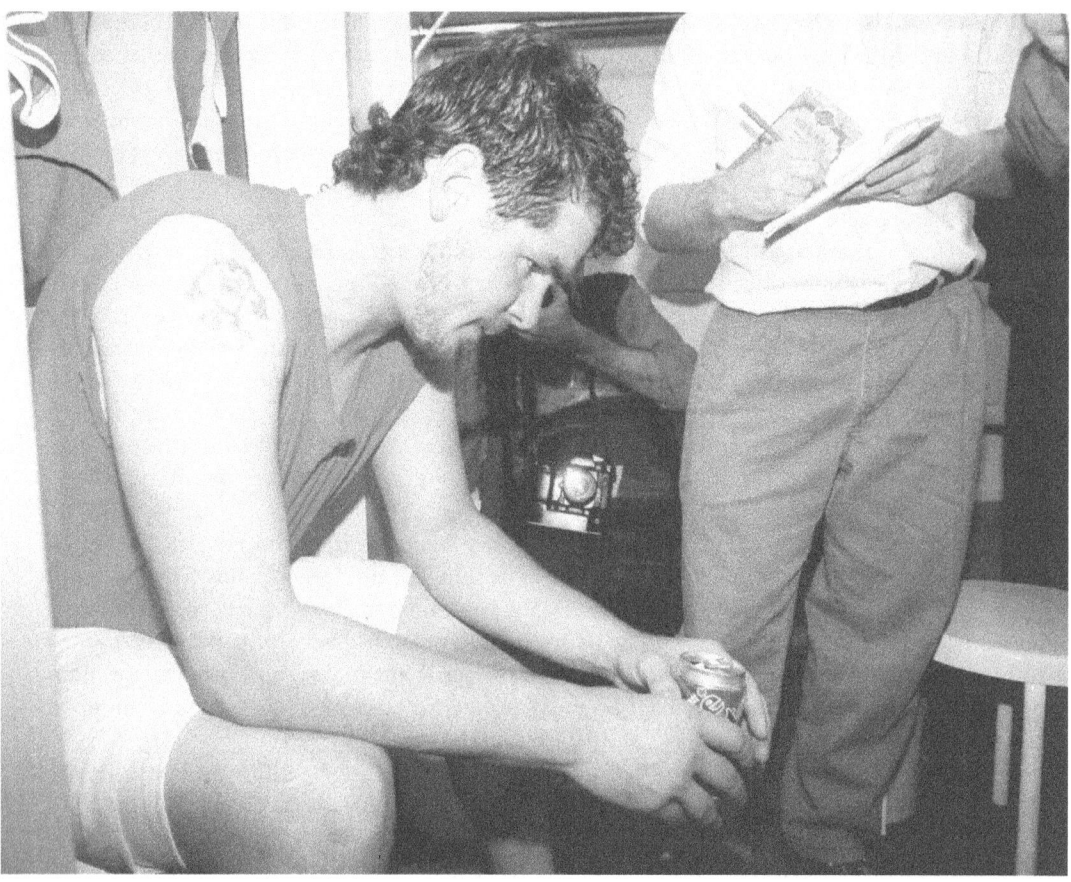

Mitch Williams of the Phillies in the locker room after giving up the Series-winning home run to Toronto's Joe Carte in 1993. "There are no excuses," he told reporters. "I didn't get the job done ... but I'll deal with it.... I'm not going to commit suicide" (AP/Wide World Photos).

That winter, the Phillies traded Williams to the Houston Astros for Doug Jones and Jeff Juden, two pitchers who together had 17 fewer saves than Williams rang up in 1993. Williams recorded six saves with the Astros before being released at the end of May. He then caught on with the Angels, returned to the Phillies, and finished his career with the Kansas City Royals without ever spending a full season with any club or recording another major league save.

Sitting in the locker room after Carter's home run, holding his Labatt's Blue, Williams told reporters, "Once I retire I'm going to get a million miles away from this game. I'm not going anywhere near it. Get as far away as I can." He returned long enough to record an interview commenting on the 1993 Series for the DVD *100 Years of the World Series*, produced by Major League Baseball in 2003. By that time he was more philosophical about Carter's home run. "Sometimes you get," he said, looking into the camera. "And sometimes you get got."

Donnie Moore: In Memoriam

After knocking around several teams early in his twelve-year career, Donnie Moore found two managers that believed in him and became a star for two short years. Then back pain, his own competitiveness, and bad luck conspired to bring it all down, and the pitch that had made him a star backfired and triggered a costly home run that became an obsession.

In the words of Bob Boone, the catcher who was behind the plate during Moore's glory years, "Moore was a journeyman pitcher until he learned the split-finger fastball. Then he became a dominant closer." Moore was in the eighth year of an unremarkable major league career when Manager Joe Torre of the Atlanta Braves showed enough faith to entrust him with the role of closer. He responded with sixteen saves for the Braves in 1984, and then was sent to the California Angels. Pitching for manager Gene Mauch of the Angels in 1985, he saved 31 games, had an ERA of 1.92, and worked two scoreless innings in the All-Star game.

Rewarded with a three-year, million-dollar-a-year contract, Moore developed back and shoulder pains during the next year, 1986. Still, with the aid of frequent cortisone shots, he managed to save 21 games and help lead the veteran Angel team to the championship of the American League West. Facing the Boston Red Sox in the League Championship Series, the Angels went up three games to one, with Moore recording a save in the third game, even though he balked in one run and allowed another on a single by Boston catcher Rich Gedman.

The fifth game of the Series proved to be a heartbreaker for Moore and the Angels. Facing elimination, the Red Sox jumped out to a 2–0 lead in the top of the second inning on a two-run Gedman home run. Then in the bottom of the second inning, Red Sox center fielder Tony Armas crashed into the outfield wall and incurred an ankle injury that was to alter the course of the game, the Angels' season, and Donnie Moore's life. Armas played on the injured ankle until the fifth inning, when he was replaced by Dave Henderson, who had joined the Red Sox late in the season and was playing hurt himself.

The Boston substitution paid dividends for California in the bottom of the sixth when Henderson lost a routine fly ball off the bat of Doug DeCinces in the sun and allowed it to drop for a double between himself and rightfielder Dwight Evans. Then, adding insult to injury, Bobby Grich, the next batter, hit a long drive to the 386-foot mark in left center. Henderson ran down the ball, leapt, captured it in his glove, and lost it over the fence when his wrist hit the top of the wall. In effect, Henderson carried the ball over the fence, so that his extraordinary effort managed to turn a double into a home run and turn a 2–1 Boston lead into a 3–2 Angel lead. California scored two more runs in the seventh and carried a 5–2 lead into the ninth inning, needing only three outs to carry the club into its first-ever World Series appearance.

Boston's leadoff hitter, Bill Buckner, guided a broken-bat single just out of the shortstop's reach. California's starter, Mike Witt, who led the team with 18 victories during the season, then struck out cleanup hitter Jim Rice for the first out. The next batter, Don Baylor, ran the count to field fence for an opposite-field home run. With one stroke of his bat, Baylor had turned around a good pitch from Witt and cut the Angels' lead to a single run.

Seemingly unfazed, Witt got Dwight Evans to pop up to DeCinces at third for the second out. With the championship only one out away, ushers, mounted policemen, and security guards gathered along the foul lines to prevent celebrating hometown fans from storming the field.

The next scheduled hitter was catcher Rich Gedman. Before Baylor homered, Gedman was the only Boston hitter to have given Witt any real trouble, collecting a single, double, and home run in three trips. Even though Witt had shown no signs of tiring or losing his effectiveness, manager Gene Mauch decided to bring in a left-handed reliever, Gary Lucas, to face the left-handed Gedman. It was a defensible strategic move, since Lucas had struck out Gedman the day before in the play-offs and the only time they had faced each other during the regular season. The strategy backfired, though, when Lucas hit Gedman on the hand with his first pitch.

As Gedman took the potential tying run to first base, Mauch relieved Lucas and brought in Donnie Moore, a right-handed pitcher to face the next hitter, the right-handed Dave Henderson. Henderson, who had played Grich's double into a home run in the sixth inning, had joined the Red Sox in August from the Seattle Mariners and had seen only limited playing time. In 51 at-bats, he had hit one home run, driven in only three runs, and batted only .196.

The crowd in Anaheim was on its feet, stomping and clapping and rooting for Moore to close out the game and the championship series. Moore threw a low pitch for a ball, then a fastball that Henderson took for strike one. Henderson swung late on the next pitch, another fastball, and the Angels were one strike away from the pennant. Henderson took the next pitch for a ball, running the count to 2-and-2, and then fouled off two pitches. Bob Boone, the Angels' catcher, saw that Henderson barely managed to foul off the first pitch, a forkball, but had come close to hitting the next one, a fastball, solidly. Worried that Henderson might be timing Moore's fastball, Boone signaled for a forkball, the split-fingered pitch that had turned Moore into a successful closer.

Moore's forkball had to be snapped off hard when it was released in order to give it enough speed so that hitters would confuse it with a fastball before it "bit" and dropped sharply when it reached the plate. The pitcher, who had received a cortisone shot the day before, didn't have it in his arm. "He pushed it," said Boone later. "It was readable. If he had thrown it hard like hundreds of others he had thrown, we would've won the thing right there."

The pitch was readable, and Henderson read it accurately, blasting it over the fence in left-center to give Boston a 6–5 lead. The crowd lapsed into stunned silence. Moore retired the next batter, but the damage had been done.

The Angels came close to taking Moore off the hook in their half of the ninth. They tied the score with a single by Boone, a sacrifice, and another single, and went on to load the bases with only one man out. But their cleanup hitter, DeCinces, hit a harmless fly to shallow right field, and when the next batter lined out softly to the pitcher, the game went into extra innings.

Mauch left Moore in the game to pitch the tenth inning, and he held the Red Sox scoreless when Jim Rice hit into a double play with one out and runners on first and third. The Angels failed to score in the bottom of the tenth and Moore was still on the mound for the top of the eleventh.

Don Baylor led off the eleventh inning for Boston. A powerful hitter who crowded the plate, he had just set a league record for being hit by pitches 35 times during the 1986 season and would go on to set a lifetime record for pitcher plunkings, collecting 267 in his 19-year career. True to form, he took first base after being hit by a Moore pitch. A single by Evans and an unplayable bunt by Gedman loaded the bases, and Dave Henderson returned to

Donnie Moore of the Anaheim Angels. He became an all-star reliever when he developed a split-finger fastball, but the pitch failed him in the 1986 American League Championship Series, when Dave Henderson of the Red Sox sent it out of the park and erased the ninth-inning lead that would have sent the Angels to the World Series for the first time in their history (National Baseball Hall of Fame Library, Cooperstown, N.Y.).

the batter's box. Henderson came through again, putting Boston ahead with a sacrifice fly to deep center. By now, it was apparent to everyone in the park but Mauch that Moore had little left. When the next batter drove Brian Dowling to the wall for a spectacular catch, even Mauch saw the light. He brought in Chuck Finley to replace Moore, who left the mound to a resounding chorus of boos.

Finley retired the Red Sox with no further damage, but the Angels went down one-two-three in the bottom of the eleventh and lost both the game and their chance to cinch the championship at home. They went on to lose the next two games and the championship in Boston, 10–4 and 8–1, in two sloppily played contests that saw California give up seven unearned runs in the final game. It was as close as the club would come to the World Series for the next 16 years when, rechristened as the Anaheim Angels, they advanced to the fall classic and beat the San Francisco Giants in seven games.

Donnie Moore blamed himself for the Angels' failure to advance to the World Series in 1986. "I got a tired arm now," he told reporters after the game. "But I can't blame my arm. If my arm felt that bad, I wouldn't have gone out there today. I was horseshit, no other excuses, I was horseshit."

The game coverage by the Boston and Los Angeles papers was remarkably different. While the *Boston Globe* headlines focused on its team's heroics (HENDERSON SAVORS DELIVERANCE; NO CHOKING FOR GEDMAN), the *Los Angeles Times* roasted the designated goats (MOORE DID NOT HAVE ANYTHING NEAR ENOUGH; PAST VISITS ANGELS' MAUCH). Ironically, in less than two weeks the situation in Boston would be reversed and the *Globe* would be roasting its own goat (ERROR BY BUCKNER ALLOWS KNIGHT TO SCORE WINNING RUN) instead of lauding its heroes.

Moore's back and arm hadn't recovered by the 1987 season. Neither had his spirits. He made only 14 appearances early in the season and was booed incessantly by the hometown fans every time he entered a game. Finally the Angels put him on the disabled list to give his back a chance to heal and doctors a chance to diagnose his injury. Unfortunately, the healing process was slow and uncertain and doctors were unable to isolate the problem.

Both Moore and the Angels grew increasingly frustrated and the team fell out of the pennant race during the last month of the season. Once again, Donnie Moore was blamed for the team's failure. As reported by Mike Sowell in his book, *One Pitch Away:*

> One day, Donnie picked up a newspaper and read a comment by Mike Port, the team's general manager. Port called Donnie a "malingerer." He said Donnie should "get out there and pitch." "Instead of whining about hurting his rib cage, he should have been out there earning his money," Port said in the newspaper. "What do we pay him $1 million for? ... He's supposed to be in shape. We should be getting our money's worth."

This unjust and unprecedented attack cut Moore to the quick. He'd pitched through pain throughout his career with the Angels. Finally after the 1987 season had ended, a back specialist isolated the source of the pain, a bone spur near Moore's spinal column. It took five hours of surgery to remove the calcium deposit and relieve the nerve irritation.

Moore returned to the mound in 1988, but never regained his All-Star form. The Angels relieved him of his closer role and released him in August of that year. On Bob Boone's recommendation, the Kansas City Royals gave him a contract in 1989 and assigned him to their Omaha farm club, but he fared no better there than he had with the Angels a year earlier. The Royals released him on June 12, and he was out of baseball for good.

Moore's life continued to spiral downward after his release. Prone to heavy drinking and angry outbursts, he separated from his wife and was forced to sell their home. On July 18, five weeks after his final release from the Royals, he put three bullets into his estranged wife, who miraculously survived, and then turned the gun on himself.

Interviewed by *The Sporting News*, Moore's agent Dave Pinter said:

> Ever since he gave up the home run to Dave Henderson, he was never himself again. He blamed himself for the Angels not going to the World Series. He constantly talked about the Henderson home run. He couldn't get over it. I tried to get him to go to a psychiatrist, but he said, "I don't need it, I'll get over it...." But he couldn't get over it. That home run killed him.

Following Moore's death, Thomas Boswell wrote in his *Washington Post* column,

> Nobody will ever be able to prove that the haunting memory of giving up Dave Henderson's home run in the 1986 American League playoffs led Moore to commit suicide. Maybe, someday, we'll learn about some other possible cause. But right now, what some people are saying aloud and many are thinking, is that this "goat" business isn't funny any more.

Chapter Seven

Gopher Balls II

> "I think I'm one of the few pitchers whose career took off after losing a big game like the one against the Pirates."
>
> Ralph Terry
> Quoted in *Heartbreakers*
> by John Kuenster

◆ ◆ ◆ ◆

Escaped Goats: Two Pitchers Who Shed Goat Horns

Many pitchers have given up walk-off home runs in crucial games without being branded as scapegoats. And a few who have been branded have managed to shed their goat horns by the time their careers ended.

Ralph Terry: Redemption

The first home run to decide a league play-off game in the ninth inning was Bobby Thomson's shot off Ralph Branca in 1951. The first home run to decide a World Series in the ninth inning of the deciding game occurred nine years later in the seventh game of the 1960 World Series, when Bill Mazeroski of the Pirates homered in the bottom of the ninth to give Pittsburgh a 10–9 win over the New York Yankees. The pitcher who gave up Mazeroski's historic round tripper was Ralph Terry, a gangling, 21-year-old right hander from Big Cabin, Oklahoma.

The 1960 Climax. The year 1960 saw one of the most exciting climaxes in World Series history. While the Yankees dominated the Pirates statistically throughout the Series, scoring twice as many runs as the National League entry and setting new Series records for the most hits, most runs, and highest batting average, Pittsburgh survived drubbings of 16–3, 10–0, and 12–0, to win three contests by much narrower margins and force a seventh game.

The Pirates jumped off to a 4–0 lead in the first two innings of the deciding contest, but the Yankees came back with a run in the fifth, four runs in the sixth, and two more in the eighth to go ahead 7–4. Yankee reliever Bobby Shantz, who had given up only one hit and held the Pirates scoreless for five innings, appeared to be in command when pinch-hitter Gino Cimoli led off the bottom of the eighth with a single to right center. The outcome of the Series turned on the next play, when Pirate leadoff hitter Bill Virdon slapped a hard grounder straight at Yankee shortstop Tony Kubek. The ball appeared to be destined for a 6-4-3 double-play when it hit a pebble, took a nasty hop, caught Kubek in the throat, and dribbled off toward second base. The shortstop dropped as if he'd been shot and began coughing up blood. By the time second baseman Bobby Richardson retrieved the ball and called time out to get help for Kubek, both runners were safe. Instead of a double play which would have left nobody on with two outs, the Pirates had men on first and second with nobody out.

When the next batter, Dick Groat, singled home a run, Yankee manager Casey Stengel called in Jim Coates to replace Shantz. The move appeared to work at first, as Coates got two quick outs on a sacrifice and a short fly to right field. When Roberto Clemente bounced a grounder to the right side of the infield, though, Coates was slow covering first, allowing Clemente to reach base and Virdon to score the Pirates' sixth run. Catcher Hal Smith then homered over the left-field wall to put Pittsburgh ahead 9–7. Stengel replaced Coates with Ralph Terry, who got the third out, but the damage had been done.

The Yankees struck back in the top of the ninth. Singles by Bobby Richardson, ex–Pirate Dale Long, and Mickey Mantle tallied one run and left men on first and third with one man out. When Yogi Berra smashed a hard one-hopper down the first-base line, the Pirates' first baseman, Rocky Nelson, who had been guarding the line to hold Mantle close to the base, backhanded the ball and stepped on first for the second out.

Nelson pivoted to throw to second, expecting to nail Mantle for the third out. Instead of running to second however, Mantle instinctively dove back into first, eluding the tag of the surprised Nelson. Mantle's alert move avoided the double play, kept the inning alive for the Yankees, and allowed the tying run to score from third. The next batter grounded out, sending the game to the bottom of the ninth with the score tied 9–9.

The first man up in the bottom of the ninth was number eight hitter Bill Mazeroski, the popular Pirate second baseman, better known for his glove work than his batting prowess. Terry's first pitch to Mazeroski was high and inside. Too high, thought Yankee catcher John Blanchard, who called time out, went to the mound, and warned Terry to keep his pitches low in the strike zone. The next pitch came in high and hard, still too high, and left the same way. As Mazeroski rounded first, he saw the ball clear the ivy-covered wall in left-center field and began leaping and waving his right arm overhead as he rounded the bases, scored the Series-winning run, and was mobbed by his jubilant teammates.

Arthur Daley of the *New York Times* drew a direct parallel between Ralph Terry and Ralph Branca, saying Mazeroski's blast "brought back memories of Bobby Thomson's pennant-winning homer for the New York Giants in 1951." "I don't know what the pitch was," a disconsolate Terry told *Times* beat reporter Louis Effrat, "All I know is it was the wrong one."

"I was up and down in the bullpen five times during that game," Terry said later in John Kuenster's book *Heartbreakers*. "I had almost thrown a full game in the bullpen.... By the time they called me in, I had nothing left. I couldn't blacken your eye if I hit you with a fastball."

"By spring training the next year I had forgotten the game," Terry told Kuenster, "but some writers wanted to know if I had suffered any trauma from getting beat in the big one. I said, 'No, why should I?' It was my first World Series."

In the late fifties and early sixties, the Yankees were regular participants in the World Series, so it wasn't unrealistic for Terry to believe his first Series would not be his last. The year 1960 had been Terry's first full year as a Yankee starter, and he won ten games while losing eight. In 1961, the year after the Mazeroski blast, he improved to sixteen and three and the Yankees, riding Roger Maris' 61 home runs and a record-breaking number of 240 team round trippers, returned to the World Series. They dispatched the Cincinnati Reds four games to one, with Terry absorbing the only Yankee loss. The next year, 1962, Terry led the league in wins with 23 and won the Cy Young award. The Yankees made their third consecutive trip to the World Series, and fate provided Ralph Terry with a chance for redemption.

The 1962 Comeback. The Yankees squared off against the San Francisco Giants in the 1962 Fall Classic. It was a see-saw Series, with neither team able to win two consecutive games. Terry lost Game Two as the Yankees suffered a 2–0 shutout at the hands of Giant pitcher Jack Sanford, but he came back to beat Sanford 5–3 in Game Five, pitching a complete game and gaining his first World Series victory in five decisions.

After heavy rains in San Francisco shut down the Series for three days, the Giants won Game Six to set up a seventh game rematch between Terry and Sanford. Both pitchers were in top form. Terry retired the first seventeen batters he faced, losing his bid for a perfect game when Sanford singled with two out in the bottom of the sixth. Sanford was nearly as effective, holding the Yankees to a single run that scored on a double play after New York had loaded the bases with none out in the top of the fifth inning.

The effectiveness of the two pitchers owed a debt to the notorious winds of San Francisco's Candlestick Park. In covering Game Seven, *Los Angeles Times* columnist Jim Murray wrote:

> The game had all the offensive fury of a pillow fight. When the wind blows in, as it did Tuesday, Candlestick park is a maximum security stockade for pitchers. A prisoner could get out of Alcatraz easier than a ball could go over that wall of wind.
>
> The Yankees had the gopher ball champion of the Western Hemisphere on the mound in Ralph Terry, who had given up 42 home runs this season. But when you get enough wood on the ball for a home run in the Candlestick wind, the second baseman gets under it.

The wind helped to preserve Terry's shutout in the seventh inning when Willie McCovey, who had homered off the Yankee pitcher in Game Two, connected solidly with a ball that, according to Murray, "if the wind hadn't been blowing, would have spent the night in Reno." The wind knocked McCovey's drive down into the soggy grass in deep center field, where Mantle recovered it in time to hold the lanky Giant left fielder to a triple. Terry saw to it that McCovey advanced no farther than third by fanning Orlando Cepeda for the third out of the inning.

The Yankees carried their 1–0 lead into the bottom of the ninth with Terry still on the mound, having given up only two hits in the previous eight innings. Pinch-hitting for the pitcher, Matty Alou led off the inning by dragging a bunt past Terry for a base hit. The next two batters, Matty's brother Felipe Alou and Chuck Hiller, both failed to lay down sacrifice bunts and wound up striking out. That brought Willie Mays to the plate. In his previous at-bat, Mays had driven Tom Tresh to the wall in left field, where he made a spectacular catch to rob Mays of a double. This time Mays slashed an outside pitch to the right-field corner and got his double.

The rain-soaked outfield grass slowed Mays' hit just enough to allow right fielder Roger Maris to hustle over to the line and cut the ball off before it reached the wall. Maris wheeled and made a perfect throw to second baseman Bobby Richardson, whose relay to home plate caused the Giant third-base coach to hold Alou at third.

The Giants, who had come from behind in the ninth inning to win the National League pennant in a play-off with the Dodgers, appeared to have set the stage for another comeback. With the tying run on third and the winning run on second, the next scheduled batter was cleanup hitter Willie McCovey, who had hit Terry hard throughout the Series. With first base open, the logical move was to walk the left-handed batting McCovey intentionally and pitch to the right-handed Orlando Cepeda, who was batting an anemic .156 for the Series.

Yankee manager Ralph Houk called time and went to the mound to confer with Terry, asking him whether he'd rather pitch to McCovey or Cepeda. Terry said he'd just as soon go after McCovey, and Houk decided to let his staff ace try to finish the job he'd started. "Terry was the only one who wanted to pitch to McCovey," Jim Murray wrote, " he was also the only one with the baseball." In his book, *100 Years of the World Series*, Eric Enders calls Houk's decision to let Terry pitch to McCovey "one of the worst strategic decisions in World Series history."

After the game, Houk defended his decision to reporters by saying, "We agreed we would sort of pitch around McCovey, not give him anything good to hit." Commenting on this strategy, Jim Murray wrote in the *Los Angeles Times*, "Pitching around McCovey is about as simple as pitching around the Empire State Building. Any pitch that stays in the ball park looks good to him. And with his reach he can hand a bat to a man in the second tier."

Terry wanted to pitch McCovey high and in, but his first pitch was high and away and the lanky Giant yanked it into the upper deck in right field. Fortunately for the Yankees, McCovey came around a little too early and the heavy Candlestick winds pushed the ball into foul territory. Terry hit his high-inside target with the next pitch, and McCovey lashed a hard line drive that had game-winning base hit written all over it until it slammed into the glove of second baseman Bobby Richardson for the final out.

In the clubhouse celebration that followed, Richardson said that McCovey's ball was hit so hard that if it had been "a yard to one side or the other ... I wouldn't have had a chance at that ball." Thus, Ralph Terry narrowly escaped being a goat for the second time in two years. Instead, his shutout sealed the victory for the Yankees, he was voted the Most Valuable Player of the Series, and the newspapers trumpeted his redemption.

The *Los Angeles Times* headlined RALPH TERRY GRATEFUL FOR SECOND CHANCE, and went on to quote the recently redeemed right-hander at length. "I'm the luckiest man in the country ... this has to be the greatest game I have ever pitched. More than that, this is a personal triumph for me. It wipes away two years of worry, two years of doubt."

Ralph Terry of the Yankees is hoisted on the shoulders of his teammates after he retired Willie McCovey of the Giants on a line drive to win the seventh game of the 1962 World Series 1–0 and help to erase the memory of his fatal seventh-game final pitch to Bill Mazeroski two years earlier (National Baseball Hall of Fame Library, Cooperstown, N.Y.).

The *Times* went on to explain that "the reference was obvious ... Terry has never forgotten his 'goat' role in the 1960 World Series." "I've tried to forget it, but people just wouldn't let me," he said, explaining that "People were always reminding me of it. Only this morning I got an anonymous letter from a fan in Pittsburgh. He reminded me of that home run ball I threw to Mazeroski and said that he was looking for me to throw another one like it today."

Terry later admitted that as he stood on the mound watching his manager retreat to the dugout after they decided to pitch to McCovey, his mind flashed to his fatal confrontation with Mazeroski in 1960. This time, though, the hard-hit ball that followed the mound conference proved fatal for the opposition. The *Los Angeles Times* headline over the game's box score neatly summarized the story of the game: GIANTS TERRY-FIED. "Thank God for the opportunity ... seldom does a man get a second chance. I'll be eternally grateful," Terry told reporters.

Terry pitched in relief for the Yankees in two more World Series, in 1963 against the Dodgers and in 1964 against the Cardinals, without earning a decision. An indication that he had exorcised the ghost of his 1960 gopher ball and come to terms with the pressures of pitching in big games can be found in a story told by Jim Bouton in Mike Blake's *Baseball Chronicles*. Bouton was nervous about making his first world Series start for the Yankees against the Dodgers in 1963. He sat on the bench all alone, fixating on the pressure, when Terry sat down beside him and asked, "Are you nervous, kid?"

"I can hardly breathe, Ralph," Bouton replied.

Terry put his arm around Bouton's shoulder, looked him in the eye and said,

"Remember one thing out on the mound today. Whatever happens, there are five hundred million Chinese communists out there who don't give a shit."

Bouton reports that "I laughed so hard I almost choked on my gum, and I was still laughing when the umpire said, 'Play ball.'"

Terry went on to play twelve years in the big leagues, winning 107 games and losing 99. His career actually blossomed after the 1960 Mazeroski homer, and his 1962 win over the Giants effectively eradicated his image as a scapegoat.

Dennis Eckersley and Gimpy Gibby

The first game of the 1988 World Series ended in a confrontation of epic proportions. The Most Valuable Player of the National League, Kirk Gibson of the Los Angeles Dodgers, came to bat against the premier reliever of the American League, Dennis Eckersley of the Oakland A's, with two out in the bottom of the ninth, the Dodgers down by a run, and the tying run on first base. The drama of the confrontation was heightened by the fact that Gibson, hobbled by a pulled left hamstring and sprained right knee, was not expected to play in the game and could barely make it to the plate under his own power. Once in the batter's box, Gibson fouled off Eckersley's first two pitches awkwardly, but then ran the count to 3-and-2 and pulled a back-door slider into the right-field seats for a 5–4 come-from-behind Dodger victory over the heavily favored A's.

The Principals. The drama of the situation and the background of the two principals have combined to make Gibson's home run off Eckersley one of the most memorable in baseball history. Dennis Eckersley came up to the major leagues with Cleveland in 1975 and quickly established himself as a force in the Indians' starting rotation, pitching a 1–0 no-hitter against the Angels in 1977. The Indians traded the 23-year-old Eckersley to the Red Sox just before the start of the 1978 season, in part because his wife's affair with teammate Rick Manning had become a distraction for all concerned. During his first season in Boston, Eckersley divorced his wife and won 20 games. Over his first five years with the Red Sox, he went on to compile a record of 76 wins and 53 losses and was selected for the All-Star team in 1982. In 1983, however, arm problems and alcoholism began taking their toll. His ERA ballooned to 5.61 runs per game, and the Red Sox traded him to the Cubs with another player for Bill Buckner early in the 1984 season.

After two years of resurgence with the Cubs, Eckersley's record dropped to six wins and eleven losses in 1986 and he was traded to the Oakland A's before the start of the 1987 season for three minor leaguers. The trade to Oakland, coupled with a self-imposed six-week stay at a treatment center where he came to terms with his alcoholism, marked a turning point in Eckersley's life and career. When he arrived in Oakland, manager Tony La Russa and pitching coach Dave Duncan converted him to a relief pitcher, where his pinpoint control and competitive nature made him one of the most successful closers the game has ever known. In 1988, his first full year as a reliever, he saved 45 games, one short of what was then the major league record, and went on to save all four of Oakland's wins over Boston in the American League Championship Series before coming up against Kirk Gibson in the first game of the World Series.

Kirk Gibson was an All-American wide receiver for Michigan State who elected to pursue a professional career on the diamond with his hometown Detroit Tigers, but who continued to approach baseball as if it were a contact sport. His all-out style of play cost him dearly throughout his career. In eleven big league seasons, he played in only 1,114 games, missing roughly thirty percent of his teams' contests during seven trips to the disabled list. When he was healthy enough to play, however, his competitive spirit, speed, and fence-busting power were an inspiration to his teammates and a curse to opposing players. In 1984 he led the Tigers to their first championship in 16 years, hitting 27 homers and driving in 91 runs during the regular season, batting over .400 as the Tigers swept the Kansas City Royals in the League Championship Series, and homering twice in the decisive fifth game of the World Series against the San Diego Padres.

Dennis Eckersley, whose conversion from starter to reliever when he was traded from the Chicago Cubs to the Oakland A's marked a turning point in his career (**National Baseball Hall of Fame Library, Cooperstown, N.Y.**).

Joining the Los Angeles Dodgers as a free agent in 1988, Gibson was named the National League's Most Valuable Player as he led the Dodgers to the pennant and supplied the key elements of the offense needed to crush the heavily favored New York Mets in the League Championship Series. Characterized by the *Washington Post*'s Tom Boswell as a "stubble-bearded, punk-cut road warrior," Gibson homered in the twelfth inning to win Game Four of the Championship Series, then came back the next day to bang out a three-run homer that keyed the Dodgers' 7–4 victory in Game Five. When the Mets, who had won ten of eleven regular-season games against the Dodgers came back to tie the Championship Series at three games apiece, Gibson drove in the first run of the decisive final contest with a sacrifice fly before leaving the game after aggravating his pulled left hamstring and spraining his right knee. His injuries were so serious that he wasn't expected to play in the opening game of the World Series and even sat out the pre-game ceremonies.

The Confrontation. Gibson spent the entire opening game in the clubhouse and was on the trainer's table, with icepacks on both legs, watching the game on TV when the A's brought in Dennis Eckersley to protect their 4–3 lead in the bottom of the ninth. The A's four runs had come in a batch on a second-inning grand slam by Jose Canseco. The Dodgers had scored twice in the first on a Mickey Hatcher home run and added another run in the sixth. There had been no scoring since the sixth inning and there was every expectation that Eckersley, who had blown only one save opportunity all year, would keep the Dodgers at bay in the ninth.

As the game entered its final phase, Dodger TV announcer Vin Scully lamented Gibson's absence, saying that "the spearhead of the Dodger offense, who saved them in the League Championship Series, will not see any action tonight." The announcement energized Gibson, who, according to the *Washington Post*'s Boswell, "growled 'Bullshit,' and broke out of his ice wrap like the Thing coming to life."

Gibson yanked on his uniform, began practicing his swings on a batting tee beneath the stands, and sent word to Dodger manager Tommy Lasorda that he was available to pinch-hit if needed. He was needed. Eckersley got two quick outs, but then walked pinch hitter Mike Davis. It was an uncharacteristic lapse for the Oakland reliever, who had walked only eleven batters all year, and it cost him dearly.

As Davis was batting, Lasorda, not wanting to advertise Gibson's availability to the A's, sent weak-hitting Dave Anderson to the on-deck circle and kept the National League MVP hidden in a corner of the dugout. While Davis trotted to first with the potential tying run, Lasorda recalled Anderson and brought Gibson out of hiding. Gibson's emergence surprised not only the A's but the crowd as well, and the hometown fans erupted with cheers as their local hero, fortified with shots of Xylocaine and cortisone, left the dugout and hobbled to the plate.

"He needed a long time to get up there, so it was driving me nuts," Eckersley sad later. "You've got your foot on their neck and you want to put them away." Eckersley set about putting the batter away, getting two quick strikes on outside corner fastballs that Gibson barely fouled off. Hopping with pain after each aborted swing, Gibson continued to foul off pitches and worked the count to three-and-two.

The runner Davis stole second base on one of the pitches that missed the plate, offering the A's a tactical choice. With first base open, they could walk the left-handed Gibson and pitch to the Dodgers' right-handed leadoff hitter, Steve Sax, whose on-base percentage was fifty points below Gibson's and who lacked the slugger's power. The A's chose not to put the winning run on base intentionally, but to continue to pitch to Gibson, who, catcher Ron Hassey noted, "didn't look too good on his swings."

By the time the count ran to three-and-two, Gibson thought he knew what to expect. The Dodgers' scouting report said that Eckersley favored a back-door slider on the full count, a pitch that began off the outside corner of the plate to left-handed batters and snapped back at the last minute for the finishing third strike. Hassey called for the back-door slider and Gibson, forewarned, hit it into the right-field stands for a 5–4 Dodger victory. Photos of the event show Gibson, balanced awkwardly on his right foot, following through with the bat in his right hand as Hassey holds his catcher's mitt low over the outside corner of the plate, an empty target.

The on-deck hitter, Steve Sax, claimed that Gibson hit the home run with one hand. He traversed the bases on his two game legs, alternately thrusting both arms in the air and pumping his right fist like a piston. It was Gibson's only appearance in the Series, but Lasorda claimed the A's were never able to recover from the blow and credited the hit with winning the Series as well as the first game. Actually, another Dodger, Orel Hershiser, deserves at least as much credit for the Dodgers' five-game Series victory as Gibson. Hershiser, who finished the season pitching six straight shutouts and an unprecedented, record-setting, fifty-nine consecutive scoreless innings, continued his pursuit of perfection by shutting out the A's on three hits in Game Two, putting the Dodgers up two games to none. After the teams split the next two games, Hershiser came back to win Game Five and the Series by a score of 5–2 on a five-hitter.

The Aftermath. Eckersley, a favorite with fans, players, and the media, bore up well under post-game and post–Series questioning. Noticing that NBC was interspersing its post-game coverage of Gibson's gimpy trot with footage from the 1984 movie *The Natural*, with its larger-than-life light-bank shattering climactic home run, the reliever said, "It got so I began thinking I had given up a home run to Robert Redford." It's ironic that the pitcher who coined the term *walk-off piece* for a game-ending homer would be victimized by one of the most famous walk-off pieces of all time.

The Gibson home run marked the first time a World Series game had ended with a come-from-behind home run. Bobby Thomson's home run had ended a play-off game, Mazeroski's had come with the score tied, and Joe Carter's Series-winning blast off Mitch Williams was five years in the future. Over the years, Gimpy Gibby's home run has, if anything, increased in importance and become a part of baseball iconography. A panel of local sports writers voted it the greatest moment in Los Angeles sports history. The sheer drama of the confrontation between the injured Gibson and the super-reliever Eckersley was unmatched, and the outcome so unlikely that the section of Los Angeles renowned for manufacturing Hollywood endings would have found it unbelievable.

Through it all, Dennis Eckersley managed to keep the home run and his role in delivering it in perspective. When he was traded to the A's he was a washed-up starting pitcher who had endured his first wife's affair with his best friend, a broken marriage, alcoholism, three trades, and career-threatening injuries. Converted to a premier reliever, he managed to scrap the "washed-up" label and shed most of the other baggage as well. Interviewed the year after the Gibson home run when he was continuing to post unprecedented numbers as a reliever, he told Thomas Boswell, "This is a second chance for me. Not too many people get a second chance. I am just so happy about what has happened to me that I don't want to stop. I've been so lucky, how could I be (upset about Gibson's homer)? You wouldn't be very appreciative if you acted that way, would you?"

Eckersley went on to spend nine seasons with the Oakland A's, establishing himself as one of the greatest relief pitchers of all time. At the height of his dominance in 1992, he saved 51 games, won seven, lost one, posted a 1.91 era, and was voted both the League Cy Young award and the Most Valuable Player award for that year. Oakland traded him to St. Louis before the start of the 1996 season, where he rejoined manager Tony La Russa and pitching coach Dave Duncan and posted 66 saves over two years. He rejoined Boston as a free agent in December 1997 and finished his career with the Red Sox in 1998. He retired with 390 saves (third on the all-time list), as well as 197 wins, and was elected to the Hall of Fame the first time his name appeared on the ballot.

In a tearful speech on the occasion of his induction into the Hall of Fame in July 2004, Eckersley broke down when talking about his alcoholism and his family. A brief video presentation accompanying the induction focused on shots of Eckersley registering saves but included the familiar clip of the Gibson home run trot. Former Giant broadcaster Lon Simmons, who was honored with the Ford Frick Award for broadcasting personnel on the day of Eckersley's induction, later told him, "I'm sick and tired of seeing Gibson pumping his fist and running the bases."

Eckersley responded "So am I." But, just as he had when besieged by reporters in the days and months following the home run, he kept the matter in perspective. "He had that moment, a meaningful moment," Eckersley said, referring to Gibson. "But have a nice life, Kirk, I'm in the Hall of Fame."

A Few Who Were Never Crowned

Bob Lemon and the Long and Short of It

One of the most written-about games in baseball history is the first game of the 1954 World Series between the Cleveland Indians and New York Giants. The Indians won 111 games that year, an American League record, and boasted one of the greatest pitching staffs ever assembled, a roster that included Bob Lemon (23 wins), Early Wynn (23 wins), Mike Garcia (19 wins), Art Houtteman (15 wins), and Bob Feller (13 wins). On the strength of their pitching staff and record-setting performance, the Indians were heavily favored to beat the Giants, who had a few weapons of their own, including two native Alabamans, a 23-year-old Willie Mays and a lesser-known 27-year-old pinchhitter named James Lamar "Dusty" Rhodes.

Dennis Eckersley holding his Hall of Fame plaque at his Cooperstown induction in 2004. When Kirk Gibson's 1988 home run at Eckersley's expense was shown on the video accompanying the induction ceremony, the pitcher said later, "Have a nice life, Kirk. I'm in the Hall of Fame" (National Baseball Hall of Fame Library, Cooperstown, N.Y.).

The Catch. Game One of the Series, played at New York's Polo Grounds, went into the eighth inning tied at two runs apiece, with Bob Lemon pitching for the Indians and Sal Maglie pitching for the Giants. Larry Doby led off the top of the eighth for the Indians by drawing a walk, and cleanup hitter Al Rosen singled him to second. That brought up Vic Wertz, Cleveland's powerful first baseman, who had already reached Maglie for three hits, including a triple that had driven in both the Indian runs. In the light of Wertz' success against Maglie, Giant manager Leo Durocher changed pitchers and brought in Don Liddle to face the Indians' first baseman.

Wertz turned on Liddle's first pitch and hit a long drive to deep center field. The oval-shaped Polo Grounds had the deepest center field in baseball, with the fence 490 feet from home plate at its farthest point. Giant center fielder Willie Mays, who had been playing Wertz shallow to cut off the potential run, turned his back to the plate at the crack of the bat and ran flat out toward the wall in right-center field. He made a spectacular over-the-shoulder catch about ten feet from the wall, and in a single motion whirled and threw the ball back to the infield, losing his hat and his balance in the process. Mays wound up on his hands and knees in front of the wall, but the ball wound up in the hands of second baseman Davey Williams, who was able to hold Rosen on first and keep Doby from advancing farther than third base on the long fly-out. Durocher lifted Liddle after Wertz' drive and brought in Marv Grissom to pitch to the next Indians batter. As Liddle left the mound, he passed the incoming Grissom and said, matter-of-factly, "Well, I got my man."

Mays' catch and throw, one of the most memorable fielding plays in Series history, proved to be the turning point in the game, as the Indians subsequently loaded the bases without scoring, and the 2–2 tie held through the first nine innings.

The Chinese Home Run. Vic Wertz led off the top of the tenth for Cleveland with his fourth hit of the day, a drive into the right-center field gap that Mays' adroit fielding held to a double. The next hitter sacrificed, moving Wertz' pinch runner to third, but the Indians failed to score when Bill Glynn, pinch-hitting for catcher Jim Hegan, struck out and Lemon lined out to first base.

Lemon struck out the first Giant to bat in the tenth, but then walked Willie Mays. Mays, who had noticed that Hegan's replacement, catcher Mickey Grasso, seemed nervous warming up Lemon before the inning began, promptly stole second base. The Indians walked the next batter, Hank Thompson, to set up a possible inning-ending double play. At that point, Leo Durocher called back the next hitter, future Hall of Famer Monte Irvin, to send up pinch hitter Dusty Rhodes.

Rhodes had served the Giants well in a part-time role that year, batting .341 and knocking out 15 home runs in only 164 at-bats. The pinch hitter swung under Lemon's first pitch, a curve, and lofted a high, lazy fly toward right field. Here again the dimensions of the Polo Grounds came into play. While the oval-shaped field had the longest center-field fence in the majors, it compensated by having the shortest distances down the left- and right-field lines. When Rhodes' hit went into the air, the right fielder, Dave Pope, drifted over to catch it, and the second baseman, Bobby Avila, raced after it as well, confident that either he or Pope could make the catch. With Avila and Pope in pursuit, the wind pushed the ball out of their reach, just over the short right-field wall. Pope ran out of room and leapt uselessly against the eleven-foot concrete wall and Avila watched helplessly below it as the ball caromed off the first row of seats and bounced back onto the field for a game-winning three-run home run.

Rhodes' pop-up became a textbook example of a Chinese home run. Before the days of politically correct speech, the term was used to denote a "cheap" home run that barely made the seats in a ballpark with constricted dimensions. The term was popular in the 1950s but went out of use when the Giants moved to San Francisco in 1958 and the Polo Grounds were demolished. In fairness, the ethnic implications of the term were questioned even before political correctness was rampant. The *Baseball Dictionary* reports that sportswriter Jimmy Cannon, writing in a 1956 article in the *Baseball Digest*, defined *Chinese Home Run* as "A cheap homer which would be called something else if the Chinese had enough influence."

Referring to the influence of the Polo Grounds' unique dimensions on the game's outcome, Indians manager Al Lopez was quoted in the next day's *Washington Post* as saying, "The longest out and the shortest home run of the season beat us, that's all." In any other park, Wertz' 450-foot drive in the eighth would have been a home run, while Rhodes' 258-foot pop-up would have been an easy out. When he saw Rhodes' hit disappear over the lip of the right-field wall,

Cleveland's Dave Pope leaps high against the short right-field wall of the Polo Grounds in a futile attempt to catch the wind-blown pop-up off the bat of Dusty Rhodes that won the first game of the 1954 World Series for the Giants. The home run off Bob Lemon was so poorly hit that Cleveland second baseman Bobby Avila (1) thought he might have a play on the ball (National Baseball Hall of Fame Library, Cooperstown, N.Y.).

Bob Lemon threw his glove into the air in disgust. In a famous photograph, he threw the glove again at a photographer taking his picture as he returned to the dugout. Rhodes observed later, "Lemon's glove went farther than the ball."

The Aftermath. While the next day's newspapers heaped superlatives on Mays' spectacular catch, they focused most of their attention on Rhodes' decisive home run. In the years since, however, "The Catch" has worked its way into baseball lore as one of the most famous fielding plays in history, eclipsing the home run that decided the game. The Indian players agreed that Mays' catch was the turning point in the game, and the Series as well. Cleveland never recovered from its first-game defeat, losing four games in a row as Rhodes continued his pinch-hitting heroics. After tying the second game with a pinch-hit single in the fifth inning, he stayed in the game to win it with a two-run homer in the seventh inning. He finished the four-game Series with a .667 average and seven runs batted in.

The 1954 World Series was easily the high point of Rhodes' career. An indifferent fielder, he left major league baseball in 1959 after seven years as a part-time player with the Giants. Although his Series exploits gained him a reputation as a clutch hitter, his lifetime average as a pinch hitter was .186, considerably lower than his overall average of .253.

None of the newspaper accounts of the day suggested that Lemon be fitted with goat horns for giving up the Rhodes homer. He had, after all, held the Giants to two runs over nine innings and induced Rhodes to hit a pop-up that in another park might have been caught by the second baseman. A converted infielder, Lemon spent thirteen years with the Indians, winning 207 games in a career that included seven 20-win seasons. After retiring as a player, he managed the Royals, White Sox, and Yankees and was voted into the Hall of Fame in 1976. Noted for his laid-back style, he never let his setbacks as a player or manager affect him. "I had my bad days on the field," the *Biographical Encyclopedia of Baseball* quotes him as saying, "but I didn't take them home with me. I left them in a bar along the way."

The Ordeal of Byung-Hyun Kim

In 2001, the 22-year-old Byung-Hyun Kim had what was probably the worst World Series ever experienced by a relief pitcher. Only the third Korean-born pitcher to reach the major leagues, Kim was full of promise, a submarining closer with uncommon speed for his underhand delivery. Replacing the injured Matt Mantai as closer for the Arizona Diamondbacks in 2001, he saved 19 games in 23 opportunities and struck out 113 batters in only 98 innings, for an eye-catching average of 10.4 strikeouts every nine innings.

Playing at home, the Diamondbacks won the first two games of the 2001 World Series against the Yankees behind the pitching of the two staff aces, Curt Schilling and Randy Johnson. On returning to New York, barely six weeks after the tragedy of 9/11, the Yankees won the third game 2–1 behind Roger Clemens.

Game Four. Curt Schilling started Game Four for the Diamondbacks on only three days of rest and held the Yankees to one run over the first seven innings. With Arizona leading 3–1 in the bottom of the eighth, manager Bob Brenly decided to replace Schilling with Byung-Hyun Kim. All but two of Kim's appearances during the regular season had started in the ninth inning. The early wake-up call didn't appear to bother him, however, as he struck out all three of the Yankees he faced in the eighth. In the ninth, though, with Paul O'Neill on first base after a broken-bat single and two men out, Tino Martinez hit the first pitch he saw from Kim, a rising fastball over the heart of the plate, into the center-field bleachers to tie the game.

An obviously shaken Kim walked the next batter, Jorge Posada, and gave up an infield single to David Justice before striking out Shane Spencer on a 3-and-2 pitch to send the game into extra innings.

In a move that provided fuel for second-guessers, Brenly left Kim in the game to face the Yankees in the bottom of the tenth. "B. K. throws a lot of pitches every day," the manager told reporters after the game, "It wasn't really pushing him beyond what he can do." In his second trip through the Yankee batting order, Kim induced the first two batters he faced to fly out and got a quick two strikes on Derek Jeter. The patient Jeter battled back, taking a few close pitches and getting used to Kim's underarm motion. When Kim left a slider up and over the plate, the Yankee shortstop met it squarely with an inside-out swing and drove it to the right-field corner, where it just cleared the fence for the game-winning homer.

Game Five. The next day, the Diamondbacks scored twice in the sixth inning and held the Yankees scoreless through eight, so that the score stood at 2–0 going into the bottom of the ninth. Here Brenly called on Kim once again, asking him to do what he'd failed to do in Game Four: protect a two-run lead. Since Kim had worked three innings and thrown sixty-two pitches the night before, this move was openly questioned by reporters and commentators. Even Roger Angell, whose lyrical accounts of the game in the *New Yorker* often explore strategy in depth but rarely criticize managerial decisions, parenthetically questioned Kim's reappearance on short rest, asking, "What was he doing here, anyway?"

Once again, Brenly defended his decision, saying, "He's our closer. I called down to the bullpen. They said his stuff was electric. We were certain he was fine. He wanted to pitch. He wanted the ball. The way he warmed up, there was no reason not to use him." Kim gave up a leadoff double to Jorge Posada, but then seemed to settle down, getting Shane Spencer and Chuck Knoblach out before facing veteran Scott Brosius, needing just one more out to save the game.

He didn't get the out. Instead, he left a slider out over the plate and Brosius nailed it, hitting it into the left-field stands for a game-tying home run. Not only had lightning struck twice in the same place, it was a rare form of heat-seeking lightning. Only once before in Series history had a team come from two runs down to tie a game with a home run in the bottom of the ninth, and now the Yankees had done it two nights in a row.

As Brosius raised his arms in triumph and began his home-run trot, Kim shrank into a despairing crouch at the foot of the mound, assuming a "See No Evil" pose by covering his eyes with his pitching hand and glove. His infielders gathered around to offer support, and veteran first-baseman Mark Grace provided a conciliatory hug. Brenly joined the support group and yanked Kim, replacing him with Mike Morgan, who closed out the inning. The Yankees put the game away in the twelfth inning, when rookie Alfonso Soriano drove in Chuck Knoblach with the winning run and put New York up three games to two in the Series.

The next day's newspapers conjured up comparisons with a familiar roster of pitching scapegoats. Kim was "Ralph Branca times two," the first pitcher since Mitch Williams to blow two saves in a World Series. Fortunately, his teammates saved him from eternal goatdom by

Arizona reliever Byung-Hyun Kim crouches on the mound after giving up a game-tying two-run home run in the bottom of the ninth inning for the second night in a row, an unprecedented event in World Series history (AP Photo/Rusty Kennedy).

salvaging the last two games and winning the Series. When the two teams returned to Arizona, Randy Johnson won Game Six handily, 15–2, and the Diamondbacks staged a comeback of their own in the ninth inning of Game Seven to defeat the vaunted Yankee closer Mariano Rivera and take home the championship.

The Aftermath. Even though Kim's blown saves didn't cost the Diamondbacks the Series, they had to be hard on his psyche. Arizona General Manager Joe Garagiola, Jr., told the *New York Times* that "When he first came to the majors, in 1999, Kim would become distraught if he gave up a single. He thought his job was to get all the hitters out." Thus, there was justifiable concern as to whether Kim would be able to function effectively as a closer in the aftermath of his massive Series failure. If his blown saves bothered him, though, it wasn't immediately apparent from his performance on the mound. In the next year he rebounded from his horrific humiliation and turned in his best season ever, winning eight games, saving thirty-six, and recording a 2.04 ERA.

In spite of his success as a closer, Kim was never entirely comfortable in the role. According to a *New York Times* report, he always considered himself a starting pitcher at heart, perhaps because starters commanded more respect than closers in his native South Korea. In deference to his wishes, and the return to form of one-time closer Matt Mantai, the Diamondbacks converted Kim to a starting pitcher in 2003 and then traded him to Boston shortly after the season began. An all-star as a closer, Kim was no more than a serviceable starter in Boston, and his aloof nature and difficulties with English, which were tolerated during his days as a successful closer in Arizona, grated on a few of his Red Sox teammates. When late-season struggles on the mound in 2003 drew criticism from the press and boos from Fenway Park crowds, Kim alienated hometown fans still further by giving them the finger after he was booed during the introductory ceremonies preceding Game Three of the American League Championship Series against Oakland.

Arm troubles and a general lack of effectiveness plagued Kim in 2004. His earned-run average ballooned to 6.23 and he spent time shuttling between Boston and the Red Sox's Pawtucket farm club. By the end of spring training in 2005, Kim was frustrated and unhappy. He had lost almost 10 mph from his once scary fastball, his slider was no longer sharp, and his future was uncertain. Just before the start of the season, the Red Sox traded Kim to Colorado for two minor leaguers, calling the two-year, $10 million deal they gave him in 2004 "a mistake." Ironically, the wire service reports covering the trade identified Kim as "a World Series hero for the Arizona Diamondbacks in 2001," an indication of the memory loss that can result when a pitcher's mistakes don't cost his team the Series. If the Diamondbacks hadn't rallied in the final inning of Game Seven, Kim wouldn't have been remembered as a Series "hero," but would have taken his place in the pen beside such lifelong goats as Branca and Buckner.

Other Walk-off Home Runs

Dusty Rhodes' home run off Bob Lemon marked only the second time in history that a World Series game had ended with a "walk-off home run"— Dennis Eckersley's term for a homer that ends the game instantly by driving in the winning run in the bottom half of the final inning. Since 1954, there have been thirteen such walk-off homers in World Series play. Except for Kirk Gibson's home run off Eckersley in Game One of the 1988 Series and Joe Carter's home run off Mitch Williams to end the 1993 Series, all have come with the score tied. Gibson's and Carter's blasts were the only two to bring their team from behind to win, and the home runs of Carter and Bill Mazeroski were the only two to end the Series itself.

From the 1960s on, Series games have ended in walk-off home runs often enough so that there have been few attempts to saddle the losing pitchers with goat horns. In fact, the task of identifying the pitchers giving up these home runs would make a trivia quiz capable of stumping all but the most ardent baseball fans. A complete list of the walk-off home runs that have ended Series games appears below.

Come-from-Behind Walk-Off Homers

Year	Pitcher/Club	Hitter/Club	Game/Inn.	Score	Series Winner
1988	Dennis Eckersley/A's	Kirk Gibson/Dodgers	One/Ninth	5–4	Dodgers
1993	Mitch Williams/Phils	Joe Carter/Blue Jays	Six/Ninth	8–6	Blue Jays

Walk-Off Homers Ending Tie Games

Year	Pitcher/Club	Hitter/Club	Game/Inn.	Score	Series Winner
1949	Don Newcombe/Dodgers	Tommy Henrich/Yankees	One/Ninth	1–0	Yankees
1954	Bob Lemon/Indians	Dusty Rhodes/Giants	One/Tenth	5–2	Giants
1957	Bob Grim/Yankees	Eddie Mathews/Braves	Four/Tenth	7–5	Braves
1960	Ralph Terry/Yankees	Bill Mazeroski/Pirates	Seven/Ninth	10–9	Pirates
1964	Barney Schultz/Cards	Mickey Mantle/Yankees	Three/Ninth	2–1	Cardinals
1975	Pat Darcy/Reds	Carleton Fisk/Red Sox	Six/Twelfth	7–6	Reds
1988	Jay Howell/Dodgers	Mark McGwire/A's	Three/Ninth	2–1	Cardinals
1991	Charlie Liebrant/Braves	Kirby Puckett/Twins	Six/Eleventh	4–3	Twins
1999	Mike Remlinger/Braves	Chad Curtis/Yankees	Three/Tenth	6–5	Yankees
2001	Byung-Hyun Kim/D'backs	Derek Jeter/Yankees	Four/Tenth	4–3	D'backs
2003	Jeff Weaver/Yankees	Alex Gonzalez/Marlins	Four/Twelfth	4–3	Marlins

Except for Ralph Terry, whose fastball to Mazeroski lost the Series as well as the game, none of the pitchers who gave up walk-off home runs with the score tied were ever seriously measured for goat horns, and Terry shed his horns by "retiring" McCovey to end the 1962 Series.

Keys to the Goat Pen

Given the number of home runs that have decided the outcome of crucial games, it's surprising that the list of pitchers stigmatized for throwing gopher balls isn't longer. The list is clearly headed by the names of Ralph Branca, Mitch Williams, and Donnie Moore. Branca made the pitch he wanted to make, Williams put his fastball in the wrong place, and Moore didn't get enough on his forkball. The end result was the same. Their pitches left the park and their failure marked them for life.

There's one other point of similarity between Branca, Williams, and Moore. In every case, victory was in their grasp as they stood on the mound. The opposing club had to come from behind to beat them, and a late-inning home run led to their downfall. Pitchers have rarely been stigmatized for giving up walk-off home runs with the score tied. There have been eleven such home runs in World Series history, and the names of the pitchers who served up the gopher balls are no more than footnotes.

The mere fact that an opponent comes from behind isn't enough to stigmatize a pitcher. Defeat must come with the thunderclap of a home run. Four successive singles may add up to four bases and a come-from-behind win, but it won't earn a pitcher a place in the pantheon of failure. Neither will three successive singles, a wild pitch and an error. Just ask Bill Buckner, who took the fall for the pitchers who really lost Game Six to the Mets.

Thirty years after he gave up Bobby Thomson's home run, Ralph Branca commented on the selective nature of the moving finger that had singled him out in *Bums*, Peter Golenbock's oral history of the Brooklyn Dodgers.

It's thirty years now, time to bury it. Sisler hit a home run off Newcombe and won a pennant for Philadelphia, and Mazeroski hit a home run off Ralph Terry to win the World Series, and Bench hit a home run off somebody to win the pennant in a playoff game, and you never hear about those things. Chambliss's home run off Littell. You don't hear about that. Bucky Dent's home run off Torrez. He hung him a slider inside. But you don't hear about that. The only reason you hear about Branca–Thomson is it was in New York, and there was a great rivalry between the Dodgers and Giants.

CHAPTER EIGHT

Errant Throws

"Who was I supposed to throw the ball to? Klem?"
Heinie Zimmerman
Addressing reporters who wondered why he chose to chase
Eddie Collins across the plate rather than throw home

◆ ◆ ◆ ◆

Wild throws by fielders have contributed to the loss of many crucial World Series games, but the memories of these misplays typically have not survived the post-season. One player whose fielding blunders cost his team dearly in the World Series is remembered more for a botched run-down play than for the wild throw that led to the run-down.

Scapegoat: Zimmerman and the Chase

Heinie Zimmerman played for thirteen years in the major leagues, between 1907 and 1919. A strong hitter with a lifetime batting average of .295, he led the National League in home runs and batting average in 1912, and in RBIs in both 1916 and 1917. His poor fielding offset his hitting, and he led National League third basemen in errors for three consecutive years when he played for the Chicago Cubs. His weak character was an even greater liability than his poor fielding, and he was banned from baseball in 1919 along with the notorious Hal Chase for trying to get his Giant teammates to throw late-season games against the Cubs and Cardinals.

Aside from the scandal of his banishment, Zimmerman is best known for an incident in the sixth and final game of the 1917 World Series, when he chased Eddie Collins of the White Sox across home plate with the first run of the game. With the White Sox leading the Giants three games to two, Collins led off the fourth inning of the sixth game by hitting a ground ball to Zimmerman at third. Zimmerman fielded the ball and threw it wildly past Walter Holke at first base, allowing Collins to take second. The next batter, Shoeless Joe Jackson, lifted an easy fly to right field that Dave Robertson dropped, putting runners on first and third.

With two runners on base through no fault of his, Giant pitcher Rube Benton bore down and got the next hitter, Happy Felsch, to hit a one-hopper back to him. Benton saw that he had Collins caught off third base and ran toward the White Sox runner. When Collins started back toward third, Benton threw the ball to Zimmerman. Collins braked, reversed direction, and headed for home. Zimmerman threw the ball to catcher Bill Rariden to start a rundown. Rariden brought the ball down the baseline toward Zimmerman, tightening the vise on Collins, who was caught between the two Giants. When the White Sox runner started back toward third, the catcher threw the ball to Zimmerman, who tried to tag Collins. At that point, Collins reversed field and dashed past Rariden toward the plate. Seeing no one covering home, Zimmerman was forced to chase after the speedy Collins himself. It was an unequal foot race, with Collins playing hare to Zimmerman's tortoise. Zimmerman chased Collins all the way home, as the crowd and his teammates shouted, "Throw the ball. Throw the ball."

"Who was I supposed to throw the ball to? Klem?" Zimmerman asked later. Indeed, the newspaper photographs of the incident show that the only individual near home plate when Collins scored was umpire Bill Klem. Neither pitcher Benton nor first baseman Holke thought to back up the botched rundown by covering the plate.

While Zimmerman was chasing Collins home, Jackson and Felsch raced happily around the bases, so that the White Sox not only scored a run but wound up with runners on second and third. The next batter, Chick Gandil, singled them both home, giving the white Sox a 3–0 lead on three unearned runs. The Sox added another unearned run in the ninth and won the game and the Series, four games to two.

The New York newspapers loudly blamed Zimmerman for the Giants' loss. The first page of the *Times* announced the White Sox win with the headline ZIM'S BLUNDERS ARE FATAL. The lead story in the *Times* called the futile chase "one of the stupidest plays that has ever been seen in a world's series," and went on to describe Collins "gathering speed and gaining in every jump" while "Heinie's feet were behaving as if they were having a hard time keeping out of each others' way."

The coverage in the Chicago papers was somewhat more circumspect. The *Tribune* carried a photo of Zimmerman leaping over Collins as the White Sox runner slid home safely with the run under the caption ZIM'S PRIZE BONER, but noted in the accompanying story that "It wasn't entirely Zimmerman's fault, either. Collins had the whole Giant team up in the air on the play they are blaming on Zimmerman."

Baseball Magazine called Zimmerman's losing race "the greatest bone-play of all time," and neither the magazine nor the *New York Times* coverage ever mentioned the failure of both Benton and Holke to back up the rundown play by covering home. The *Times* reporters forestalled any attempt to shift the blame by writing, "No matter whether an alibi can be established for Zimmerman or not, the spectators were in no mood to accept it and already they have enthroned Zimmerman with that select few headed by Fred Merkle."

In his year-by-year account of the World Series published in 1949, sportswriter Fred Lieb notes that

> New York writers and fans made Zimmerman almost as much of an all-time Giant goat as Fred Merkle for his failure to touch second base in 1908 and Fred Snodgrass for his expensive muff in the 1912 Series. However, some baseball men were fair enough to ask why neither Benton nor first baseman Holke covered the plate after the procession passed Rariden, but McGraw always contended Zim's error was in maneuvering the play so that Collins was chased toward the plate instead of away from it.

Whatever culpability one assigns to Zimmerman for his futile and fatuous chase, it was his wild throw that had allowed Collins to reach base in the first place. In addition, Lieb points out, "even if Zimmerman hadn't chased Collins home in the sixth game, Heinie would have been voted the goat of 1917. As McGraw's cleanup hitter, he came out of the Series with the sorry average of .120 and only three hits in twenty-five times at bat." Furthermore, an earlier wild throw by Zimmerman in Game Five helped the White Sox to the victory that put them up three games to two going into the fateful Game Six.

Looking back on the 1917 Series from the perspective of 2001, Bill James notes in his *Historical Baseball Abstract* that "Zimmerman must have played as badly in that series as anyone ever," and raises an interesting but ultimately unanswerable question in the light of Zimmerman's subsequent banishment for fixing games and his shadowy role in helping to rig the 1919 World Series: "It is not possible to know exactly when Zimmerman began throwing games, and

Heinie Zimmerman of the Giants, who chased Eddie Collins of the White Sox across home plate with the first run of Game Six of the 1917 World Series. When the Sox won the game and the Series, the *New York Times* called the botched rundown "one of the stupidest plays that have ever been seen in the world's series," but didn't note that it was the failure of Zimmerman's teammates to cover home plate that made the chase necessary (National Baseball Hall of Fame Library, Cooperstown, N.Y.).

thus we can never be certain that when he lost the 1917 World Series almost single-handedly, he wasn't doing it on purpose."

Clearly, there must have been more underhanded rigging of baseball games in the period between 1910 and 1919 than ever came to light in the Black Sox scandal and the banishing of Zimmerman and Hal Chase. Baseball betting by players was hardly a secret at the time, as witnessed by this article, printed in its entirety as part of the *Chicago Tribune*'s coverage of the White Sox victory in 1917.

Zim's Race with Collins Costs Cap Herzog $1,700

New York, Oct. 16. (Special.) When Heinie Zimmerman ran Eddie Collins over the home plate with the first run in the final world's series game it was noticed that Capt. Herzog talked to Umpire Evans. Herzog was not protesting on anything, though. Here are his exact words: "Bill, did you ever see anything like that? I have $1,700 riding on this ball game and that's the shortest run for $1,700 that I ever heard of."

In the light of the Pete Rose scandal, it seems incredible today that such an account would have been part of the public record in 1917.

After raising the issue of Zimmerman's culpability in 1917, Bill James wrote a fitting epitaph for the player, contrasting him with the notorious fixer Hal Chase, who had been rigging games for at least ten years.

Zimmerman was not Hal Chase. He was not a heavy drinker, as Chase was, not a charmer, and he had not been throwing games for ten years. He had been, and he should have remained, a lovable eccentric. He wanted more. He got less. His dishonesty and his World Series blunder have long since supplanted any other memory of him.

Escaped Goats

Buck Herzog, Art Fletcher, and the Series Error Record

Buck Herzog and Art Fletcher were trash-talking, tough-as-nails infielders with John McGraw's National League champion New York Giants in 1911. Between them, Herzog at third and Fletcher at short made seven errors in the World Series against Connie Mack's Philadelphia Athletics, with five of these errors coming in the crucial third game.

The series was tied at one game apiece and the Giants led the third game 1–0 with Christy Mathewson pitching and one man out when Philadelphia third baseman Frank Baker came to the plate. Baker had led the American League in home runs that year with nine round-trippers and his home run off a Rube Marquard fastball had won Game Two for the A's and been discussed at length in the newspapers of the day. Several observers, including Marquard teammate Mathewson, declared that the pitcher never should have thrown Baker a fastball. "Baker's home run was due to Rube's carelessness," wrote Mathewson (or his ghostwriter), "Prior to the game, John McGraw went over all of the Athletics' hitters in a clubhouse talk and paid special attention to Baker. Marquard was told just what not to pitch to Frank. Well, Rube pitched just what Baker likes."

When Baker came up in the ninth inning the next day against Mathewson, he had presumably read the newspapers. Knowing what to expect from Matty, he got a pitch to his liking and deposited it in the right-field seats. Round trippers were a rare commodity in 1911, and when the A's third baseman produced two in successive Series games he was ever after known to the press and public as "Home Run" Baker.

Although it made his reputation, Baker's home run only tied the score. Coming as it did off the near-invincible Mathewson, however, it let the air out of the feisty Giant team, which imploded in the eleventh inning. Eddie Collins singled to open the top of the eleventh for the A's, bringing up Baker for another shot at Mathewson. This time Baker was only able to manage a little bouncer to third. Herzog charged the ball, picked it up, and, in his haste to get an out, threw it away. It was Herzog's third error of the game, and it left A's runners on second and third. The next batter, Danny Murphy, hit a grounder that Fletcher fumbled for his second error of the game, allowing Collins to score the go-ahead run. Harry Davis followed with a single that put the Athletics up 3–1.

The Giants got one run back in the bottom of the eleventh, but couldn't overcome the weight of Herzog's and Fletcher's five errors and lost the game 3–2. The next day's newspapers focused on Baker, laying the foundation for his canonization as "Home Run" Baker. In addition to tying the game in the ninth with his home run, Baker had stood fast at third base against a spikes-high slide by Fred Snodgrass in the tenth inning. Snodgrass was out on the play, but it left Baker with a torn uniform and several ugly gashes. The newspapers took Snodgrass to task as much for his poor judgment in trying to take third on a short passed ball as for his spikes-high slide, generating a flood of angry letters and a few death threats toward the Giants' center fielder.

In focusing on the heroics of Baker and the brutal slide of Snodgrass, the newspapers overlooked the poor fielding of Herzog and Fletcher, which actually cost the Giants the game. The *Washington Post* predicted in banner headlines that the DEFEAT OF MATHEWSON PRACTICALLY DECIDES OUTCOME OF WORLD'S SERIES. This observation proved prescient, as Philadelphia won the Series four games to two, helped along by sixteen Giant errors—a record for a six-game series.

Herzog and Fletcher contributed seven of the Giants' sixteen errors, but neither player was fitted with goat horns. Even the *New York Times,* usually quick to assign blame to Giants' players, focused their coverage on Baker's heroics.

Fletcher went on to establish a record for the most Series errors by a single player, committing twelve miscues in twenty-five games with the Giants in their losing efforts in 1911, 1912, 1913, and 1917. The press of the day barely noted this fact (as compared, for example, with the roasting of Roger Peckinpaugh in 1925 for his single Series record of eight errors), since the record stretched over a long period of time and was as much a measure of the Giants' success in reaching the fall classic as of Fletcher's ineptitude.

Herzog and Fletcher both played for thirteen years in the majors and put in unsuccessful

Buck Herzog and Art Fletcher, Giant infielders who together made five errors and cost their team Game Three of the 1911 World Series. New York made a record sixteen errors in the six-game series, but the team's fielding miscues were overshadowed by the long-ball heroics that earned Philadelphia's third baseman the nickname "Home Run" Baker (Library of Congress, Prints and Photographs Collection).

stints as managers after they left the Giants. As player–manager for the Reds, Herzog never finished higher than seventh in an eight-team league, while Fletcher managed the Phillies for four years without ever finishing higher than sixth.

Vern Stephens' Brown-out

The hapless St. Louis Browns were the last of the original sixteen American and National League teams to reach the World Series. It took them until 1944 to register a first-place finish, which they managed with a team of 4-Fs and returning veterans in a league weakened by the war-time absence of most major stars.

Prior to 1944 the Browns had been perennial second-division finishers. A sportswriter who computed the composite record of all American League teams through 1944 found the Browns solidly entrenched in last place, 837 games behind the first-place Yankees.

The Browns' opponents in the 1944 World Series were their cross-town rivals, the St. Louis Cardinals. The Cardinals, who managed to retain the services of such stars as Stan Musial, Harry Brecheen, Marty Marion, and the brothers Walker and Mort Cooper throughout the war, were easily the class of the National League, having won pennants in the two preceding years and a total of seven through 1944.

In spite of their disparate pedigrees, the Browns surprised the Cards early in the World Series, winning two of the first three games and barely missing winning all three. The Cardinals fought back, winning two in a row to go up three games to two.

In Game Six, the Browns led 1–0 when the Cardinals put runners on first and third with one out in the bottom of the fourth inning. Cardinal batter Whitey Kurowski hit a hard smash that shortstop Vern Stephens fielded cleanly. But Stephens threw wildly to second, pulling second baseman Don Gutteridge off the bag. The runner on third scored the tying run on the error, and the Browns, who might have been out of the inning if Stephens' throw had been on the money and Gutteridge was able to turn the double play, were left facing runners on first and second.

After Marty Marion popped up for the second out, Emil Verban singled home the go-ahead run. Verban, normally a weak hitter who had been lifted for pinch hitters in the first two games, went on a hitting tear after being angered by the fact that his wife had been seated behind a pole when the Browns took over as home team in the shared Sportsman's Park. According to Fred Lieb in his invaluable reference, *The Story of the World Series*, Verban's hot Yugoslav blood was aroused by this slight, and he hit .412 for the series. Pitcher Max Lanier followed Verban with a single that brought Kurowski home and put the Cardinals up 3–1. Neither team scored after the fourth inning, and the Cards won their fifth world title.

The next day's newspapers highlighted the three-hit pitching of Cardinal starter Max Lanier

Ray Sanders scores the go-ahead run for the Cardinals against the Browns in the final game of the 1944 World Series. The tying run had scored earlier in the inning when Browns' shortstop Vern Stephens threw wildly to second in an attempt to start a double play after fielding a grounder hit by Whitey Kurowski (National Baseball Hall of Fame Library Cooperstown, N.Y.).

and reliever Ted Wilks, and mentioned Stephens' error only in passing. His error was only one of ten made by the Browns in the Series, against one for the Cardinals, and their loose play had as much to do with their Series loss as the Cardinal pitching, which produced a record-tying 49 strikeouts in the six-game series. Another fact that kept Stephens free of goat horns was his timing. His error occurred in the fourth inning, leaving the Browns five innings to overcome their two-run deficit.

The Browns finished third in 1945, and then tumbled to their accustomed second-division lodgings in 1946, when they finished in seventh place. After that, they never posted a winning percentage above .400, departing St. Louis to become the Baltimore Orioles in 1954.

Vern Stephens didn't accompany the Browns on their slide into obscurity. Nicknamed Junior, he was a straight-A student in high school, where he was judged too small to make the baseball team. After building himself up, he played American Legion baseball, attracted the interest of major league scouts, and made his debut with the Browns in 1941. He became a legitimate star during the war years, when a trick knee and asthma kept him out of the service. Traded from the Browns to the Red Sox in 1948, he adapted well to Fenway Park and, batting fourth behind Ted Williams, led the league in RBIs in 1949 and 1950. An eight-time All-Star, he moved from shortstop to third base in 1951 when his old knee injury began to limit his mobility and retired from baseball in 1955.

Today, Stephens' stint with the Browns and his misplay in the 1944 World are all but forgotten. Instead, his biographies focus on his glory years with the Red Sox and his hard-drinking lifestyle, which led to an early death at the age of 48.

Al Kaline's Near-Perfect Throw

Official scorers will almost always award errors on wild throws by infielders handling batted balls. Exceptions are made in the case of close plays if the scorer believes a good throw would have failed to retire the runner and the runner gets no extra bases as a result of the errant throw. The general presumption, however, is that an accurate throw from the infielder would have resulted in an out.

This presumption does not hold in the case of throws from the outfield. In general, an outfielder can miss his cutoff man, airmail throws beyond the reach of any player without a stepladder, and miss his target by half the distance from home plate to third base without incurring an error, so long as runners do not advance beyond the base they were aiming for when the throw was made. The presumption in this case is that the runner will arrive safely at his intended goal. Errors are awarded only when throws from the outfield are so wild, or so mishandled, that runners take extra bases.

Ironically, an outfielder is more likely to be charged with an error on an accurate throw that arrives at the base at the same time as the runner than on an inaccurate throw that draws the fielder far enough from the base so that he has no chance to make a play. When the ball and a sliding runner arrive simultaneously at the base, the possibility of an error is multiplied. The runner may deflect the throw or obscure the fielder's vision enough so that the ball skips through and allows the runner to take an extra base. In such a case, scorers usually assign an error to the outfielder whose only crime was to put his throw right on the money.

Hall of Fame outfielder Al Kaline of the Detroit Tigers was charged with an error under this set of circumstances in the crucial opening game of the 1972 American League Championship Series between the Tigers and the Oakland A's. The Tigers, representing the American League's Eastern Division, were favored to beat the Western Division Champion A's. In the three years since the league had been split into two divisions and the World Series contender decided by a best-of-five championship play-off, the representative of the American League's

Western Division had not won a single game from the Eastern Division Champions. The Eastern Division Orioles swept the Western Division Twins in 1969 and 1970, and held the A's winless in 1971.

The first game of the 1972 ALCS went into extra innings, with Catfish Hunter of the A's and Mickey Lolich of the Tigers each holding the opposition to a single run. When Al Kaline homered in the top of the eleventh to give the Tigers a 2–1 lead, it looked as if Detroit was going to carry on the winning tradition of the Eastern Division. Kaline was in his twentieth year with the Tigers, having joined them fresh out of high school in 1953. He was one of the few modern-day players to make the majors without spending so much as an inning in the minor leagues, and in 1955, at age 20, his .340 average made him the youngest player to win a big-league batting championship. By 1972, Kaline was far enough removed from his youthful batting championship to have earned the nickname "old bones" and have won eleven gold gloves as a right fielder in recognition of his powerful throwing arm.

Mickey Lolich, who had held the A's to a single run through ten innings, gave up a single to Oakland Captain Sal Bando leading off the eleventh inning. Athletics' manager Dick Williams, who ran his team as if his salary depended on the number of players he got into his lineup, sent pitcher John "Blue Moon" Odom in to run for Bando. Odom decided on his own to steal second and was sliding into the base when Mike Epstein sliced a single into left field. Intent on his steal attempt, Odom was late in realizing Epstein had delivered a hit that could have sent him to third and was forced to remain at second. The pinch runner's failure to advance proved costly when the next hitter, Gene Tenace, bunted too hard toward third and forced out Odom.

With Mike Hegan pinch-running for Epstein at second and Tenace at first, Williams sent Rookie Gonzalo Marquez in to bat for second baseman Dal Maxvill. Williams treated the keystone sack as an equal-opportunity position for a string of weak-hitting second basemen, and Marquez was the third pinch hitter to bat for a second baseman that day. He came to the plate against Chuck Seelbach, who had replaced Lolich, and fouled off five two-strike pitches before bouncing a single between first and second base.

Right fielder Kaline handled the ball cleanly and, conceding the tying score to the lead runner, Hegan, gunned a perfect throw to third baseman Aurelio Rodriguez in an attempt to cut down the slower trailing runner, Gene Tenace. The throw arrived at the same time as the Oakland catcher, who slid in head first and evidently blocked Rodriguez' view, as the ball skipped under the third baseman's glove. Unfortunately, the pitcher Seelbach had expected Kaline to throw home and was backing up home plate instead of third base, so that the ball rolled unimpeded all the way to the box seats, allowing Tenace to leap up and score the winning run.

Because Tenace scored on the play, the official scorer properly charged Kaline with the error that led to the unearned run, although most of the press coverage acknowledged that the throw was on target and the run could have been prevented if Seelbach had backed up third instead of home. One newspaper, the *Los Angeles Times*, unjustly applied the g-word to the Detroit right fielder, noting that "When Kaline homered in the top of the 11th, it looked like the old pro, playing in his 20th major league season, would be the hero. Moments later, though, he was the goat." Shirley Povich of the *Washington Post* put the matter in perspective when he wrote:

> Kaline was no more responsible for that winning run than any fan in front of any television set. He grabbed up Marquez's single to right and made the proper play, a rifle throw on target to third to head off the winning run, but the damn thing never took any kind of bounce and went skidding past third baseman Aurelio Rodriguez's glove.... Not only did (Charles O.) Finley's A's destroy the myth the West couldn't win a playoff game, but now they had a 1–0 lead in the playoff, and a glowing chance to get into the World Series.

Oakland catcher Gene Tenace is safe at third as the throw from right fielder Al Kaline eludes the glove of Detroit third baseman Aurelio Rodriguez. When no one backed up the play, Tenace got up to score the winning run in the eleventh inning of Game One of the 1972 American League Championship Playoff (©Bettmann/Corbis).

The opening A's win proved to be a crucial one. They won the play-off over the Tigers three games to two, and went on to win the World Series, the first of three consecutive World Championships for the upstart Green and Gold Athletics.

Al Kaline was never seriously measured for goat horns for the throw that led to the Tigers' defeat in the first play-off game. A reigning superstar and one of the most popular players ever to wear a Tiger uniform, he retired in 1974 after spending his entire 22-year career with Detroit and was elected to the Hall of Fame in 1980, his first year of eligibility.

Summing Up

Throwing errors tend to be less prevalent than fielding errors. It's generally harder to catch the ball in the first place than throw it accurately, and the fielder can always elect not to make a throw if he is in an awkward position or sees that the play is hopeless. A few infielders, like Steve Sax and Chuck Knoblach, have developed mental blocks that stifle their ability to throw the ball accurately after they've caught it, but these represent the exception rather than the rule. And outfielders making wild throws are rarely charged with errors unless their throws are so far off line that runners are able to take an extra base.

Of the examples cited in this chapter, only Heinie Zimmerman is remembered as a classic goat, and that is because he wound up chasing Eddie Collins across home plate, not because his wild throw put Collins on base in the first place. Vern Stephens' error occurred in the fourth inning of the final World Series game, leaving his team time to recover, and the Herzog/Fletcher meltdown occurred in the final inning of Game Three, so that it wasn't seen as the proximate cause of the Giants' World Series loss. In any case, the Giants' errors in Game Three were overshadowed by "Home Run" Baker's heroics.

Al Kaline's fielding credentials and popularity were such that he wouldn't have been fitted for goat horns even if he'd airmailed a throw into the seats behind third base to allow the A's to draw first blood in the 1972 ALCS. As it was, he made a perfect throw that happened to arrive at the same time as the runner and skipped by the third baseman. And it was his home run that had given his Tigers the lead in the top of the eleventh. In all, hardly a performance likely to tarnish a Hall of Fame reputation.

Chapter Nine

Weak-Fielding Pitchers

"I didn't have a good grip. The ball took off. I think that was the key to the game."
Mariano Rivera
Quoted in *Sports Illustrated*
following Game Seven of the 2001 World Series

◆ ◆ ◆ ◆

It's axiomatic that pitchers can't hit. While there have been exceptions to this rule, from Babe Ruth to Mike Hampton, the exceptions are so rare that the American League relieved pitchers of the responsibility for hitting by introducing the designated hitter in 1973. What is often overlooked is that most pitchers don't field very well either. There are, of course, exceptions to this rule as well. Converted infielders like Bob Lemon and Bucky Walters fielded their position quite well. For the most part, however, pitchers have historically performed just as poorly with their gloves as with their bats.

This shortcoming is reflected in fielding averages. In 2004, pitchers in the aggregate compiled a lower fielding average, .958, than players at any other position. Averages at other positions ranged from .960 for third basemen to .997 for first basemen, and weighed in at .985 overall. Viewed another way, pitchers made 4.2 errors for every hundred chances, as compared with 1.5 errors per hundred chances for the rest of their teammates.

There are many reasons for the poor fielding performance of pitchers. With the mound only 60 feet, six inches away from home plate, they have little time to react to hard-hit line drives back through the box, and the follow-through of many pitchers leaves them in awkward fielding positions even if they are able to react. The careers of several pitchers have been shortened by line drives back to the box. Hall of Fame pitcher Dizzy Dean had his career shortened when Earl Averill broke the pitcher's toe with a line drive in the 1937 All-Star Game. He wound up announcing games for the Cards and Browns. Promising Indians fireballer Herb Score was never able to regain his form after a line drive off the bat of Gil McDougald caught him flush in the face in 1957, and he, too, wound up announcing games for the club that had counted on his services as a pitcher.

The Bungled Bunt Defense

One of the most common errors recorded by pitchers is the wild throw made in an attempt to force the lead runner in a sacrifice situation. In many ways, the worse the bunt, the tougher the play for the pitcher. If the batter lays down a good sacrifice bunt, guiding and deadening the ball so that there is no chance for an out anywhere but first, the play becomes routine. Field the bunt and make the play at first. If the bunt is poorly placed and/or tapped so hard that there is a possibility of forcing the lead runner, the play becomes much more complex for the pitcher.

The pitcher finishes his follow-through facing the plate, with his concentration on the catcher and hitter. As he moves in to field a bunt, his back is turned toward the base runners, so he must rely on his instincts, a sneak peek, or his catcher to let him know if there is a chance of forcing the lead runner. An infielder or catcher fielding a bunt has a better angle on the play and knows what kind of a jump the base runners have gotten. But the pitcher is typically charging toward the plate or the baselines, focusing on the rolling ball and relying on his catcher to call the play over the noise of the screaming crowd. On the run, the pitcher must field the ball, decide, whirl, plant, and throw. If he decides to target the lead runner, there is a natural instinct to rush the throw, since the runner has gotten a head start toward the base. Even if the pitcher decides to make the play at first, the split second used to check the runners and make the decision may force a "hurry-up" mentality that increases the chances for error.

Designated Fielders?: Escaped Goats

While no one has suggested replacing the pitcher with a designated fielder, most ball clubs take steps to minimize the number of fielding plays a pitcher needs to make in the course of a game. High pop-ups that could be taken by the pitcher are traditionally handled by nearby infielders or the catcher while the pitcher directs traffic. Over the years, the number of fielding plays made by pitchers in big league games has gradually grown smaller and smaller, reaching 1.8 plays per game in 2004. Even so, World Series history is replete with examples of pitchers whose bungled plays on bunts have cost their team crucial games. Several of these misplays helped to decide contests already described in this book.

Bullet Joe Bush's "Whimsical Throw"

The third game of the 1914 World Series between the Boston Braves and the Philadelphia A's was marked by an uncharacteristic lapse on the part of Braves second baseman Johnny Evers. With the score tied 2–2 in the top of the tenth inning, Evers fielded a hot shot off the bat of Frank Baker as one run scored and then held the ball, apparently dazed, while another runner, Eddie Murphy, dashed home to make the score 4–2 (see Chapter 1). Evers escaped a goat label when Boston tied the score in the bottom of the tenth on a home run by Hank Gowdy, a walk, a redemptive single by Evers himself, and a sacrifice fly. The game stayed tied until the bottom of the twelfth, when Gowdy, who batted .545 in the Series, doubled to lead off the inning. Les Mann went in to run for Gowdy, and after pinch hitter Larry Gilbert was walked intentionally, Herbie Moran tried to move both runners along with a sacrifice bunt. As things turned out, he moved them much farther than he had planned. The A's pitcher, Bullet Joe Bush, fielded the bunt, checked the progress of the runners, and threw wildly past Frank Baker at third in an attempt to force Mann, who scored the winning run as Baker tracked down the errant throw.

The newspapers of the day focused their attention on the seesaw nature of the game and the Braves' comeback, and generally made no attempt to cast the young Bush in the role of a goat. The *New York Times* coverage was typical, giving Bush's gaffe no more attention than Evers' redemption in their headlines:

NERVE-RACKING STRUGGLE
Mack Pitcher's Wild Throw
Gives Braves Three Straight
In the World Series

Cartoon shows Bullet Joe Bush making a wild throw to Athletics third baseman Frank Baker after fielding a bunt. Baker missed the ball, which allowed the Braves to score the winning run in the twelfth inning of Game Three of the 1914 World Series. Card images show Baker (left) and Bush *(Card images: Library of Congress, Prints and Photographs Division; 1914 cartoon by Wallace Goldsmith of the* Boston Globe*).*

**Evers, After Tip Is Dropped,
Singles, Paving Way for Tying Run—
Atones for Bad Play**

The *Times* correspondent waxed poetic in his first paragraph.

A giddy toss to third base by Joe Bush in the twelfth inning brought today's contest at Fenway Park to an abrupt end and gave the Boston Braves the third game of the world's series over the Athletics by a score of 5 to 4. The whimsical throw by Bush was fraught with tragedy for the Mackmen, making a last desperate stand to hold their fading glory. On this foolish bit of a schoolboy's error hinged the most nerve-racking struggle that has ever been played in the national classic.

Several newspapers softened their coverage of Bush's error with a reminder that a year earlier, as a rookie, he had beaten McGraw's Giants in a crucial World Series game. Bush was traded to the Red Sox in 1918 as Connie Mack dismantled his championship club and the pitcher then went to the Yankees in 1922 as part of the group of Red Sox that followed Babe Ruth from Boston to New York and contributed to the Curse of the Bambino. In addition to his two World Series with the Athletics, he pitched in three more Series, in 1918 with the Red Sox and in 1922 and 1923 with the Yankees. His record over five Series was two wins and five losses, but he posted a respectable 2.67 ERA and his wild throw in 1914 has come to have no more impact on his reputation or record than any of his other Series decisions.

Nelson Potter's Double Dip

As described earlier in Chapter Eight, the 1944 "Trolley Series" between the St. Louis Browns and St. Louis Cardinals went to the Cardinals in six games, with the decisive runs scoring after Vern Stephens threw wildly to second in an attempt to start a double play. The Series might have had a vastly different outcome, however, had it not been for a number of Brown misplays in the second game, which included a sequence in which Browns pitcher Nelson Potter was charged with two errors after fielding a sacrifice bunt. Manager Luke Sewell thought this accounting was somewhat generous—he counted six screw-ups on the play. Quoted in William B. Mead's book *Even the Browns,* Sewell recalled the play, which began when the Cardinals' Max Lanier tried to move Emil Verban, who had singled to lead off the third inning, to second base with a sacrifice. As Sewell told the story,

> We made six misplays on the ball. That's pretty difficult. He (Lanier) popped a little ball down the third-base line. Potter and Christman came over to it. They looked at each other and let the ball drop, and Potter picked it up and he rolled it up his arm. That's two misplays. He threw it to Gutteridge at first. Little Don was trying to hold his foot on the bag and get the ball, when he should have gotten off and caught the ball. It went down into right field. That's three. Chet Laabs let it hit that right field wall there, reached over to pick it up and it rolled through his legs. That's four. He picked the ball up and fumbled on his pickup, that's five, and threw it away at second base. That's six misplays on one ball.

The official scorer awarded Potter two errors on the play, which ended with runners on second and third. The runner on third, Emil Verban, subsequently scored on a groundout.

The Browns gave up another unearned run in the fourth inning when third baseman Christman fumbled a potential double-play ball, and eventually lost the game 3–2 in eleven innings. Since the Browns won Games One and Three, a win in Game Two would have put them up three games to none. At that time, no club had ever come back from such a deficit. (In fact, it would take another fifty years before a ball club turned the trick.) It could be argued, therefore, that the Browns' sloppy play in the third and fourth innings of Game Two cost them the Series.

Neither the press nor the fans castigated Potter for his double miscue. It was just one of a series of misplays by the error-prone Browns, who made ten errors to the Cards' one in the six-game Series. Besides, Potter had managed to keep the power-laden Cardinals from scoring any earned runs during his six innings of work in the second game.

Calvin Schiraldi: One Throw Away

Of all the "what ifs?" associated with Game Six of the 1986 World Series, here's one that is rarely mentioned: If Calvin Schiraldi fields a bunt cleanly in the eighth inning, the game never goes to extra innings, the Curse of the Bambino is dispelled eighteen years early, and Bill Buckner is comfortably retired in the Boston area with nothing more on his mind than his eventual consideration by the Veteran's Committee of Baseball's Hall of Fame.

Schiraldi came into Game Six to pitch for Clemens, who left after seven innings with a blister on his pitching hand, a bleeding middle finger, and a 3–2 Red Sox lead. A Red Sox rookie, Schiraldi had been called up in mid-season and worked his way into the closer role, saving nine games during the regular season and posting a 1.41 ERA. He lost one game in the League Championship Series against California when he gave up a home run to Brian Dowling, but he redeemed himself by saving the turnaround fifth game lost by Donnie Moore and he struck out five of the last six batters he faced in the pennant-clinching seventh game.

The first batter Schiraldi faced in the eighth inning of World Series Game Six was pinch-hitter Lee Mazzilli, who singled sharply to right field. The next batter, Lenny Dykstra, laid down a sacrifice bunt. The pitcher fielded it cleanly, but as he hurried to nail Mazzilli at second, he bounced his throw in the dirt and both runners were safe. The play was scored as a sacrifice and a fielder's choice. A poor choice, as it turned out. If Schiraldi had taken the easier out at first base, or made a better throw to second, the outcome of the game might have been much different. As it was, the Mets had runners on first and second with nobody out.

Wally Backman followed Dykstra with another bunt. This time Schiraldi made the safe play and threw to first to force the batter, but that left the Mets with runners on second and third and only one out. After walking Keith Hernandez intentionally to load the bases, Schiraldi threw three straight unintentional balls to Gary Carter. At that point, wrote Peter Gammons in his subsequent dissection of the game for *Sports Illustrated*, "the NBC camera honed in on his face: Calvin looked exactly like a 24-year-old rookie who has suddenly realized that half the nation is watching him. 'It just happened that when I screwed up, it was in the World Series,' he said."

Carter swung at the 3-and-0 pitch and drove the ball deep to left field, where it was caught by Jim Rice as Mazzilli tagged up and scored the tying run. The score remained tied through nine innings, and the rest, as they say, is history. Schiraldi's failure to get an out on Dykstra's eighth inning bunt has been overshadowed by the three hits he gave up in the tenth, Stanley's wild pitch, and Buckner's error. If Schiraldi fields the bunt successfully, though, and gets an out at second (or even at first), the rest *isn't* history.

Schiraldi was charged with the loss in Game Six, but the Fates weren't through with the rookie reliever. He was called into Game Seven to replace starter Bruce Hurst with the score tied in the seventh inning and promptly gave up a home run to leadoff hitter Ray Knight. The home run was followed by two more hits and a wild pitch before Schiraldi finally retired a batter and was replaced by Ron Sambito. By the time the inning was over, the Mets had a 6–3 lead and were never headed, so that Schiraldi was saddled with the loss in both the sixth and seventh games of the 1986 World Series.

Schiraldi's World Series losses set the tone for the remainder of his career. He never regained the form of his rookie year, and the Red Sox traded him to the Cubs at the end of the 1987 season. He spent a year as a starter with Chicago, winning nine games and losing thirteen, and then returned to his relief role. The Cubs traded him to the Padres near the end of the 1989 season and he spent two mediocre years in San Diego before his arm went dead and he ended his career with the Texas Rangers at age thirty in 1991. Although the press placed the blame for the 1986 Red Sox collapse squarely on the shoulders of Bill Buckner, Schiraldi was never able to shake his own share of that responsibility. When interviewed by Mike Sowell for his 1995 book, *One Pitch Away*, the pitcher was quoted as saying, "I wouldn't wish anything that happened to me on my worst enemy."

Dave Stewart and the Defunct Dynasty

In 1990, the Oakland A's appeared in their third consecutive World Series with a team that featured Bash Brothers Jose Canseco and Mark McGwire, MVP Rickey Henderson, and staff ace Dave Stewart, who turned in his fourth straight twenty-win season. The team was billed as a dynasty, and their Series opponents, the Cincinnati Reds, were given no more chance of upsetting the Oakland juggernaught than the Christians had of outlasting the lions in the Roman Coliseum. Jose Canseco, the highest-paid player in the game at the time, ranked his club with the greatest of all time and repeatedly predicted a Series sweep.

After three Series games had been played, it looked as if Canseco's prediction of a sweep might be accurate, with one glaring exception: it was the A's who were in danger of being swept. Every aspect of the American League champion's game failed them in the first three games. Staff ace Stewart was hammered by the Reds as Cincinnati won the first game 7–0. In the second game, two misplayed fly balls by Canseco contributed to a 5–4 A's loss, and the Reds won Game Three 8–3 when a McGwire error in the third inning led to six unearned runs.

In the fourth game, it looked as if the A's twenty-two-game winner Dave Stewart had regained his form, shutting the Reds down for the first seven innings. Unfortunately, the A's had managed only one run off of Reds starter Jose Rio over this span, and Oakland went into the eighth inning with a slim 1–0 lead. Barry Larkin led off the top of the eighth with a single, and went to second when Herm Winningham, with two strikes on him, beat out a bunt that A's catcher Jamie Quirk was slow to field. With runners on first and second, Paul O'Neill dropped down another sacrifice bunt that looked to be an easy play for Stewart. Rushing unnecessarily, the pitcher hurried his throw to second baseman Willie Randolph covering first and pulled a lunging Randolph off the bag into foul territory. An accurate throw would have nailed O'Neill by a wide margin, especially because the Reds' right fielder pulled a muscle on his way to first and hobbled the last twenty feet to the bag. Randolph was unable to recover in time, and the limping O'Neill was safe at first. As Thomas Boswell observed in the *Washington Post*, "Stewart could have rolled the ball to first in time."

With the bases loaded, Glenn Braggs grounded into a force out that scored Larkin and moved Winningham to third. Hal Morris followed with a sacrifice fly that put the Reds ahead 2–1. Because of Stewart's throwing error, one of the runs scored by the Reds was unearned, and that unearned run stood up as the margin of victory when the A's failed to score in their last two at-bats. "We got beat on a couple of bunts we didn't play, a ground ball and a fly ball," said A's manager Tony LaRussa. The A's proved ungracious in defeat, claiming that their 103 regular season wins, twelve more than the Reds managed, proved that they were the better team. Dave Stewart went so far as to claim that the Reds wouldn't have been in the Series if they had played in the A's division of the American League.

None of the sportswriters covering the Series tried to hang goat horns on Stewart after the A's ignominious loss. He had, after all, held the Reds to one earned run over nine innings in the final game. Besides, there was plenty of blame to go around. Canseco and McGwire had each contributed crucial misplays in earlier games, and Canseco had hit so poorly, producing only one hit in twelve at-bats (albeit a grand slam), that LaRussa had kept him out of the starting lineup in the fourth and final game.

Dave Stewart pitched for the A's until 1993, when he joined the Toronto Blue Jays as a free agent.

Dave Stewart, ace of the 1988 Oakland Athletics' pitching staff, whose hurried, wild throw to first on a Paul O'Neill bunt loaded the bases for the Cincinnati Reds in the eighth inning of the final World Series game that year. The error helped to turn a 1–0 Oakland lead into a 2–1 deficit and a series sweep for Cincinnati (National Baseball Hall of Fame Library, Cooperstown, N.Y.).

He returned to the A's in 1995, retiring from active service midway through that year after logging 168 wins over a 16-year career. His biographical sketches tend to overlook his two losses in the 1990 World Series, focusing instead on his postseason successes, which included two awards as the MVP of the American League Championship Series, and another MVP award for the A's four-game sweep of the Giants in the 1989 World Series.

Mariano Rivera: No Relief from the Best Reliever Ever

The 2001 World Series between the New York Yankees and Arizona Diamondbacks, one of the most memorable of all time, was decided by an uncharacteristic throwing error made by a usually reliable reliever in the ninth-inning of the seventh game. The reliever was the Yankees' Mariano Rivera, arguably the greatest closer of all time, and certainly the most dominant relief pitcher in the history of post-season play.

The 2001 Series was a nail-biter's nightmare, with the New York Yankees becoming the first team in World Series history to win two consecutive games after trailing going into the ninth inning. New York won Games Four and Five after making up two-run deficits with ninth-inning home runs off of the hapless Arizona closer Byung-Hyun Kim (see Chapter 7). The wins put the Yankees up three games to two in the Series, and came in their home park before a New York audience still recovering from the shock of the 9/11 attack on the World Trade Center.

When the Series returned to Arizona's Bank One Ballpark, Randy Johnson and his Diamondback teammates forced a seventh game by bludgeoning the Yankees with a score of 15–2. The win set up a classic pitching confrontation between two twenty-game winners, Curt Schilling of the Diamondbacks and Roger Clemens of the Yankees, for the World Championship. Both starters pitched well, and the score was tied 1–1 going into the eighth inning when Alfonso Soriano homered to give the Yankees a 2–1 lead.

With a 2–1 lead, Yankee manager Joe Torre called upon his relief ace Mariano Rivera to get the final six outs of the game. Rivera had been close to automatic in this situation, making 52 postseason appearances without a loss and saving a record seventeen postseason games for the Yankees. Rivera lived up to his billing as the best reliever in World Series history by striking out three of the four hitters he faced in the bottom of the eighth, holding the Diamondbacks to a harmless single.

After Randy Johnson, pitching in relief, sat the Yankees down one-two-three in the top of the ninth, Rivera returned to the mound needing only three outs to extend his record string of World Series saves and give New York their fourth consecutive World Championship. Veteran first baseman Mark Grace led off the inning with his third single of the night. The next batter, Damian Miller, dropped down a routine sacrifice bunt to start the play that proved to be the Yankees' undoing. Rivera fielded the ball cleanly but decided to try for the force play at second instead of taking the safer out at first. In his haste to nail the lead runner, Rivera threw the ball past shortstop Derek Jeter, putting runners on first and second with no one out.

The next batter, pinchhitter Jay Bell, tried to sacrifice, but his bunt reached Rivera so quickly that the pitcher was able to accomplish what he'd failed to do one play earlier, force out the lead runner. The failed sacrifice attempt left runners on first and second, and the Yankees were one out closer to the championship.

The Diamondbacks then duplicated the Yankee feat in Games Four and Five, coming from behind to tie the score in the ninth inning. Tony Womack doubled down the right-field line, bringing home the pinch runner who was on base courtesy of Rivera's error. Rivera next threw a pitch that grazed Craig Counsell's hand, loading the bases, and forcing Yankee manager Torre to make a choice of defensive alignments. He chose to move his infielders in to play for the

Mariano Rivera's attempt to nail the lead runner after fielding a sacrifice bunt goes past shortstop Derek Jeter into center field and puts Diamondback runners on first and second with nobody out in the ninth inning of Game Seven of the 2001 World Series. Both runners eventually scored to give Rivera his first post-season loss and end the Yankees' string of consecutive World Series wins at three (Solomon Chuck/*Sports Illustrated*).

force at the plate on a ground ball. The strategy backfired when the next hitter, Luis Gonzalez, looped a broken-bat single over the drawn-in infield to score the winning run. The looper, which barely reached the outfield grass and would have been caught easily by Jeter from his normal position, handed Rivera his first World Series loss.

Rivera's reputation and past performance saved him from the fate of Ralph Branca, Mitch Williams, Donnie Moore, and others who had the misfortune of standing on the mound while a championship slipped away. He'd made a good tight pitch to Gonzalez, sawing off his bat, only to watch the ball loop over the drawn-in infield. His own culpability for the wild throw that turned the inning sour was lost in the shuffle of subsequent events. After all, he was still the best post-season reliever ever, and he still held the record for most World Series saves.*

---

*As this chapter was being completed, Detroit pitchers set a record by making five errors in the 2006 World Series. This was two more than any staff had ever committed and contributed to a total of eight unearned St. Louis Cardinal runs. In the final game, St. Louis went ahead for good when pitcher Justin Verlander threw wide of third trying to force the lead runner in a two-on, one-out situation, eventually allowing two unearned runs to score. The play mirrored a wild throw to third by Tiger reliever Joel Zumaya that contributed to the Tigers' loss in Series Game Three. "That exact play was something we worked on all of Spring Training," Verlander told reporter Jason Beck. "It gets very repetitive, and I missed. I hadn't done it all season long. It was one of those fluke plays." The play mirrored a wild throw to third by Tiger reliever Joel Zumaya that contributed to the Tigers' loss in Series Game Three (and the wild throw by Bullet Joe Bush that cost the Athletics Game Three of the 1914 World Series).

CHAPTER TEN

Passed Balls

> When you give the Yankees a reprieve, they get up out of the chair and electrocute the warden.
>
> — Hearst newspaper columnist Henry McLemore, commenting on the aftermath of Mickey Owen's passed ball on October 5, 1941 (quoted in the *Washington Times* obituary for Mickey Owen, July 18, 2005).

♦ ♦ ♦ ♦

The official rules of baseball reserve the term *passed ball* for certain misplays on pitched balls. A catcher is charged with a passed ball "when a runner, or runners, advance because of the catcher's failure to hold or to control a legally pitched ball which should have been held or controlled with ordinary effort." When the third strike is a passed ball, allowing the batter to reach first base, the official scorer awards a strikeout, but charges the catcher with a passed ball.

Scapegoat: Mickey Owen and the Dodger Debacle

The most famous passed ball in baseball history occurred in the fourth game of the 1941 World Series between the Dodgers and the Yankees when Dodger catcher Mickey Owen failed to hold a third strike that would have sealed a Dodger victory.

The 1941 World Series was the first of ten memorable October meetings between the Yankees and the Dodgers. It marked the first World Series appearance for the Dodgers in twenty-one years, while the Yankees had won four of the five previous World Series. The two clubs split the first two games in New York, with identical scores of 3–2.

The third game was just as tightly contested, with the Yankees' Marius Russo and the Dodgers' Fat Freddie Fitzsimmons pitching scoreless ball for seven innings. With two out in the seventh, however, Russo lined a pitch off Fitzsimmons' knee. The ball ricocheted into the glove of shortstop Pee Wee Reese for the third out, but Fitzsimmons was forced to leave the game, and his pitching career never really recovered after his knee healed.

Dodger manager Leo Durocher replaced Fitzsimmons with Hugh Casey in the eighth inning. One of the premier relief pitchers of his day, Casey posted a lifetime winning percentage of .641 (75 wins against 42 losses), but had a reputation for losing his poise if the breaks of the game went against him. In a key late-season game against the Pirates, Casey was so incensed by a balk call that brought in the tying run that he threw four consecutive "message" pitches at the head of the hitter, Al Lopez, walking him semi-intentionally. In the next day's newspaper, a reporter observed, "Casey threw the ball right where he wanted to four times in a row. He should have control that good all the time." Having put the potential winning run on first base in a fit of pique, Casey then grooved a pitch to a weak-hitting shortstop, Alf Anderson, who drove in the winning run with a triple that was only his third extra-base hit of the year.

Casey had been warming up in the Dodger bullpen during most of Game Three, but proved unable to finish up the shutout Fitzsimmons had started. After getting the Yankee leadoff hitter in the eighth inning to fly out, he gave up a hard-hit single to Red Rolfe. With Rolfe moving on a hit-and-run play, the next batter, Tommy Henrich, hit a grounder just beyond the reach of the Dodger first baseman. The second baseman fielded the ball and would have thrown Henrich out, except that Casey failed to come off the mound in time to take the throw at first base. Rattled, the pitcher surrendered successive singles to Joe DiMaggio and Charlie Keller, putting the Dodgers down 2–0 and bringing Durocher out of the dugout to replace Casey.

The Dodgers eventually lost the game 2–1, and fell behind the Yankees in the series, two games to one. That made Game Four a must-win game for Brooklyn, since they couldn't afford to give the Yanks a three-to-one Series lead. At that time, no team had ever come back from a three-to-one deficit to win the Series, and the Dodgers would have little hope of doing so against a Yankee team that had won four of the five previous world championships.

Although faced with a must-win situation, the Dodgers had fallen behind 3–0 by the fourth inning of Game Four. The deficit might have been greater, but with two Yankees on base and two out in the fourth inning, Mickey Owen, who had set a record for catchers that year by handling 509 consecutive chances without an error, blocked what looked like a certain wild pitch and caught Phil Rizzuto in a rundown for the third out.

The Dodgers scored twice in the bottom of the fourth to narrow the margin to 3–2, but the relentless Yankees stormed back and loaded the bases with two out in the top of the fifth inning. At that point, Durocher brought in Hugh Casey, who had been charged with the loss one day earlier. This time Casey closed out the inning successfully, getting the dangerous Joe Gordon on a fly to left field for the third out.

In the bottom of the fifth, Pistol Pete Reiser homered with Dixie Walker on second base to give the Dodgers a 4–3 lead. Casey stayed on the mound to protect that lead effectively through the sixth, seventh, and eighth innings, allowing only two Yankee base runners over that span. The first two Yankee batters in the ninth inning also failed to reach base, grounding out weakly to the second baseman and to Casey himself. That left the Dodgers one out away from a 4–3 win that would even the Series at two games apiece.

The batter standing in the way of a Dodger win was Tommy Henrich, the Yankees' number-three hitter. Dubbed "Old Reliable" by the press, Henrich had been anything but reliable up to that point in the Series. At the time he stood in the batter's box against Casey, he had collected only two hits in the four games and was batting .142. Henrich watched Casey's first three pitches go by with the bat on his shoulder, taking a ball and two called strikes. He got his bat on the next pitch, fouling it off, and then worked the count to 3-and-2.

Casey's full-count pitch was a sharp breaking curve that fooled Henrich completely. He committed himself, saw that the ball was breaking wide of the plate, tried to hold up, but went through with his swing, missing the pitch. Umpire Larry Goetz threw up his right hand, signaling the third out, and the Brooklyn fans began to run onto the field.

Unfortunately, the pitch fooled Mickey Owen as well. It caromed off his glove and rolled toward the Dodger dugout, where police guards were coming out to control the celebrating crowd. Owen retrieved the ball in front of the dugout steps, but it was too late to make a play on Henrich, who reached first safely.

It was suggested after the fact that the reason both Henrich and Owen had so much trouble with Casey's 3-and-2 pitch was that the pitcher had loaded the ball with saliva and thrown an illegal spitball.

"It wasn't a spitter," Owen told Donald Honig. "It was a curve, as good a curve ball as Casey

Dodger catcher Mickey Owen chases the missed third strike to Tommy Henrich that could have ended Game Four of the 1941 World Series in a 4–3 Brooklyn win but instead opened the floodgates for a 7–4 Yankee victory (National Baseball Hall of Fame Library, Cooperstown, N.Y.).

ever threw, and missing it was my own fault. Casey had two curve balls, a big curve and a short quick one. He'd been throwing the short quick one for five innings. We had only one sign for the curve ball. I gave him the sign and he threw the big curve. I should have had it, but it got away from me."

The curve had gotten away from Owen, but the game hadn't gotten away from the Dodgers. Not yet, anyway. Even though Henrich had reached first base, they still needed just one more out to nail down their win. But that out didn't come soon enough. Working rapidly, the rattled Casey gave up a hard-hit single to Joe DiMaggio. He then got two quick swinging strikes on Charlie Keller, bringing the Dodgers within one strike of victory for the second time in the inning.

At that point in the game, both Owen and Durocher agreed later, they should have tried to settle Casey down. But both the catcher and the manager appeared to be in shock, "... paralyzed by the cataclysm," according to the *New York Times*. "It was like a punch on the chin. You're stunned. You don't react," Owen said later. "I should have gone out to the mound and stalled a little." Durocher said much the same thing. Quoted by Robert W. Creamer in *Baseball in 1941*, the manager said:

> That's where I pulled a rock. I told the writers that if they really wanted to get to the reason why we lost the game they should blame me. Casey gets two quick strikes on Keller and we're only one strike away from winning. My mistake was that for the first time in my life I was shell-shocked. I should

have got off the bench and gone out to the mound to talk to my pitcher in a spot like that. Especially after what happened. I got to go out there and talk to him, slow him down. I got to say to him, Look, you got this guy where you want him. Take your time. Waste a couple of pitches. Maybe he'll go after a bad one. Instead, I sat on my ass and didn't do anything. And Casey comes right back in with a pitch and Keller hits it off the wall for a double.

Keller's double scored both Henrich and DiMaggio and put New York ahead 5–4. But the Yankees weren't done yet. Casey walked Bill Dickey and gave up another long two-run double to Joe Gordon. In a matter of minutes, the shell-shocked Dodgers saw what looked like a game-ending strike-out turn an apparent victory into a 7–4 deficit. It was a deficit they couldn't overcome, as Yankee reliever Johnny Murphy sat them down one-two-three in the bottom of the ninth to give New York the victory and their third Series win against a single loss. The Yankees closed out the Series the next day, beating a disheartened Dodger team by a score of 3–1 to secure their fifth World Series championship in six years.

Writing in the *New York Times* the day after the debacle, John Drebinger reported:

> It couldn't, perhaps, have happened anywhere else on earth. But it did happen yesterday in Brooklyn, where in the short space of twenty-one minutes a dazed gathering of 33,823 at Ebbets Field saw a World Series game miraculously flash two finishes before its eyes.
> The first came at 4:35 of a sweltering afternoon, when, with two out and nobody aboard the bases in the top half of the ninth inning, Hugh Casey saw Tommy Henrich miss a sharp-breaking curve for a third strike that for a fleeting moment had the Dodgers defeating the Yankees, 4-to-3, in the fourth game of the current classic.
> But before the first full-throated roar had a chance to acclaim this brilliant achievement there occurred one of those harrowing events that doubtless will live through all the ages of baseball like the Fred Snodgrass muff and the failure of Fred Merkle to touch second.

After lumping Mickey Owen with the classic Giant goats Snodgrass and Merkle, Drebinger went on to claim that the loss was "easily the darkest hour that Flatbush ever has known," a claim that would be challenged ten years later by Branca's home-run pitch to Bobby Thomson.

The *New York Times* headline the next day read, "Owen Shoulders Entire Blame for Blunder Which Opened Gates to Yanks." "It was my fault," Owen told reporters. "I should have had the ball." That was his story the day after the Dodgers' hard luck loss, and it was still his story over sixty years later.

Joseph Wallace, writing in his book, *World Series: 100 Years, an Opinionated Chronicle*, noted that Owen's lifelong reputation as a goat was secured by the newspaper reports of the day and the continuing coverage that followed them. In the intervening years, several articles were written to ensure that Owen would be remembered as a Series goat. *Collier's* Magazine in 1942 did a piece entitled "The Mystery of the Missed Third Strike," *Life* magazine profiled Owen twenty-four years later in 1966, the *New York Post* headlined, "One that got away haunts Owen" in 1985, and the 1991 World Series Program had a 50-year look back at Owen's 1941 passed ball.

Brooklyn fans were more forgiving than the press. When Owen came to bat for the first time the day after his passed ball paved the way for the Dodgers' loss, they rose and gave him a standing ovation.

Owen caught for the Dodgers until 1945, when he joined the Navy. On his return from the service, he jumped to the outlaw Mexican League, then decided he'd made a mistake, only to find himself banned from professional baseball until 1949. When the ban was lifted, he caught for three seasons for the Chicago Cubs and served as a player–coach and player–manager in the minor leagues for two years before returning to the major leagues for a final season with the Boston Red Sox in 1954.

Owen had a full life after retiring from major league baseball. He served as sheriff of Greene County, Missouri, for many years, ran unsuccessfully for Lieutenant Governor in that state, and founded a baseball camp for promising young players before succumbing to complications from

Alzheimer's disease in 2005. Notwithstanding his other accomplishments on and off the diamond, his obituaries and the entries under his name in biographical dictionaries all lead off with an account of the 1941 passed ball. The following opening paragraph from the *Biographical Encyclopedia of Baseball* is typical:

> Catcher Mickey Owen's failure to catch a third strike in Game 4 of the 1941 World Series against the New York Yankees ranks as one of the most dramatic moments in baseball history — and one of the most heartbreaking for Brooklyn fans.

The official scorer of Game Four absolved Hugh Casey of any blame for the dropped third strike by declaring it a passed ball, thereby adding Mickey Owen's name to the list of legendary baseball goats. It was Casey, however, who subsequently surrendered a single, two walks, and two doubles to give the Yankees a 7–4 lead and qualify as the losing pitcher. Casey got a modicum of revenge in Game Four of the 1947 World Series against the Yankees, when he came in to face Tommy Henrich with the bases loaded and one out in the top of the ninth inning and the Dodgers down 2–1. He threw one pitch, which Henrich bounced back to the mound for an inning-ending double play. Casey then retired to the bench to watch Yankee pitcher Bill Bevens walk two batters and give up a two-run game-winning double to Cookie Lavagetto in the bottom of the ninth. The double was the Dodgers' first hit of the game, and it not only broke up Bevens' no-hitter, but also made Hugh Casey the winning pitcher on the strength of his one pitch to Henrich. He went on to set an individual record for the most games pitched in a Series, appearing in six of the seven games in 1947 and finishing all six.

Casey was released by the Dodgers after the 1948 season, but he signed on with the Pirates, where he won four games in 28 relief appearances before being sent to the Yankees to help with their stretch drive for the pennant. The 1949 season was his last in the major leagues. He spent the 1950 season pitching in the minors for his hometown Atlanta Crackers before retiring from the game.

Casey had a reputation as a hard-drinking hell-raiser and numbered among his exploits a knock-down, drag-out, bare-fisted fight with Ernest Hemingway in Havana. He did not adjust well to life outside the baseball limelight. While on the phone with his estranged wife in 1951, he denied charges that he had fathered an illegitimate son, threatened suicide, and ended his own life with a shotgun blast to his neck. His obituary in the *New York Times* did not mention his aborted strikeout of Henrich in the 1941 World Series, but praised his glory days as a Brooklyn reliever, even though the picture accompanying the obituary showed him in a Yankee cap.

Escaped Goats

Boss Schmidt and the Gathering Darkness

Mickey Owen's passed ball in 1941 wasn't the first dropped third strike to affect the outcome of a World Series game. The first game of the 1907 Series between the Tigers and the Cubs marked the Tigers' first appearance in a World Series, and in addition to the 24,397 fans watching the game at Chicago's West Side Park, another 12,000 gathered in downtown Detroit to follow the game's progress on a gigantic bulletin board erected by the *Detroit Free Press*. Another group of fans, residents of nearby Blue Hill, Illinois, a neighbor of Chicago, got inning-by-inning updates from carrier pigeons released from the ballpark.

Wild Bill Donovan, the Tigers' starting pitcher, held a 3–1 lead going into the bottom of the ninth inning when player–manager Frank Chance, Chicago's "Peerless Leader," led off the inning with a single to right field. Donovan hit the next batter, Harry Steinfeldt, putting runners on first and second. Johnny Kling popped out trying to bunt the runners along, and Johnny Evers hit what looked like a game-ending double-play grounder to third baseman Bill

Boss Schmidt of the Detroit Tigers, who let a third strike get by him with two outs in the bottom of the ninth of the first game of the 1907 World Series. Schmidt's passed ball allowed the Chicago Cubs to tie the score and sent a Series game into extra innings for the first time in history. The game ended in a tie when it was called on account of darkness in the twelfth inning (Library of Congress, Prints and Photographs Division).

Coughlin. Unfortunately, Coughlin, the Detroit captain, booted the ball, loading the bases. The next batter, Frank Schulte, grounded out to the first baseman, scoring Chance and moving the runners up to second and third. Chance sent Del Howard in to bat for shortstop Joe Tinker, who had struck out three times against Donovan. It looked as if Howard would do no better, as Donovan got two quick strikes on him and then called catcher Boss Schmidt to the mound for a conference, promising to end the game by striking out the hitter with "the best curve you ever saw." Schmidt went back behind the plate and Donovan delivered the advertised curve. Howard swung and missed, but the curve got by Schmidt as well, allowing Howard to reach first as Steinfeldt raced home with the tying run.

With Howard on first and Johnny Evers on third, Chance sent up another pinch hitter, Pat Moran, to bat for the pitcher Orval Overall. Moran never got a chance to swing the bat, as Johnny Evers tried to steal home, only to be tagged out by Schmidt. The attempted steal wasn't necessarily a bad gamble, since Schmidt, playing with a broken bone in his throwing hand, had turned in one of the worst fielding performances ever by a catcher in a Series game, allowing seven stolen bases and making two errors. Even so, the catcher proved equal to the task of handling Donovan's pitch and tagging the sliding Evers, sending the game into extra innings.

Schmidt nearly allowed the winning run to score from third in the bottom of the tenth inning when he was slow in returning the ball to the pitcher and the Chicago runner, Jimmy Slagle, attempted a delayed steal of home. Donovan quickly threw the ball back to Schmidt, but the throw eluded the catcher and rolled into the crowd. It appeared that the winning run had scored, but Umpire Hank O'Day ruled that the batter Steinfeldt had interfered with Donovan's return throw, calling the runner out and sending the game into the eleventh inning.

The two teams struggled through two more scoreless innings before the umpires called the game on account of darkness at the end of the twelfth, causing the first extra-inning game in Series history to end in a tie. While Schmidt's passed ball in the bottom of the ninth cost the Tigers a victory, therefore, it didn't result in a Chicago win.

The next day's newspapers offered a variety of views of the game. The *Chicago Tribune* praised the "sensational play" of both teams, while the *New York Times* spread the blame for the Tigers' ninth inning collapse equally among Donovan, who hit Steinfeldt with a pitch, Coughlin, who booted a double-play ball, and Schmidt. The *Detroit Free Press*, on the other hand, laid the blame for the outcome squarely on the shoulders of their team's catcher, headlining SCHMIDT'S PASSED BALL RESULTS IN TIE IN NINTH and noting that the catcher's poor overall play was "the surprise of the game."

The Cubs went on to win the next four games and the Series, holding the Tigers, with their vaunted outfield of Sam Crawford, Davy Jones, and the young Ty Cobb, to three runs over the four-game span. In the face of this four-game sweep, it is difficult to argue that Schmidt's muffed third strike in Game One had any impact on the outcome of the Series. It certainly didn't earn him anywhere near the notoriety of Mickey Owen's thirty-four years later.

After 1907, Boss Schmidt played four more years for the Tigers, participating in two more World Series and averaging two errors in each. He retired from the majors in 1912 and returned to his native state of Arkansas, where he lived in relative obscurity.

Jimmie Wilson, the "Almost Goat"

The 1931 World Series is generally remembered as the Series in which Cardinal rookie Pepper Martin, the "Wild Horse of the Osage," ran wild, batting .500, stealing five bases, and almost single-handedly thwarting the Philadelphia Athletics' bid for a third consecutive world championship. The Cardinals defeated the Athletics, four games to three, with Martin making a running, lunging catch in center field to cut off a Philadelphia rally for the final out of the series.

The Cardinals' first win of the series was put in jeopardy by a bonehead play on the part of their usually reliable catcher, Jimmie Wilson. Nursing a 2–0 lead in the ninth inning, Cardinal pitcher Wild Bill Hannahan lived up to his nickname by walking two batters, putting runners on first and second with two men out for pinch hitter Jimmy Moore. With a one ball and two strike count, Moore swung and missed a low pitch that Wilson dug out of the dirt. Instead of tagging Moore or throwing the ball to first base, the catcher unaccountably threw the ball to third baseman Jake Flowers.

Thinking he had struck out, Moore turned and headed for the dugout. Believing the game to be over, Flowers and Wilson also started off the field. However, third base coach Eddie Collins, realizing that the third strike had hit the dirt, began "Waving his arms like a wild Zulu" and yelling for Moore to run to first. Moore finally got the idea and reached first base safely as hometown fans stormed the field to celebrate. They wound up milling around as the Cardinals argued their case with the umpires. In the end, plate umpire Nallin ruled that Moore had reached first base safely and restored enough order so that the game could continue. As a result of Wilson's misplay, the Athletics had the bases loaded and their leadoff hitter, Max Bishop, at the plate in a situation in which a single could tie the game and an extra-base hit could put the A's ahead.

Hallahan went back to work, threw a called strike to Bishop, and then got him to hit a foul fly that first baseman Jim Bottomley caught crashing into the temporary grandstands behind first base. Bottomley's catch ended the game and took Wilson off the hook. The next day's papers highlighted the ninth-inning drama, with the *St. Louis Post Dispatch* headlining

> MARTIN STEALS GAME
> WITH DARING EFFORTS
> WILSON ALMOST "GOAT"

and the *Philadelphia Inquirer* publishing a caricature of Wilson over the title "Almost Goat."

Wilson's blunder cost the Cardinals nothing, and his status as an almost-goat was soon forgotten, lost in the excitement over the heroics of Pepper Martin and the remaining Series games. When modern histories of the World Series mention Wilson, they overlook his 1931 blunder and focus on his performance in the 1940 Series, when he was a 40-year-old coach for the Cincinnati Reds and came out of retirement to replace the injured Ernie Lombardi for the last two weeks of the season and the seven-game World Series against the Detroit Tigers. Wilson contributed to the Reds' victory by batting .353, throwing out the only runner who tried to steal against him, and stealing a base himself.

The fact that Wilson's 1931 gaffe is forgotten today reflects the sometimes overlooked fact that baseball is a team game. Hallahan and Bottomley followed their catcher's blunder by getting a crucial out. If Hugh Casey and his Dodger teammates had managed to retire either Joe DiMaggio or Charlie Keller in 1941, Mickey Owen would be remembered today as the ex-sheriff of Greene County, Missouri, and the catcher who set a record for consecutive chances without an error. Instead, he'll forever be frozen in time flipping off his mask to chase down Tommy Henrich's missed third strike.

Passed Balls From 1903 to the Present

Passed balls are relatively rare events, occurring roughly once every seventeen games. They can vary greatly from player to player and team to team, and it is therefore difficult to assess their full impact statistically. Nonetheless, passed balls have figured in the outcome of a number of crucial baseball games. Mickey Owen's passed ball helped send the Dodgers to their World Series loss in 1941. In 1985, after Don Denkinger's bad call at first base and Jack Clark's missed pop-up, it was Darrell Porter's passed ball that put two Kansas City Royals in a position to score the tying and winning runs on Dane Iorg's base hit.

The appearance of the passed ball and its evil twin, the wild pitch, in so many crucial World Series losses causes one to wonder whether these misplays are over represented in Series games. Is it possible that professional players, in the glare of the national spotlight, self-destruct more often than they do during the regular season? Do pitchers trying to "put a little extra" on the ball raise the incidence of passed balls and wild pitches significantly in postseason play?

Jimmie Wilson of the Cardinals, who was labeled an "Almost Goat" when he failed to throw to first base after catching a bounced third strike with two out in the ninth inning of the first game of the 1931 World Series against the Athletics. Wilson's gaffe loaded the bases for the A's, who failed to score when Card first baseman Jim Bottomley made a circus catch of a foul ball off the bat of Max Bishop (National Baseball Hall of Fame Library, Cooperstown, N.Y.).

Exhibit 10.1
Passed Balls Per Game: Season vs. Series

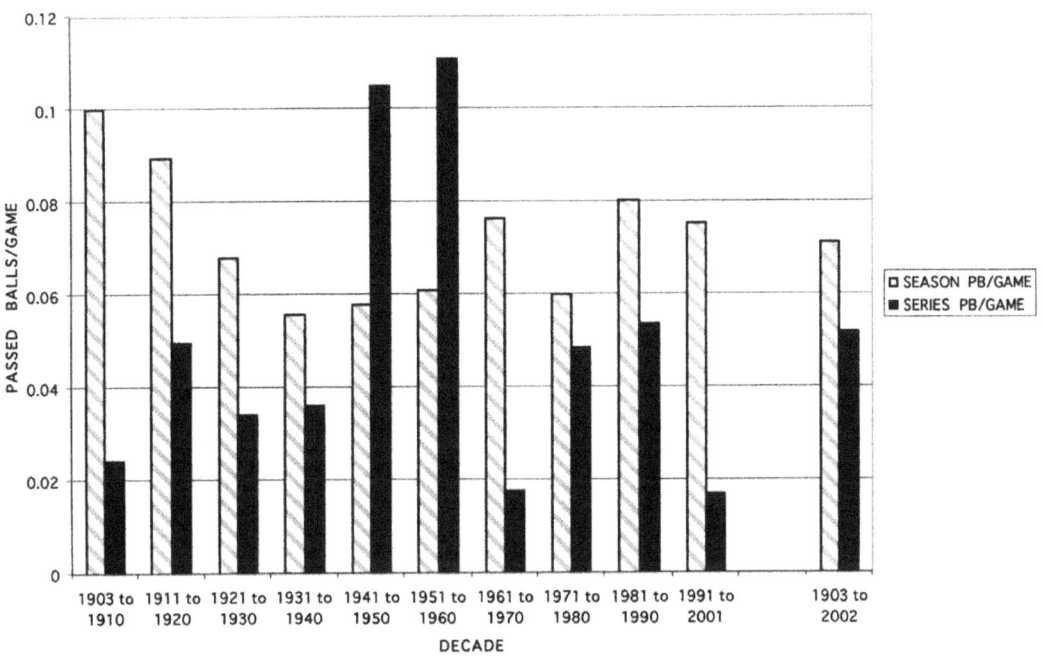

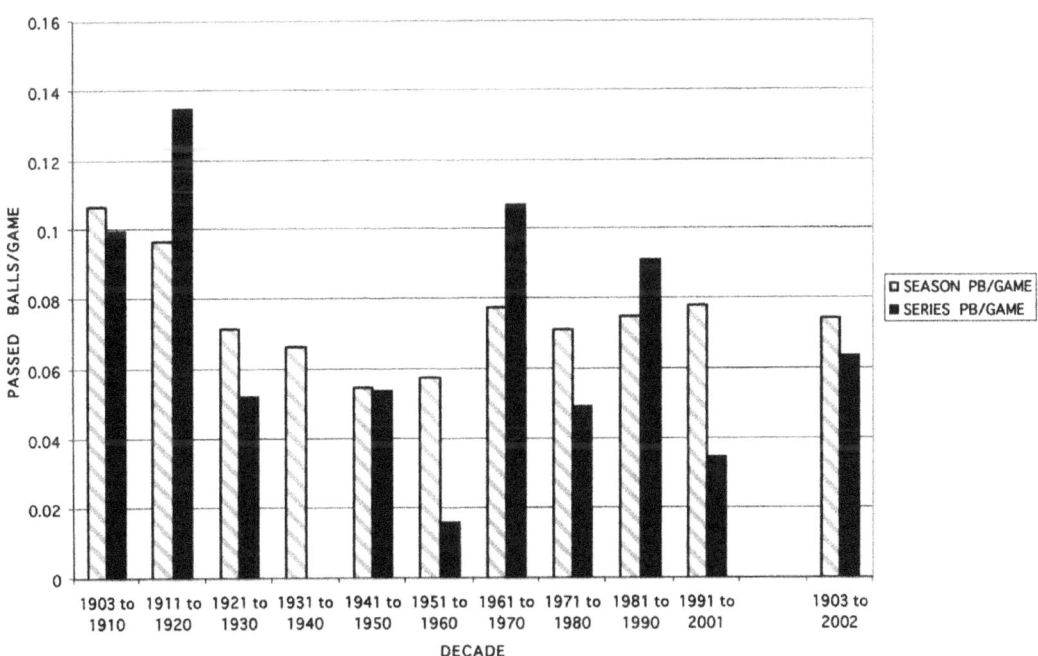

Graphs compare the decade-by-decade incidence of passed balls allowed by pennant-winning teams during the season and during the World Series.

Exhibit 10.1 traces the incidence of passed balls per nine innings by pennant-winning teams during the regular season and the World Series. Two charts are given, one for World Series winners and one for World Series losers. Statistics are organized by decades in an attempt to normalize the wide swings in annual data, which are heavily dependent on catcher skills and the composition of a team's pitching staff.

A few patterns are evident in the cross-hatched bars graphing the seasonal incidence of passed balls. Passed balls were more frequent in the early ears of modern baseball, then dropped steadily as equipment improved, gloves became larger and better padded, and hard-to-hit pitches like the emery ball and spitball, which were also hard to catch, were outlawed. After bottoming out around the 1940s, seasonal passed balls began rising slightly in the 1960s and subsequent decades.

Between 1903 and 2002, the number of passed balls per season logged by teams headed for the World Series ranged from three to twenty-six. At the low end of the scale, the two opponents in the 1975 Series, Cincinnati and Boston, with their Hall of Fame catchers Johnny Bench and Carlton Fisk, registered just three passed balls apiece. Three teams, the 1906 Cubs, 1960 Pirates, and 1964 Yankees had as many passed balls in the World Series as Bench and Fisk allowed over the entire 162-game season in 1975.

Many teams have gone through the World Series without being charged with a passed ball. The events have been so rare that the measure of "Passed Balls per Series Game" charted in Exhibit 10.1 fluctuates wildly from decade to decade. An overall season vs. Series comparison of passed balls per game for the first hundred years of the fall classic appears at the far right-hand side of each graph. It shows that the passed balls registered by Series winners dropped 27% below their seasonal record (.07 passed balls per game during the season vs. .05 per game during the Series), while Series losers experienced a slightly lower drop-off of 14% (from .07 passed balls per game during the season to .06 in the series). Thus, there is no evidence that the incidence of passed balls has increased in postseason play. If anything, it has decreased. Both winning teams and losing teams fielded better behind the plate in the Series than they had during the season. The most logical explanation for this is that teams tend to play their best catchers throughout the Series, whereas first-string catchers are typically rested and replaced by second-string backstops at intervals during the long season.

CHAPTER ELEVEN

Wild Pitches

> That ball rode so far over (catcher) Kleinow's head that he couldn't have caught it standing on a step ladder.
>
> Kid Elberfeld,
> New York Highlander shortstop,
> on the Jack Chesbro wild pitch that
> cost the Highlanders the 1904 pennant

♦ ♦ ♦ ♦

The evil twin of the passed ball is the wild pitch. A pitcher is charged with a wild pitch "when a legally delivered ball is so high, or so wide, or so low that the catcher does not stop and control the ball by ordinary effort and, as a result, a runner, or runners advance." It's the job of the official scorer to determine whether a missed pitch that allows a runner to advance is a passed ball (a ball that the catcher should have handled) or a wild pitch (a ball that would have required extraordinary effort on the part of the catcher). When the third strike is a wild pitch, allowing the batter to reach first base, the official scorer awards a strikeout, but charges the pitcher with a wild pitch.

Scapegoat: Jack Chesbro and His "Revolutionary" Pitch

Since 1900, no pitcher has ever surpassed Jack Chesbro's single-season victory record of 41 wins in 1904. But he will always be remembered for one errant pitch in the final inning he worked that year.

Jack Chesbro was given the nickname "Happy Jack" in the mid–1880s when he worked as an attendant at the state mental hospital in Middletown, New York, and pitched for the hospital team. He turned pro in 1895 and reached the majors in 1899 with the Pittsburg Pirates. After reaching the majors, he improved steadily and began experimenting with a new pitch, the spitball, in 1902. The pitch, which was then legal and new to the baseball world as well as Chesbro, helped him lead the league in victories that year with 28.

In 1903, Chesbro jumped to the newly formed New York Highlanders of the fledgling American League, where he won 21 games. The Highlander club, which would be renamed the Yankees ten years later, finished fourth that year, seventeen games behind the pennant-winning Boston Pilgrims, soon to become the Red Sox. The next year, on the strength of Chesbro's unprecedented 41-win season, the Highlanders challenged the Pilgrims for the league championship. The two teams exchanged the lead throughout the season, with neither club falling more than two-and-one-half games out of first place.

On Friday, October 7, the Pilgrims had a half-game lead over the Highlanders, and the two clubs had five games left to play with each other. The pennant would go to the club that won three of the five remaining games. Chesbro got the Highlanders off to a good start by winning the first of the five games in New York 3–2. As the teams boarded the train for a Saturday double-header in Boston, Chesbro volunteered to start one of those contests as well. The Highlanders' manager, Clark Griffith, who had wanted Chesbro to remain in New York and rest up for the final two games of the series, observed that Chesbro had just pitched on Friday and couldn't expect to pitch all of the team's games.

"You want to win the pennant, don't you?" Chesbro said. Faced with the logic of this argument, Griffith named Chesbro to pitch the first game of the Boston double-header. Chesbro started well, but was rocked for six runs in the fourth inning and New York lost the game 13–2. The Highlanders dropped the second game as well, losing 1–0 to the 37-year-old Cy Young, and returned home needing to win both of the season's final two games to capture the pennant.

Sunday baseball was illegal in both Boston and New York, so the last two games of the season were scheduled as a double-header on Monday, October 9, at the Highlanders' Hilltop Park. The blue laws gave Chesbro a day of rest, and he was tapped to pitch the first game of the Monday double-header, his third crucial start in four days. The extra work didn't seem to faze Happy Jack, as he shut Boston out for six innings while New York forged a 2–0 lead in the fifth on the strength of three singles, one by Chesbro himself, and two walks.

Boston tied the score in the top of the seventh without the benefit of a cleanly hit ball. Candy Lachance reached first base on a slow grounder, and Hobe Ferris drove a single through the legs of second baseman Jimmy Williams. After the two runners had been sacrificed to second and third, the pitcher Bill Dinneen hit a grounder that the second baseman caught cleanly but threw badly to home trying to keep Lachance from scoring. His throw hit the dirt and bounced away from the rookie catcher Red Kleinow, allowing both Lachance and Ferris to score. In the opinion of the correspondent for the *New York Sun*, "Ferris's run could have been shut off had Chesbro been spryer in getting to the plate to help out Kleinow."

The two teams were still tied at two runs apiece when Boston came to bat in the top of the ninth. The leadoff hitter, catcher Lou Criger, legged out a slow roller to short, was sacrificed to second, and reached third on an infield out. With two outs and Criger on third, Chesbro got two quick strikes on shortstop Freddy Parent, and then wasted a pitch outside for ball one. Everybody in the park expected Chesbro to try to finish Parent off with his signature pitch, the spitball, which Happy Jack claimed he could make drop anywhere from two inches to a foot-and-a-half.

Chesbro did indeed throw the spitball, but it didn't drop at all. Instead, it sailed high over the head of the catcher for a wild pitch that allowed the tie-breaking run to score from third. To add insult to injury, Parent eventually singled, but there is no telling what he would have done if Criger hadn't already scored and Chesbro hadn't been shaken up by his own wild pitch.

Although New York put runners on first and second in the bottom of the ninth, they failed to score and Boston won the game and the pennant. The newspapers of the day didn't speculate on whether Chesbro's pitch carried too much or too little saliva, whether it slipped from the pitcher's hand, or whether he overthrew it, trying to put just a little extra on the two-strike pitch. For its part, though, the *New York Sun* did not feel that Chesbro had become unnerved by the pressure of the situation. "Happy Jack is always a cool customer in the box," its correspondent wrote. "It simply happened that at this most crucial of moments he made a wild pitch."

The *New York Times* headline placed the blame for the loss on "Errors by Williams and Chesbro." The *Boston Globe* was more magnanimous. Whereas the *Globe* lead following their double-header win on Saturday had gloated, "THE MIGHTY CHESBRO DRIVEN TO THE BENCH," their banner headlines after their pennant-cinching victory on Monday trumpeted,

BOSTON CHAMPIONS
CAPTURE THE PENNANT
New York Is Beaten in the Great Contest
After Making a Gallant Fight.

And the story beneath the banner led off with the claim that the Pilgrims' win was the "greatest victory ever won in outdoor sport."

The Pilgrims had no chance to follow this "greatest victory ever" with an even greater triumph in the World Series. The Boston team had beaten Pittsburg in the first World Series ever played a year earlier, and the day his Pilgrims cinched the pennant, Boston team owner and president John I. Taylor sent the following open message to Manager John McGraw of the National League champion New York Giants:

Dear Sir:

As the Boston Club today won the championship of the American League, I challenge your club to play for the championship of the world. Of course, if you refuse to play, we hold the title by default, but I should prefer to win it on the diamond, in a series of five or more games.

As to the gate receipts, I am willing that all should go to the players. A reply tonight will greatly oblige.

Yours truly,
John I. Taylor

Jack Chesbro of the New York Highlanders, who set a record for single-season victories with 41 in 1904, but lost the American League pennant for his team when he threw his signature pitch, the spitball, over the head of catcher Red Kleinow in the ninth inning of the next-to-last game of the season to allow the Boston Pilgrims to win the game and cinch the league championship (**National Baseball Hall of Fame Library, Cooperstown, N.Y.**).

McGraw and Giants owner John T. Bush, upset over the invasion of their New York territory by the Highlanders and the poaching of prime National League players like Chesbro by the upstart American League teams, rejected Taylor's offer and refused to meet the Pilgrims in a championship series.

It's ironic that the day after the Boston Pilgrims won the pennant as a result of a misdirected spitball, a *Boston Globe* columnist, Tim Murnane, wrote an article claiming that this newfangled pitch would "revolutionize baseball fully as much as the curve did twenty years ago." Observing that the "batsmen of the American League say that it is utterly impossible to hit the ball square," he predicted that the public would be so outraged over the resulting "light stick work" and a scarcity of runs that they would demand a rule change. Murnane suggested that eliminating the foul strike would redress the balance and enable batters to regain their lost footing.

He also observed, on the basis of Chesbro's heavy pitching load that year, that the spitball must put less strain on the arm than fastballs and curves, and predicted that pitchers who mastered the spitter would naturally assume more and more of their teams' pitching assignments. In actuality, of course, relatively few pitchers ever mastered the spitter, which was outlawed in 1920. At that time, only seventeen pitchers (roughly one per team) were using the pitch, and those seventeen were allowed to continue throwing it until their playing days ended.

Jack Chesbro's playing days were finished well before the spitter was outlawed. He never repeated his 41-win season, but then, the *Biographical Encyclopedia of Baseball* observes, "neither has anyone else."

He "slumped" to nineteen wins in 1905, regained his form in 1906 to log his fifth season with twenty or more wins, and then had two seasons in which his earned run average remained low but his won/lost record dropped below .500. He appeared to lose his effectiveness entirely at age 35 in 1909, starting only ten games, and was out of baseball the next year.

Chesbro's wild pitch cast a pall on his 41-win season and haunted him for the rest of his life. In an attempt to remove the stigma, his wife and a group of friends campaigned to have the official scorer's ruling changed from a wild pitch to a passed ball, thereby shifting the blame to the rookie catcher Kleinow. Commenting on this effort, the Highlanders' 1904 shortstop, Kid Elberfeld, told a reporter years later that there was no way the pitch could have been ruled a passed ball, saying, "That ball rode so far over Kleinow's head that he couldn't have caught it standing on a step ladder."

Chesbro was voted into the Hall of Fame in 1946, fifteen years after his death in 1931. His *New York Times* obituary confirmed his fear that he would be remembered primarily for his 1904 wild pitch, announcing

> JACK CHESBRO DIES;
> FAMOUS AS PITCHER
> Veteran, whose Wild Throw
> Once Cost New York American Pennant, Expires at 56.

Escaped Goats

John Miljus vs. the 1927 Yankees

The pennant-winning 1927 Yankees, the Yankees of Babe Ruth, Lou Gehrig, and "Murderers' Row," are judged by many to be the greatest baseball team of all time. The team won 110 games, Ruth hit 60 home runs, and Gehrig drove in 175 runs, all records at that time. Odds makers established them as clear favorites over the National League champion Pittsburgh Pirates before the World Series began. Indeed, baseball legend claims that the Yankees took a significant step toward winning the Series the day before it began by staging a power-laden batting practice exhibition that sent ball after ball careening out of Forbes Field while the awe-struck Pirates watched from the stands. The Pirate players themselves always debunked this legend, claiming either that they hadn't really watched or were too professional to be impressed by batting practice prowess.

The Yankees swept the Pirates in four games, but the play-by-play results suggest that the National Leaguers had less to fear from the Yankee bats than from their own shaky defense. Only two home runs left the park in the four games, both hit by Ruth, but the Pirates made seven errors, and nearly every error resulted in a Yankee run. The Yankees took the first game 5–4, scoring three unearned runs in the third inning on a fumbled grounder, two walks, a single, and a botched rundown. The American Leaguers' 6–2 victory in the second game included runs that came across as a result of an outfield error, a wild pitch, and a hit batsman. The Pirates scored only one run on three hits off Herb Pennock in losing Game Three, an 8–1 laugher, but helped the Yankees to six runs in the seventh with two late throws on attempted force plays before Ruth hit a three-run homer.

The fourth and final game was more tightly contested than the first three. Both teams scored a run in the first inning, and Ruth sent the Yankees ahead 3–1 with a two-run homer in the fifth. It looked as if the Bambino's home run might be the margin of victory when the Yankee defense, errorless through the first three games, fell apart in the top of the seventh. Two Pirates reached base when the Yankee pitcher, Wilcey Moore, covering first, dropped a throw from Gehrig and shortstop Tony Lazzeri bobbled a grounder. A sacrifice bunt, a single, and a sacrifice fly brought the two runners home to tie the score at three all.

The Pirates brought in relief pitcher John Miljus to face the Yankees in the seventh inning. Nicknamed the "Big Serb," Miljus, a Pittsburgh native, had spent more time in the minors than in the majors following his debut in 1915. The year 1927 was easily his best in the big leagues, when he won eight games, lost three, and posted a 1.90 earned run average, less than half his career ERA. The *New York Times* characterized him as "a curve-ball pitcher who failed in Brooklyn and has kicked his way around the 'bushes.'" His performance in the Series was anything but bush league, as he had held the Yankees scoreless for four innings in relief in Game One. He continued to blank the Yanks in the seventh and eighth innings of Game Four, but Pittsburgh was unable to score in the eighth and ninth and the game moved to the bottom of the ninth with the score still tied at three all.

Miljus began the ninth inning by walking Yankee center fielder Earle Combs on four straight balls. Shortstop Mark Koenig then beat out a bunt down the third-base line, putting runners on first and second. Facing Babe Ruth, whom he had gotten out on a double-play grounder in the seventh, Miljus let fly a wild pitch that sent the runners to second and third. Pirate manager Donnie Bush then decided to walk Ruth intentionally, loading the bases with nobody out. According to the *New York Times*, Ruth chided Miljus each time a pitch went wide, pleading "Give me a chance!" and promising "The Buster will do it if I don't!" referring to on-deck hitter Lou Gehrig.

The Buster didn't do it, as Miljus buckled down and fanned Gehrig, but that still left him in a position where a sacrifice fly would end the game and the Series. The Big Serb voided that option by fanning the next hitter, Bob Meusel, as well. It looked as if Miljus might actually pitch his way out of the jam, and the Pirate infielders and outfielders, who had moved in for a possible play at the plate, retreated to their normal playing depth as Yankee shortstop Tony Lazzeri stepped into the batter's box. Just one year earlier, Lazzeri had failed dismally in a similar situation, striking out against Grover Cleveland Alexander with the bases loaded and two men out in the final game of the World Series won by the St. Louis Cardinals.

John Miljus of the Pirates, who struck out Lou Gehrig and Bob Meusel with the bases loaded and the score tied in the ninth inning of Game Four of the 1927 World Series, only to see the Yankees win the game and sweep the series when he put his second wild pitch of the inning out of the reach of catcher Johnny Gooch (National Baseball Hall of Fame Library, Cooperstown, N.Y.).

Lazzeri began his at-bat against Miljus in the same way he had against Alexander a year earlier, driving a long foul into the left-field bleachers for strike one. Then the script changed dramatically as Miljus threw his second wild pitch of the inning, a fastball that rose and sailed off catcher Johnny Gooch's glove, passed over his shoulder, and rolled to the box seats as Combs raced home with the Series-winning run.

Miljus stood on the mound, stunned and dejected, finally leaving the diamond with his Pirate teammates as Yankee fans stormed the field to celebrate. In *The Story of the World Series*, Fred Lieb notes that "many observers have contended the play should have been scored as a passed ball for catcher Johnny Gooch," but the play went into the books as a wild pitch and marked the only time in history that the Series had ended on an errant offering.

Second-tier headlines in both the *New York Times* and *Pittsburgh Press* identified Miljus' wild pitch as the proximate cause of the Pirates' loss, but the accompanying stories expressed admiration and sympathy for the pitcher. Syndicated articles under the bylines of Ruth, Gehrig, and Hans Wagner all struck a sympathetic note. The article under Ruth's name was typical:

> And the man I'm sorriest for in the whole series is John Miljus. There's a pitcher. He has plenty, that fellow, and all the nerve and courage in the world along with it. Losing a big game and a series on a wild pitch as he did is about the toughest thing that can happen. Particularly after he struck out Gehrig and Meusel with the bases full.
> But that's baseball.

Both the *Pittsburgh Press* and the *New York Times* summoned up the ghost of Jack Chesbro in covering the story. *Times* correspondent Richards Vidmer wrote:

> It took John Miljus, Pittsburgh's' roving right hander, ten trying years to work his way from the minors to a permanent job in the major leagues. Yesterday he went from triumph to tragedy in the short span of one inning.
> ...
> More than two decades ago Jack Chesbro threw a pennant away for the Yanks (sic) in the last game [sic] of the season. Perhaps the debt was being settled by the hand of fate at this late date.

For some reason, Miljus' wild pitch never achieved the notoriety of Chesbro's and the press never awarded the Big Serb a place in the pantheon of goats occupied by such figures as Merkle, Snodgrass, and Mickey Owen. Maybe he got milder treatment from the Gotham press because he was playing against a New York team rather than for one. It certainly can't be argued that Miljus' wild pitch cost the Pirates the World Series. Even if he had gotten Lazzeri out, the game would have gone undecided into extra innings, New York had already won three games, and nobody ever expected the Pirates to have much of a chance against the Yankee juggernaught anyhow. In effect, Miljus' ninth inning performance was viewed as a last Christian swat at a lion's nose before the carnage ended and the Coliseum crowd went home with its blood lust sated.

As an indication that most of the press viewed, and continues to view, the outcome of the Yankee–Pirate series as a foregone conclusion, Eric Enders, in *100 Years of the World Series*, wrote that the 1927 contest was the "least interesting series ever played." And Paul Gallico, writing at the time in the *New York Daily News*, observed, "The slapstick is mightier than the bludgeon, and for that reason the New York Yankees are the baseball champions of the world; and if ever a dramatic ball game came to a sillier ending, I would like to be informed."

Bob Moose and the Bad Bounce

Two strong, evenly matched teams squared off against each other in the best-of-five playoff series to decide the National League championship in 1972. The Cincinnati Reds' "Big Red Machine" had won the National League pennant two years earlier in 1970 and the Pittsburgh

Pirates, led by Roberto Clemente, had won the pennant and World Series one year earlier in 1971. Both teams had dominated their respective divisions in 1972, leading their nearest competition by more than ten games, and both boasted such a strong mix of power, speed, and pitching that it was the common contention that the National League Championship Series marked the real face-off between the strongest teams in baseball. The winner's subsequent meeting with the American League champion would be little more than an afterthought with a preordained conclusion.

Given that buildup, it was hardly surprising that the Reds and Pirates split the first four games of the series, or that just one run separated the two teams in the ninth inning of the deciding game. The Pirates took the field in the bottom of the ninth at Cincinnati's Riverfront Stadium holding a slim 3–2 lead. To protect that lead, Manager Bill Virdon brought in his ace reliever, Dave Giusti, who had won 7 games and saved 22 for the Pirates during the regular season. Giusti protected the lead through four pitches to the Reds' cleanup hitter Johnny Bench, who, with two strikes on him, parked a palm ball in the right-field seats for an opposite-field home run that tied the score. Visibly upset, Giusti then gave up singles to Tony Perez and Dennis Mencke, putting runners on first and second with nobody out. At that point, Roger Angell, who was watching the game on TV, reported in the *New Yorker*, "The expression on Giusti's face (seen in close-up) was almost too stricken, too private, to look at."

Virdon put Giusti out of his misery by replacing him with Bob Moose, a young, heavy-set right hander who had started thirty games for the Pirates in 1972, posting a won–lost record of 13 and 10 and an ERA of 2.91. The first hitter Moose faced, Cesar Geronimo, flied out to Roberto Clemente on the warning track in right field, deep enough to allow pinch runner George Foster to advance from second to third after the catch. When the next hitter popped up to the shortstop, Reds manager Sparky Anderson sent Hal McRae up to pinch-hit for his pitcher. Moose threw two breaking pitches to McRae, running the count to one-and-one, and then tried to put a little extra on a low outside slider. The ball hit the dirt in front of catcher Manny Sanguillen and bounced crazily beyond him for a wild pitch. Sanguillen ran down the ball, but Foster had scored the winning run by the time he retrieved it and he flung it into centerfield in disgust as the Reds mobbed Foster.

Newspaper photos of the pitch show Sanguillen's glove sweeping across the ground in an attempted backhand catch as the ball disappears over his right shoulder. The distance between the ball and the glove suggests that the Pirates were the victims of a phenomenally bad bounce, but had Sanguillen slid over to block the ball instead of trying to backhand it, he still might have averted disaster.

"Just a regular old slider away," Moose told reporters while puffing a cigarette in the locker room afterward. "It hit the dirt and went straight up. I don't know if it was the spin.... All I know, it went straight up in the air. What can I do? If it goes straight it bounces off Sanguillen's chest."

The press reports in both Pittsburgh and Cincinnati treated Moose sympathetically. No blaring headlines measured him for goat horns. The banner heading in the *Cincinnati Enquirer* simply announced REDS WIN PENNANT, while the *Pittsburgh Press* headline called out the pitch without mentioning Moose (REDS WIN ON WILD PITCH, 4–3) and went on to praise Bench's home run. In the light of future events, a few of the players' post-game quotes are worth noting. "That game represented the World's Championship," Pete Rose said. "I know we've got to beat the American League, but the two best teams in baseball played in this playoff." One hopes Rose didn't back his boasting with any wagers, since his Reds lost the World Series to the Oakland A's in seven tightly contested games.

Another quote is more poignant. The *Pittsburgh Press* describes a post-game scene in the Pirates locker room, with Roberto Clemente standing and shouting across the lockers to a

Hal McRae of the Cincinnati Reds watches as a pitch from Bob Moose of the Pirates bounces over the shoulder of catcher Manny Sanguillen to let in the winning run in the final game of the 1972 National League Championship Series (Associated Press).

dejected Dave Giusti, "Pick up your head. Don't quit now. We go home and come back in February.... Long as you mope they're going to have something to write about," he said, pointing to the reporters. "I don't want anybody writing about the Pirates moping." Of course, Clemente didn't come back the next February. He was killed in a plane crash that December, while on a mercy mission to aid Nicaraguan earthquake victims.

Bob Moose also suffered an untimely death. His pitching career after 1972 was interrupted by a series of injuries and physical breakdowns, including elbow problems, knee surgery, and an operation on a life-threatening blood clot. He recovered enough to become the Pirates' leading relief pitcher in 1976, but died on his 29th birthday in an auto accident just after the season ended while driving to a party at a golf course owned by former Pirate Bill Mazeroski. His *New York Times* obituary didn't mention the wild pitch that had cost the Pirates the pennant four years earlier.

Wild Pitches from 1903 to the Present

Bill James, in his *Historical Abstract of Baseball*, introduce an index of self-destructive acts for pitchers. These include wild pitches, hit batsmen, balks, and pitchers' errors. These are relatively rare events, which can vary greatly from player to player and team to team, and it is

Exhibit 11.1
Wild Pitches per Game: Season vs. Series

WINNING TEAMS

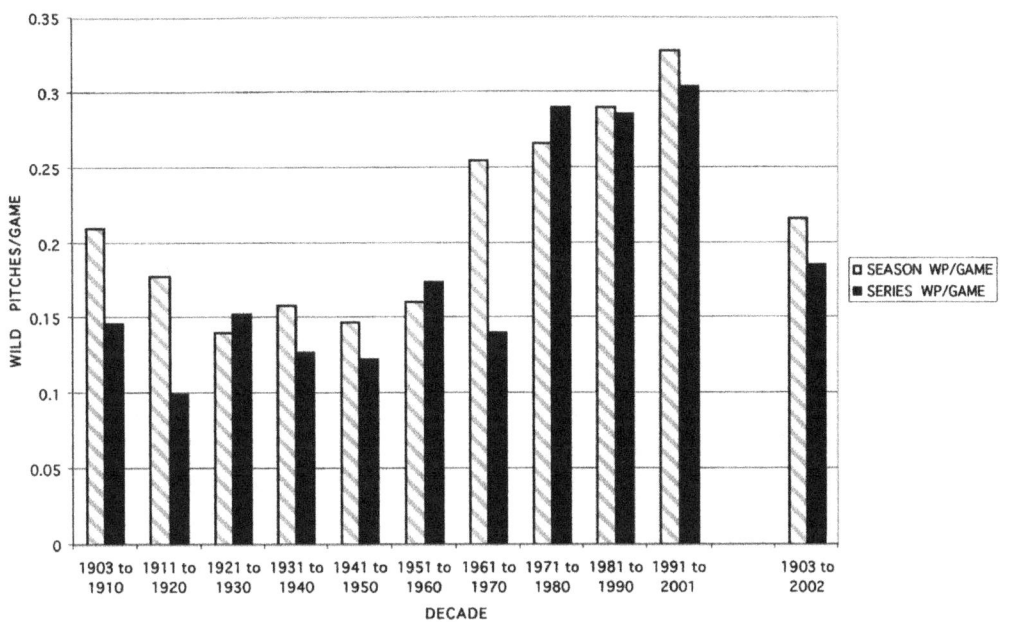

LOSING TEAMS

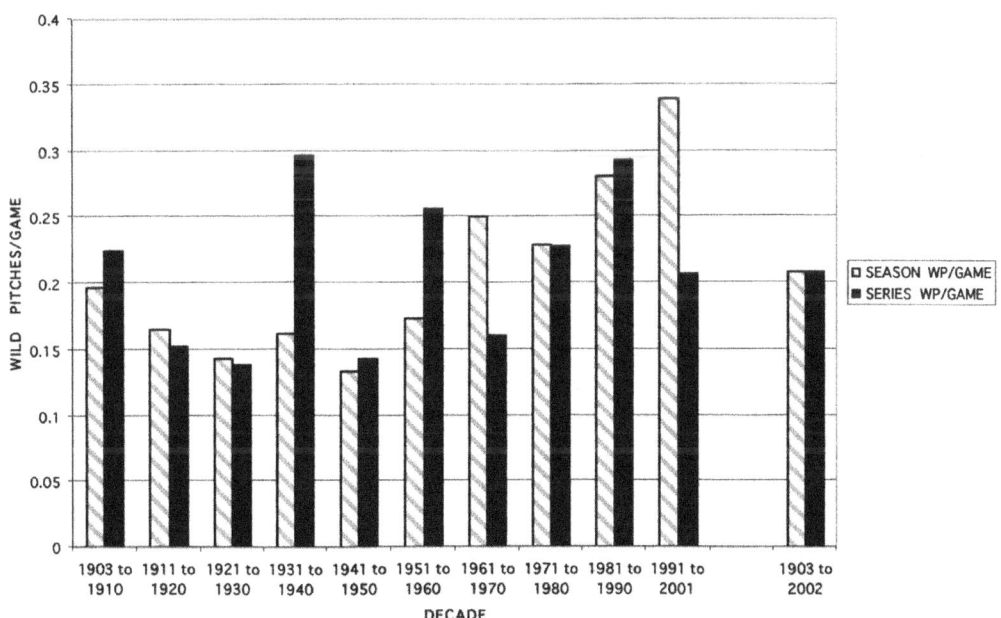

Graphs compare the decade-by-decade incidence of wild pitches allowed by pennant-winning teams during the season and during the World Series.

therefore difficult to assess their full impact statistically. Nonetheless, wild pitches have figured in the outcome of a number of crucial baseball games. In addition to those of Chesbro, Miljus, and Moose, Bob Stanley's wild pitch to Mookie Wilson in the sixth game of the 1986 Series had at least as much to do with the Red Sox loss as Bill Buckner's failure to handle Wilson's grounder. As with passed balls, the seeming prevalence of wild pitches in crucial situations raises the question of whether such situations give rise to an increase in misplays, as pitchers try to put a "little extra" on the ball.

Exhibit 11.1 presents two decade-by-decade graphs of the number of wild pitches per game thrown by the staffs of pennant-winning teams during the season and the subsequent World Series. As in the case of passed balls in Chapter Ten, the data have been split to separate the records of winning and losing teams. There are certain similarities between the incidence of passed balls and wild pitches logged by pennant-winning teams over the course of the last century. As with passed balls, the number of wild pitches in a season by pennant winners started high in 1903, then dropped as catchers' equipment improved, reaching a low in the 1940s. The number of wild pitches per game then began to rise, doubling for both Series winners and Series losers between the 1940s and 1990s. Over that period, the average number of wild pitches increased from roughly .17 per game to around .34 per game. One factor explaining this marked rise was a scoring change in which a pitcher was charged with a wild pitch (or a catcher with a passed ball) if a batter reached first base after a third strike eluded the catcher. Prior to 1957, pitchers or catchers were awarded errors if the batter reached first base, but no wild pitch or passed ball was recorded. The rise of knuckle-ballers over the last half-century is another factor which might help to explain the increase in wild pitches.

The lowest number of wild pitches recorded in one season by a pennant-winning team was 9, logged in 1919 by the Chicago White Sox team that went on to throw the World Series. The highest number was 83, roughly one every other game, recorded by the 1993 Toronto Blue Jays, whose staff ace, Juan Guzman, contributed 26 wild pitches by himself. Ironically, the next highest number of wild pitches logged in a season by a pennant-winning team was 74, recorded by the Blue Jays' series opponents, the Philadelphia Phillies, whose closer was Mitch "Wild Thing" Williams. The Blue Jays lowered their wild pitch output to one in every third game in beating the Phillies, although Joe Carter's walk-off home run in Game Six off Williams had a lot more to do with the Blue Jay victory than any reduction in their wild pitch output.

Viewed over the 100+ year history of the World Series, championship teams lowered their wild pitch production by 14% below their season numbers during the Series, while Series-losing teams showed no difference between season performance and Series performance. Thus, while losing teams did not throw any more wild pitches per game in the aggregate than they had during the regular season, winning teams threw fewer. Since wild pitches are a relatively rare event, however, the season–series difference registered by winning teams represented a savings of only one wild pitch every thirty-three games, hardly enough to make a difference in the Series outcome, unless the wild pitch was delivered with a runner on third base in the bottom of the ninth inning of a tie game. Ask Johnny Miljus.

CHAPTER TWELVE

Asleep at the Switch

> During the long season, attention is dispersed among all the teams of both leagues. In October, all attention falls upon these two, the last teams standing on a field. They have at once arrived in Oz and are prepared to bid it farewell. What the do upon these green fields will be remembered through the winter and in some cases, for life. And the players surely know this. If they disgrace themselves, the disgrace will follow them into old age.
> Pete Hamill
> "Faith, Hope, and Charity"
> 1989 World Series Program

♦ ♦ ♦ ♦

In the lexicon of baseball mistakes, mental errors weigh more heavily than physical errors in the eyes of managers, broadcasters, and fans. A throw to the wrong base is less likely to be forgiven than a dropped fly ball. And a perceived lack of hustle, as evidenced by a failure to run out an easy grounder or back up a throw from the outfield, is the unforgivable sin. No fans ever remember giving less than a hundred percent when they played as amateurs, and they won't accept anything less from professionals.

Scapegoat: Ernie Lombardi and the Schnozz's Snooze

Cincinnati Reds catcher Ernie Lombardi was the victim of one of the most unfair charges of lackadaisical play ever levied by the press. Lombardi, a lumbering mountain of a man whose nose was so long it poked through his catcher's mask and earned him the nickname "Schnozz," spent seventeen years in the major leagues, played in five All-Star games and two World Series, was the only catcher ever to win two batting championships, caught Johnny Vander Meer's consecutive no-hitters in 1939, and won the National League's MVP award that same year.

If Lombardi wasn't the slowest player ever to play in the majors, he was, at the very least, in the words of Bill James, the slowest player ever to play the game well. The fastest players of his day could circle the bases in the time it took Lombardi to huff and puff his way to second base. He was so slow that outfielders sometimes threw him out at first base on what seemed to be safe hits and infielders took to playing him several feet back on the outfield grass to improve their chances of flagging down his hard-hit drives, confident that their long throws would beat the slow-footed catcher to first base. Acknowledging this situation, Lombardi once told Dodger shortstop Pee Wee Reese, "You had been in the league for five years before I realized you weren't an outfielder."

Given the way opposing teams stacked their defenses against him, it is all the more remarkable that Lombardi managed to hammer out enough line drives to compile a lifetime batting average of .306. But Lombardi isn't remembered today for his batting average, which could have been at least thirty points higher if he had possessed merely average speed, or for his All-Star

Ernie "Schnozz" Lombardi, the lumbering Cincinnati Reds backstop who compiled a .306 lifetime batting average over a seventeen year Hall-of-Fame career in spite of being one of the slowest players ever to set his sluggish feet on a baseball diamond (National Baseball Hall of Fame Library, Cooperstown, N.Y.).

appearances and MVP award. Rather, he is forever defined by the play that let in the final run of the 1939 World Series.

Lombardi's Reds had been beaten in the first three games of the Series by the New York Yankees and were tied 4–4 in the top of the tenth inning of Game Four. With Yankees on first and third and one out, Joe DiMaggio lashed a single to right field. The runner on third scored easily, and when the Cincinnati right fielder failed to handle the ball cleanly, the runner on first, Charlie Keller, who carried just as much heft as Lombardi and was nicknamed "King Kong," rounded second and third and thundered toward the plate.

Keller arrived at home plate at the same time as the ball and reportedly collided with Lombardi, jarring the ball loose from his glove and leaving the catcher lying dazed with his back to the plate. DiMaggio, whose hit started the play, rounded third, saw Lombardi lying still with the ball about five feet away, and hustled in to score on a hook slide before anyone could retrieve the ball and make the tag.

The next day's newspapers labeled the play "Schnozz's Snooze" and saddled the catcher with lasting blame for his tenth-inning "reclining act." The idea that Lombardi should be labeled a goat was absurd on the face of it and represents one of the most unfair miscarriages of justice in baseball history. The run scored by DiMaggio was hardly crucial — it padded the Yankees' lead from two runs to three runs, changing the final score from 6–4 to 7–4. Keller scored ahead of DiMaggio because the right fielder, Ival Goodman, had let the Yankee Clipper's single roll past him and made a late throw home. Keller himself was on base courtesy of a grounder booted by the Reds' shortstop, Billy Meyers, who had also muffed a double-play toss in the ninth to allow the Yankees to tie the score. The Reds' pitcher, Bucky Walters, publicly faulted himself for not backing up the plate on Goodman's throw. In the Series as a whole, the Yankees had routed the Reds in four games, outscoring them 20–8 overall.

Lombardi never said much about the play, except to note that the day was hot and he "felt dizzy." The real injustice of the goat horns awarded by the media for "Schnozz's snooze" was not evident until years later, when Reds pitcher Johnny Vander Meer revealed the real cause of Lombardi's inattention. The throw from right fielder Goodman had short-hopped the catcher's protective cup, leaving Lombardi doubled over in pain. "Anybody but Lombardi, they would have had to carry him off the field," Vander Meer said.

Ernie Lombardi (4) lies dazed near the plate as Joe DiMaggio slides home with the final run of the 1939 World Series. The newspapers labeled the play "Schnozz's Snooze" and attributed Lombardi's reclining act to a collision with "King Kong" Keller, who preceded DiMaggio across the plate. In actuality, a late throw from right fielder Ival Goodman had shorthopped the catcher's protective cup, leaving him prostrate with pain (National Baseball Hall of Fame Library, Cooperstown, N.Y.).

A review of the game films tends to confirm Vander Meer's story. The ball arrived before Keller, who leapt past the catcher to score and claimed afterward that he never touched Lombardi. Certainly Lombardi never executed the "beautiful somersault" described by the reporter covering the game for the *Cincinnati Enquirer*. Given today's TV coverage, with instant replays and ESPN's post-game analysis, it's likely that the cause of Lombardi's inactivity would have been clear and he never would have been subjected to public ridicule. There were no replays in 1939, however, and reporters' faulty perceptions, coupled with the tendency to "print the legend" and fit a story to Lombardi's comic image, saddled the catcher with an unearned reputation that haunted him for the rest of his life.

The winter following Lombardi's "snooze" the Reds management used the play as one argument for cutting his salary. This ploy resulted in the first of several well-publicized holdouts on the part of the popular catcher. His disagreements with management were a strong factor in his move from the Reds to the Boston Braves in 1942 and from the Braves to the New York Giants in 1943. Lombardi was named to the All-Star team with both the Braves and the Giants and was released by the Giants in 1947. He played one more year in the minor leagues with his hometown Oakland Oaks before retiring from baseball.

After retiring, Lombardi managed a liquor store in San Leandro, California, and grew steadily more despondent. By 1953, his depression had advanced to the point that he agreed to be committed to a sanitarium in Livermore. In route to the sanitarium, he and his wife stopped to spend the night with Lombardi's sister. While visiting, Lombardi shut himself in the bathroom found a razor blade, and cut his throat from ear to ear. His wife found him still alive, bleeding profusely, and begging to be allowed to die.

Lombardi fought with the ambulance attendants summoned by his wife, but they managed to stabilize his wounds and convey him to the sanitarium. Once there, shock treatments helped him to stave off depression. He returned to the Bay Area and worked for several years as a press box attendant for the San Francisco Giants following their move from New York to the West Coast. He quit in 1963 after being insulted by a young writer and dropped out of public view for nearly ten years.

Stories about Lombardi resurfaced in 1974 when a reporter spotted him helping out at a gas station during the energy crisis. The reporter recognized Lombardi's burly build and protruding nose and printed an interview that depicted the former catcher as an angry old man, bitter at having been ignored by the baseball establishment and passed over by the Hall of Fame in Cooperstown.

By that time fellow catchers Gabby Hartnett and Bill Dickey, both contemporaries of Lombardi's, had been elected to the Hall, and he lambasted the Veterans Committee responsible for elections, saying, "If they voted me into the Hall of Fame, I wouldn't accept. They've waited too long and they've ignored me too long." He went on to acknowledge, "That sounds terrible, but I'm bitter. All anybody wants to remember about me is that I couldn't run."

Lombardi saw another contemporary catcher, Al Lopez, inducted into the Hall of Fame before Ernie died in Santa Cruz, California, in 1977. His *New York Times* obituary did in fact mention his lead-footed lack of speed, turning it into a back-handed compliment by quoting remarks made by Arthur Daley of the *Times* the year Lombardi left the New York Giants.

> When you look back on him and his 17 years in the majors, you almost come to the conclusion that he was the greatest hitter of all time. Every hit he made ... was an honest one. Where a Ty Cobb would scratch out hundreds of infield singles as a result of his flashing speed afoot, Lumbering Lom did all his running in the same spot. He ran on a treadmill and couldn't outrace a snail, even with a head start.

True to form, the *Times* also called up the "single play Lombardi is most remembered for," devoting a paragraph of the obituary to "Ernie's Snooze."

The Veterans Committee finally voted Ernie Lombardi into the Hall of Fame in 1986, nine years after his death. His sister, Rita Lenhardt, accepted the award gratefully and graciously, without any trace of bitterness, and insisted that Ernie, the genial giant, would have done the same.

Escaped Goats

Jack Lapp and Larry Doyle's Fadeaway Slide

In the 1911 World Series between the New York Giants and Philadelphia A's, the A's quickly went up three games to one, largely on the strength of the two home runs in two days that turned Frank Baker into "Home Run" Baker. Both teams then endured six days of rainouts, after which Connie Mack's Athletics appeared poised to take home their second consecutive world championship. The A's took a 3–1 lead into the ninth inning of the fifth game, only to see the Giants tie the score on a pair of doubles and a Josh Devore single.

The A's failed to score in their half of the tenth inning, and the gathering dusk made it seem unlikely that the game would go on much longer. The first batter to hit in the Giants' half of the tenth was second baseman Larry Doyle. In the third inning, Doyle had dropped a potential double-play throw that opened the door to all three Athletics runs. Since that time, he had tried to atone for his error with his hitting, and had two singles and a double to his credit when he stood in against incoming Athletics pitcher Eddie Plank. Doyle continued his quest for atonement with a hard double down the left-field line off Plank. He then slid safely into third base, avoiding Frank Baker's tag, when the pitcher tried to turn Fred Snodgrass' sacrifice bunt into an out at third.

One out later, Fred Merkle lifted a deep fly to right field. Danny Murphy caught the ball along the foul line and threw home immediately. Doyle tagged up and easily beat Murphy's throw home, executing a graceful fadeaway slide. While Doyle's slide home was graceful, it lacked the required accuracy, and his extended foot remained at least eight inches above the plate as he slid past it. The Athletics' catcher Jack Lapp had moved away from the plate to take Murphy's off-line throw and didn't see Doyle miss the plate. Assuming the game was over, Lapp ran for the clubhouse with the rest of his teammates as overjoyed Giants fans streamed onto the field.

One figure that did not leave the field was Bill Klem, the umpire-in-chief. He remained at home plate, waiting to see if any of the Athletics would appeal the play. When none did, he left the field, allowing the score to stand.

In a post-game interview, Klem stunned reporters by announcing that Doyle had missed home plate, and his declaration was corroborated by the game's official scorers. The umpire noted that as he was preparing to leave the diamond, Giants manager John McGraw passed by on his way from the third-base coach's box to the dugout and asked, "Did you see it, Bill?"

"I certainly did," Klem replied.

"What would you have done about it if they had appealed?" McGraw asked.

Klem responded that if the A's had appealed he would have given his decision as he saw it, adding, "But you see what a mess I would have gotten myself into," presumably referring to the fact that the Giant fans celebrating on the field would have been none too happy to learn that the winning run had been discounted.

"Well, I would have protected you," McGraw replied as he walked away.

"I would have declared Doyle out if the appeal had been made," Klem reiterated. "But none was made."

Catcher Jack Lapp of the Philadelphia A's failed to notice that the Giants' Larry Doyle missed the plate as he slid home with what appeared to be the winning run in the tenth inning of Game Five of the 1911 World Series. When the Athletics didn't appeal the play, the run stood and the Giants won 4–3. A's manager Connie Mack later said that third baseman Frank Baker had observed Doyle's failure, but the A's elected not to "take advantage of a technicality" with the celebrating hometeam crowd streaming over the field (Library of Congress, Prints and Photographs Division).

When informed of the incident, National League President Thomas J. Lynch backed Klem, saying "Since no appeal had been registered on the field the score would stand as a 4–3 victory for New York."

No attempt was made to fit catcher Jack Lapp with goat horns for failing to notice that Doyle had slid past home plate without touching it. Lapp, who was getting a reputation as a "Giant Killer" for throwing out ten of the fourteen Giants who attempted to steal during the Series, was clearly busy fielding Murphy's throw during Doyle's slide. A few newspapers accused the entire Athletics' club of inattention (The *Los Angeles Times* headline read DOYLE MISSED PLATE BUT QUAKERS SLEPT), but A's captain Harry Davis deflected these barbs with the following statement:

> When I reached the bench, Baker told me that Doyle had not touched the plate, but I would not make any claim for the point then with the crowd all over the field. It would have been impossible to continue the game. To all intents and purposes, Doyle scored the winning run, and we can take a beating without claiming technicalities.

A's manager Connie Mack echoed this attitude in supporting his players. "My players know that Doyle did not touch the plate," Mack is quoted as saying in Eric Enders' *100 Years of the World Series*. "It was the most pleasing moment in my life when not one of them tried to take advantage of a technicality." McGraw, who admitted that Doyle hadn't touched the plate, complimented Davis and Mack on their "prudence and sportsmanship."

Given the treatment of Fred Merkle three years earlier for failing to touch a base, and the general view of early 1900s baseball as a no-holds-barred game populated by roughnecks, it's refreshing to learn not only of Mack's gentlemanly response to Doyle's gaffe, but also of the scrappy McGraw's willingness to defend Klem in the event that an appeal had been lodged.

The Athletics' forbearance was rewarded the next day, when they ran roughshod over the Giants, defeating them 13–2 behind Chief Bender's four-hit pitching, to take the World Series championship back to Philadelphia for the second consecutive year.

Art Wilson and the Greatest Game Ever Pitched

Most of the games described in these chapters deal with post-season contests when championships are at stake and the eyes of the nation are focused on the participants. In theory, at least, every baseball game, post-season or not, holds the prospect of immortality, the possibility of creating heroes and goats for the ages. One such game, called "the greatest game ever pitched" by John Thorn in his book *Baseball's Ten Greatest Games*, took place before a scant 2,500 spectators on May 2, 1917, between "two mediocre teams, playing on the worst field in the big leagues under conditions that would make Bowie Kuhn blush."

The two teams were the Cincinnati Reds and Chicago Cubs, destined to finish the season in fourth and fifth place, respectively. The field was Chicago's Weeghnan Park. Built in 1914 for the ill-fated Federal League, the park would eventually be refurbished and reborn as Wrigley Field. The temperature at game time was thirty-eight degrees, with a chill wind blowing off Lake Michigan. According to Thorn, "the arctic conditions ... caused the topsoil dumped on the cowpasture of a playing field to crack and shift," leaving seams in the surface of the grassless infield.

But the real story of the day was not the field or the weather. The real story turned out to center on the two pitchers. The starter for the hometown Chicago Cubs was Jim "Hippo" Vaughn, who Thorn characterized as "a very good pitcher with some very bad ball clubs." By the end of the season, the fire-balling lefty would win 23 games for the fifth-place Cubs, and by the end of his career he would register 178 victories, amassing a .565 winning percentage for teams that posted a collective winning percentage of .495.

Vaughn's opponent on the mound that day was Cincinnati's Fred Toney. A native of rural Tennessee, Toney was allegedly discovered by a minor league executive who saw him wandering barefoot down a mountain road carrying three dead squirrels he had felled with thrown rocks. Toney rewarded the executive's interest by going on to a successful pitching career. In 1909, he pitched a seventeen-inning no-hitter for Winchester Kentucky in the Blue Grass League. It was a harbinger of things to come. He went on to pitch for twelve years in the majors, winning 139 games for four different teams. In 1917, the year he participated in "the greatest game ever pitched," he won 24 games, including complete-game victories in both ends of a doubleheader.

Toney and Vaughn came up through the minor leagues at the same time, and the May 2 game in Chicago was not the first time they had faced each other. "We had met several times dating back to our days in the American Association," Toney recalled years later. "I usually won because I'd let Vaughn get a hit off me and he'd get so tired running the bases our batters would get to him and we'd win."

In their May 2, 1917, face-off in Chicago, Toney foreswore his strategy of allowing Vaughn to get a hit so that he would wear himself out. Vaughn got no hits that day. And neither did any other Cub. But Vaughn was equally tough on the Cincinnati hitters. At the end of nine innings, neither team had scored a run, and neither team had registered a base hit.

A double no-hitter is one of the rarest occurrences imaginable in baseball. It had never happened before at any level of professional baseball, and it hasn't happened since. On any given day, the odds against pitching a no-hitter are roughly 600 to 1. That makes the odds that both pitchers will record no-hitters around 360,000 to 1, an occurrence so rare that it is not likely to happen again in the major leagues until sometime between 2100 and 2200.

Both Vaughn and Toney would undoubtedly have preferred that their no-hit efforts had been saved for a day when their own teams weren't stymied at the plate, since the zero-to-zero tie forced them to continue pitching into the tenth inning. Vaughn was the first to put his achievement on the line in the top of the tenth inning. The first Cincinnati batter popped out to the catcher, but the next hitter, shortstop Larry Kopf, lined a clean single between first and second for the first hit of the game.

His no-hitter gone, Vaughn still had hopes of winning the game. He got the next hitter, Greasy Neale, to fly out to center fielder Cy Williams. With two outs and a runner on first, clean up hitter Hal Chase came to the plate. The National League's leading hitter the previous year, Chase would be suspended by his manager Christy Mathewson the next year for throwing games. It was not the first time the smell of fixed contests surrounded Chase. He would be banned from baseball in 1919, the unchallenged holder of the live-ball record for rigged games.

Chase lined a ball to center that Cy Williams played a little too cautiously. The center fielder managed to get both hands on the sinking liner, but dropped it for an error, putting runners on first and third.

Chase stole second on the first pitch to the next hitter, Jim Thorpe, as catcher Art Wilson held the ball rather than risk a throw that would give Larry Kopf the chance of scoring from third. Praised as the greatest athlete of the half-century, Thorpe excelled at nearly every sport he tried except baseball, and it was his summer stint in the minor leagues for $60 a month while in college that violated his amateur status and caused the Olympic Committee to strip him of the gold medals he won in the decathlon and pentathlon at the 1912 Olympics in Stockholm.

Thorpe swung lustily at Vaughn's second pitch, a curve, and managed to hit a dribbler up the third-base line. Vaughn hurried over to make the play himself. Realizing he had little chance of throwing out the speedy Thorpe, he shoveled the ball to catcher Art Wilson in an attempt to keep Kopf from scoring.

It appeared that Wilson wasn't expecting the throw, because it bounced off his chest protector and fell at his feet without his even raising his arms to try for the catch. Kopf, who had started for the plate and stopped when he saw Vaughn make the throw home, scored as Wilson stood transfixed. "He was just paralyzed," Vaughn said later. "The moment Kopf saw the ball drop he started for the plate, but Wilson just stood there. I looked over my shoulder and saw Chase round third and head home too, so I shouted at Art, 'Are you going to let him score, too?'"

Roused from his trance, Wilson picked up the ball and tagged the sliding Chase for the third out, but the damage had been done.

Presented with a 1–0 lead, Toney still had to retire the Cubs in the bottom of the tenth to protect his own no-hitter. He struck out the first batter, second baseman Larry Doyle, and then faced the Cubs' cleanup hitter, first baseman Fred Merkle. Merkle, who had been victimized by the Cubs for failing to touch second base as a rookie with the Giants in 1908, left New York in 1916 and eventually wound up with the team that had been responsible for his "bonehead" nickname. So far, Merkle had the only hard-hit ball off Toney, a line drive to third baseman Heinie Groh in the second inning. This time Merkle connected again, lofting a deep drive that left fielder Manuel Cueto caught with his back up against the fence.

Center fielder Cy Williams, still smarting from the error that set up the lone Cincinnati run, was the last batter to stand in the way of Toney's no-hitter. Williams had always hit well against Toney, and the Reds pitcher had treated him cautiously all day, walking him twice. Working carefully, Toney ran the count to 2-and-2 on Williams and then put a pitch too close to the heart of the plate. Williams ripped it to deep right field, with Jim Thorpe giving chase. Thorpe dived for the ball, missed it, and it caromed off the grandstand, foul by inches. What happened next varies from account to account. When Thorpe returned the ball to the infield, it either was or was not inspected by plate umpire Al Orth. Whether or not it was inspected, the same ball that had ricocheted off the wall wound up in Toney's hands with a scuff mark the size of a silver dollar marring its surface. Toney could hardly believe his good fortune, since a scuffed ball thrown with the speed of his fastball would do unhittable tricks. Toney missed the plate with his first scuffed

Catcher Art Wilson of the Cubs, who "froze" at home plate as a throw from pitcher Hippo Vaughn bounced off his chest protector and the Reds scored the only run of the game in the tenth inning of the "double no-hitter" pitched by Vaughn and Fred Toney of the Reds in 1917 (National Baseball Hall of Fame Library, Cooperstown, N.Y.).

pitch, running the count full, and then fanned Williams with a pitch that dropped at least eight inches under his flailing bat.

Williams' strikeout secured Toney's no-hitter, at that time only the fourth in history to go more than nine innings. Vaughn, of course, lost both his no-hitter and the game in the tenth inning. His catcher, Art Wilson, was disconsolate, reportedly sobbing and apologizing, "I just went out on you, Jim—I just went tight."

Given the rarity of the occurrence, the double no-hitter received relatively little attention in the press of the day. The *New York Times* limited its account of the game to four paragraphs, leading off with headlines that failed to mention either Vaughn or Toney.

NO HITS, NO RUNS
FOR NINE INNINGS
Reds Nose out Cubs in Tenth
By 1 to 0 when Kopf and Jim Thorpe Get Singles

Of course, the game was played in the nation's Second City and did not involve any of the clubs based in New York. The *Chicago Tribune* gave the contest more play, publishing a full-length column under the headline,

CUBS HITLESS
AS TONEY WINS
IN 10TH, 1 TO 0

They acknowledged the rarity of the event, and focused on Williams' dropped fly as the deciding error in the tenth inning, saying only that Vaughn's throw home on Thorpe's roller hit Wilson on the shoulder about the time that Kopf scored. The fact that the official scorer didn't charge an error on the play and credited Thorpe with an infield hit helped to expiate Wilson's trance-like performance.

The *Cincinnati Enquirer* devoted nearly a half page of coverage to the game, headlining,

TONEY PITCHES FIRST NO-HIT GAME OF SEASON IN NATIONAL LEAGUE

(Two no-hitters had already been pitched in the American League.) Its account of the game ignored Wilson's gaffe entirely, reporting only that the winning run scored on a "scratch hit in front of the plate by Jim Thorpe."

Quoted in the *Enquirer*, Reds manager Christy Mathewson called the contest "the greatest game ever pitched," and it regularly shows up in lists of Baseball's Ten (or Twenty, or Fifty) Greatest Games. Its luster has dimmed a little with time. As *The Bill James Historical Baseball Abstract* reports:

> When I was a kid the double no-hitter was one of the most famous games in baseball history, but you rarely hear about it anymore, because baseball history has become the purview of the television people, who aren't interested in anything for which there is no tape.

Art Wilson spent eleven years in the National League and two years in the Federal League and retired with a respectable .261 batting average. It is fortunate for his reputation that he dozed off in early May in a game between Cincinnati and Chicago. Although the game achieved national prominence because of its singularity, reports focused, quite properly, on the achievement of the opposing pitchers rather than the game's outcome or the manner in which the winning run was scored. As another catcher, Ernie Lombardi, found out twenty-two years later, it's another matter entirely to appear to be dozing off in the final game of the World Series against the New York Yankees.

CHAPTER THIRTEEN

Misjudgments and Miscommunication

"What we've got here is failure to communicate."
Pronounced by Chain-Gang Boss (Strother Martin)
over prostrate body of Cool Hand Luke (Paul Newman)
From *Cool Hand Luke* (Warner Brothers, 1967)
Screenwriters: Donn Pearce and Frank R. Pierson

◆ ◆ ◆ ◆

In addition to outright errors, batted balls can be misplayed in a number of ways that don't show up in a box score or subject miscreants to long-term blame. Fielders can position themselves poorly, get late starts, misjudge the flight of the ball entirely, or play Alphonse and Gaston with a teammate. All of these actions can cause balls which should be caught to drop safely, and most will be scored as safe hits rather than fielding errors.

Poor positioning, slow starts, and misjudged flies can be just as costly as muffed flies that clank off outfielders' gloves for obvious errors, and they are often invisible to all but the most knowledgeable fans. Ironically, examples of such "invisible" errors are to be found in many of the games which have spawned lifelong goats, and often have had just as much impact on the outcome of those games as the visible and heavily publicized misplays of the designated miscreants.

Escaped Goats

Turkey Mike Donlin: 1908 (the Merkle Game)

In the game that demonized Fred Merkle, the Giants and Cubs were tied 1–1 in the bottom of the ninth. The lone Cub run had scored off Mathewson on an inside-the-park home run by Joe Tinker, whom Matty called "the worst man I have to face in the National League." The home run was helped considerably by the slowness of right fielder "Turkey" Mike Donlin, who was hobbled by a painful charley horse. (So many of the Giants were injured at the time that manager McGraw allegedly entered the clubhouse asking, "How are my cripples?" Merkle was playing in place of regular first baseman Fred Tenney, whose legs were so painful he had to be bandaged from the waist down.) Donlin limped over to Tinker's hit, tried to intercept it with a kick save, missed, and managed to turn what should have been a double into a home run. Had he been free of injury and saved the run, the Giants might have won the game 1–0, and Merkle would never have come to bat in the bottom of the ninth.

Christy Mathewson and Cy Seymour: 1908 (the Play-off Game)

In the eyes of many, including the Cubs' Johnny Evers, the play-off game forced by Merkle's boner was also decided by an outfield misplay that didn't show up in the box score. With New York leading 1–0 in the third inning, the first Cub batter was Mathewson's nemesis, Joe Tinker. Wary of Tinker's success against him, Mathewson signaled center fielder Cy Seymour to play deep. Seymour ignored the signal and actually took a few steps closer to the infield instead of moving back. When Tinker drove the ball to deep center, Seymour ran back as fast as he could, but missed the ball by a few feet and it rolled into the crowd for a triple. The triple was the linchpin of a four-run rally that carried the Cubs to a 4–2 victory and the National League championship. In Evers' view, however, "If Seymour had played a deep field, as he was commanded to do, the probabilities are that New York would have won the pennant." Mathewson himself, who felt that his arm was "dead" on the day of the play-off, declined to blame Seymour for the loss. In his book *Pitching in a Pinch*, the Hall of Fame pitcher said, "Cy knew as much about playing the Cubs hitters as I did."

"Turkey" Mike Donlin in 1906, wearing the uniform advertising the Giants' 1905 championship that John McGraw hoped would intimidate other teams. (It failed to intimidate the Cubs, who won the pennant that year.) In the 1908 "Merkle Game," right fielder Donlin, hobbled by a charley horse, was slow getting to a Joe Tinker hit that he misplayed into an inside-the-park home run for the Cubs' only run of the game (Library of Congress, Prints and Photographs Collection).

Art Fletcher: 1912 (the Snodgrass Game)

In the game that undid Fred Snodgrass, the Red Sox and Giants went into extra innings tied at 1–1. The lone Red Sox run had come in the seventh inning when, with one out and nobody on, Boston manager Jake Stahl fisted a blooper into short left center, between shortstop Art Fletcher, left fielder Red Murray, and center fielder Snodgrass. Shortstop Fletcher backtracked and called for the ball. At the last minute, however, he pulled up short and gave way to the outfielders as the ball fell safely just beyond his reach. Mathewson was so unnerved by this gaffe, which was scored as a double, that he walked the next batter on four straight balls, putting runners on first and second.

The next hitter popped up for the second out, but pinch hitter Olaf Hendricksen swung late on a two-strike fastball, hitting it down the third-base line where it ricocheted off the bag for a double, scoring Stahl. If Fletcher (or Snodgrass or Murray, who were put off by Fletcher's

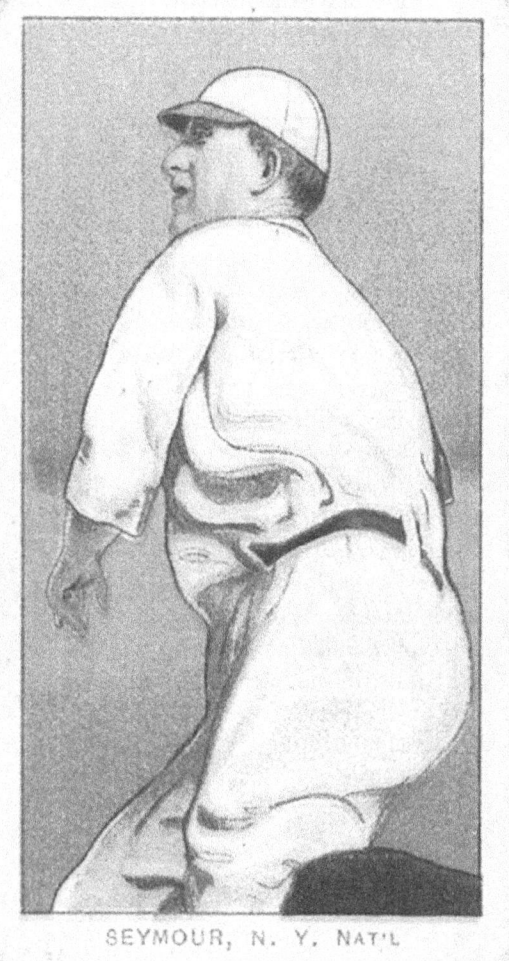

A disagreement between Christy Mathewson and Cy Seymour over positioning preceded the Joe Tinker triple that keyed the Cubs' four-run rally and their 4–2 victory in the 1908 play-off game. Seymour ignored Matty's signal to play deeper and actually moved in slightly just before Tinker's long drive sailed just out of his reach (Library of Congress Prints and Photographs Division).

initial call) had caught Stahl's blooper, the Giants might have won the game in nine innings, sparing Snodgrass the embarrassment of his tenth-inning muff. Even after his muff, Mathewson, Merkle, and Meyers congregated around Tris Speaker's foul pop-up, improvising an Alphonse, Gaston, and Friend act that allowed the ball to drop untouched and gave Speaker the life he needed to double in the tying run. After the game, manager McGraw appeared to be more disturbed by the mental errors that let Stahl's and Speaker's balls drop safely than in the physical error represented by Snodgrass' muff. When asked how he reacted to the Snodgrass misplay, McGraw said later, "I'll tell you how I reacted. I gave him a $1,000 raise."

Mark Koenig and Bob Meusel: 1926 (the Meusel Muff)

The fatal fourth inning for the New York Yankees in 1926 was marked by an error by shortstop Mark Koenig, who bobbled a grounder that he might have turned into an inning-ending double play, and a dropped fly ball by left fielder Bob Meusel that allowed the first run of the inning to cross the plate. In-between these two obvious errors, Koenig and Meusel suffered a communications lapse that allowed a bloop hit by Chick Hafey to drop between them. The consensus among sportswriters was that either could have caught the ball, but neither did. Hafey advanced to second on Meusel's muff and scored the third (and ultimately deciding) run of the game on a single by shortstop Tommy Thevenow. Since Koenig and Meusel already shared the blame for the two official errors that were recorded in the inning, there is little point in trying to apportion the responsibility for Hafey's bloop hit between them. In any case, the relief performance of Pete Alexander was the dominant story of the game and overshadowed the sloppy play of both Koenig and Meusel.

Charlie Dressen and Gil Hodges: 1951 (the Shot Heard 'Round the World)

The "Shot Heard 'Round the World" might never have sounded if Brooklyn manager Charlie Dressen had paid more attention to the positioning of first baseman Gil Hodges in the fateful ninth inning of the decisive 1951 Dodgers-Giants play-off game. The Giants came to bat in the bottom of the ninth down 4–1 and facing a tiring Don Newcombe. Their leadoff hitter, Alvin Dark, stroked a single that glanced off the glove of first baseman Hodges and rolled between him and Jackie Robinson into right field.

As the next hitter, Don Mueller, came to the plate, Hodges chose to guard the line and hold Dark close to first base, creating a wide gap between himself and the second baseman. It's not known whether Hodges took this position in response to a signal from Dressen, or whether Dressen just wasn't paying attention to his first baseman's position. Either way, the manager was definitely derelict in his duty. Hodge's positioning didn't make sense. With the Giants three runs down, Dark was no threat to steal. And there was no point in guarding the line against a double, since a double still wouldn't have put the tying run in scoring position.

"We all knew that Hodges was out of position," utility infielder and future major league manager Dick Williams, watching from the Dodger bench, recalled later. "But we couldn't say anything. Charlie ran his own ship and if we told Dressen he would have pinched our heads off."

Another person who noticed that Hodges' positioning left a big hole between first and second was Don Mueller, the Giants' batter. Mueller, who was known as "Mandrake the Magician" for his wizardry with the bat, took advantage of the opening by guiding a single through the gap between Hodges and Robinson.

Hodges lunged for Mueller's hit and barely missed it. Had he been positioned normally, there is little question that he would have caught the ball and, at the least, turned it into a force out, or, at best, a double play. A double play would have all but finished the Giants, leaving them with nobody on base, two outs, and a three-run deficit to overcome. A force-out would have left New York with a runner on first and one out. Had the inning played itself out from that point as it did on October 3, 1951, Thomson's home run would have only tied the game. But neither of these alternative futures came to pass. Mueller's single eluded Hodges, put Giants on first and third with nobody out, and the rest is history.

Willie Davis and Ron Fairly: 1966 (the Davis Drops)

After Dodger center fielder Willie Davis made three errors in the fifth inning of the second game of the 1966 World Series to help the Baltimore Orioles to a 3–0 lead, Frank Robinson led off the sixth inning with a long drive to right center. Both Davis and right fielder Ron

Dodger center fielder Willie Davis and right fielder Ron Fairly both brake and allow a long fly from Frank Robinson that either man could have caught to fall between them for a triple. The Dodgers made six errors in the game, including three by Davis in a single inning (both Series records), as the Orioles won 6–0 (AP/Wide World Photos).

Fairly arrived on the scene in time to catch the ball, but executed an Alphonse and Gaston act that allowed the ball to drop safely for a triple. Robinson later scored the fourth run of the game on a single by Boog Powell. Dodger manager Walter Alston, who refused to blame Davis for the balls he lost in the sun, was less compassionate when he discussed the Robinson triple that fell between Davis and Fairly. "Either one could have caught the ball," Alston said, and both fielders confirmed this observation. "Willie hollered for me to take it at the last second," Fairly said. "I could have caught it if I'd continued after it, but I hesitated."

Curt Flood: 1968 (Brock's Stand-up Play)

The 1968 World Series, which some say turned on Lou Brock's failure to slide home in the fifth inning of the fifth game, was stretched to seven games after the Detroit Tigers came back from a three-games-to-one deficit to tie the St. Louis Cardinals at three games apiece. Mickey Lolich of the Tigers and Bob Gibson of the Cardinals each pitched shutout ball for the first six innings of the seventh game. In the seventh inning, with two men on and two men out, the Tigers' Jim Northrup hit a line drive to deep center. Curt Flood, one of the best fielding center fielders of all time, misjudged the ball. He came in at first, then turned, slipped in the wet grass, and chased the ball toward the fence. The ball sailed over his head and bounced safely 400 feet from the plate for a two-run triple.

The next hitter, Bill Freehan, doubled in Northrup for the third run of the inning and what proved to be an insurmountable Tiger lead. Detroit won the game and the Series, snapping a string of seven straight Series victories by Cardinal pitcher Bob Gibson. Sportswriter Bob Broeg called Flood's stumble "the $100,000 slip," summoning up the image of Snodgrass' now inflated $30,000 muff. While Flood has since become a more recognizable name in baseball history than

Snodgrass, it is not because he slipped on the outfield grass at Busch Stadium in October of 1968, but because he quit baseball at the peak of his career in 1969 to protest a proposed trade to Philadelphia by unsuccessfully challenging baseball's reserve clause and its anti-trust status in court.

Marty Barrett and Bob Stanley: 1986 (the Buckner Boot)

In the much-discussed final inning of Game Six of the 1986 World Series, a communications breakdown occurred between Red Sox second baseman Marty Barrett and pitcher Bob Stanley. Were it not for this breakdown, the Red Sox might have gotten out of the inning with the score still tied and Bill Buckner would have been spared the lifelong embarrassment of missing Mookie Wilson's grounder. The miscommunication occurred just after Stanley's wild pitch sent Kevin Mitchell across the plate with the tying run. Ray Knight of the Mets took second on the pitch and, anxious to be able to score the winning run in the case Wilson singled, stretched his lead off second as Stanley prepared to pitch.

Seeing Knight's lead, second baseman Barrett signaled for a pickoff, broke for second, and waited for Stanley to whirl and catch Knight off base. Stanley, perhaps flustered by the fact that his wild pitch had just sent the tying run home, missed the signal entirely, and Barrett watched in frustration as the pitcher delivered the ball to the plate instead of second base. Wilson fouled the pitch off, and Knight returned to second. "We had Knight picked off," Barrett told Peter Gammons later.

Bob Stanley of the Red Sox pitches inside to the Mets' Mookie Wilson in the tenth inning of the storied Game Six of the 1986 World Series. After Stanley's wild pitch to Wilson tied the score, the pitcher missed the signal for a pick-off play that players and announcers believed would have caught Ray Knight off second base and ended the inning before Knight scored on Wilson's grounder to Bill Buckner (National Baseball Hall of Fame Library, Cooperstown, N.Y.).

Watching from the TV broadcasters' booth, Vin Scully agreed with Barrett, announcing that Knight would have been a dead duck if Stanley had only turned and thrown the ball to second. Knight himself agreed with this assessment. "If it had been a good throw I would have been out," he told Mike Sowell in *One Pitch Away*. He then added the kind of rationalization that drives baseball statisticians crazy. "But I'd rather be out at second than out at home on a base hit, so I just kept getting a bigger and bigger lead." Obviously, if Knight had been picked off second, he never would have had a chance to score, while the right kind of hit (or, as it turned out, a first baseman's error) would have allowed him to score without a play at the plate regardless of the length of his lead.

Of course, there is no assurance that the Red Sox would have caught Knight off base for the third out, even if Stanley had picked up the pickoff signal. The move would have required perfect timing and an on-target throw. But at least three of the observers, Barrett, Scully, and Knight himself, thought the Sox had the runner dead to rights. Since the score was already tied, there is also no assurance that Boston would have gone on to win Game Six — the arms in both bullpens were depleted by that time. However, a successful pickoff would have made a huge difference to at least one participant: Bill Buckner would be able to enjoy a peaceful retirement without having to endure jokes that he once failed to catch the team bus when it went between his legs.

Defensive Misplays

Bill James, in *The Fielding Bible* by John Dewan, introduces the term *Defensive Misplay* for "any play which is not an error (or a passed ball) on which the fielder surrenders a base advance or the opportunity to make an out when a better play or a different play would have or might have gotten the out or prevented the advance."

James has been rigorous in listing fielding plays that fit this definition. They include misjudged flies that land for hits, balls lost in the sun, infielders who run into each other trying to make a catch, and outfielders who fail to communicate and let catchable balls drop between them. He judges that these misplays are more than twice as common as recorded errors, but they have not been counted by traditional scoring methods.

As shown in this chapter, defensive misplays that didn't make the scorebook affected the outcome of games that made lifelong goats of such players as Fred Merkle, Fred Snodgrass, Ralph Branca, and Bill Buckner. These were close, crucial games that have been analyzed to death, but the importance of uncredited misplays in these storied games suggests that such miscues are likely to be found affecting the result of any close contest.

The outcome of crucial games can hinge on a number of small incidents, many of which never show up in the box score. Goat horns are usually assigned to the obvious candidate, the outfielder who lets a late-inning fly slip through his fingers, the infielder who bobbles a grounder while the winning run scores, the man without a chair when the music stops. But the outfielder who comes in on a fly ball that sails over his head or the infielder who positions himself poorly can be just as guilty as the more obvious goats maligned by the press and fans. A baseball game is made up of tiny failures, a hesitation here, a slip there, that can in the end be just as decisive as a glove-clanking two-base error or a walk-off home run.

CHAPTER FOURTEEN

Managerial Misfires

> There are only two kinds of managers. Winning managers and ex-managers.
> — Gil Hodges
> Manager, New York Mets

> When you have a responsible job you've got to accept the responsibility.
> — Birdie Tebbetts
> Manager, Cleveland Indians

♦ ♦ ♦ ♦

In football, the term *Monday Morning Quarterback* refers to those individuals who second-guess the decisions of their teams' coaches during the previous weekend's contests. But baseball is played day in and day out, and the calendar for second-guessing runs seven days during each week of the season. Managers' decisions are constantly questioned by the fans in the stands and the viewers at home who scream "Take the bum out!" at their TV set in the late innings of close games. But the fans shouting "Take the bum out!" are often counterbalanced by those yelling "Don't bring that guy in!" at other TV sets. In the end, the players perform well or poorly, decisions are vindicated or not vindicated, and fans are placated by wins or see their team endure losses that could have been avoided if only their manager had heeded the advice given freely to the unresponsive TV screen.

Bill James has written that "a manager earns his daily bread in the gun sights of 30,000 rifles." This pressure takes its toll: of the twenty-five most successful managers in the history of the game, James estimates that at least eighteen were alcoholics.

Managers are rarely remembered for their decisions in specific games. Each day brings a new set of circumstances and a new batch of decisions. Over the course of a season, these decisions tend to even out. James has also speculated that "the percentage calculations which drive strategic decisions in baseball are normally so close and so complicated that it is categorically impossible to state with any assurance what the correct course of action would be." That is, most strategic decisions are so close that managers might fare just as well by flipping coins. Even when the "correct" (i.e., highest percentage) course of action can be identified, the vagaries of chance are such that a good decision can be followed by a poor outcome, or vice versa.

In the long run, managers tend to be hired, or fired, on the basis of their won–lost records, which usually depend more on the skill of their players than the quality of their strategic decisions. Still, there are a few cases in baseball history in which decisions that went wrong have cost managers their jobs or, at the least, sullied their reputations.

Scapegoats: Grady Little and Pedro Martinez

Personnel changes, particularly those involving the removal and replacement of pitchers, have been among the most second-guessed managerial decisions in the major leagues. One of the most controversial of these decisions, and one of the few that has actually cost a manager his job, was Grady Little's decision not to remove Pedro Martinez in the eighth inning of the deciding game of the American League Championship Series in 2003.

Grady Little managed for many years in the minor leagues and served time as a bench coach for the Cleveland Indians and Boston Red Sox before being named Red Sox manager for the 2002 season. In 2003 he led the Red Sox to their first postseason appearance since 1999, and beat Oakland to earn a spot in the American League Championship Series, where his team pushed their long-time rival, the hated New York Yankees, to a seventh and deciding game. Going into the bottom of the eighth inning of that game, the Red Sox led the Yankees 5–2, with their best pitcher, Pedro Martinez, on the mound.

Martinez had pitched masterfully up to that point, limiting the Yankees to two solo home runs by Jason Giambi. After getting the first out in the eighth, however, Martinez began to falter. Derek Jeter doubled on a 0-2 pitch, and Bernie Williams singled him in to make the score 5–3. When another double sent Williams to third and put the tying run on second base, Little was faced with a decision: stick with his ace or go to his bullpen of one of the relievers who had been effective against the Yankees in earlier games. Little elected to stick with Martinez, who gave up a broken-bat bloop hit to Jorge Posada that tied the score. At that point, Little finally went to his bullpen pitchers, who held the Yankees scoreless for two innings but gave up a game-winning home run to Aaron Boone in the bottom of the eleventh inning.

The Boston press and the seers on talk radio crucified Little for his decision. Everyone knew, the second-guessers ranted, that Martinez lost his effectiveness after a hundred pitches, a milestone he reached at the end of the seventh inning. Few blamed Martinez, who defended his manager's decision, saying, "(Little) asked me if I had enough bullets in my tank to get them out and I said yes. I would never say no." Little explained his decision by saying, "Pedro Martinez has been our man all year long and in situations like that he's the one I want on the mound over anybody we could bring out of the bullpen."

A subsequent statistical study by Bill Felber, in *The Book on the Book*, suggests that Little's decision wasn't the no-brainer that the second-guessers made it out to be. Even deep in the game, after facing twenty-seven batters, statistics showed that Martinez was likely to retire seventy-seven percent of the batters he faced, a slightly better percentage than was recorded by any of the fresh arms available in the Boston bullpen on that day. So the decision was a close one. It's not likely, though, that Grady Little pored over statistics before making his decision. He went with his gut, stuck with his ace, and the Red Sox went on to lose the lead in the eighth inning and the game in the eleventh. Of course, there's no guarantee that the Red Sox would have held the lead if Little had changed pitchers. But he didn't, and when the Red Sox lost the pennant, Grady Little lost his job.

The Red Sox released Little within a month after Aaron Boone's home run sent New York to the World Series in place of Boston. The Red Sox management insisted that it wasn't only his decision to stick with Martinez that led to his dismissal. It was true that Little, an old-line manager who relied more on his instincts than on statistics, was out of step with the new Red Sox front office, which preached salvation through statistics with the fervor of religious converts.

Still, there is scarcely any doubt that Little would have kept his job if he had won the ALCS and taken Boston to its first World Series since their heartbreaker against the Mets in 1986. (There is also little doubt that he would have lost his job if he'd pulled Pedro and the bullpen had failed to hold the lead and win the game.)

As it was, the Boston press put Little on a pedestal next to Buckner in their pantheon of patsies. In the words of the *Boston Herald* following the Red Sox loss, Little would be "scorched throughout the winter, perhaps forever. Deservedly so ... fingers will be pointed. Blame will be assigned. That's life. That's Boston." Observing the press treatment of Little, Peter Gammons of ESPN observed, "this goes beyond vilification. This is pure, unadulterated hatred for a wonderful, decent man who has a large part in the centrifugal force that held together a team that had a few dysfunctional parts."

What came to be recognized as Little's (not Martinez's) failure took on a broader symbolic meaning. When John Kerry, the Democratic candidate for president, replaced his campaign manager in the midst of the 2003 election runup, he explained his actions to the press by saying he didn't want to make "Grady Little's mistake" of sticking with his starter too long, and was going to his bullpen. The Red Sox also marketed a Grady Little "Bobble-arm" doll, built like a "bobble-head" doll but with a stationary head and a left arm that bobbled, simulating a manager's call to the bullpen.

Grady Little, manager of the Boston Red Sox in 2002 and 2003. His decision to stick with his staff ace, Pedro Martinez, in the eighth inning of Game Seven of the 2003 American League Championship Series continues to stir controversy. Martinez gave up three runs to allow the Yankees to tie the score, New York won in the eleventh on an Aaron Boone home run, and Little lost his job in the off-season (National Baseball Hall of Fame Library Cooperstown, N.Y.).

Ironically, Terry Francona, Little's successor at the Red Sox helm, repeated "Grady Little's mistake" in the heat of the 2004 pennant race against the Yankees. Francona left Pedro Martinez in a late–September game in the eighth inning to protect a 4–3 lead over the Yankees. Pedro, at 101 pitches entering the inning, gave up a game-tying home run to Hideki Matsui, and, still pitching, gave up the go-ahead run as well. The Red Sox lost the game 6–4, but Francona escaped permanent vilification when his team came back from a 3-games-to-0 deficit in the ALCS to defeat the Yankees and went on to sweep the Cardinals in the World Series, bringing Boston its first championship in eighty-six years.

Following his dismissal by Boston, Grady Little was hired by the Cubs as a front-office advisor. After a year at this position, he was assigned the role of roving catching instructor in the minor leagues, quite a comedown for a man who won 188 games in two seasons as Boston's manager and logged the fifth-best winning percentage of the forty-three managers who had led the team. He lost a game and his job on the basis of a decision that had at least as much chance of succeeding as failing. As a result of that decision, though, he wound up touring the minor leagues for two seasons before being hired to manage the Los Angeles Dodgers in 2006.

Escaped Goats

Personnel Moves That Backfired

Bucky Harris and Walter Johnson. Over seventy-five years before Grady Little was pilloried in the press for sticking with his best pitcher, another second-year manager, Bucky Harris of the Washington Senators, was criticized for leaving his ace, Walter Johnson, on the mound too long in the seventh game of the 1925 World Series.

Even though he'd been staked to a 4–0 lead over the Pittsburgh Pirates in the first inning of the seventh game, the 37-year-old Johnson, the best pitcher of his day and arguably the best pitcher ever, saw the Pirates tie the score 6-all in the seventh inning. A Roger Peckinpaugh home run gave the Senators a 7–6 lead, but the Pirates came back with three runs in the eighth to cap the scoring at 9–7 and win the world championship.

To say the least, Johnson was pitching under extenuating circumstances. This was the game that was played in fog and rain so thick that the infielders often couldn't see the outfielders. Four of the Pirates' last five runs were unearned, coming courtesy of a misplayed pop-up by shortstop Peckinpaugh in the seventh and a botched grounder by the same player in the eighth inning.

The field conditions, which Ring Lardner likened to playing in a bowl of Chicken-à-la-King, and Fred Lieb said made the outfielders look like "ghoulish figures in a tragedy on the Scottish moor," contributed not only to playing errors but also to questionable umpiring calls. In the late innings, drives launched by Pirate hitters Carey and Cuyler were called fair by umpires who couldn't see the foul lines and went for doubles over the strenuous protests of Washington outfielders closer to the plays. Johnson refused to blame the weather conditions for his performance, saying, "It was as fair for one as for the other," but there is little doubt that his performance on a clear day would have come closer to his winning outings in Games One and Four of the Series, when he gave the Pirates only one run in eighteen innings.

There was plenty of blame to spread around for Washington's loss. The press singled out Peckinpaugh, the American League's Most Valuable Player, who made a record-setting eight errors in the series; Commissioner Landis, for insisting that the seventh game be played under dismal weather conditions; the umpires, for their poor guesswork on fog-shrouded calls; and Bucky Harris, for sticking with his ace starter throughout the sodden contest.

As in the case of Pedro Martinez years later, little public blame was directed at Johnson himself. Criticism of player–manager Harris, at twenty-eight the youngest manager in the major leagues, came from an unlikely source. American League President Ban Johnson, who hadn't attended the game or observed the sloppy field conditions firsthand, sent Harris a public telegram criticizing him for his "sentimental" insistence on sticking with Johnson, stating that the Senators "LOST THE SERIES FOR SENTIMENTAL REASONS. THIS SHOULD NEVER OCCUR IN A WORLD SERIES."

Harris responded by saying that Ban Johnson's remarks were "gratuitous and should have been left unsaid," adding that "We have no alibis. The breaks were somewhat against us, but our team went down fighting and I feel that we will be in the thick of it next year." He later defended his use of Walter Johnson by saying, "If I had it to do over again, I still would have stuck with old Barney. With all the chips down, and on such a day I would rather have gambled on Johnson than any other pitcher on the staff."

League President Johnson retaliated by calling the manager's loyalty to his ace pitcher the "crudest blunder in the history of baseball," but the press tended to side with Harris. The *Washington Post* averred that the "great majority of fans will accept the statement of 'Bucky' Harris that the defeat of the Washington club was due to the 'breaks' of the game," and went on to consider Harris' options.

> Let it be considered for a moment what would have been the opinion of critics if Harris had taken Johnson out of the game and sent in Ferguson or Zachary or Reuter. If he had done this and then had lost the game, he would have been blamed by the multitude and dubbed "the greatest bonehead in baseball." His critics would have insisted that if he had permitted Johnson to remain in the game, the team could not have lost. But Harris chose to keep Johnson at work, notwithstanding the anticipated criticism. Had Barney won, Harris would have been a great manager.

U. S. President Calvin Coolidge is flanked by Washington's "Boy Manager," Bucky Harris, on his right and "Big Train" Walter Johnson (with ball) on his left. Harris received a public reprimand from the American League president, Ban Johnson, for sticking with his ace, Walter Johnson, in the seventh game of the 1925 World Series against the Pirates. The Big Train gave up three runs, only one of which was earned, in the eighth inning to lose the game and the world championship 9–7 (Library of Congress, Prints and Photographs Division).

The Senators' management also showed their support for Harris in defeat. Owner Clark Griffith kept Harris on as manager through 1928, when he traded him to Detroit, where Bucky immediately became the Tigers' manager. Griffith subsequently rehired Harris for two more managing stints with the Senators, in 1935 and 1950. In all, Harris managed for 29 years in the major leagues, amassing a total of 2,157 victories, a total exceeded by only five other managers. He was elected to the Hall of Fame by the Veterans Committee in 1975, two years before his death.

Charley Dressen and Ralph Branca. Given the earth-shattering impact of Bobby Thomson's 1951 "Shot Heard Round the World," it was inevitable that Brooklyn Manager Charley Dressen would be second-guessed for bringing in Ralph Branca to pitch to Thomson. The *Brooklyn Eagle* headlines the next day read, "FANS PUT BLAME ON DRESSEN AND BRANCA," and the accompanying article reported that Dressen was hanged in effigy from a lamppost at 75th Street and 3rd Avenue. Local columnists speculated that Dressen, whose loss to the Giants in the play-offs marked the end of his first year as manager of the Dodgers, would not be rehired by Dodger owner Walter O'Malley.

Charley Dressen had a reputation, largely self-inflicted, of being one of the smartest managers in baseball. He was not shy about sharing his vaunted image of his own brilliance with anyone within earshot and quite a few just beyond earshot. On the field, he accepted few suggestions from his players and coaches, and dictated every aspect of his team's play. During the season, and in the first two play-off games with the Giants, he gave explicit instructions to the bullpen concerning which pitchers should be warming up during which innings. In the third and deciding play-off game, however, he bombarded bullpen coach Clyde Sukeforth with calls asking, "Who's ready?" instead of dictating his own warm-up choices.

From the seventh inning on, two pitchers had been warming up in the Dodgers' bullpen: Carl Erskine and Ralph Branca. They were both throwing when the Dodgers broke a 1–1 tie and built a 4–1 lead in the top of the eighth inning. In the eyes of bullpen coach Sukeforth, Branca was pitching better than Erskine, who appeared to have a sore arm. When the Giants scored once in the bottom of the ninth to make the score 4–2 and had runners on second and third with Thomson coming to bat, Dressen called the bullpen once more to ask "Who's ready?" and Sukeforth responded that Branca was throwing well but that Erskine had just bounced a curve in the dirt. "Gimme Branca," Dressen said.

When Branca reached the mound, Dressen handed him the ball with the all-purpose instruction, "Get this guy out," and returned to the dugout to watch his pitcher throw a fastball across the heart of the plate. Thomson took it for strike one. Branca followed that strike with a high inside heater that Thomson tomahawked into the left-field stands to give the Giants the pennant.

When questioned by the press about his selection of Branca, who had already given up a home run to Thomson in Game One of the play-offs, Dressen did what any self-proclaimed genius would do—he blamed Clyde Sukeforth for the ill-fated choice. "In the papers, Charley told everyone it was my fault," Sukeforth told Peter Golenbock in *Bums, an Oral History of the Brooklyn Dodgers*. "He never said anything to me, but you know Charley. I expected it. Charley was always critical and outspoken when things didn't go right, but it was always to his credit if something turned out good. But that's Charley. I knew him for years."

Over the winter, O'Malley surprised the press by keeping Dressen on as manager and letting Sukeforth go. "The newspapers started to make a big fuss over the oldest man in point of service in the organization being let go over one pitch," Sukeforth said, "and they played it up pretty good." In the face of the bad press, O'Malley relented and asked Sukeforth to return. Sukeforth refused, and found work as a coach with the Pirates, where he rejoined Branch Rickey, who had brought Sukeforth to Brooklyn during Rickey's earlier tenure as the Dodgers' general manager.

Dressen went on to manage the Dodgers for two more years, winning the National League pennant both years and losing to the Yankees in the World Series both years. The ballplayers Dressen managed during those two years formed one of the greatest teams in baseball history. They included four future Hall of Famers (Jackie Robinson, Duke Snider, Pee Wee Reese, and Roy Campanella) and All-Stars at nearly every position. These were the Dodgers that were immortalized in Roger Kahn's *The Boys of Summer*. In Dressen's view of the world, though, according to Peter Golenbock in *Bums*, Charley Dressen was responsible for winning the National League pennants in 1952 and 1953, while "the ballplayers lost the World Series."

When the 1953 season ended, Dressen had spent three years at the helm of the Dodgers, won two National League pennants, and narrowly lost the third in the ninth inning of the most famous play-off game in baseball history. At that moment, Bill James wrote, "Charley Dressen ... had one foot in the Hall of Fame and one foot on a banana peel. Unfortunately, all of his weight went on the banana peel."

Dressen, who had been operating on year-to-year contracts at the insistence of Walter O'Malley, decided his performance warranted a multi-year agreement. O'Malley didn't believe in multi-year contracts for managers, fearing that he might want to cut an unsuccessful manager loose and be forced to pay him for not managing. O'Malley refused to offer Dressen a multi-year pact, and Dressen refused to sign a one-year contract. To end this standoff, O'Malley fired Dressen and replaced him with Walter Alston, then a little-known manager in the Dodger farm system.

After leaving the Dodgers, Dressen managed Oakland in the minor leagues for a year, and then had a series of jobs with lackluster major league teams that lacked not only luster, but also personnel equivalent to those on the Dodger team he left. In 1955 he took over a sixth-place Washington Senators team and managed them to seventh- and eighth-place finishes. In 1961, he joined a second-place Milwaukee team and was let go after failing to improve their performance in two years. In 1963 he signed on with a fifth-place Detroit Tiger team and managed to raise them as high as fourth place before suffering a terminal illness in the middle of the 1966 season.

Dressen's Brooklyn replacement, Walter Alston, managed the Dodgers under twenty-three successive one-year contracts, the third-longest tenure for a manager of a single team, bettered only by Hall of Fame managers Connie Mack and John McGraw. During those twenty-three years, Alston's teams won seven pennants and four World Series, and he joined Mack and McGraw in the Hall of Fame in 1983.

Clyde Sukeforth, who had scouted Jackie Robinson for Branch Rickey when he was with the Brooklyn Dodgers, went on to coach and scout several years with the Pirates under Rickey. During that time he spotted a raw young outfielder in the Dodgers' minor league system and recommended that Rickey draft the outfielder away from the Dodgers. The outfielder was Roberto Clemente, who played eighteen seasons for the Pirates, won four batting titles, twelve Gold Gloves, and became the all-time Pirate leader in games played, at-bats, hits, singles, and total bases. He was elected to the Hall of Fame on the first ballot after perishing in a plane crash while delivering supplies to earthquake victims in Nicaragua.

Over fifty years after "The Shot Heard 'Round the World" was fired, Ralph Branca is still being introduced as "the man who gave up Bobby Thomson's homer." His manager, Charley Dressen, on the other hand, has been reduced to a mere footnote to the event. In fact, it can be argued that Dressen's successor, Walter Alston, and even his bullpen coach, Clyde Sukeforth, had a more lasting effect on baseball than Dressen himself.

Gene Mauch and Donnie Moore. The 1986 postseason, with its late-inning heroics and sudden reversals of fortune, was a utopia for second guessers. But few managerial moves received more attention from armchair tacticians than Gene Mauch's call to the bullpen with the California Angels one out away from eliminating the Boston Red Sox in the American League Championship Series.

The Angels came into the ninth inning ahead of Boston three games to one and up 5–2 with their ace, Mike Witt, on the mound and cases of celebratory champagne being wheeled into their locker room. Witt surrendered a soft single to Bill Buckner, struck out Jim Rice, and saw Don Baylor muscle his best pitch, a curve ball on the outside corner, over the left-field fence to cut California's lead to 5–4. When Dwight Evans popped out, the Angels were one out away from their first World Series appearance.

The next scheduled hitter was Rich Gedman, a left-handed batter who had hit Witt hard all day, reaching him for a single, double, and two-run homer. Mauch elected to remove his right-handed starter in favor of a left-handed reliever, Gary Lucas, who had struck out Gedman earlier in the series. The strategy backfired when Lucas hit Gedman on the hand with his first pitch. That brought journeyman outfielder Dave Henderson, a right-hander, to the plate. Mauch countered with his right-handed closer, Donnie Moore, who got two strikes on Henderson and watched him foul off two more pitches before hitting the home run that put the Red Sox ahead 6–5.

The Angels tied the game in the bottom of the ninth, but lost it in the eleventh, when Henderson hit a sacrifice fly off Moore to put the Red Sox ahead for good, 7–6. The two teams then returned to Boston, where the Red Sox won the next two games handily, 10–4 and 8–1. "I don't think we ever should have had to come back here," Donnie Moore said after the two Red Sox home wins had denied the Angels their first trip to the World Series. He brooded over the Game Five loss that made the trip necessary for the next three years, and his part in that loss contributed to his 1989 suicide.

Second guessers were quick to point out that if Mauch had left Witt in to pitch to Gedman, even if he'd walked the catcher or hit him the way Lucas had, the Angels would have been left with Witt facing Henderson instead of Moore, who was pitching with a sore shoulder and a rib cage full of cortisone. Witt had made Henderson look overmatched in the outfielder's only previous at-bat that day, striking him out with two men on base. Mauch defended his decision to replace Witt vehemently. "I'd seen enough of Rich Gedman against Mike Witt for one day," he told reporters, referring to the Boston catcher's home run, double, and single in three trips, "and I'd never seen Gedman do anything but strike out against Gary Lucas."

In covering the Angels' Game Five loss, the *Los Angeles Times* brought up visions of past seasons when Mauch had his teams knocking on the door of a World Series appearance only to be turned away at the last moment.

- In 1964, Mauch's Phillies held a six-and-a-half game lead over the St. Louis Cardinals with only 12 games to play, but lost the pennant when Mauch elected to use his two best starters, Chris Short and Jim Bunning, on short rest in a two-man rotation that proved ineffective.
- In 1982, Mauch's Angels won the first two games of a best-of-five play-off against the Milwaukee Brewers, but lost the final three games when Mauch was second-guessed for starting Tommy John on only three days of rest. Ironically, Mauch was also criticized for *failing* to bring in a left-handed reliever to face a left-handed batter, the move he'd made with Gary Lucas in the ninth inning of Game Five in 1986. In 1982 he had let right-hander Luis Sanchez pitch to left-handed Cecil Cooper with two out and the bases loaded in the seventh inning of the deciding game. Cooper singled, driving in the two runs that turned a 3–2 Angel lead into a 4–3 deficit and took the Brewers to their first World Series.

The tone of the newspaper coverage of Mauch's 1986 ALCS failure was more sorrow than second-guessing. Local columnists didn't demand his head on a platter. Mauch had managed four different teams for twenty-six years without ever taking his teams to the World Series, the longest record of futility endured by any manager. He retired after the 1987 season, when the Angels dropped from first to last place in the American League's West Division.

Mauch's decision to replace Mike Witt with Gary Lucas, which started the Angels' downfall in 1986, wasn't necessarily a bad one. It was certainly defensible, and the odds initially seemed to be in Mauch's favor. Unfortunately, his good decision produced a bad outcome that left Mauch a perpetual spectator at Baseball's Fall Classic.

Defensive Oversights

John McNamara and Bill Buckner. After coming from behind to defeat the Angels in the 1986 ALCS, the Boston Red Sox went on to lose the World Series to the New York Mets in seven games after coming within one strike of winning the Series in six games. Game Six, of course, featured the Mets' own come-from-behind victory, when they wiped out a 5–3 Boston lead in the bottom of the tenth inning, scoring the winning run when Mookie Wilson's grounder slid under Bill Buckner's glove and passed through the first baseman's legs into short right field.

Throughout the season, Red Sox manager John McNamara would often bring Dave Stapleton in as a late-inning defensive replacement for first baseman Bill Buckner, whose aching legs made him something of a liability in the field. Indeed, Stapleton had taken the field as a backup first baseman in each of the four Red Sox victories over California in the ALCS and in their three previous World Series wins over the Mets. The second-guessers, whose numbers multiplied in this particular postseason, wanted to know why McNamara hadn't made that switch in the tenth inning of Game Six. McNamara responded to the criticism by noting that "Buckner has a soft pair of hands. He catches what he gets to." Of course, no one was questioning Buckner's hands. Or his heart. It was his legs which were at issue, specifically his bandaged and painful ankles, which limited his range at first base and caused spectators to wince in sympathy whenever he ran the bases.

McNamara never adequately explained why he had failed to replace Buckner with Stapleton in the crucial tenth inning. He said once that he only brought Stapleton in when a pinchrunner was needed for Buckner, but an examination of the box scores shows that Stapleton often entered games purely for his defensive contribution. So why didn't he come in when defense was needed in Game Six? Roger Angell speculates that McNamara sentimentally wanted Buckner to be on the field with the rest of the first team when the Red Sox claimed a World Series title for the first time in 68 years. It's equally possible that, in the heat of the moment, the manager simply neglected to make the change he'd made throughout the season. (Earlier in the game, Davey Johnson, the Mets' manager, had failed to make a double switch when he brought in reliever Jesse Orosco in to get the last out of the eighth inning and was forced to remove him for a pinch hitter in the Mets half of the ninth. The double switch is a fairly standard move for National League managers, but Johnson apparently forgot to make it under the late-inning pressure of the big game.) In any event, even if Dave Stapleton had replaced Buckner and made the play on Mookie Wilson perfectly, there is no guarantee that the Red Sox would have gone on to win the Series. By that time, the Mets had already tied the score, so that the game would have gone to the eleventh inning and its outcome is anybody's guess.

McNamara managed Boston for another year and a half. In 1987, the Red Sox dropped to fifth place, twenty games behind the Detroit Tigers, and McNamara was released halfway through the 1988 season. He came back to manage Cleveland in 1990 and half of 1991, and the California Angels for a half season in 1996.

John McNamara managed for nineteen years in the major leagues, leading a variety of teams that included Oakland, San Diego, Cincinnati, California, Boston, and Cleveland. He had the reputation of being a low-key manager and was once fired for being "too nice." His record as a manager is mostly undistinguished and he is primarily remembered for raising the Red Sox from a fifth-place finish in 1985 to the American League championship in 1986. He is also remembered, and criticized, in Boston for failing to replace Buckner with Stapleton in Game Six of the 1986 World Series, but it is Buckner, not McNamara, who will wear goat horns to his grave.

Danny Ozark and Greg Luzinski. The failure of John McNamara to insert a late-inning defensive replacement in a crucial game was not without precedent. In 1977, Philadelphia outfielder Greg Luzinski had an all-star year, batting .309 with 39 home runs and 130 RBIs to help the Phillies finish atop the National League's Eastern Division. Nicknamed "The Bull" because of his hulking, muscle-bound presence, he not only hit with the strength of his nickname but sometimes fielded as if he had hooves instead of a glove. For this reason, manager Danny Ozark often replaced Luzinski with fleeter, more sure-handed outfielders when the Phillies had a late-inning lead.

The best-three-out-of-five National League Championship Series between the Phillies and the Western Division Champion Los Angeles Dodgers was tied at one game apiece when the Phillies scored two runs in the bottom of the eighth inning to break a tie and take a 5–3 lead. As the Dodgers came to bat in the top of the ninth, the situation called out for Ozark to replace Luzinski with light-hitting Jerry Martin, a better glove man who had served as a late-inning defensive replacement for much of the year. Ozark chose not to make the move.

When the Dodgers grounded into two quick infield outs, it seemed that Ozark's decision would have no bearing on the game's outcome. With two out, however, the 38-year-old Vic

Davalillo reached first on a drag bunt and the 39-year-old pinch hitter Manny Mota drove a pitch to deep left field. Luzinski chased after the ball, leapt, and got his glove on it as he ran up against the fence. But the ball glanced off the leather and bounced off the fence before he could corral it. When he finally retrieved the ball, Luzinski's throw to the infield eluded second baseman Ted Sizemore, allowing Mota to take third as Davalillo scored. With the Dodgers only one run down, the next batter, Davey Lopes, scorched a line drive that caromed off third baseman Mike Schmidt's glove toward shortstop Larry Bowa. Bowa picked off the ball and made a strong throw to first that appeared to beat the fleet Lopes, but the umpire ruled that the hitter was safe and the tying run scored on the play.

Upset by the umpire's call and the presence of Lopes on first, Phillies pitcher Gene Garber made a bad situation worse by loosing a wild pickoff throw that allowed Lopes to advance to second base. Bill Russell followed with a single to center that scored Lopes with the go-ahead run. The Phillies failed to score in the bottom of the ninth, and instead of going up two games to one over the Dodgers in the best-of-five series, they fell behind by that margin. The Dodgers closed out the Series the next day, beating the Phillies 4–1 in a rain-soaked contest to win the National League pennant.

When asked by reporters why he hadn't replaced Luzinski with Martin in the top of the ninth, Ozark responded that Luzinski was scheduled to be the third batter up in the bottom of the inning and he didn't want to take the Bull's bat out of the lineup in the event that the Dodgers tied the score. As Charles Maher of the *Los Angeles Times* pointed out, however, "With a two run lead in the ninth, you need Luzinski's bat less than you don't need his glove."

Luzinski and Ozark have escaped permanent enshrinement in Baseball's Hall of Shame largely because the Bull's boot was not the easy play that Buckner's (or much earlier, Snodgrass') appeared to be. Photos of the attempted catch show Luzinski splayed against the outfield wall with the dropping ball about a foot above his outstretched glove. While it is true that a better, fleeter fielder might have made the catch, it's also true that the play was difficult enough so that the official scorer awarded Mota a double instead of charging Luzinski with an error.

Strategic Second-Guessing

Tom Lasorda and the Pitch to Jack Clark. One of the most-discussed managerial moves of the 1980s occurred in the sixth game of the 1985 National League Championship Series between the Los Angeles Dodgers and St. Louis Cardinals. The Cardinals held a three-to two lead in games, but the Dodgers led 5–4 in the ninth inning and needed just one more out to force a seventh game. Runners were on second and third with two outs when Jack Clark, the Cardinals' cleanup hitter, came to the plate against relief pitcher Tom Niedenfuer.

Dodger manager Tommy Lasorda was faced with a decision. He could pitch to Clark, or, with first base open, he could walk Clark, a right-handed batter, and let Niedenfuer, also a righty, pitch to lefty Andy Van Slyke. Clark had been a much stronger batter than Van Slyke in the play-offs, but Niedenfuer had struck out both Clark and Van Slyke with runners on first and third just two innings earlier.

Lasorda chose to allow Niedenfuer to pitch to Clark. The Dodger catcher, Mike Scioscia, signaled for a fastball and set up his glove as a target just off the outside corner of the plate. Niedenfuer's pitch missed Scocia's target and cut across the heart of the plate, where it met Clark's bat and flew some 450 feet across the left-field fence, giving the Cardinals a two-run lead. The Cards held that lead through the bottom of the ninth and advanced to the World Series.

Everybody and his brother, uncle, and next-door neighbor claimed that it was obvious that Lasorda should have walked Clark to get to Van Slyke. Thomas Boswell of the *Washington Post* framed the argument for the prosecution as follows:

All the glory this sunny day should have gone to Clark. But it won't. The exclamation point Clark wrote beside his name will always stand side by side with the question mark that now accompanies Tom Lasorda's name. What many in the crowd of 55,200 here wanted to know is why Clark ever got to hit.

Writing in the *Los Angeles Times*, Mike Downey expressed the opinion of the hometown fans.

> He (Lasorda) should not have pitched to him. That is all there is to it. He should have walked Jack Clark, or hit Jack Clark in the ribs with a change-up, or offered Jack Clark several billion dollars to leave the bat on his shoulder. Anything but pitch to him.

The Cardinal players and manager also added their voices to those in favor of walking Clark. "I'd have walked him," said Cardinal third baseman Terry Pendleton. "You don't pitch to a guy who's been beating people in the ninth inning for nine years when you can get to somebody who has one hit in the play-offs (Van Slyke was one for ten). Let Van Slyke beat you."

"When you manage a baseball team, you only have one guess," said Cardinal manager Whitey Herzog. I'm not second-guessing, but I thought possibly they'd walk him." Herzog went on to avoid a second guess by elaborating with a third guess: "I've always figured that if I can pitch to a guy making $1.3 million a year or a guy making $100,000 a year, I pitch to the guy making $100,000."

Lasorda defended his decision, saying, "If I walk Clark, they have the bases loaded and we can't put the next guy anywhere. I want him (Niedenfuer) to make Clark go for a bad pitch, go to his weakness."

In his *Guide to Baseball Managers*, Bill James backed Lasorda's choice more vigorously. After reiterating that the percentage calculations which drive baseball's strategic decisions are usually too close and complex to favor one course of action strongly, he said, "This case is an exception. Lasorda's decision, although it didn't work out, was unquestionably the correct one. To load the bases with a one-run lead to let a right-hander pitch to a left-handed hitter (Van Slyke) would have been lunacy."

The post-game second-guessing did not affect Lasorda's reputation, confidence, popularity, or tenure as a manager. He managed the Dodgers for twenty-one years, from the time he succeeded Walter Alston in 1976 to 1997, when he suffered a heart attack in mid-season. During those years he led the Dodgers to six division titles, four National League pennants, and two World Series championships. Often quoted as saying he "bled Dodger blue," he was voted into the Hall of Fame in 1997.

Bucky Harris and the Walk to Pete Reiser. Any list of the greatest baseball games ever played usually includes the fourth game of the 1947 World Series between the New York Yankees and the Brooklyn Dodgers, which came within an eyelash of featuring the first no-hitter in Series history. The Yankees were up two games to one in the Series, and went into the bottom of the ninth inning of the fourth game leading the Dodgers by a score of 2–1. The real story of the game was Yankee pitcher Floyd "Bill" Bevens, who had held the Dodgers hitless through the first eight innings. Bevens had achieved that feat by serving the Dodgers a steady diet of mostly unhittable fastballs. Those that were hit well found their way into the gloves of the Yankee outfielders, Lindell, DiMaggio, and Henrich, each of whom made at least one spectacular catch to preserve Bevens' bid for immortality.

Unfortunately, Bevens' fastballs were not only unhittable, but were largely uncontrollable as well. Bevens walked eight batters through the first eight innings, one short of the World Series record, and two of those walks, coupled with a sacrifice bunt and a groundout, had led to a Dodger run in the fifth inning. In reviewing the game and the stellar work of the Yankee outfielders, Shirley Povich of the *Washington Post* quoted the old baseball adage, "The greatest outfielder in the world can't field a base on balls."

Notwithstanding his wildness, Bevens stood on the mound in the bottom of the ninth only three outs away from a feat no one had accomplished at that time: a World Series no-hitter. He got the first out quickly in a familiar fashion when Hank Edwards hit a long drive that chased left fielder Johnny Lindell to the wall for the catch. Bevens then issued Carl Furillo a free pass to tie the record for World Series walks, but got the second out when Spider Jorgensen popped out to first baseman George McQuinn in foul territory.

With two outs and a runner on first, Dodger manager Burt Shotton made two key personnel moves. He sent reserve Al Gionfriddo in to run for Carl Furillo and brought in his last left-handed hitter, Pistol Pete Reiser, to bat for pitcher Hugh Casey.

Gionfriddo, a short, little-used outfielder, had come to the Dodgers from Pittsburgh early in the year in one of the housekeeping moves made by Branch Rickey to rid the Dodgers of players who objected to serving alongside of Jackie Robinson. In return for Gionfriddo and $100,000 in cash, the Dodgers dealt pitcher Kirby Higbee, their biggest winner in 1946, catcher Dixie Howell, and two other players to the Pirates. Assessing the deal, columnist Dick Young speculated that Gionfriddo had been thrown into the trade merely to "carry the money in a satchel from Pittsburgh."

While Gionfriddo was a minor role-player, Pete Reiser, whom Shotton sent up to bat for the pitcher, was another story entirely. A tragic figure, Reiser won a batting championship as a 22-year-old rookie with Brooklyn and was thought by experts to have the tools to be one of the greatest players in the game. His all-out play, however, brought him into contact with too many concrete outfield walls, and a series of concussions, broken bones, and severed tendons greatly shortened his career. After a particularly severe crash into the Ebbets Field wall early in the 1947 season, he'd been given the last rites by a priest, and columnist Red Smith counted at least eleven times when he had been carried off the playing field on a stretcher. His career as a full-time player was essentially finished by the time he turned 28, an age when most players hit their prime.

Reiser came to the plate to bat against Bevens hobbled by an ankle injury he'd sustained sliding into second base on the previous day. Still struggling with his control, Bevens ran the count to 2-and-1 on Reiser when Shotton flashed the steal sign to Gionfriddo. It wasn't a bad gamble, as the Yankee catcher Yogi Berra had been having so much trouble throwing out potential base stealers that *New York Times* columnist Arthur Daley suggested that Yogi take out burglary insurance. Even with a stumbling start, Gionfriddo slid safely into second under a high throw from Berra.

With Gionfriddo on second and a 3-and-1 count on Reiser, Yankee manager Bucky Harris made a move that contradicted seventy-five years of accumulated baseball wisdom. He ordered Bevens to walk Reiser intentionally, putting the potential winning run on first base. The walk, the tenth issued by Bevens, set a new record for World Series largesse by a single pitcher.

Shotton wasn't finished with his own managerial moves. He sent Eddie Miksis in to run for the hobbled Reiser and brought in a utility infielder, Cookie Lavagetto, to hit for leadoff man Eddie Stanky. On the face of it, this second substitution didn't appear to make much sense. The two men, Stanky and Lavagetto, were essentially the same hitter, light-hitting, right-handed middle infielders with little power. If anything, Stanky, who led the National League in walks for three seasons, would have seemed to be the better choice against the wild Bevens.

Lavagetto swung and missed Bevens' first pitch and then justified Shotton's hunch by lining the second pitch, an outside fastball, high off the right-field wall. The ball caromed trickily off the uneven wall and eluded right fielder Tommy Henrich long enough for Gionfriddo to score the tying run and Miksis, on base as a result of the intentional walk to Reiser, to convert the potential winning run into the actual winning run. With one pitch, Bevens had managed to lose not only his no-hitter, but the game as well.

Questioned by reporters after the game, Bucky Harris defended his unorthodox decision to put the winning run on base intentionally.

> I'd do it again; tomorrow if I had to. You've got the tying run on second after Gionfriddo steals. A single drives it home and the winning run's on first anyhow. The count is three-and-one and Reiser is a long-ball hitter. I'm not going to give him a chance to whack one over the fence. I suppose it was against baseball legend to order that pass but the second guess is always the best one, and I got only one.

After tying the Series at two games apiece, the Dodgers and Yankees split the next two games, with reserve outfielder and satchel carrier Al Gionfriddo making a spectacular catch of a DiMaggio drive to stave off a Yankee comeback in the sixth game and preserve it for the Dodgers. The Yankees won the seventh game 5–2 behind five strong innings of relief pitching by Joe Page to give Bucky Harris his second world championship. (It was his first appearance in the fall classic since he'd been publicly criticized by Ban Johnson for sticking too long with Walter Johnson in the rain-soaked seventh game of the 1925 World Series.)

Bill Bevens injured his arm during the 1947 Series and never regained the fastball that had carried him so close to immortality in Game Four. Ironically, the three unlikely heroes of that game, Bevens, Gionfriddo, and Lavagetto, were released by their teams during the off-season and never appeared again as players in a major league uniform.

Decisions and Outcomes

Most difficult managerial decisions are toss-ups that have roughly the same chance of success or failure as the next best alternative. It follows that "good" decisions (i.e., decisions more likely to produce a positive outcome than alternative courses of action) can produce bad outcomes nearly as often as "bad" decisions with a slightly lower probability of success. Thus, Tommy Lasorda's decision to pitch to Jack Clark, arguably a "good" decision with a higher likelihood of success than an intentional walk, led to a home run that cost the Dodgers the National League pennant. Bucky Harris's decision to walk Pete Reiser probably had a slightly lower chance of success than risking a 3-and-1 pitch from Bill Bevens, and could be classified as a poor decision that led to a bad outcome, the loss of the no-hitter and the Series game. Any decision, good or bad, that leads to a bad outcome is fodder for baseball's omnipresent second-guessers.

Good decisions that produce good outcomes are seldom remarked on by the press. Neither are bad decisions that produce good outcomes. Ralph Houk's 1962 decision to let Ralph Terry pitch to Willie McCovey with a 1–0 lead, Willie Mays on second, and Matty Alou on third in the ninth inning of the seventh game has been called "one of the worst strategic decisions in World Series history." McCovey had hit Terry hard throughout the Series, and the on-deck hitter, Orlando Cepeda, was batting an anemic .156 in the postseason and was zero for the Series against Terry. All the odds cried out for Terry to walk McCovey and pitch to the right-handed Cepeda, but Houk and Terry chose to pitch to McCovey. The powerful left-handed hitter saw his home run bid on Terry's first pitch pushed foul by the heavy winds at Candlestick Park and then lashed a screaming line drive that had game-winning hit written all over it until it collided with Bobby Richardson's glove for the final out of the Series. In the light of this improbable but successful outcome, Houk's decision has rarely been second-guessed.

Managers may be second-guessed daily, but their reputations rarely suffer as a result of this spectator sport. They are judged on the basis of their wins and losses, a cumulative record that has more to do with the quality of their players than the quality of their strategic decisions. Players may be awarded goat horns for an errant pitch, a dropped fly ball, or a botched grounder, but managers are seldom scarred for life for the decisions that led to these plays.

A losing record may cause a manager to be fired, but few have been fired for losing a particular game. The case of Grady Little, who was let go shortly after he stuck with his ace Pedro Martinez one batter too long in the 2003 ALCS, is a glaring exception to this general observation. It appears, however, that the significant philosophical differences between Little, a traditional manager, and the new Red Sox brain trust, which relied heavily on statistics, had as much to do with the loss of his job as Aaron Boone's home run.

CHAPTER FIFTEEN

Fan Interference

Every true baseball fan daydreams about the ball they will one day catch, perfecting the link between that fan and the game that he or she loves.
Tim Wiles
"The Joy of Foul Balls"

It seems to me that those who deplore the animal instincts of spectators at ball games (by Darwinian theory, the instinct to reach out for baseballs comes to us from the great anthropoids, who reach out for coconuts) are ignoring the facts of baseball.
John Lardner
Ball Fans and Other Primates

♦ ♦ ♦ ♦

The holy grail of every baseball fan is the souvenir ball that is plucked from the air in the midst of several pairs of clutching hands. In the fan's fantasies the quest for the grail ends with a clean, bare-handed catch of a ball arcing off the bat of a favorite player. It's more likely, however, that the quest will end after a couple of caroms, a few fluffed grabs, and a scramble beneath folding seats. That's if it ends at all. Tim Wiles, in an article in *The National Pastime*, calculated the odds that a randomly chosen fan will take a foul ball home to be 1300 to 1.

Historical Perspective

In the early 1900s, the odds that a fan would take a souvenir ball home were even longer than 1300 to 1. Foul balls were not always fair game. At the beginning of the last century, balls were comparatively expensive, and fans were encouraged, and sometimes even forced, to return fouls to the field of play. Many clubs stationed roaming employees in the stands to retrieve fouls caught by fans. One club that took exception to this practice was Chicago's National League entry, whose owner at the time, Charles Weeghman, announced that fans attending the Cubs' home games would be allowed to keep balls landing in the stands.

The Cubs were in the minority, however, and the habit of hounding the fans to return foul balls persisted. Some fans resented this practice and either hid foul balls or heaped abuse on the employees charged with retrieving them. A 1915 article in *The Sporting Life* bemoaned the fact that "The practice of concealing balls fouled into grandstands or bleachers has reached disgusting proportions in New York, where it is far more common than anywhere else."

Face-offs between fans and club-paid ball-hawks slacked off during World War I, when all parties agreed to donate all fouls hit into the stands to the armed services. With the cessation of hostilities overseas, however, hostilities between fans and ball-hawks resumed. The matter finally came to a head in 1921 when a Polo Grounds usher verbally chastised a New York Giants fan for failing to surrender a foul ball. When the fan, whose name was Reuben Berman, angered the usher further by throwing the ball to another group of spectators several rows away, security personnel removed Berman from his seat, threatened him with arrest, and escorted him out of the ballpark after refunding his ticket price.

The infuriated Berman sued the Giants for $20,000, claiming that he had suffered humiliation, mental and bodily distress, and loss of reputation. The case went to trial, and Berman was awarded $100 for his treatment at the hands of Polo Grounds employees. Although the settlement was much smaller than the plaintiff had sought, the judgment led the Giants to change their policy of demanding that fans return foul balls, and other teams soon followed suit. So today's fans have this decision, known as Reuben's Rule, to thank for clearing a major obstacle from the path of their pursuit of the holy grail.

As a lifelong fan who has attended well over 100 major league games, I can testify to the difficulty of taking a foul ball home. The closest I ever came was one afternoon in Cleveland's Municipal Stadium when I was eleven years old. The game between the Cleveland Indians and the last-place Philadelphia Athletics was sparsely attended, and I had moved down the left-field line to take an empty seat in the front row, where I thought I was more likely to catch a foul ball. Kermit Wahl, a little-used utility infielder for the Athletics, got around too quickly on a curve and lined it into the empty seats about twenty rows behind me. I clambered up the aisle after the ball, but two teenagers got to it just ahead of me. As I started back down the cement steps, I noticed that Wahl's line drive had knocked a piece off one of the stadium seats when it rattled into the stands. That green sliver of wood, a little larger than a dagger, graced my bedroom wall throughout my high school years, the centerpiece of a butcher-paper exhibit that charted the Indians' history from the 1900s on and featured bubble-gum cards of every player on their current roster.

The urge to acquire a foul ball doesn't diminish with age. In March of 2000, two friends and myself played hooky from a Mystery Writers convention in Tucson to attend an exhibition game between the Arizona Diamondbacks and the Chicago Cubs. We were told that the game was likely to be sold out, and were speeding along the expressway behind Tucson's Electric Park when we encountered a tangle of traffic just beyond the park's outfield fence. As we inched along in stop-and-go traffic, the cause of the tie-up became clear. An elderly driver had abandoned his car in the middle of the expressway to chase after a baseball that had cleared the outfield fence and bounced across the tree-lined median into the opposing traffic lanes.

The three of us watched in wonder, commenting on the blatant stupidity of certain fans, while the derelict driver worked his way back through three lanes of oncoming vehicles holding his prize aloft. As he got behind the wheel of his abandoned car and traffic began to move again, we heard a sharp clang and saw another ball bounce off our fender toward the curb. Instead of joining the moving line of vehicles, I kept our car braked as one friend jumped out to hold back traffic while the other chased down the rolling ball in the adjacent lane.

The Primal Urge

According to former *Newsweek* columnist John Lardner, a fan's need to reach out for baseballs is a primal urge that can be traced to the primate's need to reach out for coconuts. Unfortunately, if a fan's reach is long enough to extend into the field of play, this urge can result in severe penalties.

To illustrate this point, Lardner describes two incidents occurring in games played by the Philadelphia Phillies during the red-hot 1950 pennant race with the Dodgers and subsequent World Series with the Yankees.

> in the closing days of the 1950 pennant race, when the Philadelphia Phillies were edging toward the championship with the red-blooded apathy characteristic of National League teams about to meet the

Yankees in the World Series, there was a game in Brooklyn at which a subdebutante from Canarsie or Red Hook reached out from her box seat and touched a baseball lightly on its jowls. The umpires ruled interference and a Philadelphia run scored from third base....

In this case, retribution followed as the night the day. The maiden and a girl friend were led weeping from the ball park by heavy-handed minions of the law, like a couple of Anne Boleyns en route to the scaffold. Justice in Brooklyn is swift and terrible. It's getting so a girl can't even make book there, let alone reach out of bounds to fondle a ball in play.

The Brooklyn announcer, Red Barber, acting as the "informal guardian of the city's morals," lectured his radio audience on the intrinsic evil of interfering with falling baseballs. In Lardner's view, however, the magnetic attraction between fan and ball was more a matter of human nature than a moral flaw. He reports that he

> was thinking about this matter of dignified baseball vs. human nature a few days later during the World Series in Philadelphia. Philadelphia is a town where human nature is rampant up till closing hours. In the third inning of the first game of the series, John Mize of the Yankees hoisted a foul fly to right field. While Del Ennis of the Phillies was waiting close by the grandstand for the ball to come down (which even the 1950 ball will do, if given enough time) a cash customer, probably a mad-dog type, lunged out and deflected the potato out of Ennis's reach.
>
> What Mr. Barber would have said about that, if the air had been at his disposal, I hesitate to think.... Fortunately the guilty fan will be able to live with himself in future years, because (a) Mr. Barber was not at the microphone, and (b) Mize popped out on the next pitch. Otherwise, though the fan paid about $6.50 for his constitutional right to deflect baseballs hit to his neighborhood, he would have been a mighty miserable deflector.

Because Mize popped out on the next pitch, the incident of the lunging fan did not affect the course of the game, which the Yankees won 1–0, and was not deemed worthy of mention in the next day's write-ups in the *Philadelphia Inquirer* and the *New York Times*. There have been several cases, however, in which grasping fans have affected the course of championship games, altering both the outcome of the games and the lives of the fans themselves.

Scapegoat: Cub Fan Needs Witness Protection Program

In theory, at least, so long as a fan's reach does not extend into the field of play, the innate urge to gather in falling horsehide will not be found to interfere with the game itself. Umpires will assess no penalties for anything that happens to the ball once it has reached the confines of the stands. This doesn't mean that other spectators might not react unkindly to a fan who succumbs to the urge at an untimely moment, even if the ball has left the field of play.

The Botched Catch. In the sixth game of the 2003 National League Championship series between the Cubs and Marlins, a Chicago Cub fan incurred the wrath of an entire city for trying to catch a foul ball that had drifted into the left-field seats. The Cubs led the Marlins three games to two in the best-of-seven series, and were ahead 3–0 in the top of the eighth with Mark Prior, their staff ace, on the mound. When the first Marlin batter flied out, the Cubs were only five outs away from their first World Series appearance in fifty-eight years, the longest absence experienced by any of the original major league franchises.

After Juan Pierre doubled, Luis Castillo worked the count to 3-and-2 and then lofted a foul fly toward the left-field stands. Cub outfielder Moises Alou positioned himself next to the eight-foot wall and seemed ready to make a leaping catch when a spectator in the front row reached for the ball and deflected it away from Alou's glove. Alou landed without the ball, threw his glove down in disgust, and screamed at the hapless fan. The fan's earphones kept him from hearing Alou's words, but there was no mistaking the left fielder's body language. Everyone in the park was blaming the fan for costing the Cubs a crucial out.

Although the missed out proved to be crucial, it was hardly guaranteed. Alou had to time

his leap perfectly, extend his glove over the wall and the railing that topped it, catch the ball just as it disappeared from his view, and bring it back over the rail without losing it. It was a play he could make, and he claimed later he would have made, but it wasn't a sure thing. Had the spectator reached over the rail into the playing field, the umpires would have ruled the batter out for fan interference. But the ball had clearly dropped beyond the rail into the first row of seats. Alou was infringing on the fan's territory, not vice versa.

Evidently upset over the missed opportunity, Prior put his next pitch where no one could catch it, a wild throw that not only put Castillo on first but also allowed Juan Pierre to advance to third. Ivan Rodriguez scored Pierre with a single, but the next batter, Miguel Cabrera, hit a slow, easy grounder to shortstop Alex Gonzalez. Gonzalez set himself to go to second for what looked like a sure force-out of Cabrera, but the usually sure-handed shortstop bobbled the ball, loading the bases. Derek Lee then unloaded them with a double that tied the score and left Marlin runners on second and third. That caused Cub manager Dusty Baker to replace Prior with Kyle Farnsworth, but the reliever had no better luck stopping the Marlins. By the time the Cubs finished imploding, Florida had an 8–3 lead that stood as the final score, forcing the series to a seventh game. Chicago lost that game the next day, 9–6, after squandering a 5–3 lead, and the hapless fan was made the scapegoat for the Cub's fifty-eighth consecutive failure to reach the World Series.

The Reaction. The Cub fan's reign as scapegoat began immediately after Moises Alou threw his hissy fit. As the Cubs started to disintegrate on the field and lose their Game Six lead, the fan was booed, spat upon, pelted with peanuts, doused with beer, and showered with shouts of "Kill him" and "You cost us the World Series." The vilification didn't stop until he was escorted out of the park by security personnel with his jacket pulled up over his head, both to protect him from thrown objects and to preserve his anonymity.

The next morning's newspapers didn't print the fan's name, but he was outed on the Internet and subsequent editions identified him as Steve Bartman, a 26-year-old securities analyst, youth baseball coach, and lifelong Cubs fan. His identification fueled a cottage industry of eBay entrepreneurs who auctioned off upwards of 200 items, including a T-shirt showing a boy urinating on Bartman's name, thong underwear with a Cub logo and the legend "Steve Bartman Sucks," and copies of Bartman's high school yearbooks. One wag parodied the MasterCard "Priceless" ad campaign, writing: "Tickets to the Cubs game: $200; Chicago Cubs hat: $20; A 1987 Walkman: $10; Fucking up your team's chances of winning the World Series: Priceless."

Illinois Governor Blagojevich joined in the assault, calling Bartman's aborted grab "stupid" and suggesting that the Cub fan join a Witness Protection Program. Bartman himself provided a public apology saying he was "truly sorry" and explaining that "I had my eyes glued on the approaching ball the entire time and was so caught up in the moment that I did not even see Moises Alou, much less that he may have had a play."

The Aftermath. By the next year, Steve Bartman had taken his place alongside Mrs. O'Leary's cow as an eternal blight on the city of Chicago. Sportswriters regularly invoked his name, threatening to plague slumping players with the Steve Bartman treatment. The first time the world

---

Opposite: Chicago Cubs fan Steve Bartman deflects a foul ball out of the reach of Cub left fielder Moises Alou in the eighth inning of Game Six of the 2003 National League Championship Series. The Cubs subsequently imploded, allowing a 3–0 lead to turn into an 8–3 loss to the Florida Marlins, and followed that with a loss the next day that kept the Cubs out of the World Series for the 58th consecutive year. Since the ball was clearly in the stands, there was no interference call, and Bartman was within his rights to try for the catch. Even so, he was pelted with peanuts and doused with beer by outraged Wrigley Field fans, and received enough threatening mail so that the Illinois governor offered him the safety of a Witness Protection Program AP Photo/Amy Sancatta).

champion Marlins visited Chicago the next season, Florida's starting pitcher, Carl Pavano, left four free passes in the name of Steve Bartman at the Wrigley Field box office as a not-so-private joke. Ironically, the ball that Bartman deflected never wound up in his possession. A local attorney retrieved it and sold it at auction for $113,000 to a Chicago restaurateur who burned the ball in a public exorcism and included the ground-up remains in a savory sauce.

The name of Steve Bartman resurfaces regularly in the sports pages as background material whenever fans misbehave, new scapegoats are crowned, teams experience sudden reversals, or the curse of the Cubs' winless streak is written up. As often as not, writers bend the facts to fit the legend that Bartman interfered with a ball that was in play rather than a ball that had reached the stands. A 2005 article in the *Seattle Times* had Bartman lunging for a catch in foul territory and knocking away the ball that could have been the final out of the eighth inning, thereby misrepresenting both Bartman's action and the number of outs at the time.

The Injustice. By its very nature the public process of creating a scapegoat is likely to be shortsighted and unjust, but few scapegoats have been as unfairly treated as Steve Bartman. A lifelong Cubs fan, he paid his way into the park, kept to his seat, and didn't extend himself or his limbs into the playing area. The ball came to him, and he obeyed his primal instinct and reached for it. All but a handful of the 40,000 fans in Wrigley Field that evening would have done exactly the same thing, and half of that handful would have been protecting their own delicate digits, not the Cubs' pennant chances. Photos of the event show dozens of other hands reaching out toward Bartman and the ball. They paid their money and were exercising their God-given right to grab a ball that had left the field of play.

The newspaper headlines trumpeted CUB FAN'S FOLLY and charged Bartman with the loss, but his supposedly ill-considered grab left the Cubs no worse off than they had been. Castillo was still at bat with a count of 3–2. Instead of concentrating on the paying customers, the newspapers might have directed the search for scapegoats toward the well-paid participants on the playing field.

- Cub pitcher Mark Prior, who was paid to get batters out, unleashed the wild pitch that put Castillo on first and moved Juan Pierre over to third;
- Cub shortstop Alex Gonzalez, who was paid to field grounders, botched an easy bouncer that he could at a minimum have converted into the second out;
- Cub manager Dusty Baker, who was paid to make tough decisions, stuck with his ace pitcher at least one batter too long and watched as a double tied the game. Two days later, in Game Seven of the ALCS, Grady Little of Boston would make the same mistake with the same immediate result. Of the two managers, only Baker returned to lead his team the next year.

Well after the event, perhaps moved by the spirit of a Chicago Christmas, *Sun Times* columnist Jay Mariott theorized that some of the blame for the Cubs debacle might rest with Alou himself, and suggested that the left fielder owed Bartman a letter of apology. (He couldn't just phone Bartman, because the fan's notoriety had forced him to obtain an unlisted number.) Mariott wrote that the left fielder's public mini-tantrum might have communicated a panicky "this can't be happening" feeling to his teammates.

If Alou keeps his cool, maybe Alex Gonzalez keeps his cool and doesn't make the error. If Alou keeps his cool, maybe Mark Prior doesn't suddenly lose it. And if Alou keeps his cool, maybe Steve Bartman isn't the guy who periodically shows up on "ESPN SportsCenter" montages, wiping away moisture from under his eye.

After all, as Yogi Berra observed long before Steve Bartman was born, "Baseball is 90% mental. The other half is physical."

Escaped Goats: Yankee Fan Lends a Hand

The atrocious public reaction to Steve Bartman contrasts sharply with the press treatment of Jeffrey Maier, a 12-year-old New Jersey resident whose illegal glove work helped the Yankees win the first game of the 1996 American League Championship Series.

The Yankees were trailing the Baltimore Orioles 4–3 in the bottom of the eighth inning when rookie-of-the-year candidate Derek Jeter hit a long fly to right field. Orioles outfielder Tony Tarasco backed up to the fence and positioned himself to make a leaping catch. As the ball descended, however, the young Yankee fan stuck his black little-league glove into the playing field and scooped it away from Tarasco into the stands.

"It was like a magic trick," Tarasco said later. "The ball just disappeared. To me, it was a routine fly ball and I was camped under it, ready to close my glove ... and all of a sudden a glove stuck out. We almost touched gloves. The kid not only reaches out, he reaches down."

Unfortunately for the Orioles, right-field umpire Rich Garcia didn't believe in magic, and evidently didn't notice the 12-year-old magician. In Garcia's view, the ball was destined for the stands. He ruled that the Jeter hit was a home run, tying the score at 4–4. Tarasco and Oriole manager Davey Johnson argued vehemently that Maier had interfered with the catch, but their arguments only moved Garcia to eject Johnson from the game.

The tied game went into extra innings and the Yankees won it in the eleventh on an undisputed home run by Bernie Williams. TV replays clearly showed that Maier had reached out into the field of play to deflect the ball into the stands. Watching the replay in the umpire's locker room after the game, Garcia admitted that Maier had interfered with the play. He didn't believe, however, that Tarasco could have caught the ball. The most the umpire was willing to acknowledge was that the ball probably wouldn't have left the park without Maier's help. In which case, the proper call would have awarded Jeter a ground-rule double, not a home run.

Maier didn't actually catch the ball cleanly. It rolled up his arm and dropped into the front row of seats, where another fan snatched it away. Even though he lost the ball, the twelve-year-old became an instant celebrity. TV cameras showed him riding on the shoulders of fans in the right-field stands, and NBC interviewed him as part of their post-game show. It turned out he was playing hooky from school, on the strength of a note claiming he had an appointment with his orthodontist.

Jeffrey Maier's fifteen minutes of fame stretched into twenty-four hours when ABC put him and his family up at the Plaza Hotel so that he could get up early the next day and appear on *Good Morning America*. That appearance was followed by a guest shot on *Live with Regis and Kathie Lee*, ABC's morning talk show. The *New York Daily News* joined the media feeding frenzy with a front-page "Kid Glove" story. *News* personnel also took the Maiers to lunch at the All-Star Café in midtown Manhattan and then transported them by limousine to the second game of the ALCS, where they provided the family with seats directly behind the Yankee dugout.

Perhaps fearing that they might launch an epidemic of fan interference, the Yankees were uncharacteristically restrained in their treatment of the guests of the *Daily News* and failed to acknowledge the presence of the Maiers on the Stadium's public address system. Yankee manager Joe Torre tried to put the adulation accorded the boy in perspective by saying, "I think it's glorifying the wrong thing." Yankee fans were not so restrained in acknowledging Maier's partner in crime. The loudest cheers at the Game Two introductions were reserved for umpire Rich Garcia, whose blown call on Maier's interference kept the Yankees in Game One long enough to claim their eleventh-inning victory. Local politicians couldn't resist the temptation to elbow their way into the media spotlight trained on the twelve-year-old. Mayor Rudolph Giuliani and Governor George Pataki rushed to defend Maier's action, and Senator Alphonse D'Amato called his interference "almost a miracle."

Twelve-year-old Jeffrey Maier reaches into the field to deflect a Derek Jeter fly ball into the Yankee Stadium stands before it could reach the outstretched glove of Oriole outfielder Tony Tarasco in the first game of the 1996 American League Championship Series. Umpire Rich Garcia failed to see the interference and improperly ruled that the Jeter hit was a game-tying home run. When the Yankees won the game in the eleventh inning, Maier was carried off on the shoulders of celebrating Yankee fans and feted by national TV and the New York press for his action, which should have earned him ejection from the park (AP Photo/Ron Frehm).

The Orioles protested the outcome of Game One, but league president Gene Budig denied the protest, noting that an umpire's judgment call cannot be appealed, even though Garcia later admitted publicly that, had he initially seen Maier, he would have called interference and not a home run. Bolstered by their Game One gift, the Yankees went on to take the Championship Series four games to one.

Baltimore manager Davey Johnson, who was ejected from the game by Garcia and upset over the hero's treatment accorded Jeffrey Maier, said, "I never like to believe that one play can win or lose a game, but this is as close as you're ever going to see." Yankee manager Joe Torre countered by observing, "Controversial calls are a part of the game. Some go your way, some don't. Hell, this is no different than if an umpire missed a double play or something."

In Johnson's defense, the difference between a proper call on the play and the call Garcia made marked the difference between a potential out and a game-altering home run. A huge difference. By way of contrast, an (improper) ruling of interference on the ball that Steve Bartman deflected away from the glove of Moises Alou would have meant the difference between a potential out and another pitch to a batter with a 3-and-2 count.

Hometown media bias is evident in the treatment of both the Bartman and Maier incidents. The Chicago papers assumed that hometown player Moises Alou would have caught the Castillo foul if Bartman hadn't deflected the ball. The New York papers, and Rich Garcia in hindsight, assumed that the visiting Oriole Tony Tarasco would have missed the catch if Maier hadn't gotten his glove in the way. Of the two outfielders, though, Tarasco had the easier play. Alou had to leap and get his glove in position over a railing to catch a ball that was disappearing from view, while Tarasco only had to leap for a ball falling in full view.

It's difficult not to sympathize with Jeffrey Maier, a twelve-year-old Yankee fan afforded the opportunity to catch a home-run ball off the bat of Derek Jeter. It's understandable that he would follow his primal instincts and reach out into the field of play. Just watch the fever spread among older, more experienced fans whenever a foul ball lands in their vicinity. What is less justifiable is the position taken by the New York media and politicians in making Maier a hero for an action that should have gotten him expelled from the game.

It's ironic that Jeffrey Maier, a fan who interfered illegally with play in a championship game would be feted and treated as a hero, while Steve Bartman, who didn't reach into the field of play, is castigated and hounded as an enemy of the people. Again, the Maier enshrinement reflects both the power and the bias of the New York media. His treatment would have been very different if he'd scooped an Oriole fly ball into the stands. Bobby Bonilla, a Bronx native and the Oriole outfielder replaced by Tarasco, described this difference eloquently when he observed of Jeter's drive, "if one of the Orioles had hit it, the kid would have been strung up on Throg's Neck Bridge."

Just ask Steve Bartman.

Chapter Sixteen

Blown Calls

> When you miss one, you know you're gonna get hollered at, and when you're an umpire, no matter what you do, someone's gonna holler at you.
>
> John Kibler
> National League Umpire, 1963 to 1989

> You're blind, ump, you're blind, ump.
> You must be out of your mind, ump.
>
> Richard Adler and Jerry Ross
> "Six Months out of Every Year"
> From *Damn Yankees*

♦ ♦ ♦ ♦

The first sentence of the official rules of baseball stipulates that:

Baseball is a game between two teams of nine players each, under direction of a manager, played on an enclosed field in accordance with these rules, under jurisdiction of one or more umpires.

Maligned though they may be, umpires are essential to the game. Anyone who has tried umpiring at any level, from the sandlots to the majors, can attest that it is a tough, demanding job. Ford Frick, one-time National League president and commissioner of baseball for fifteen years, is on record as saying that, "Good umpires are tougher to find than good ballplayers."

On a good day, nobody notices the umpire. On a bad day, though, thousands of fans boo him, players confront and curse him, and managers kick dirt on his shoes. A major league umpiring team makes upwards of 300 decisions a day, many of them close enough to go either way, ensuring a disagreement from one side or the other. When even close calls generate arguments, all hell can break loose on those rare occasions when an umpire makes a call that is blatantly and obviously wrong. In this age of omnipresent cameras, stop-motion photography, and instant replays, the evidence of a blown call is immediately brought before the bar of the radio and TV audience, debated on *Baseball Tonight*, and recycled in the next morning's sports pages. In theory, at least, over the course of a long 162-game season, blown calls, like bloop hits and bad hops, will even out. In a short, best-of-seven championship series, however, bad calls have influenced the outcome of crucial games, and even the World Series itself.

Scapegoat: Don Denkinger's Death Threats

Blown post-season calls by umpires inevitably resurrect the story of Don Denkinger and his role in the 1985 Series outcome. This story also featured a botched pop-up by Jack Clark and a passed ball by Darrell Porter and has been related in earlier chapters. Whitey Herzog's Cardinals led the Kansas City Royals three games to two and held a 1–0 lead going into the bottom of the ninth inning of Game Six. Throughout the season and post season, the Cards had never been beaten when they carried a lead into the ninth inning, winning 91 times, and now they found themselves just three outs away from the world championship.

The first batter up in the ninth for Kansas City, pinchhitter Jorge Orta grounded a slow roller that first baseman Jack Clark fielded and threw to pitcher Todd Worrell covering first. The throw appeared to arrive well in advance of Orta, but Denkinger spread his palms in the "safe" call. TV replays clearly indicated that Orta was out, and the Cards argued vehemently, with Worrell pointing out that Orta's foot had landed on his own after the ball was in his glove, but Denkinger stood his ground and Orta stood on first. Steaming over the injustice, the Cardinals promptly fell apart. A misjudged pop-up, a solid single, a passed ball, and a broken-bat blooper off the bat of Dane Iorg brought the tying and winning runs across the plate.

Cardinal manager Herzog blasted the umpires in a post-game interview. "The two best teams are supposed to be in the World Series," he ranted in the *New York Times*. "They ought to have the best umpires in it too. I think it's a disgrace. It's a joke. We haven't got one call from those American League umpires in this thing. You want my opinion? It stinks."

Herzog aimed his sharpest barbs at Denkinger, who was scheduled to be the plate umpire

The base reference for blown calls is umpire Don Denkinger's ruling on Kansas City's Jorge Orta, which affected the outcome of the 1985 World Series. With the Cardinals clinging to a 1–0 lead and three outs away from winning the championship, Denkinger called Orta safe at first leading off the ninth inning. Cardinal pitcher Todd Worrell argued, and TV replays confirmed, that the ball was in his glove when Orta's foot landed on his shoe. With the help of a botched pop-up, a single, a passed ball, and a bloop hit, the Royals turned the bad call into a 2–1 victory to even the Series and blew out the Cardinals the next day to win the championship (Ronald C. Modra, *Sports Illustrated*).

in Game Seven the next day. "And we got that guy behind the plate tomorrow," he said. "We got about as much chance of winning as a monkey."

Herzog's observation proved prescient. The Cards imploded the next day. They hadn't played at a high enough level to overcome the bad call on Orta and win Game Six, but they played at such a low level in Game Seven they disgraced themselves. Plate umpire Denkinger ejected both Herzog and relief pitcher Joaquin Andujar for arguing balls and strikes as the Royals scored six runs in the fifth inning and gave the Cardinals an 11–0 shellacking behind 21-year-old Cy Young winner Bret Saberhagen.

Ignoring the Cardinals' failure to hit throughout the Series—they batted a measly .185 and scored only 13 runs in the seven games—and their self-immolation in the final two games, the St. Louis management, press, and fans placed the blame for their loss squarely on the shoulders of Don Denkinger. The St. Louis *Post Dispatch* led the attack by referring to the umpire as "Jesse James," and a local disc jockey gave out the phone number and address of Denkinger's home in Waterloo, Iowa, so that fans could harass him in the off-season.

Denkinger admitted that he'd made a bad call after viewing the replay and conferring with Commissioner Peter Ueberroth. "I got myself caught in a position nobody likes," the umpire said, as quoted in Eric Enders' *100 Years of the World Series*, "I had to depend on watching the foot and listening for the sound of the ball in the glove, but the crowd was so loud I couldn't hear it.... When I found out I missed it, I was just sick. But you have to leave it there. No one ever missed one intentionally."

After the Series, Denkinger arrived home in Waterloo to find bags full of hate mail and death threats. Local police patrolled his block to provide protection, and the hate mail eventually subsided. Denkinger went on to umpire for 13 more years, retiring in 1998 after 31 years of active service to become an evaluator and supervisor of umpires. To this day, though, fans in St. Louis grouse that his call cost them the 1985 World championship, and he has become the poster boy for controversial Series calls.

Escaped Goats

Doug Eddings and the Not-Yet-Out Call

The White Sox and Angels were tied 1–1 with two out and no one on base in the bottom of the ninth of the second game of the 2005 American League Championship Series. When Sox catcher A. J. Pierzynski, swinging wildly with two strikes on him, missed a low breaking split-finger fastball from Angel pitcher Kelvim Escobar, it appeared that the game would go to extra innings. Plate Umpire Doug Eddings pumped his right fist in a "you're out" motion as Angel catcher Josh Paul rolled the ball back toward the mound and began running for the visitor's dugout.

Pierzynski took two steps across home plate toward the hometeam dugout, then dropped his bat and ran toward first base while the Angels stood by and watched. The batter reached first base without a play and was ruled safe by Eddings. In the ensuing dust-up, Eddings explained to Angel manager Mike Scioscia that he ruled that catcher Paul had trapped the ball, so that the receiver needed to tag Pierzynski or throw the ball to first for a force-out. What about the apparent thumb-up "out" call? According to Eddings, that was his "mechanic" for a third-strike call, not an "out" call.

Pierzynski was allowed to stay at first base, and the ruling proved costly to the Angels. Pinch runner Pablo Ozuna stole second base and then scored the winning run when Joe Crede lashed a double to left field. The White Sox didn't lose another post-season game, winning the championship series four games to one and sweeping the Astros in the World Series.

Catcher Josh Paul insisted that he had caught the ball cleanly. "As a catcher, naturally, if the ball bounces, you're going to pick it up and try to tag him or throw it to first. I didn't need

With the score tied 1–1 in the bottom of the ninth of Game Two of the American League Championship Series in 2005, White Sox hitter A. J. Pierzynski swung and missed at a low breaking pitch for what appeared to be the final out of the inning. After pumping his fist in an apparent "out" call, umpire Doug Eddings ruled that Angel catcher Josh Paul had trapped the ball, and Pierzynski took first in the ensuing confusion. Joe Crede then won the game for Chicago with a double (AP Photo/Charles Rex Arbogast).

to do that because I caught it." Replays of the controversial pitch appeared to confirm Paul's claim that he caught the ball before it hit the ground.

Even so, veteran catchers commenting on the play observed that Paul should have tagged Pierzynski anyhow, "just to make sure." "If it's questionable, you tag the guy. You have to," said Jason Kendall of the Oakland A's. It's not a mistake Paul is likely to make again. In the future, receivers crouched in front of Eddings can be expected to tag batters following any third-strike catch made below the kneecaps.

Granting that Paul's failure to follow through with a "just in case" tag was a mistake, the play started with Eddings' bad call. The video replay showed that the call was a close one, but, of course, Eddings didn't have the benefit of a replay. He also didn't ask for help from other members of his umpiring team, and compounded his mistaken call with a thumb-up "out" gesture that essentially froze every Angel except Paul, who, with his back to Eddings, was rolling the ball toward the mound. In the absence of the gesture, the pitcher Escobar might have fielded the rolling ball and tossed it to first ahead of Pierzynski.

After the game, Eddings defended his decision, but faulted himself for failing to "sell" the trap call by saying "no catch." He insisted that he never verbally called Pierzynski out, and reiterated his claim that he pumped his closed fist after every strike call, and that it shouldn't be confused with his "out" call. Needless to say, the Angels were far from satisfied with this explanation. *L. A. Times* columnist Bill Plaschke wrote, "Missing the trap call is understandable. Explaining that an 'out' call is a "'not-yet-out' call is utter nonsense."

Credit Pierzynski with a heads-up play. He had the presence of mind to comprehend the situation and take advantage of it. A catcher himself, he had been victimized by a similar play in San Francisco a year earlier, when Red Sox pitcher Bronson Arroyo wound up on first courtesy of a mishandled third strike.

Addressing the press after the game, Angel manager Mike Scioscia, an ex-catcher himself, focused on Eddings' thumb-up "out" call, saying, "he rang him up with his fist," but then took a longer view of the situation with an observation that spoke well for his professionalism. "We didn't play at a high enough level tonight to win the ball game," he told reporters. "That's the bottom line. You have to play at a high enough level so that if there's a call you don't get, or something happens, a bloop hit, or whatever it might be, you have to play at a high enough level ... to absorb that. We just didn't get it done tonight."

The box score of the game bears out Scioscia's classy analysis. The Angels made three errors, and the first White Sox run came in the first inning after pitcher Jarrod Washburn overthrew first base to allow leadoff hitter Scott Posednick to reach second base. Posednick moved to third and later scored on a Jermaine Dye groundout. *Baseball Weekly* columnist Paul White observed that poor timing compounded Eddings' problem. If his missed call had led to a first-inning run, and Washburn's misplay had come in the ninth, Eddings' call would have been forgotten and Washburn would have been measured for goat horns. As it was, Eddings joined a not-so-select list of arbiters whose controversial calls helped to decided crucial play-off games and World Series outcomes.

Press coverage of the Eddings call inevitably invoked the name of Don Denkinger and his blown call twenty years earlier. The *Los Angeles Times* called the Eddings affair "Denkinger Squared," and *Baseball Weekly* interviewed Denkinger just after he'd called Eddings to offer sympathy and support.

Ken Burkhart's Behind-the-Back Call

The first game of the 1970 World Series between the Baltimore Orioles and the Cincinnati Reds featured a play in which all the participants performed so ineptly that, according to John G. Robertson in *Baseball's Greatest Controversies*, "it is used in umpiring instructional videos to demonstrate how *not* to make a call."

The Reds came up in the bottom of the sixth inning with the score tied at 3–3. The first Cincinnati batter, Lee May, scorched a hot shot toward third but was thrown out, a victim of the first of many sensational fielding plays Series MVP Brooks Robinson would turn in that October. Oriole pitcher Jim Palmer then walked Bernie Carbo, who was singled to third by Tommy Helms. Pinch hitter Ty Cline swung over a pitch and chopped it high in the air off home plate. Catcher Elrod Hendricks moved a few feet down the third-base line to take in the ball as soon as it dropped within reach. Umpire Ken Burkhart moved with him so that he would be in a position to call the ball fair or foul. Hendricks snatched the ball out of the air in fair territory and was transferring it to his throwing hand when he heard Palmer yell "Tag him." In concentrating on the falling baseball, both Hendricks and Burkhart had ignored the runner Carbo, who made an ill-advised attempt to score from third on Cline's high bouncer.

Seeing Carbo bearing down on the plate, Hendricks whirled to tag him and collided with umpire Burkhart, who had stood in place after calling Cline's hit fair. Burkhart fell to his knees, blocking Carbo's path to the plate and Hendricks' path to Carbo. Hendricks lunged over the umpire, tagging Carbo with his glove as the runner tried to slide around the downed umpire. Burkhart wound up on the seat of his pants, raising his fist in an "out" call.

A series of stop-action photographs in the paper the next day showed that Hendricks did in fact tag Carbo with his glove before the runner's foot touched home plate. Unfortunately, the ball was still in the catcher's throwing hand as he applied the glove-hand tag. It might not have mattered, since Carbo's slide took him wide of the plate, but Carbo touched the plate inadvertently on his way back to argue with Burkhart.

The photos also clearly showed that Burkhart had his back turned at the time of the phantom tag. Rather than admit his call was guesswork, he insisted later that he saw the play over his shoulder. Against all the evidence, Hendricks was convinced that he had made a valid tag and Carbo swore that his hook slide had caught the plate. Thus, all three participants claimed to have carried out their assigned tasks successfully, even though the photographic record showed that all three had failed miserably.

Umpire Ken Burkhart manages to entangle himself with Oriole catcher Elrod Hendricks as Cincinnati's Bernie Carbo tries to score from third on a high bouncer near home plate. Hendricks reaches around Burkhart to tag the sliding Carbo with his empty glove (AP/Wide World Photos).

Burkhart makes the mistaken "out" call from the seat of his pants as Carbo, who missed home plate with his slide, comes back to argue, inadvertently touching home (and thereby scoring) on the return trip (AP/Wide World Photos).

Burkhart's blown call cost the Reds a run and effectively stifled their rally. The next batter lined out to center for the third out and Cincinnati failed to score again in the game, losing 4–3 when Brooks Robinson homered in the top of the seventh.

Reds manager Sparky Anderson took a remarkably relaxed view of Burkhart's role in the game's outcome, damning the umpire with faint praise in a UPI release.

> I don't want any umpire out there to be crucified when he's not wrong. Burkhart was not wrong. Sure, the way the play developed, my man was safe. But if Burkhart's not there, it's a routine play and Carbo's out by ten feet. He called him out because he knew he blocked off Hendricks. We got beat 4-to-3 and I'm not mad at anybody. If we got a few more runs, no one would even be talking about this play. The umpires are honest and sincere and they're trying to do a good job. I'm not going to jump on them.

Baltimore went on to win the Series four games to one, so it's hard to make the case that Burkhart's blown decision cost the Reds the championship. Given the fact that he made it on his butt with his back turned, his call remains one of the most ignominious in Series history.

Burkhart never again umpired in a World Series, retiring from active duty in 1973. He'd started his career as a pitcher, winning 19 games and losing 8 for the Cardinals in 1945, his rookie year. An arm injury had kept him out of the armed services and forced him to deliver the ball with an unusual shot-put motion, and he faded from the majors as the veteran players returned from World War II. He made it back to the bigs as an umpire in 1957, serving for seventeen years without missing a regular season game, and finished his career as a supervisor of umpires.

Bill Stewart and the Timed Pickoff

The first game of the 1948 World Series between the Cleveland Indians and the Boston Braves was marred by a missed call that cost Bob Feller, the premier power pitcher of his day, his chance to record a World Series win. Lou Boudreau, the player–manager of the Indians, had worked out a timed pickoff play with his pitching staff. Boudreau would flash the signal for the play from his shortstop position, count to three, and arrive at second base just in time to take a pickoff throw from the pitcher. To make sure umpires didn't miss the play, he would let them in on the signal, an open glove resting against his left knee. Because the three National League umpires assigned to call the Series had never seen the play, Boudreau took special pains to alert them to the timed move prior to the first game of the Series. National League umpire Bill Stewart, a 15-year veteran who was umpiring in his third World Series, reportedly resented Boudreau's attempt to educate the umpiring crew, boasting that he'd never been caught off guard by a pickoff play.

The first game of the Series shaped up as a tight pitching duel between Feller and Braves ace Johnny Sain. Feller allowed only one hit through the first seven innings, but Sain matched him pitch-for-pitch and both teams were scoreless when the Braves came to bat in the bottom of the eighth. A walk, a sacrifice, and an intentional pass put runners on first and second for the Braves when Sain came to the plate. The runner on second, Phil Masi, edged off second base

With no score in the eighth inning of the first game of the 1948 World Series, a pickoff throw from pitcher Bob Feller to the Indians' player–manager Lou Boudreau appears to catch the Braves' Phil Masi off second base. To Boudreau's dismay, umpire Bill Stewart rules Masi safe, and the Brave subsequently scores the only run of the game to saddle Feller with a loss in his first World Series appearance (National Baseball Hall of Fame Library, Cooperstown, N.Y.).

to give himself a better chance of scoring if Sain managed a hit, and Boudreau flashed the pickoff sign. The shortstop counted to three and arrived at second base at the same time as the pickoff throw from Feller, a little ahead of the surprised Masi. Boudreau caught the throw and applied the tag to Masi's shoulder as he dove head-first back to the bag. It appeared to everyone in the park that the pickoff was successful, except that the runner Masi wasn't the only one caught napping by the play. Bill Stewart, umpiring at second base, was as surprised as the runner and called Masi safe. Masi subsequently scored on a single by Tommy Holmes.

The Indians failed to score in the top of the ninth, and Boston won the opening game of the Series 1–0. Photos in the next day's newspapers clearly showed that Boudreau had tagged Masi well before the runner's hand reached second base, so that the run that beat Feller and the Indians was tainted by Stewart's blown call. Since the Indians eventually won the championship four games to two, the blown call didn't affect the Series outcome, but Bob Feller, who lost four years of his Hall of Fame career to World War II and pitched for Cleveland in an era when the New York Yankees dominated American League play, was never able to add a World Series win to his illustrious record.

Art Passarella and the Six-Column Photograph

Johnny Sain, the pitcher who bested Bob Feller in the first game of the 1948 World Series courtesy of Bill Stewart's blown call, was on the other end of a flagrantly bad decision in the fifth game of the 1952 World Series.

With the Dodgers and Yankees even in the Series at two games apiece and tied 5–5 in the bottom of the tenth inning of the fifth game, Sain, now pitching in relief for the Yankees, came to bat against Carl Erskine of the Dodgers. With no runners on, Sain hit a ground ball back through the middle of the diamond. Second baseman Jackie Robinson made a fine backhand stop and threw the ball to first. It appeared that Sain beat the throw, but umpire Art Passarella called the runner out. Both Sain and first-base coach Bill Dickey argued vehemently but futilely. The call stood, and the Dodgers won the game 6–5 when Duke Snider doubled home the deciding run in the eleventh inning.

United Press photographs validated the arguments of Yankees Sain and Dickey. They showed Sain's foot coming down on first base when the ball was still several feet away from the outstretched glove of Dodger first baseman Gil Hodges. When shown the photographic evidence, Baseball Commissioner Ford Frick indicated that Passarella had made a bad call. The *New York Times* quoted Frick as saying, "If I owned a newspaper, I'd blow that picture up to six or eight columns. The boys have missed a few in the past and they will miss a few in the future." The picture accompanying the quote was blown up to cover six columns. It marked one of the few times in baseball history when a commissioner has been openly critical of his umpiring staff.

John Mize, the Yankee first baseman whose fifth-inning home run accounted for three of the Yankee runs and who nearly tied the game in the bottom of the eleventh when his bid for a second homer was kept in the park by the glove of a leaping Carl Furillo, was especially critical of the umpiring around first base. Knowing that Passarella operated an umpiring school in the off-season, Mize said, "There's a guy who should be going to an umpiring school, not running one.... If the call had been right and Sain was on," he speculated, "it could have been a different ball game."

Actually, it's unlikely that Sain's reaching first would have changed the outcome of the game. While it's much more difficult to speculate on the impact of a blown "safe" call that creates an unearned out than a blown "out" call that leaves a runner on base, Dodger pitcher Carl Erskine was particularly effective that day. He sat the Yankees down in order in every inning

Umpire Art Passarella calls Yankee pitcher Johnny Sain out at first, even though Sain clearly beat the throw to Dodger first baseman Gil Hodges in the tenth inning of Game Five of the 1952 World Series. When the Dodgers won the game 6–5 in the eleventh, this photograph appeared in the next day's newspapers and elicited an open criticism of the call from Baseball Commissioner Ford Frick (National Baseball Hall of Fame Library, Cooperstown N.Y.).

except the fifth, when the Bronx Bombers scored all five of their runs. Thus he pitched nine perfect innings, retiring the last nineteen men he faced (counting Sain) in order. Erskine recalled the aftermath of his feat in his *Tales from the Dodger Dugout*:

> Johnny Sain was waiting for me the next day and gave me a real chewing out for getting such an undeserved win. He was really worked up over the call (by Passarella). After enduring his sour grapes for several minutes, I said, "Johnny, who got the win in the 1948 World Series when Masi was picked off second base?" What goes around, comes around.

It's unlikely that Passarella's call affected the outcome of the fifth game, and it certainly didn't affect the outcome of the Series, since the Yankees came back to win it four games to three.

Passarella retired from umpiring the next year after serving thirteen years in the major leagues. The Associated Press announcement of his retirement said that "Passarella refused to comment on his reasons or on his plans, other than to say that he hoped 'to remain in baseball in some capacity.'" His hopes to stay in the game weren't fulfilled, but he went on to pursue an acting career that included a role in the film *Damn Yankees* and ten years as a police sergeant alongside Michael Douglas and Karl Malden in the TV series *The Streets of San Francisco*.

Other Calls and Consequences

Career Consequences. While managers and players may argue vehemently on the field, most tend to accept bad calls as a part of the game and recognize that a winning team must play at a high enough level to overcome the temporary setback of a botched decision. Fans are less forgiving, but few umpires have achieved the level of notoriety accorded to scapegoats like Fred Merkle, Mickey Owen, and Bill Buckner. Don Denkinger's name invariably surfaces whenever a controversial call surfaces in a play-off game, but Denkinger umpired for thirteen years after the 1985 World Series and had built enough respect by the time he retired from the field to be named a supervisor of umpires. Other umpires remembered for conspicuously blown calls have also been rewarded in this fashion. Both Ken Burkhart, who made the behind-the-back call on Bernie Carbo, and Rich Garcia, who failed to see Jeffrey Maier's intrusive glove, went on to become umpire supervisors.

Of the umpires discussed in this chapter, only Art Passarella's career may have been affected adversely by his blown call. Even though his mistaken "out" call against Johnny Sain and the Yankees had little impact on the outcome of the game (and certainly no impact on the outcome of the World Series), it marked one of the few times in which the commissioner of baseball acknowledged publicly than an umpire had blown a call. Coincidentally (or perhaps not), it was the only call cited in this chapter that went against a New York team, and the only blown call the *New York Times* saw fit to blow up to a six-column treatment. Passarella resigned the following year, refusing to discuss his decision, but expressing a hope (which never materialized) that he might stay in baseball in some capacity.

Other Calls. Blown calls by umpires have figured in more than one of the scapegoat stories cited earlier in this book. As already noted, Don Denkinger's blown call on Jorge Orta in the 1985 World Series jump-started Kansas City's comeback and helped to deflect scapegoat

Umpire Hank O'Day, whose 1908 ruling on Fred Merkle was called the "worst decision in the history of baseball" by Hall of Fame umpire Bill Klem forty-three years after it helped to cost the Giants the pennant (Library of Congress, Prints and Photographs Division).

status from Jack Clark's botched pop-up and Darrell Porter's passed ball. After viewing the videotapes, Rich Garcia admitted he blew his home-run call when Jeffrey Maier interfered with Tony Tarasco and carried Derek Jeter's fly ball into the stands. Doug Harvey's "out" call when Lou Brock failed to slide in the 1975 Series still generates controversy in St. Louis, but the call was so close that repeated examination of the film fails to support a conclusion one way or the other. And Bill Klem, the first umpire to be inducted into Baseball's Hall of Fame, called Hank O'Day's ruling on Fred Merkle's blunder "the worst decision in the history of baseball" forty-three years after it helped to cost the Giants the 1908 pennant. Klem argued that O'Day had been wrong to accept a technicality and ignore "perhaps half a century of custom, usage, tradition, and the intent of the rule."

In the second edition of his *Historical Baseball Abstract*, Bill James supported Klem's argument, writing that if Merkle's action was, in fact, common practice, "then the umpire used poor judgment in deciding to commence enforcement of the rule at that particular moment, when the pennant was on the line."

A Chickenshit Call. The injustice of enforcing a technicality for the first time at a key moment in a championship race came home to me personally when I was managing my son's little-league team, a minor-league team for players 9 and 10 years old. Major-league teams in our area of California were run by dedicated coaches who scouted young talent and fielded teams of 11- and 12-year-olds (with a few promising younger players) year after year, whether or not they had a son in the system. Almost half the teams in the minors were run by dedicated non-parents waiting for a coaching slot to open up in the major leagues. The other half were coached by volunteer parents like myself.

Because the dedicated "semiprofessional" coaches spent time scouting youngsters from year to year and had a keener eye for talent than the "amateur" parent–coaches like myself, their teams were usually the stronger entries in the league. When my son Wayne was ten, though, our team, the Pacific Union Bank, was tied for the league lead with a team managed by one of the dedicated major-league coaches-in-waiting. In a head-to-head late-season meeting that was to decide the league championship, the two teams were tied 6–6 going into the final inning. In the top of the inning, our right fielder, an enthusiastic nine-year-old named Richie, who was playing in the shadow of his ten-year-old brother and whose arms and legs never seemed to be on the same page, made a rare trip to first base courtesy of a walk and went to second on an infield out. When the next batter hit a ball off the opposing shortstop's glove, Richie took off for third and, ignoring (or, more likely, not even seeing, since third base was largely uncharted territory for him) the third-base coach's signal to hold up, rounded the base and headed home.

The opposing shortstop retrieved the ball and, with plenty of time to nail Richie at the plate, looped a throw well over the catcher's head, nearly clearing the top bar of the backstop. As the catcher backed up to retrieve the ball, Richie slid into home in a cloud of dust and jumped up with a triumphant smile on his face, proud to have scored the go-ahead run. Proud, that is, until we heard the umpire call "you're out."

Richie turned around, red-faced, and I hurried to the plate. Non-confrontational by nature, I'd always tended to accept umpires' decisions without complaining, but I could feel my non-confrontational resolve fading fast. By the time I arrived at home plate, the umpire, a neighbor, had taken off his mask and folded his arms across his ample chest in an imitation of a major-league arbiter. "The runner is out," he repeated. "The rules forbid sliding into home plate."

Stopped short by his statement, and by my belief that adults have no business arguing with little-league umpires, all I could muster was, "You've got to be kidding."

The umpire reached into his hip pocket and pulled out a small black book. "It's against the rules."

"But teams have been doing it all year," I said. "Where's the harm? The catcher wasn't anywhere near the plate."

The umpire refolded his arms. "I don't care. It's against the rules."

Richie was jumping up and down waving his arms disjointedly, and shouting "He never touched me. He never touched me."

I decided to imitate a big-league manager and get between my player and the umpire. I grabbed Richie by one flailing arm and turned him around. "It's okay," I said. "You're right. He never touched you."

"Then why am I out?"

Embarrassed that I had blithely assumed little-league rules were just big-league rules on a tighter diamond, I got Richie headed back to our bench and said, "There's a rule against sliding home." Then I shrugged my shoulders and raised my voice a little and added "Evidently," loud enough for the umpire to hear with as much sarcasm as I could muster under the circumstances.

Richie, not worried that the umpire might hear, said, "Well, it's a chickenshit rule."

The word *chickenshit* didn't sit well with my umpiring neighbor. "You're out of the game, young man," he shouted.

Richie's face turned red again, tears formed in his eyes, and I could see the baby of a great big tantrum pushing its way toward birth as he tried to turn back to the umpire. Fortunately, I had a firm enough grip on his scrawny forearm to keep him headed back to our bench. "Don't worry, I said. We'll beat them anyhow." But we didn't beat them. We failed to score in our half of the inning and lost the game and our hold on first place when they pushed across the winning run in their half.

After that day, I never saw my neighbor without thinking of the way he'd turned Richie into a miniature Fred Merkle by invoking an obscure rule. The memory came back in full force some years later when he left our driveway after a short visit. Our driveway curves downhill and can be difficult to negotiate in the dark, so we installed a light on a pole at the head of the hill. Unfortunately, we put the pole a little too close to the drive itself, and every couple of years a visitor would misjudge the curve at the top of the slope, back into the light pole, and knock it over.

The following scene would then repeat itself. The embarrassed driver would ring our doorbell, apologize, and offer to pay for the light standard. I'd always decline the offer, explaining that all we had to do was replace a four-foot length of pipe and a junction box, and that by now we had a lot of experience doing it. When my neighbor, the ex-umpire, left, I had just closed the door when I heard the familiar snap of the light pole. I waited at the door for the expected ring, but it didn't come. Finally, I peeked through the blinds and watched my neighbor squat beside the broken pole, examine his bumper, size up the fallen light standard, glance up and down the street, look down at our house, get back inside his car, and drive away. It was a chickenshit thing to do, but somehow I wasn't surprised.

Chapter Seventeen

Errors, Scapegoats, and Escaped Goats

> It is designed to break your heart. The game begins in the spring, when everything else begins again, and it blossoms in the summer, filling the afternoons and evenings, and then as soon as the chill rains come, it stops and leaves you to face the fall alone, You count on it, you rely on it to buffer the passage of time, to keep the memory of sunshine and high skies alive, and then, just when the days are all twilight, when you need it most, it stops.
>
> A. Bartlett Giamatti
> Future commissioner of baseball, 1977

♦ ♦ ♦ ♦

Scapegoats are distinguished by errors that they have made, or were judged to have made, at critical moments of crucial games. But not all errors are created equal. Apparent mental errors such as Fred Merkle's blunder seem to weigh more heavily in the creation of scapegoats than physical misplays. And some physical errors brand a player for life, while other players can make the same mistake under similar circumstances and escape with nothing but a single sentence in the next day's newspaper. The fly ball Fred Snodgrass dropped in Game Seven of the 1912 World Series marked him for life, and his "$30,000 muff" headlined his obituary. On the other hand, Max Flack dropped a fly ball to let in the two runs that beat the Cubs in the final game of the 1918 World Series, but his name is virtually unknown today, even to diehard Cubs fans.

The stories in this book make it clear that errors have helped to decide a large number of pennant races and post-season games. This fact raises a number of questions: Do post-season pressures lead to more errors than a team makes in regular season play? And what sorts of conditions combine to cause one player to be branded for life as a scapegoat while another escapes opprobrium all together?

Errors in the Season and Series

First, there's the question of post-season misplays: Do teams become more error-prone in crucial World Series games? And are losing teams consistently more error-prone than winning teams? Exhibit 17.1 traces the incidence of errors per nine innings by pennant-winning teams during the regular season and the World Series. Two charts are given, one for World Series winners and one for World Series losers. Statistics are organized by decades in an attempt to normalize the wide swings in annual data and highlight trends over time.

A few patterns are evident in the cross-hatched bars graphing the seasonal incidence of

Exhibit 17.1
Errors Per Game: Season vs. Series

WINNING TEAMS

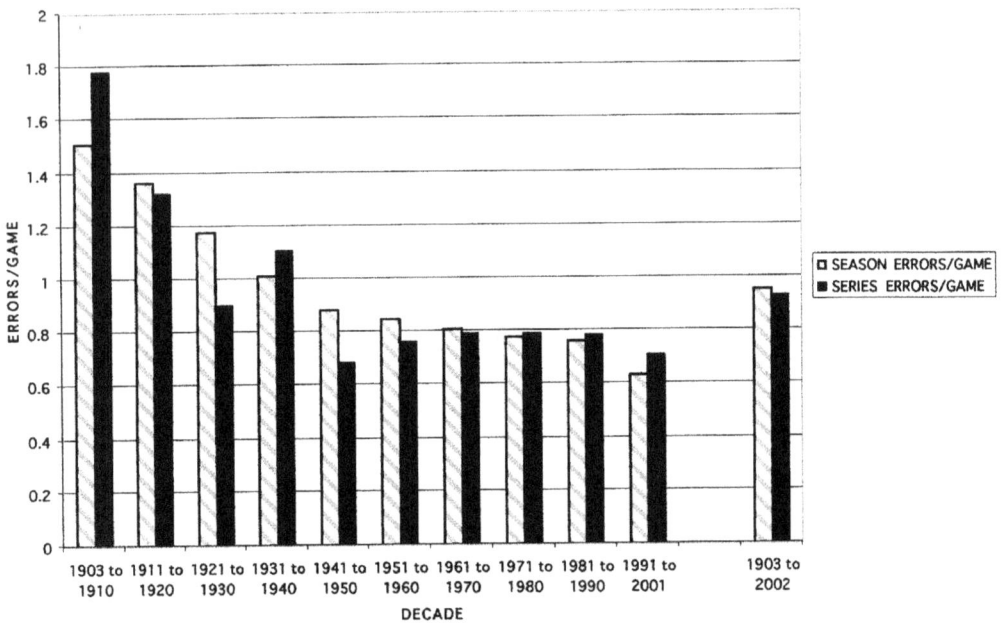

LOSING TEAMS

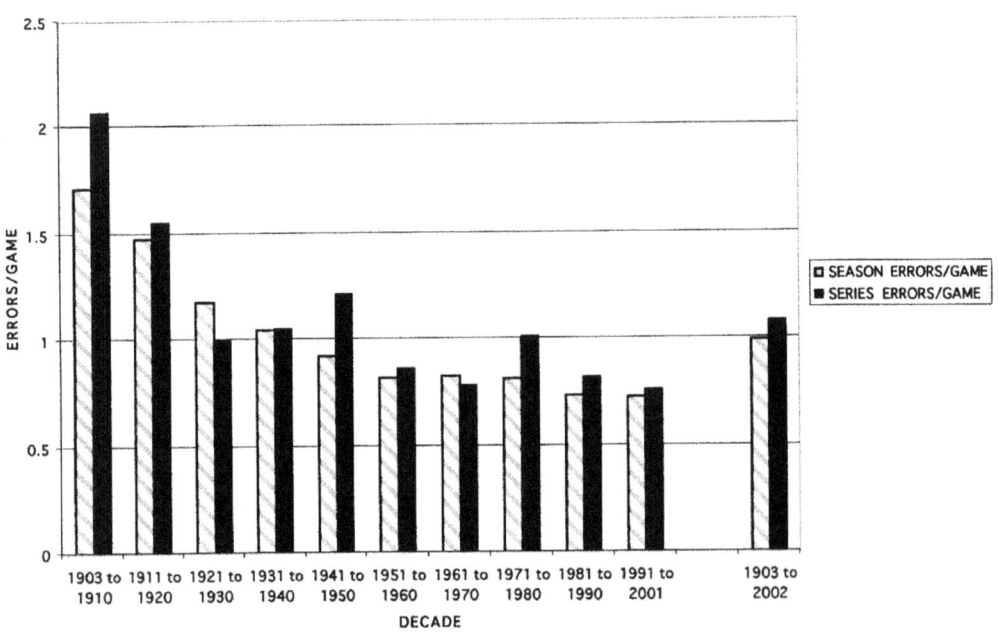

Graphs compare the decade-by-decade incidence of errors per game allowed by pennant-winning teams during the season and during the World Series.

errors. Miscues were much more frequent in the early years of modern baseball, then dropped steadily as park conditions improved, ground crews grew, equipment got better, and gloves became larger and better padded. The average number of errors per game dropped from over 1.5 in the decade before 1910 to less than half that number in the 1990s.

From 1903 to 1910, World Series participants (both winners and losers) made more errors per game in the Series than they had during the regular season. After this jittery start, there's no clear relationship between season and Series error rates. An overall season vs. series comparison of errors per game for the first hundred years of the fall classic appears at the far right-hand side of each graph. It shows that the number of errors per game registered by Series winners dropped slightly below their season record (from .95 errors per game during the season to .93 during the Series), while the Series losers experienced a slight increase in their error rate (from .99 errors per game during the season to 1.08 during the Series). In the long run, bad breaks and errors tend to even out, but this leveling process takes longer than a single Series, or even a single decade.

Over the 100+ year history of the World Series, then, the number of errors per game registered by Series participants was not significantly different from the number registered during the season. Of course, working with averages can mask a few key distinctions. Fred Snodgrass' fielding percentage during the 1912 season was exactly the same, .947, as his fielding percentage during the 1912 World Series. But the one error he made in the Series haunted him for life.

Characteristics of Scapegoats and Escaped Goats

Exhibits 17.2 and 17.3 contain two matrices that associate each player labeled as a "scapegoat" or "escaped goat" with a number of key characteristics. Listed in rough order of their importance, these characteristics are:

1. Did the misplay lead to the loss of a game and/or a championship?
2. Was the player a recognized "superstar?"
3. Did the misplay occur in the late innings (defined as the seventh inning or later)?
4. Did the player perform for a team covered by the East Coast press (here defined as Boston, New York, Philadelphia, Baltimore, or Washington)?
5. Did the misplay cause his team to forfeit a lead *and* lose the game? and
6. Could the misplay be classified as a mental error?

Lost Games and/or Lost Championships

By way of covering all the analytical bases, it should be self-evident that players whose teams win key games, pennants, and world championships get a free pass out of the goat pen. Baseball is a team game, and players whose teams have come back to bail them out of bad spots include Johnny Evers, who helped his Braves battle back after he had held the ball while the A's scored a crucial tenth-inning run in the 1914 World Series, and Byung-Hyun Kim, whose Diamondbacks rebounded to win the 2001 World Series after he had given up game-tying home runs to the Yankees in the ninth inning of two consecutive losses.

Exhibit 17.2
Scapegoat Characteristics

Scapegoat; Pos, Team	Year	Transgression	Lost Lead	East Coast Press	Late Innings	Not a Superstar	Mental Error
Bartman, Steve; fan, Cubs	2003	Tried for pop-up in stands, possibly preventing Alou catch					•
Branca, Ralph; p, Dodgers	1951	Gave up Bobby Thomson's "Shot Heard 'Round the World"	•	•			
Buckner, Bill; 1b, Red Sox	1986	Muffed grounder allowed winning run to score in WS Game 6	•	•	•	•	
Chesbro, Jack; p, Highlanders	1904	Wild pitch let in winning run, costing NY pennant chance	•		•	•	
Denkinger, Don; umpire	1985	Blew call at first, opening door for Royals win in WS Game 6		•	•	•	
Gowdy, Hank; c, Giants	1924	Caught foot in mask, dropped foul pop-up			•	•	•
Lombardi, Ernie; c, Reds	1939	"Snoozed" at home plate as DiMaggio scored final WS run			•	•	•
Merkle, Fred; 1b, Giants	1908	Failure to touch second negated Giant win, forced playoff	•			•	•
Moore, Donnie; p, Angels	1986	Gave up go-ahead homer and lost Game 5 of ALCS	•		•	•	
Owen, Mickey; c, Dodgers	1941	Dropped third strike opened door for Yanks win in WS Game 4	•	•	•	•	•
Peckinpaugh, Roger; ss, Nats	1925	Made record eight errors in 1925 World Series				•	
Pesky, John; ss, Red Sox	1946	Allegedly held ball while Slaughter scored Series-winning run	•		•	•	•
Snodgrass, Fred; cf, Giants	1912	Dropped fly ball opened door for Giant World Series loss	•	•		•	
Williams, Mitch; p, Phils	1993	Gave up Joe Carter's WS Winning Home Run	•		•	•	
Zimmerman, Heinie; 3b, Giants	1917	Chased Eddie Collins home after wild throw put him on base				•	•

Exhibit 17.3 "Escaped Goat" Characteristics

Scapegoat; Pos, Team, Year Transgression / Comments	Lost Lead	East Coast Press	Late Innings	Not a Superstar	Mental Error
Andrews, Mike. 2b, A's. 1973. Botched two grounders in 12th to help cost A's WS Game 2 *"Fired" by Owner Finley, reinstated by Commissioner Kuhn*			•	•	
Bartell, Dick. ss, Tigers. 1940. Held ball while game-tying run scored in Series Game 7 *Detroit press blames crowd noise for misplay*			•	•	•
Berra, Yogi. c, Yanks. 1951. Dropped foul pop-up, jeopardizing Reynolds no-hitter. *Rescued when Ted Williams popped up a second time.*		•	•		
Brock, Lou. lf, Cards. 1968. Tried to score standing up, was tagged out. *Blunder occurred in middle innings of Game Five.*				•	
Bush, Joe. p, A's. 1914. Errant throw let in winning runs in Game 3 of Series. *Held Boston to two runs over nine innings.*		•	•	•	
Byrnes, Eric. lf, A's. 2003. Failed to touch home when throw eluded catcher, was tagged out *Blunder occurred in early innings.*				•	•
Clark, Jack. 1b, Cards. 1985. Allowed foul pop-up to drop, contributing to Series loss *Muff overshadowed by Denkinger miscall.*	•		•		
Davis, Willie. cf, Dodgers. 1966. Lost fly balls in sun, made three errors in one inning *Press and fans forgive sun-burned misplays.*				•	
Doyle, Larry. 2b, Giants. 1911. Failed to touch home with winning run in WS Game 5 *A's failed to appeal play, so run counted and Giants won.*		•	•	•	•
Durham, Leon. 1b, Cubs. 1984. Botched grounder let in tying run, set stage for NLCS loss *Homered early, error followed by three singles in 7th.*	•		•	•	
Eckersley, Dennis. p, A's. 1988. Gave up Gibson Walk-Off Home Run in Series Game 1 *Hall-of-Fame career trumps memory of Gibson home run.*	•		•		
Evers, Johnny. 2b, Braves. 1914. Held ball while run scored in 10th inning of Series Game 3 *Rescued when Braves came back to tie in 10th and win later.*		•	•	•	•
Fernandez, Tony. 2b, Indians. 1997. Botched grounder contributed to Indians Series loss *Cleveland press forgiving, focuses on two RBIs.*			•	•	
Flack, Max. cf, Cubs. 1918. Dropped fly let in winning runs of final Series game *Dropped fly let in winning runs, but occurred in third inning*				•	
Giambi, Jeremy. lf, A's. 2001. Tried to score standing up, was tagged out *Victim of extraordinary play by Jeter.*			•	•	

Scapegoat; Pos, Team, Year Transgression / Comments	Lost Lead	East Coast Press	Late Innings	Not a Superstar	Mental Error
Kaline, Al. rf, Tigers. 1972. Throwing error let in winning run in 11th inning of ALCS Game 1. *Protected by superstar status, earlier home run.*		•		•	
Kim, Byung-Hyun. p, D'backs. 2001. Gave up Game-Tying Two-Run 9th inning homers in Games 4&5 *Rescued when Diamondbacks came back to win Series.*	•		•	•	
Lemon, Bob. p, Indians. 1954. Gave up Rhodes Walk-Off Home Run in Series Game 1 *Gave up only two runs over 9 innings, Chinese homer in 10th.*			•		
Merkle & Meyers. 1b-c, Giants. 1912. Allowed foul pop-up to drop, contributing to Series loss *Muff overshadowed by press treatment of Snodgrass error.*	•	•	•	•	
Meusel, Bob. cf, Yanks. 1926. Dropped fly let in winning runs of final Series game *Muff overshadowed by press focus on Alexander heroics.*	•	•		•	
Miljus, John. p, Pirates. 1927. Wild pitch allowed winning Series run to score *Struck out three of the heavily favored Yankees.*			•	•	
Moose, Bob. p, Pirates. 1972. Wild pitch allowed winning run to score in final NLCS game *Pitch took a bad hop over catcher's shoulder.*	•		•	•	
Porter, Darrell. c, Cards. 1985. Passed ball put tying and winning runs in position in Game 6 *Muff overshadowed by Denkinger miscall.*	•		•	•	
Potter, Nelson. p, Browns. 1944. Made two errors on one play to set up go-ahead run *Muff occurred in early innings.*				•	
Rivera, Mariano. p, Yanks. 2001. Errant throw keyed winning rally in final Series game *Protected by superstar status, record-setting past.*	•	•	•		
Ruth, Babe. rf, Yanks. 1926. Thrown out trying to steal second for final out of Series *Game story focused on Pete Alexander heroics, not final out.*		•	•		
Schiraldi, Calvin. p, Red Sox. 1986. Wild throw on bunt allowed Mets to tie score in 8th of Game 6 *8th inning misplay overshadowed by Buckner's error in 10th.*	•	•	•	•	
Schmidt, Charles. c, Tigers. 1907. Dropped third strike cost Tigers opening Series game *Game stopped by darkness, so Tigers didn't lose.*	•		•	•	
Stanley, Bob. p, Red Sox. 1986. Wild pitch allowed game-tying run to score in Series Game 6 *Wild pitch overshadowed by press focus on Buckner error.*	•	•	•	•	

Scapegoat; Pos, Team, Year Transgression / Comments	Lost Lead	East Coast Press	Late Innings	Not a Superstar	Mental Error
Stephens, Vern. ss, Browns. 1944. Errant throw keyed winning rally in final Series game *Muff occurred in early innings.*		•		•	
Stewart, Dave. p, A's. 1990. Errant throw keyed winning rally in final Series game *Hard to fault pitcher who gave up one earned run in 9 innings.*	•		•	•	
Tejada, Miguel. ss, A's. 2003. Stopped to argue interference call, was tagged out *Blunder occurred in early innings.*					•
Terry, Ralph. p, Yanks. 1960. Gave up Mazeroski Series-winning Home Run *Redeemed by getting McCovey for last out of 1962 Series.*		•	•	•	
Tolan, Bobby. cf, Reds. 1972. Error provided margin of difference in WS finale. *Error occurred in first inning.*				•	
Wagner, Honus. ss, Pirates. 1903. Made six errors in first World Series *Protected by superstar status.*	•				
Wilson, Art. c, Cubs. 1917. Inattention allowed winning run in "Double No-Hitter" *Game story focused on "Double No-Hitter."*	•		•	•	•
Wilson, Hack. cf, Cubs. 1929. Lost too fly balls in sun to contribute to 10-run inning *Press and fans forgive sun-burned misplays.*	•				
Wilson, Jimmy. c, Cards. 1931. Misplayed third strike prolonged final inning *Rescued when A's failed to score after misplay loaded bases.*			•	•	•

Superstar Immunity

As Exhibit 17.2 shows, no superstar has ever been fitted with permanent goat horns. The two concepts are diametrically opposed, and superstar status tends to erase any blemish that might result from a serious misplay. A few diamond legends have been guilty of errors that might have condemned lesser players. Examples of superstar "escaped goats" include Mariano Rivera, whose wild throw and blown save led to a Yankee loss in the final inning of the 2001 World Series, and Honus Wagner, who was guilty of a then-record six errors in the 1903 Series. However, Rivera's dominance as a closer and his prior record-setting World Series performances overshadowed his 2001 meltdown, and Wagner's status as the premier player of his day and the greatest shortstop of all time is hardly diminished by his poor showing in the 1903 Series.

Late-Inning Prerequisite

Fans and the media make allowances for errors that occur early in games, apparently assuming that teams will have several opportunities to recover in later innings. This allowance for early inning misplays has helped several potential scapegoats to escape lasting infamy. Max

Flack's error let in the two decisive runs of the final 1918 World Series game in the third inning; Eric Byrnes and Miguel Tejada each cost the Oakland A's a much-needed run in the sixth inning of the game that could have won the American League Divisional Series; and the Browns' Vern Stephens loosed the wild throw that contributed to all the Cardinal scoring in the fourth inning of the final 1944 World Series game between the two St. Louis teams. Of the unlucky thirteen scapegoats listed in Figure 17.2, only Heinie Zimmerman earned his horns in an inning earlier than the seventh. But Zimmerman's pursuit of Eddie Collins looked like a mental blunder to the fans in the stands and the hometown press, and it didn't help his case that his team's hometown press was located in New York City.

East Coast Press

The fact that they played for teams outside the East Coast media centers has softened the press treatment of several players who might otherwise be prominent scapegoats. In 1940, Dick Bartell of Detroit actually did what Johnny Pesky of Boston was unfairly accused of doing six years later: he held the ball while the opposing team sent a key run across the plate in Game Seven of the World Series. The Detroit press was much kinder to Bartell than the Boston press would be to Pesky. They laid the blame for Bartell's hesitation on the crowd noise and made the losing Tiger pitcher Bobo Newsom the focus of the story, lauding him as the Series hero for holding the Cincinnati Reds to 4 runs in pitching three complete games and winning two games out of those three. The *Detroit News* had also treated Boss Schmidt kindly when his passed ball cost the Tigers a win in the first game of the 1907 Series, devoting their headlines to a spectacular catch by Germany Schaefer that preserved a tie in the twelfth inning ("The Most Precious Play Ever Made," according to *News* reporter M. W. Bingay). Tiger immortal Al Kaline was also spared scapegoat treatment when his errant throw from right field allowed the Oakland A's to score the winning run in the eleventh inning of the first game of the 1972 ALCS. To be fair, Kaline had already achieved superstar status in the Motor City, and his home run in the top of the eleventh off reliever Rollie Fingers had given the Tigers a temporary 2–1 lead.

Other newspapers in other cities have treated hometown players much more kindly than the Boston press treated Pesky and Buckner or the New York press treated Merkle, Snodgrass, Zimmerman, Branca, and Mickey Owen. The grounder that Tony Fernandez botched in the eleventh inning of Game Seven against the Marlins in 1997 contributed heavily to the Indians' loss but not to the universal vilification of Fernandez, who had driven in Cleveland's only two runs of the game. Baseball historian Mike Sowell speculated in *One Pitch Away* that Buckner might not be the poster boy for blown chances if he'd botched a World Series grounder for some team other than the Red Sox.

Another contributing factor to the Buckner legend is the fact that his error was the last play of the game, so that the image of him walking off the field, clutching his empty glove, as the Mets celebrate, persists in memory and ESPN reruns. Still, the Series wasn't over. Game Seven had yet to be played. And other players have made the same lonely walk after Series-ending misplays without being branded for life. Pittsburgh pitchers John Miljus and Bob Moose both lost key post-season games when their wild pitches allowed Series-winning runs to score — Miljus in the 1927 World Series and Moose in the 1972 NLCS — but neither player was pilloried either by the Pirate fans or the Pittsburgh press.

Of the thirteen scapegoats listed in Exhibit 17.2, only two, Ernie Lombardi and Donnie Moore, played for teams outside the sphere of influence of the East Coast press. And the lumbering Lombardi, by apparently "snoozing" while DiMaggio scored, seemed to be showing a lack of hustle, a transgression that trumps all considerations of geography.

Turning Victory into Defeat

All but one of the scapegoats listed in Exhibit 17.2 botched a play in the late innings of a crucial game, and most of their misplays turned the outcome of the game around. Thus, if Fred Merkle touches second, the Giants beat the Cubs in 1908; if Branca gets Thomson out, the Dodgers win the 1951 pennant; if Moore gets Henderson out, the Angels win the 1986 ALCS; if Owen holds onto the Henrich third strike, the Dodgers win the game. The scapegoats' misplays didn't just lead to a loss, they snatched defeat from the jaws of victory.

Bill Buckner's error in the 1986 World Series is an apparent exception to this observation. By the time Mookie Wilson's grounder went through the Red Sox first baseman's aching legs, the Mets had already scored two runs to tie the game in the tenth inning. Even if Buckner had caught the ball and gotten Wilson at first, the Red Sox wouldn't necessarily have won the game. The Mets might still have prevailed in a later inning. Since New York came to bat in the tenth inning two runs down, however, the Red Sox as a team failed to hold the lead and Buckner, as the man whose muff let in the game-winning run, in effect took one for the team — or at least for Calvin Schiraldi and Bob Stanley, the pitchers who gave up the first two runs of the inning.

Two pitchers, Mitch Williams and Dennis Eckersley, have given up come-from-behind home runs to lose World Series games. Williams' pitch to Joe Carter ended the 1993 Series and earned the pitcher death threats as well as goat horns. Eckersley's back-door slider to a gimpy Kirk Gibson ended Game One of the 1988 Series, and has lived on in baseball lore because of the drama of the situation, but Eckersley's superstar status and Hall of Fame election have erased any traces of goat horns. Eleven other pitchers have given up home runs to end World Series games, but their home runs came with the score tied and have not tarnished the reputation of the hurlers, whose identities are now generally known only to family members, teammates, and trivia experts. Only Ralph Terry, whose fastball to Bill Mazeroski with the score tied in the ninth cost the Yankees the 1960 Series, was ever seriously measured for goat horns, and Terry subsequently redeemed himself by "retiring" Willie McCovey to close out the Yankees' win over the Giants in the 1962 Series.

Of the scapegoats and "escaped goats" listed in Exhibits 17.2 and 17.3, the combination of a lost late-inning lead by an East Coast team has failed to produce a scapegoat only once. Mariano Rivera's superstar status and past Series success kept him from wearing permanent goat horns when his ninth-inning error and blown save cost the Yankees the 2001 World Championship.

Mental Errors

In branding scapegoats, mental errors can trump almost all other circumstances. Teammates, fans, and even the press may forgive any physical error on the diamond, but a perceived lack of hustle or a mental mistake in a crucial situation can mark a player forever. Merkle's "boner," Pesky's "hesitation," Lombardi's "snooze," and Zimmerman's "chase" all appeared to be mental bloopers. There were mitigating circumstances in each case, but the transgressions were perceived as mental mistakes, and the fans and press were unforgiving.

Epilogue

Injustice, Failure, and Redemption

> It is grand game, a thinking man's game, and a thinking woman's game as well. It is a game which surely does not mean half of the things we take it to mean. Then again, it probably means so much more.
>
> Peter C. Bjarkman
> Quoted in *Diamonds Forever*
> Edited by W.P. Kinsella

◆ ◆ ◆ ◆

The difference between scapegoats and escaped goats can be a matter of geography, timing, and/or just plain bad luck. Many of the scapegoats dotting baseball history were largely innocent of the misplays that earned them their horns. Pesky didn't hesitate, Lombardi didn't snooze, Zimmerman had no one covering home plate to take a throw, and Merkle was just following the custom of the day. Some players, like Fred Snodgrass and Bill Buckner, were saddled with blame that should logically have been shared with several other teammates. Baseball is a team game, and it is rarely that a player manages to lose a game, let alone a World Series, all by himself. There is an e in *team*.

Baseball and Life

The ease and apparent injustice with which diamond reputations can be made or broken was brought home to me at an early age. Organized Little League baseball hadn't quite reached my hometown of Huntington, West Virginia, when I was growing up. Instead, we had a summer "midget" league presided over by the coach of the Huntington High School baseball team, Doug Greenlee. Boys between the ages of nine and twelve would show up on the first day of summer vacation and choose up sides for an eight-team league. Greenlee would work out a schedule, arrange for umpires, and sit well up in the stands behind home plate with a brown bullhorn dispensing observations, advice, and intermittent commentary. I remember once standing on third base, preening after hitting a bases-clearing triple, only to hear Greenlee's megaphone-amplified voice boom out, "Billheimer, if you don't learn to start running as soon as you hit the ball, you'll never play for me in high school. You're slow enough without standing at home plate admiring your handiwork."

I worked my way up through Greenlee's summer league from a nine-year-old who got one at-bat the whole season (I walked and was immediately replaced by a pinchrunner) to a twelve-year-old who was co-captain of the first-place team. The biggest event of the summer-league season was an all-star game played after all regularly scheduled games had been decided. I'd never played in the all-star game, but had high hopes that I'd be chosen to participate in my final year after leading my team to a first-place finish.

Greenlee selected two teams of all-stars on the basis of a tryout session presided over by himself and local high school and American Legion players. The year I was twelve, his helpers at the try-outs were Ronald and Donald Dunkle, identical twins who were outstanding American Legion athletes.

While Greenlee pitched batting practice to half the tryout group, the Dunkle twins took the other half to the outfield, where we took turns shagging flies. As a slow-footed first baseman, I remember feeling at the time that fly-chasing was an unfair test of my fielding abilities, but I took my place in line with about twenty other all-star hopefuls. When I'd advanced to the front of the line, the twin hitting fungoes — I never knew whether it was Ronald or Donald — shanked the ball so that it carried in a short arc well out of reach to my right. I hustled after the spinning ball, aware that I couldn't possibly catch up with it on the fly, but hoping that I could cut it off and make a good throw back to the twins. I caught up with the ball on the first hop, but the shanked hit bounced crazily, clanked off my glove, and fell to the ground. As I retrieved the ball and managed a weak, embarrassed throw back in, I saw the batter, Ronald (or Donald) shake his head and say to his twin Donald (or Ronald), "ball shy."

"Ball shy." The injustice of these dread words stung my ears as I ran back to take my place at the end of the tryout line. The Dunkle twin, whoever he was, hadn't been able to hit a decent fly ball, and he had the nerve to call me "ball shy." At twelve, I was a fairly good judge of my own capabilities and knew that I might be slow of foot and weak of arm, but I wasn't ball shy. My nose had been broken twice and the fingers of both my hands were splayed in different directions because I didn't have the good sense to get out of the way of balls that took tricky hops on their way toward me.

I honestly don't remember the rest of the tryout. I probably performed creditably when it came time to bat, although I may have put too much pressure on myself trying to overcompensate for the unfair assessment of my fielding skills. In any event, I didn't make the all-star team. It was my last year of eligibility, and the injustice of the "ball shy" judgment stuck with me for many years, through my career as a high school first baseman and college softball player.

It took me quite a while to put the perceived injustice done to me by the Dunkle twins into perspective. Enlightenment finally came when I graduated from college with an engineering degree and won a scholarship for graduate studies at the Massachusetts Institute of Technology. In order to attend MIT, I would need a student deferment from my draft board. I understood that these weren't difficult to obtain — it was the early sixties and the nation wasn't yet mired in Viet Nam — but I would have to return to West Virginia and show up in person at my draft board to get it.

My draft board visit took me to rural Wayne, West Virginia, the county seat of Wayne County. The clerk there was a thin, serious woman with the prominent cheekbones and drawn features common in Dorothea Lange photographs who questioned me in great detail about the utility of an advanced degree in electrical engineering. She understood the need to go to graduate school to become a doctor or a lawyer, and had given several deferments for this purpose, but mine was the first request for an engineering deferment she had encountered. After some discussion, I managed to convince her that my quest for an advanced degree was legitimate and not some ruse to avoid serving my country.

She agreed to provide the deferment, but only after lecturing me at some length about my patriotic duty to join the armed forces. The centerpiece of the lecture was a yellowed newspaper clipping thumbtacked to her office bulletin board. The clipping showed two young

Inset shows PFCs Ronald and Donald Dunkle against a background of the Huntington, West Virginia, crowd sending the local Marine Reserve unit off to Camp Pendleton in the summer of 1950 (Courtesy Paul Fulks).

Marines in fatigues shipping out from Huntington to Camp Pendleton. As the picture and caption made clear, the two recruits were identical twins—the Dunkle twins. "Those two boys didn't have to go off to war," the clerk said. "They weren't drafted. They enlisted. Just signed up and off they went to Korea." She paused to let the lesson sink in. "And only one came back." Only nineteen at the time, PFC Donald Dunkle had been killed at the Chosin Reservoir just three weeks after the twins arrived in Korea.

I did the math in my head. The Dunkle twins had shipped out for Korea within three months of proclaiming me "ball shy" and unfit for all-star service. In the light of their sacrifice, my grudge, which I'd nursed for over ten years, seemed particularly petty. Balls and strikes, wins and losses, botched plays and blown calls will always be dwarfed by the life-and-death issues outside the ballpark.

From the look on my face, the draft board clerk evidently assumed her message had hit home. "So," she said, 'I'll see you back here when your deferment runs out. By then maybe you'll be ready to serve your country."

I thanked her and told her I'd be back. But I never went back. I never needed to. By being lucky enough to be born on a date that made me too young for Korea and too old for Viet Nam, I was spared the need to make the sacrifice that the Dunkle twins made in Korea and that thousands of West Virginians would make later in Viet Nam. On a per-capita basis, West Virginia suffered more fatalities than any other state in that later conflict. The Battle of Waterloo may have been won on the playing fields of Eton, but the battles of Viet Nam were fought by men fresh from the dusty diamonds of Appalachia.

Failure and Redemption

Baseball is a team game that focuses for brief, telling moments on individual performance. The batter with two out and a runner on third, the pitcher with the bases loaded, the outfielder chasing after a long fly with runners on the move, all have their moment in the spotlight. And with that moment comes the possibility of failure. It's the price that makes success worthwhile, and it is collected with persistent regularity. Babe Ruth struck out 1,330 times. Cy Young lost 316 games. And Fred Merkle, by all reports one of the smartest players of his day, lived with the nickname "bonehead" for nearly fifty years.

To love baseball is to learn to live with failure. The best hitters fail seven out of ten times. The best teams lose forty percent of their games. Your favorite ball club can go decades without winning a World Series. But baseball also teaches that the box score isn't the only measure of performance. Solid line drives are caught for outs. Broken-bat bloopers fall in to win games. Bad bounces can decide World Series, and the breaks don't always even out. The only sensible response is to pick yourself up, dust yourself off, and show up for the next game, the next season, or the life outside the ballpark. Manny Trillo, a journeyman second baseman who played for six different teams during his seventeen-year career in the majors, captured this feeling when he said, "The best thing about baseball is that you can do something about yesterday tomorrow."

Bibliography

Adomites, Paul. *The World Series: October's Game*. Alexandria, VA: Redefinition, 1990.
Alexander, Charles C. *John McGraw*. New York: Viking, 1988.
Alvarez, Mark. *The Perfect Game*. New York: Barnes & Noble, 1993.
Anderson, David W. *More Than Merkle*. Lincoln, NE: University of Nebraska Press, 2000.
Angell, Roger. *Five Seasons*. New York: Simon & Schuster, 1977.
_____. *Game Time*. Orlando, FL: Harcourt, 2003.
_____. *Late Innings*. New York: Simon & Schuster, 1982.
_____. *Once More Around the Park*. New York: Ballantine, 1991.
_____. *Season Ticket*. Boston: Houghton Mifflin, 1988.
Astor, Gerald, Ed. *The Baseball Hall of Fame 50th Anniversary Book*. New York: Prentice-Hall, 1988.
Bak, Richard. *Cobb Would Have Caught It*. Detroit, MI: Wayne State University Press, 1991.
Barra, Allen. *Clearing the Bases: The Greatest Baseball Debates of the Last Century*. New York: Thomas Dunne Books, 2002.
Bartell, Richard, and Norman L. Macht. *Rowdy Richard*. Berkeley, CA: North Atlantic Books, 1987.
Baseball Prospectus, The. *Baseball Between the Numbers*. New York: Basic Books, 2006.
Bell, Christopher. *Scapegoats: Baseballers Whose Careers Are Marked by One Fateful Play*. Jefferson, NC: McFarland, 2002.
Blake, Mike. *Baseball Chronicles: An Oral History of Baseball Through the Decades*. Cincinnati, OH: Betterway Books, 1994.
Boston, Talmage. *1939: Baseball's Tipping Point*. Albany, TX: Bright Sky Press, 2005.
Boswell, Thomas. *Cracking the Show*. New York: Doubleday, 1994.
_____. *Game Day*. New York: Doubleday, 1990.
_____. *The Heart of the Order*. New York: Doubleday, 1989.
_____. *How Life Imitates the World Series*. New York: Doubleday, 1982.
_____. *Why Time Begins on Opening Day*. New York: Doubleday, 1984.
Boudreau, Lou, with Russell Schneider. *Lou Boudreau: Covering All the Bases*. Champagne, IL: Sagamore Publishing, 1993.
Bouton, Jim, with Neil Offen. *I Managed Good, But Boy Did They Play Bad*. Chicago: Playboy Press, 1973.
Buckley, James, Jr., and Phil Pepe. *Unhittable*. Chicago: Triumph Books, 2004.
Carmichael, John P. *My Greatest Day in Baseball*. New York: A. S. Barnes, 1945.
Carter, Craig, Ed. *The Series: An Illustrated History of Baseball's Postseason Showcase*. St. Louis, MO: Sporting News, 1988.
Cohen, Richard M., David S. Neft, and Jordan A. Deutsch. *The World Series*. New York: Dial Press, 1979.
Colbert, David, Ed. *Baseball: the National Pastime in Art and Literature*. New York: Time-Life Books, 2001.
Conner, Floyd. *Baseball's Most Wanted*. Dulles, VA: Brassey's, 2000.
_____. *Baseball's Most Wanted II*. Dulles, VA: Brassey's, 2003.
Connor, Anthony J. *Voices from Cooperstown: Baseball's Hall of Famers Tell It Like It Was*. New York: Collier Books, 1984.
Costello, James, and Michael Santa Maria. *In the Shadows of the Diamond*. Dubuque, IA: Elysian Fields Press, 1992.

Creamer, Robert W. *Baseball in 1941*. New York: Viking, 1991.
Daley, Arthur. "Downfall of the Mighty," *New York Times*, October 7, 1966.
DeValeria, Dennis, and Jeanne Burke DeValeria. *Honus Wagner: A Biography*. New York: Henry Holt, 1995.
Devaney, John, and Burt Goldblatt. *The World Series: A Complete Pictorial History*. Chicago: Rand McNally, 1972.
Dewan, John. *The Fielding Bible*. Skokie, IL: ACTA Sports, 2006.
Dewey, Donald, and Nicholas Acocella. *The New Biographical History of Baseball*. Chicago: Triumph Books, 2002.
Dickson, Paul. *The Dickson Baseball Dictionary*. New York: Facts on File, 1989.
Dugan, Ken. *How to Organize and Coach Winning Baseball*. West Nyack, NY: Parker, 1971.
Durant, John. *Highlights of the World Series*. New York: Hastings House, 1963.
Dykes, Jimmie, and Charles O. Dexter. *You Can't Steal First Base*. Philadelphia: Lippincott, 1967.
Emmons, Mark. "Seeing 'Schnozz' in a New Light," *San Jose Mercury News*, September 23, 2002.
Enders, Eric. *100 Years of the World Series*. New York" Barnes & Noble, 2003.
Erskine, Carl. *Carl Erskine's Tales from the Dodger Dugout*. New York: Sports Publishing, 2000.
Evers, Johnnie. *Baseball in the Big Leagues*. Chicago: Reilly & Britton, 1910.
Falkner, David. *Nine Sides of the Diamond*. New York: Simon & Schuster, 1990.
Felber, Bill. *The Book on the Book*. New York: Thomas Dunne Books, 2005.
Fleming, G. H. *The Unforgettable Season*. New York: Holt, Rinehart and Winston, 1981.
Frick, Ford C. *Games, Asterisks, and People: Memoirs of a Lucky Fan*. New York: Crown, 1973.
Fulks, Paul N., and Willard F. Daniels, Jr. *The Gate to Westmoreland*. Parsons, WV: McLain Printing, 2004.
Gallen, David, Ed. *The Baseball Chronicles*. New York: Carroll & Graf, 1991.
Gammons, Peter. "Game 6," *Sports Illustrated* 66, No. 14, April 6, 1987.
Gerlach, Larry. *The Men in Blue*. Lincoln, NE: University of Nebraska Press, 1980.
Golenbock, Peter. *Bums: An Oral History of the Brooklyn Dodgers*. New York: Putnam, 1984.
Gould, Stephen Jay. *Triumph and Tragedy in Mudville*. New York: Norton, 2003.
Graham, Frank, Jr. *Great No-Hit Games of the Major Leagues*. New York: Random House, 1968.
Gray, Scott. *The Mind of Bill James*. New York: Doubleday, 2006.
Gutman, Dan. *Baseball's Biggest Bloopers*. New York: Viking, 1993.
_____. *The Way Baseball Works*. New York: Simon & Schuster, 1996.
Halberstam, David. *The Teammates: A Portrait of a Friendship*. New York: Hyperion, 2003.
Hano, Arnold. *A Day in the Bleachers*. Binghamton, NY: Crowell, 1955.
Higgins, George V. *The Progress of the Seasons*. New York: Henry Holt, 1989.
Hodges, Russ, and Al Hirshberg. *My Giants*. Garden City, NY: Doubleday, 1963.
Holtzman, Jerome. *No Cheering in the Press Box*. New York: Holt, Reinhart and Winston, 1974.
Holway, John. "The Myth of Pesky's Throw," in *The Ol' Ball Game*. Harrisburg, PA: Stackpole Press, 1990.
Honig, Donald. *Baseball America*. New York: Macmillan, 1985.
_____. *Baseball Between the Lines*. New York: Coward, McCann, and Geoghegan, 1976.
_____. *Baseball When the Grass Was Real*. New York: Coward, McCann, and Geoghegan, 1975.
_____. *The Man in the Dugout*. Chicago: Follett, 1977.
_____. *October Heroes*. New York: Simon & Schuster, 1979.
_____. *The World Series: An Illustrated History from 1903 to the Present*. New York: Crown, 1986.
Hoppel, Joe, Ed. *Baseball from the Archives of the Sporting News*. St. Louis, MO: The Sporting News, 2001.
James, Bill. *The Bill James Guide to Baseball Managers*. New York: Scribner's, 1997.
_____. *The Bill James Handbook 2005*. Chicago: ACTA Sports, 2004.
_____. *The Bill James Historical Baseball Abstract*. New York: Villard Books, 1986.
_____. *The New Bill James Historical Baseball Abstract*. New York: Free Press, 2001.
_____. *The Politics of Glory*. New York: Macmillan, 1994.
_____. *This Time Let's Not Eat the Bones*. New York: Villard Books, 1989.
_____, and Rob Neyer. *The Neyer/James Guide to Pitchers*. New York: Simon & Schuster, 2004.
Judge, Mark Gauvreau. *Damn Senators*. San Francisco: Encounter Books, 2003.
Kahn, Roger. *The Boys of Summer*. New York: Harper & Row, 1972.

Kerrane, Kevin. *Dollar Sign on the Muscle.* New York: Beaufort, 1984.
_____. *The Hurlers.* Alexandria, VA: Redefinition, 1989.
_____, and Richard Grossinger. *Baseball, I Gave You All the Best Years of My Life.* Oakland, CA: North Atlantic Books, 1977.
Kinsella, W. P., Ed. *Diamonds Forever: Reflections from the Field, the Dugout, & the Bleachers.* New York: Harper Collins, 1997.
Koppett, Leonard. *The Man in the Dugout.* New York: Crown, 1993.
_____. *The Thinking Man's Guide to Baseball.* New York: Dutton, 1967.
Kuenster, John. *From Cobb to "Catfish."* Chicago: Rand McNally, 1975.
_____. *Heartbreakers: Baseball's Most Agonizing Defeats.* Chicago: Ivan R. Dee, 2001.
LaBlanc, Michael L., Ed. *Baseball: Professional Sports Team Histories,* Vol. 1. Detroit, MI: Gale Research, 1994.
Lardner, John. *It Beats Working.* New York: Lippincott, 1947.
_____. *Strong Cigars and Lovely Women.* New York: Funk & Wagnall's, 1951.
Leventhal, Josh. *The World Series: An Illustrated Encyclopedia of the Fall Classic.* New York: Black Dog & Leventhal, 2001.
Lieb, Frederick G. *Baseball As I Have Known It.* New York: Coward, McCann, and Geoghegan, 1977.
_____. *The Story of the World Series.* New York: Van Rees Press, 1949.
Littlefield, Bill, and Richard A. Johnson. *Fall Classics: The Best Writing About the World Series' First 100 Years.* New York: Crown, 2003.
Livingstone, Seth. "Denkinger Empathizes with Eddings' Plight." *USA Today Sports Weekly,* October 19–25, 2005.
Mathewson, Christy. *Pitching in a Pinch.* New York: Putnam, 1912.
McCarver, Tim, with Danny Peary. *Tim McCarver's Baseball for Brain Surgeons and Other Fans.* New York: Villard Books, 1998.
_____, with Ray Robinson. *Oh, Baby, I Love It.* New York: Villard Books, 1987.
McGraw, John. *My Thirty Years in Baseball.* New York: Boni and Liveright, 1923.
Mead, William B. *Even the Browns.* Chicago: Contemporary Books, 1978.
Murray, Jim. *The Best of Jim Murray.* Garden City, NY: Doubleday, 1965.
_____. "Willie D. Played Center Just Like It Owned Him." *Los Angeles Times,* October 7, 1966.
Nash, Bruce, and Allan Zullo. *The Baseball Hall of Shame.* New York: Pocket Books, 1985.
_____.*The Baseball Hall of Shame 2.* New York: Pocket Books, 1986.
_____. *The Baseball Hall of Shame 3.* New York: Pocket Books, 1987.
National Baseball Hall of Fame and Museum. *Baseball As America.* Washington, DC: National Geographic, 2002.
Neyer, Rob. "It Ain't Cheatin' If You Don't Get Caught." ESPN.com, February 13, 2001.
Ol' Ball Game, The: A Collection of Baseball Characters & Moments Worth Remembering. Harrisburg, PA: Stackpole Press, 1990.
Pietrusza, David, Matthew Silverman, and Michael Gershman, Eds. *Baseball: The Biographical Encyclopedia.* New York: Sports Illustrated, 2000.
Plaschke, Bill. "Umpire Is Charged with the Error." *Los Angeles Times,* October 13, 2005.
Pluto, Terry. *The Curse of Rocky Colavito.* New York: Simon & Schuster, 1994.
_____. *Our Tribe: A Baseball Memoir.* New York: Simon & Schuster, 1999.
Povich, Shirley. "West Scores Historic 1st." *Washington Post,* October 8, 1972.
Prager, Joshua Harris. "For Bill Buckner, It's Life's Small Joys That Offer a Reprieve—Missed Ball Fouled a Career, but Open Spaces of Idaho Assuage a Boston Massacre." *Wall Street Journal,* July 24, 1998.
_____. "Giants' 1951 Comeback Wasn't All It Seemed." *Wall Street Journal,* January 31, 2001.
Reach Official American League Base Ball Guide for 1909. Philadelphia: A. J. Reach, 1909.
Reichler, Joseph, Ed. *The World Series: A 75th Anniversary.* New York: Simon & Schuster, 1978.
_____, and Jack Clary. *Baseball's Great Moments.* New York: Routledge, 1989.
Reidenbaugh, Lowell. *The Sporting News Selects Baseball's 50 Greatest Games.* St. Louis, MO: Sporting News, 1986.
_____. *The Sporting News Selects Baseball's 25 Greatest Pennant Races.* St. Louis, MO: Sporting News, 1987.

Reisler, Jim. *Before They Were the Bombers: The New York Yankees' Early Years, 1903–1915*. Jefferson, NC: McFarland, 2002.
Ritter, Lawrence S. *The Glory of Their Times*. New York: Macmillan, 1966.
_____, and Donald Honig. *The Image of Their Greatness*. New York: Crown, 1979.
Robbins, Mike. *Ninety Feet from Fame*. New York: Carroll & Graf, 2004.
Robertson, John G. *Baseball's Greatest Controversies*. Jefferson, NC: McFarland, 1995.
Robinson, Ray. *Greatest World Series Thrillers*. New York: Random House, 1965.
_____. *The Home Run Heard 'Round the World*. New York: Harper Collins, 1991.
Scheinin, Richard. *Field of Screams*. New York: Norton, 1994.
Schiffer, Don, Ed. *World Series Encyclopedia*. New York: Thomas Nelson & Sons, 1961.
Schoor, Gene. *The History of the World Series*. New York: Morrow, 1990.
Schwartz, Alan. *The Numbers Game*. New York: Thomas Dunne Books, 2004.
Seaver, Tom, with Marty Appel. *Great Moments in Baseball*. New York: Birch Lane Press, 1992.
Seib, Philip. *The Player, Christy Mathewson, Baseball, and the American Century*. New York: Four Walls Eight Windows, 2003.
Shlain, Bruce. *Baseball Inside Out*. New York: Viking, 1992.
Shaughnessy, Dan. *The Curse of the Bambino*. New York: Dutton, 1990.
_____. *One Strike Away*. New York: Beaufort, 1987.
Smelser, Marshall. *The Life That Ruth Built*. New York: Quadrangle, 1975.
Smith, Curt, Ed. *What Baseball Means to Me*. New York: Warner, 2002.
Smith, Red. *Red Smith on Baseball*. Chicago: Ivan R. Dee, 2000.
Smith, Ron, Ed. *The Sporting News Chronicle of Baseball*. New York: BDD Books, 1993.
Snyder, John. *The World Series' Most Wanted*. Dulles, VA: Brassey's, 2004.
Sowell, Mike. *One Pitch Away*. New York: Macmillan, 1995.
Spink, J. G. Taylor. *Judge Landis and 25 Years of Baseball*. New York: Thomas Y. Crowell, 1947.
Stern, Bill. *Bill Stern's Favorite Baseball Stories*. Garden City, NY: Doubleday, 1949.
Stout, Glenn. "A 'Curse' Born of Hate." *Boston Baseball*, September, 2004.
_____, and Richard A. Johnson. *The Red Sox Century*. Boston: Houghton Mifflin, 2000.
Sugar, Bert Randolph. *Baseball's 50 Greatest Games*. New York: Exeter Books, 1986.
Sullivan, Dean A., Ed. *Early Innings: A Documentary History of Baseball, 1825–1908*. Lincoln, NE: University of Nebraska Press, 1995.
_____, Ed. *Middle Innings: A Documentary History of Baseball, 1900–1948*. Lincoln, NE: University of Nebraska Press, 1998.
Thomson, Bobby, with Lee Heiman and Bill Gutman. *The Giants Win the Pennant, the Giants Win the Pennant*. New York: Zebra Books, 1991.
Thorn, John, Ed. *The Armchair Book of Baseball II*. New York: Scribner's, 1987.
_____. *Baseball's 10 Greatest Games*. New York: Four Winds Press, 1981.
_____, Ed. *The National Pastime*. New York: Bell Publishing, 1988.
_____, Phil Birnbaum, and Bill Deane. *Total Baseball, the Ultimate Baseball Encyclopedia*, 8th ed. Wilmington, DE: Sport Media Publishing, 2004.
Torrez, Andrew. *Off Base: New Insights into an Old Game*. San Francisco: Woodford Press, 1999.
Torry, Jack. *Endless Summers: The Fall and Rise of the Cleveland Indians*. South Bend, IN: Diamond Communications, 1996.
Turner, Frederick. *When the Boys Came Back: Baseball and 1946*. New York: Henry Holt, 1996.
Tyglet, Jules. *Past Time: Baseball As History*. New York: Oxford, 2000.
Verducci, Tom. "Desert Classic." *Sports Illustrated* 95, No. 19, November 12, 2001.
Vizquel, Omar. *Omar! My Life On and Off the Field*. Cleveland, OH: Gray & Company, 2002.
Waggoner, Glen, Kathleen Moloney, and Hugh Howard. *Baseball by the Rules*. Dallas, TX: Taylor Publishing, 1987.
Wallace, Joseph, Ed. *The Baseball Anthology: 125 Years*. New York: Harry N. Abrams, 1994.
Wallace, Joseph. *World Series: 100 Years, an Opinionated Chronicle*. New York: Harry N. Abrams, 2003.
Ward, Geoffrey C., and Ken Burns. *Baseball: An Illustrated History*. New York: Knopf, 1994.
White, Paul. "Charmed Life Finds Way to South Side." *USA Today Sports Weekly*, October 19–25, 2005.
Wilbert, Warren N. *The Greatest World Series Games*. Jefferson, NC: McFarland, 2005.

Wiles, Tim. "The Joy of Foul Balls," in *The National Pastime*. Cleveland, OH: Society for American Baseball Research, 2005.
Will, George F. *Bunts*. New York: Scribner's, 1998.
_____. *Men at Work*. New York: Macmillan, 1990.
_____. "A Season Spoiled." *Jewish World Review*, February 8, 2001.
Williams, Ted, with John Underwood. *My Turn at Bat*. New York: Simon & Schuster, 1969.

Videos

100 Years of the World Series, Major League Baseball, 2003.
Nine Innings from Ground Zero, HBO Sports, 2004.
Reverse of the Curse of the Bambino, HBO Sports, 2004.

Index

Numbers in ***bold italics*** indicate pages with photographs.

Adler, Richard 178
Alexander, Grover Cleveland 6, 33, 34, 43, 44, 45, 133, 151, 196
Alomar, Sandy, Jr. 66
Alou, Felipe 87
Alou, Matty 87, 167
Alou, Moises 171, 172, 173, 174, 177
Alston, Walter 49, 152, 160, 161, 165
Andersen, Larry 79
Anderson, Alf 119
Anderson, Dave 91
Anderson, Sparky 135, 184
Andrews, Mike 65, 68, 69, 195
Andujar, Joaquin 180
Angell, Roger 45, 47, 48, 55, 59, 69, 96, 135, 163
Armas, Tony 81
Arroyo, Bronson 182
Averill, Earl 111
Avila, Bobby 94, ***95***

Backman, Wally 115
Baker, Dusty 173, 174
Baker, Frank 18, 19, 104, 110, 112, ***113***, 142, 143
Balboni, Steve 54, 55
Ball Fans and Other Primates 169
Bando, Sal 45, 108
Barber, Red 171
Barrett, Marty 59, 153, 154
Barrow, Ed 33
Bartell, Dick 1, 14–16, ***17***, 18, 20, 195, 198
Bartman, Steve ***172***, 173–175, 177, 194
Baseball Chronicles 11, 89
Baseball Dictionary 94
Baseball Digest 94
Baseball Hall of Shame 28, 33, 34
Baseball in 1941 121
Baseball Magazine 102
Baseball Tonight 178
Baseball Weekly 182
Baseball's 50 Greatest Games 72
Baseball's Greatest Controversies 182

Baseball's Ten Greatest Games 144
Bauer, Hank 48
Baylor, Don 81, 82, 161
Beane, Billy 31
Beck, Jason 118
Bell, Jay 117
Bell, Lester 44
Belle, Albert 66
Bench, Johnny 100, 128, 135
Bender, Chief 144
Bentley, Jack 52
Benton, Rube 101, 102
Berman, Reuben 170
Berra, Yogi 55, ***56***, 57, 86, 166, 174, 195
Bevens, Bill 123, 165–167
Big Cabin, Oklahoma 85
Big Red Machine 45, 134
The Bill James Historical Baseball Abstract 8, 17, 22, 65, 102, 136, 147, 189
Billheimer, John 200
Billheimer, Wayne 189
Bingay, M.W. 198
Biographical Encyclopedia of Baseball 63, 96, 132
Bishop, Max 125, 126
Bjarkman, Peter C. 200
Black Sox 103
Blair, Paul 47
Blagojevich, Rod 173
Blake, Mike 11, 89
Blanchard, John 86
Boggs, Wade 59
Boley, Joe 46
Boleyn, Anne 171
Bonilla, Bobby 67, 177
The Book on the Book 156
Boone, Aaron 156, 168
Boone, Bob 56, ***57***, 81–83
Boston Daily Globe 11
Boston Globe 8, 9, 15, 18, 19, 42, 43, 59, 83, 113, 130
Boston Herald 157
Boston Sunday Globe 58
Boswell, Thomas 59, 69, 70, 71, 78, 79, 84, 90–92, 116, 164
Bottomley, Jim 44, 125, 126

Boudreau, Lou ***185***, ***186***
Bouton, Jim 89
Bowa, Larry 164
Boys of Summer 73
The Boys of Summer 76, 160
Braggs, Glen 116
Branca, Ralph 3, 5, 7, 8, 9, 71–74, ***75***, 76, 77, 85, 86, 97–100, 118, 122, 154, 159–161, 194, 198, 199
Brecheen, Harry 18, 106
Brenly, Bob 96, 97
Brennan, Walter 59
Bridwell, Al 23, 28
Brock, Lou 34, ***35***, 36, 152, 189, 195
Broeg, Bob 152
Brooklyn Eagle 75
Brosius, Scott 97
Brown, Mordecai 21, 26
Bruce, L.E. 29
Buckner, Bill 1, 3, 6, 7, 8, ***9***, 10, 21, 49, 58–60, ***61***, 62, 65, 66, 67, 68, 70, 71, 81, 83, 90, 98, 114, 115, 138, 153, 154, 157, 161, 162–164, 188, 194, 196, 198, 199, 200
Budig, Gene 177
Bums 99, 160
Bunning, Jim 162
Burkhart, Ken 182, 183, 184, 188
Bush, Donnie 133
Bush, Joe 20, 58, 112, ***113***, 195
Bush, John T. 131
Byrnes, Eric 1, 29, ***30***, 31, 32, 36, 37, 38, 195, 198

Cabrera, Miguel 173
Camp Pendleton 202
Campanella, Roy 73, 160
Campaneris, Campy 45
Campbell, Bruce 15
Cannon, Jimmy 94
Canseco, Jose 91, 115, 116
Carbo, Bernie 182, 183, 184, 188
Cardinal, Jose 56
Carey, Max 63, 64, 158
Carlton, Steve 56
Carter, Gary 60, 115
Carter, Joe 3, 8, 79, 80, 92, 98, 99, 138, 199

211

Index

Casey, Hugh 7, 119–123, 126, 166
Casey, the Mighty 5
Castillo, Luis 171, 173, 174, 177
Cepeda, Orlando 87, 167
Chambliss, Chris 100
Chance, Frank 22, 24–28, 123, 124
Chase, Hal 101, 103, 145, 146
Chavez, Eric 29, 31, 32
Chesbro, Jack 129, 130, 131, 132, 134
Chicago Sun Times 174
Chicago Tribune 22, 25, 102, 124, 147
Chinese home run 94
Chosin Reservoir 202
Christman, Mark 114
Cimoli, Gino 85
Cincinnati Enquirer 25, 135, 141, 147
Clark, Jack **54**, 55, 57, 126, 164, 165, 167, 178, **179**, 180, 189, 195
Clemens, Roger 59, 71, 96, 114, 117
Clemente, Roberto 86, 135, 136, 161
Cline, Ty 182, 183
Coates, Jim 86
Cobb, Ty 125, 142
Cobb Would Have Caught It 16
Colavito, Rocky 66
Colliers 122
Collins, Eddie 6, 8, 101–104, 109, 125, 198
Combs, Earle 44, 133, 134
Connelly, Joe 19
Cool Hand Luke 148
Coolidge, Calvin **159**
Cooper, Cecil 162
Cooper, Mort 106
Cooper, Walker 106
Corps of Engineers (Huntington, WV) 10
Costas, Bob 60
Coughlin, Bill 124
Counsell, Craig 67
Cox, Billy 73
Crawford, Sam 125
Creamer, Robert W. 121
Crede, Joe 180, 181
Crews, Tim 66
Criger, Lou 130
Cueto, Manuel 146
Culberson, Leon 6, 11–14
Curse of Rocky Colavito 66, 67
Curse of the Bambino 58, 59, 61, 62, 69, 71, 113, 114
The Curse of the Bambino 9, 71
Curtis, Chad 99
Cuyler, Kiki 63, 64, 158
Cy Young Award 86, 92

Daley, Arthur 48, 86, 142, 166
D'Amato, Alphonse 175
Damn Yankees 178, 187
Dark, Alvin 73, 74, 151
Davalillo, Vic 164
Davis, Harry 104, 144
Davis, Jody 69
Davis, Mike 91
Davis, Willie 47, **48**, 49, 151, **152**, 195

Dean, Dizzy 111
DeCinces, Doug 81, 82
defensive misplays 154
Denkinger, Don 54, 55, 57, 126, 178, **179**, 180, 182, 188, 194, 195, 196
Dent, Bucky 59, 100
Derringer, Paul 18
Detroit Free Press 123, 125
Detroit News 15, 16, 198
Dewan, John 154
Diamonds Forever 200
Dickey, Bill 122, 142, 186, 187
DiMaggio, Dominic 11, 12, 13
DiMaggio, Joe 3, 6, 12, 120–122, 126, 140, **141**, 165, 198
Dinneen, Bill 130
Doby, Larry 93, 94
Donlin, Mike 148
Donovan, Wild Bill 123, 124
Douglas, Michael 187
Dowling, Brian 83, 114
Downey, Mike 165
Doyle, Larry 26, 142, 143, 144, 146, 100
Drebinger, John 46, 55, 122
Dressen, Charlie 74–76, 151, 159–161
Duncan, Dave 90, 92
Dunkle, Donald 201, 202
Dunkle, Ronald 201, 202
Durazo, Erubiel 31
Durham, Leon 65, 69, **70**, 71, 195
Durocher, Leo 76, 93, 94, 119–121
Dye, Jermaine 182
Dyer, Eddie 14
Dykstra, Lenny 78, 114, 115

Easter Bunny 79
Ebbets Field 73, 76, 166
Eckersley, Dennis 59, 66, 70, 89, **90**, 91, 92, **93**, 98, 99, 195, 199
Ed Sullivan Show 77
Eddings, Doug 180, 181, 182
Edwards, Hank 166
Effrat, Louis 86
Elberfeld, Kid 129, 132
Empire State Building 88
Emslie, Bob 23
Enders, Eric 17, 87, 134, 144, 180
Engle, Clyde 39, 40, 52
Ennis, Del 171
Epstein, Mike 108
Erskine, Carl 74, 76, 160, 186, 187
Escobar, Kelvim 180, 181, 182
ESPN 23, 141, 157, 198
ESPN SportsCenter 174
Etchebarren, Andy 47, 48
Evans, Bill 103
Evans, Dwight 81, 82, 161
Even the Browns 114
Evers, Johnny 7, 18, **19**, 20, 22, 23, 26, **27**, 28, 112, 113, 123, 124, 149, 193, 195

Fairly, Ron 151, 152
Farnsworth, Kyle 173
Felber, Bill 156
Feller, Bob 93, 185, 186

Felsch, Happy 101, 102
Ferguson, Alex 158
Fernandez, Tony 1, 10, 65, 66, 67, **68**, 71, 195, 198
Ferris, Hobe 130
Fielding Bible 154
$50,000 Muff 50, 52
Fingers, Rollie 198
Finley, Charles O. 69, 108
Finley, Chuck 83
Fischer, Bill 60
Fisk, Carleton 99, 128
Fitzsimmons, Fred 119
Five Seasons 69
Flack, Max 1, 4, 5, **42**, 43, 45, 49, 191, 195, 197
Fletcher, Art 41, 103, 104, 105, 100, 110
Flood, Curt 35, 152
Flowers, Jake 125
Ford, Whitey 3
Ford Frick Award 93
Fosse, Ray 66
Foster, George 135
Foxx, Jimmy 46
Francona, Terry 157
Frazee, Harry 58
Freehan, Bill 34, **35**, 36, 152
Fregosi, Jim 79
Frick, Ford 12, 178, 186
Fulks, Paul 202
Fullerton, Hugh 52
Furillo, Carl 166, 186

Gallico, Paul 134
Gammons, Peter 61, 71, 115, 153, 157
Gandil, Chick 102
Garagiola, Joe, Jr. 98
Garber, Gene 164
Garcia, Rich 175–177, 188, 189
Garciaparra, Nomar 31
Gardner, Larry 40, 52
Garvey, Steve 69, 70
Gedman, Rich 60, 81–83
Gehrig, Lou 7, 33, 34, 132–134
Gehringer, Charles 16
Geronimo, Cesar 135
Giamatti, A. Bartlett 191
Giambi, Jason 38, 156
Giambi, Jeremy 34, 36, **37**, 38, 195
Gibson, Bob 152
Gibson, Kirk 89–93, 98, 99, 195, 199
Gilbert, Larry 112
Gill, Warren 21, 22, 23, 26, 28
Gionfriddo, Al 166, 167
Giuliani, Rudolph 175
Giusti, Dave 135, 136
The Glory of Their Times 9, 39, 53
Glynn, Bill 94
Goetz, Larry 120
Goldsmith, Wallace 19, 41, 53, 113
Golenbock, Peter 99, 160
Gonzalez, Alex 99, 173, 174
Gonzalez, Luis 8, 118
Gonzalez, Mike 13, 14
Gooch, Johnny 133, 134
Good Morning America 175
Goodman, Ival 6, 140, 141

Index

gopher ball 72
Gordon, Joe 120, 122
Goslin, Goose 5, 63
Gossage, Goose 70
Gould, Stephen Jay 62
Gowdy, Hank 19, 50, *51*, 52, 55, 57, 112, 194
Grace, Mark 97, 117
Gradgrind 69
Grasso, Mickey 94
Greenlee, Doug 200, 201
Grich, Bobby 81
Griffith, Clark 130, 159
Grim, Bob 99
Grissom, Marv 94
Groat, Dick 86
Groh, Heinie 146
Gutman, Bill 74
Gutteridge, Don 106, 114
Guzman, Juan 138
Gwynn, Tony 70

Haas, Mule 46, 47
Hafey, Chick 44, 151
Halberstam, David 13, 14, 15
Hamill, Pete 139
Hampton, Mike 111
Hannahan, Wild Bill 125, 126
Harrellson, Ken 66
Harris, Bucky 50, 51, 157, 158, **159**, 165–167
Harrison, James 63
Hartnett, Gabby 142
Harvey, Doug 36, 189
Hassey, Ron 91
Hatcher, Mickey 91
Hearn, Jim 73
Heartbreakers 85, 86
Hegan, Jim 94
Hegan, Mike 108
Heiman, Lee 74
Helms, Tommy 182
Hemingway, Ernest viii, 123
Henderson, Dave 3, 59, 81–84, 161, 162, 199
Henderson, Rickey 79, 115
Hendricks, Elrod 182, 183, 184
Hendricksen, Olaf 149
Henrich, Tommy 3, 7, 8, 99, 120, *121*, 122, 123, 126, 165, 166, 199
Hernandez, Keith 115
Hernandez, Ramon 31, 36
Herrmann, August 29
Hershiser, Orel 66, 92
Herzog, Buck 103, 104, 105, 110
Herzog, Whitey 54, 55, 165, 179, 180
Higbee, Kirby 166
Higgins, Pinky 14–17
Hiller, Chuck 87
Hodges, Gil 73, 74, 76, 151, 155, 186, **187**
Hodges, Russ 74
Hofman, Solly 23, 28
Holke, Walter 101, 102
Holmes, Tommy 75, 186
Holway, John B. 12, 13, 14, 15
Honig, Donald 39, 51, 53, 120
Hooper, Harry 39, 40, 52
Hornsby, Rogers *33*

Horton, Tony 66
Horton, Willie 34, 35
Houk, Ralph 87, 167
House Un-American Activities Committee 9
Houtteman, Art 93
Howard, Del 26, 124
Howell, Dixie 166
Howell, Jay 99
Hoyt, Waite 44, 58
Hunter, Catfish 108
Huntington, WV 200, 202

I Ain't an Athlete, Lady 78
Iorg, Dane 55, 126, 179
Irvin, Monte 73, 74, 94

Jackson, Shoeless Joe 101, 102
Jackson, Travis 51
James, Bill 7, 17, 22, 28, 40, 65, 102, 103, 136, 139, 154, 155, 160, 165, 189
James, Jesse 180
Jansen, Larry 73
Javier, Julian 34
Jenkins, Bruce 31
Jeter, Derek 36, 37, 99, 117, **118**, 156, 175, 177, 189, 195
Jim Bowie's Letter and Bil Buckner's Letters 62
John, Tommy 162
Johnson, Ban 29, 158, 159, 167
Johnson, Davey 163, 175, 177
Johnson, Randy 96, 98, 117
Johnson, Richard 12
Johnson, Walter 50–52, 63, 64, 157, 158, **159**, 167
Jones, Davy 125
Jones, Doug 80
Jones, Sam 58
Jorgensen, Spider 166
The Joy of Foul Balls 169
Juden, Jeff 80
Judge Landis and 25 Years of Baseball 65
Justice, David 96

Kaese, Harold 15
Kahn, Roger 76, 160
Kaline, Al 107, 108, 109, 196, 198
Keller, Charlie 120, 121, 122, 126, 140
Kendall, Jason 181
Kerry, John 157
Kibler, John 178
Kim, Byung-Hyun 7, 96, *97*, 98, 99, 117, 193, 196
Kinsella, W.P. 200
Kleinow, Red 129–132
Klem, Bill 28, 101, 102, 143, 144, 100
Kling, Johnny 26, 123
Knight, Ray 3, 60, 83, 115, 153, 154
Knoblach, Chuck 97, 109
Koenig, Mark 44, 133, 150, 151
Kopf, Larry 145–147
Koppett, Leonard 48, 49
Korea 202
Koufax, Sandy 47
Kruk, John 78
Kubek, Tony 85

Kuenn, Harvey 66
Kuenster, John 85, 86
Kuhn, Bowie 144
Kurowski, Whitey **106**

Laabs, Chet 114
Labine, Clem 73, 76
Lachance, Candy 130
Lammers, Nick 37
Landis, Kenesaw Mountain 63, 65, 158
Lane, Frank 66
Lange, Dorothea 201
Lanier, Max 106, 114
Lapp, Jack **143**, **144**
Lardner, John 169–171
Lardner, Ring 63, 158
Larkin, Barry 116
La Russa, Tony 90, 92, 116
Lasorda, Tommy 91, 92, 164, 165, 167
Laurel and Hardy 47, 48
Lavagetto, Cookie 123, 166, 167
Lazzeri, Tony 6, 44, 133, 134
Leach, Tommy 25
Lee, Derek 173
Lemon, Bob 93–96, 98, 99, 196
Lenhardt, Rita 142
Leventhal, Josh 17
Lewis, Duffy 40
Liddle, Johnny 93, 94
Lieb, Fred 40, 46, 64, 102, 106, 134, 158
Liebrant, Charlie 99
Life 122
The Life That Ruth Built 34
Lindell, Johnny 165
Lindstrom, Fred 51
Littell, Mark 100
Little, Grady 156, 157, 168, 174
Live with Regis and Kathie Lee 175
Lockman, Whitey 73, 74
Lofton, Kenny 66
Lolich, Mickey 34, 108, 152
Lombardi, Ernie 1, 3, 5, 6, 9, 16, 126, 139, **140**, **141**, 142, 147, 194, 198, 199, 200
Long, Dale 86
Long, Terence 36
Lopes, Davey 164
Lopez, Al 94, 119, 142
Los Angeles Times 47, 48, 83, 87, 88, 89, 108, 165, 182
Lowe, Derek 31
Lucas, Gary 81, 161, 162
Luzinski, Greg 163, 164
Lynch, Thomas J. 144
Lyon, Bill 79

Macha, Ken 31
Macht, Norman L. 16
Mack, Connie 142, 143, 144, 161
Maglie, Sal 73, 93
Maher, Charles 164
Maier, Jeffrey 175, 176, 177, 188, 189
Major League 78
Malden, Karl 187
Mandrake the Magician 151
Mangual, Angel 45

Index

Mann, Les 112
Manning, Rick 89
Mantai, Matt 96, 98
Mantle, Mickey 86, 99
Maranville, Rabbit 19
Marion, Marty 106
Mariott, Jay 174
Maris, Roger 86, 87
Marquard, Rube 104
Marquez, Gonzalo 108
Martin, Jerry 163, 164
Martin, Pepper 125
Martin, Strother 148
Martinez, Carmello 69, 70
Martinez, Pedro 156, 157, 158, 168
Martinez, Tino 36, 96
Masi, Phil **185**, **186**, **187**
Massachusetts Institute of Technology 201
Mathews, Eddie 99
Mathewson, Christy 6, 23, 26, 28, 39, 40, 41, 52, **53**, 54, 55, 57, 104, 145, 147–149, **150**
Matsui, Hideki 157
Mauch, Gene 81, 82, 83, 161, 162
Maxvill, Dal 108
May, Lee 182
Mays, Carl 42, 58
Mays, Willie 49, 72, 75, 87, 93–95, 167
Mazeroski, Bill 85, 86, 88, 89, 92, 98–100, 136, 17, 199
Mazzilli, Lee 114, 115
McCormick, Frank 15, **16**, 17, 18, 20
McCormick, Moose 23, 24
McCovey, Willie 87, 88, 99, 167, 199
McDougald, Gil 111
McDowell, Sam 66
McGinnity, Joe 23, 28
McGraw, John 25, 26, 28, 45, 50, 52, 102–104, 113, 131, 143, 144, 148, 150, 161
McGraw, Tug 56
McGwire, Mark 99, 115, 116
McNamara, John 59, 162, 163
McNeely, Earl 51
McQuinn, George 166
McRae, Hal 135, 136
Mead, William B. 114
Mencke, Dennis 135
Merkle, Fred 1, 3, 8, 18, 21, 23, 24, **25**, 26–29, 32, 38, 39, 40, 41, 52, **53**, 54, 55, 57, 61, 62, 67, 68, 71, 102, 122, 134, 143, 144, 146, 148–150, 154, 188–191, 194, 196, 198, 199, 200
Mesa, Jose 67
Meusel, Bob 6, 7, 33, 34, 43, **44**, 45, 133, 150, 151, 196
Meyers, Billy 16, 140
Meyers, Chief 40, 41, 52, **53**, 54, 55, 57, 150, 196
Miami Herald 67
Miksis, Eddie 166
Miljus, John 132, 133, 134, 138, 196
Miller, Bing 46
Miller, Damian 117
Miller, Robby 10

Miracle of Coogan's Bluff 75
Mitchell, Kevin 60, 80, 153
Mize, John 171, 186
Molitor, Paul 79
Monday Morning Quarterback 155
Moore, Donnie 3, 8, 10, 62, 81, **82**, 83, 84, 99, 114, 118, 161, 162, 194, 198
Moore, Eddie 63, 64
Moore, Jimmy 125
Moore, Wilcey 133
Moose, Bob 134–136, 138, 196, 198, 199
Moran, Herbie 112
Moran, Pat 124
Morgan, Mike 97
Morris, Hal 116
Mota, Manny 164
Mueller, Bill 31, 32, 49
Mueller, Don 74, 76, 151
Murderers' Row 132
Murnane, Tim 131
Murphy, Charles W. 22
Murphy, Danny 104, 143, 144
Murphy, Eddie 18, 19, 112
Murphy, Johnny 122
Murray, Jim 47, 48, 87
Murray, Red 39, 149
Musial, Stan 13, 106
My Greatest Day in Baseball 26
My Turn at Bat 14
The Myth of Pesky's Throw 14

Nagy, Charles 66
Nallin, Richard 125
Nash, Bruce 33
Nasium, Jim (Edgar Forrest Wolfe) 18
Nason, Jerry 11
National Baseball Commission (members, 1909) 29
The National Pastime 169
The Natural 92
Neale, Greasy 145
Nehf, Art 46, 47
Neidenfuer, Tom 164, 165
Nelson, Rocky 86
Nen, Rob 67
The New Bill James Historical Baseball Abstract 28, 40
New York American 25
New York Daily News 75, 134, 175
New York Evening Mail 28
New York Globe 23
New York Herald 23
New York Herald Tribune 11
New York Post 122
New York Sun 130
New York Times 4, 6, 7, 8, 17, 21, 25, 33, 40, 42, 43, 44, 46, 48, 49, 52, 54, 55, 63, 98, 104, 112, 113, 121–123, 125, 130, 133, 134, 136, 142, 166, 171, 186, 188
New Yorker 55, 96
Newcombe, Don 73, 74, 76, 99, 100, 151
Newhouser, Hal 16
Newman, Paul 148
Newsom, Bobo 15, 198
Newsweek 170

Nixon, Trot 32
Northrup, Jim 152

October Heroes 53
O'Day, Hank 22–25, 28, 124, **188**, 189
Odom, Blue Moon 108
O'Farrell, Bob 33, 44
The Ol' Ball Game 12, 13
O'Leary's Cow 173
Olin, Steve 66
O'Malley, Walter 159, 160
Omar! 67
$100,000 slip 152
100 Years of the World Series 17, 87, 134, 144, 180
100 Years of the World Series (DVD) 80
One Pitch Away 3, 71, 83, 115, 153, 198
O'Neill, Paul 96, 116
Orosco, Jesse 163
Orta, Jorge 54, 179, 180, 188
Orth, Al 146
Overall, Orval 124
Owen, Mickey 1, 3, 7, 8, 61, 62, 119, 120, 121, 122, 123, 125, 126, 134, 188, 194, 198, 199
Ozark, Danny 163, 164
Ozuna, Pablo 180

Pafko, Andy 73
Page, Joe 167
Palermo, Steve 31
Palmer, Jim 47, 182, 183
Parent, Freddy 130
Partee, Ray 12, **13**
Passarella, Art 186, 187, 188
passed balls: definition 119; from 1903 to the present 126; per game, season vs. series 127
Pataki, George 175
Paul, Josh 180, 181, 182
Pavano, Carl 174
Pearce, Donn 148
Peckinpaugh, Roger 5, 7, 8, 62, 63, **64**, 65, 66, 104, 158, 194
Pendleton Terry 165
Pennock, Herb 58, 132
Perez, Tony 135
Pesky, Johnny 1, 3, 6, 8, 11–15, 17, 18, 21, 58, 71, 194, 198, 199, 200
Pfiester, Jack 23, 26
Philadelphia Inquirer 18, 79, 125, 171
Pierre, Juan 171, 173, 174
Pierson, Frank R. 148
Pierzynski, A.J. 180, 181, 182
Pinter, Dave 84
Pitching in a Pinch 26, 149
Pittsburg Post 22, 23
Pittsburgh Press 134, 135
Plank, Eddie 143
Plaschke, Bill 182
Pluto, Terry 66
Polo Grounds **24**, 72, 73, 76, 94
Pope, Dave 94, **95**
Port, Mike 83
Porter, Darrell 55, 126, 179, 189, 196

Index

Posada, Jorge 36, *37*, 96, 97, 156
Posednick, Scott 182
Potter, Nelson 113, 114, 196
Povich, Shirley 108, 165
Powell, Boog 47, 152
Prior, Mark 171, 173, 174
Puckett, Kirby 99
Pulliam, Harry Clay 23, 25, 28, *29*
Purdy, Mark 31

Quik, Jamie 116

Ramirez, Manny 31, 32, 66
Randolph, Willie 116
Rariden, Bill 6, 101, 102
The Red Sox Century 12
Redford, Robert 92
Reese, Pee Wee 73, 119, 139, 160
Reichler, Joseph L. 14, 47
Reidenbaugh, Lowell 72
Reiser, Pistol Pete 120, 165–167
Remlinger, Mike 99
Renteria, Edgar 67
Reynolds, Allie 55, 57
Rhodes, Dusty 93, 94, 95, 98, 99, 196
Rice, Grantland viii
Rice, Jim 81, 82, 115, 161
Richardson, Bobby 86, 87, 88, 167
Rickey, Branch 160, 161, 166
Rio, Jose 116
Ripple, Jimmy 15, 17
Ritter, Lawrence 9, 39, 41, 53
Rivera, Mariano 8, 98, 111, 117, 118, 196, 197, 199
Robertson, Dave 101
Robertson, John G. 182
Robinson, Brooks 182, 184
Robinson, Frank 151, 152
Robinson, Jackie 5, 73, 74, 75, 151, 160, 161, 166, 186
Robinson, Ray 77
Rodriguez, Aurelio 108, 109
Rodriguez, Ivan 173
Rolfe, Red 120
Root, Charlie 46
Rose, Pete 56, *57*, 103, 135
Rosen, Al 93, 94
Ross, Jerry 178
Ruel, Muddy 51, 52
Russell, Bill 164
Russo, Marius 119
Ruth, Babe 7, *33*, 34, 35, 42, 44, 58, 60, 66, 111, 113, 132–134, 196, 203

Saberhagen, Bret 55, 180
Sain, Johnny 185, 186, 187, 188
St. Louis Post Dispatch 15, 45, 180
St. Nicholas 79
Salem Witch Trials 9
Salsinger, H.G. 15, 16
Sambito, Ron 115
San Francisco Chronicle 31
Sanchez, Luis 162
Sandberg, Ryne 70
Sanders, Ray *106*
Sanford, Jack 87
Sanguillen, Manny 135, 136
Santa Claus 79

Sax, Steve 92, 109
Schaefer, Germany 198
Schang, Wally 19
Schilling, Curt 78, 96, 117
Schiraldi, Calvin 59, 60, 114, 115, 196, 199
Schmidt, Boss 1, 123, 124, 125, 196, 190
Schulte, Frank 124
Schultz, Barney 99
Scioscia, Mike 164, 180, 182
Score, Herb 111
Scott, Everett 58
Scully, Vin 91, 154
Seattle Times 174
Seaver, Tom 61
Seelbach, Chuck 108
Sewell, Luke 114
Seymour, Cy 26, 149, 150
Shantz, Bobby 85
Shaughnessy, Dan 9, 59, 71
Sheckard, Jimmy 26
Sheen, Charlie 61, 78
Shibe Park boo birds 9
Short, Chris 162
Shot Heard 'Round the World 72, 76, 77, 151, 161
Shotton, Burt 166
Simmons, Al 46
Simmons, Lon 92
Sisler, Dick 100
Six Months Out of Every Year 178
Slagle, Jimmy 22, 124
Slaughter, Enos 3, 6, 11, 12, *13*, 14, 15, 17, 18, 20, 58
Smelser, Marshall 34
Smith, Hal 86
Smith, Red 11, 75, 166
Snider, Duke 73, 74, 160, 186
Snodgrass, Fred 1, 3, *4*, 5–10, 21, 39, 40, *41*, 42, 43, 45, 47–49, 52–54, 57, 61, 62, 68, 102, 104, 122, 134, 143, 149, 150, 152–154, 164, 191, 193, 194, 196, 198, 199, 200
Soriano, Alfonso 36, 97, 117
Sowell, Mike 3, 62, 71, 83, 154, 198
Speaker, Tris 6, 7, 8, 39, 40, 41, 42, 49, 52, 54, 150
Spencer, Shane 36, 37, 96, 97
Spink, J.G. Taylor 65
Sport Magazine 19
The Sporting Life 169
Sporting News 84
Sports Illustrated 61, 115
Stahl, Jake 41, 149, 150
Stallings, George 19
Stanky, Eddie 166
Stanley, Bob 60, 115, 138, 153, 154
Stapleton, Dave 59, 66, 162, 163
Stark, Jayson 79
Steinfeldt, Harry 123, 124
Stengel, Casey 86
Stephens, Vern 105, 106, 107, 109, 113
Stewart, Bill *185*, *186*
Stewart, Dave 115, 116, 197
Stockton, J. Roy 15
The Story of the World Series 46, 64, 106, 134
Stout, Glen 12

The Streets of San Francisco 187
Sukeforth, Clyde 74, 76, 159–161
Sullivan, Billy 15, *16*
The Summer Game 47
Sutcliffe, Rick 69

Tales from the Dodger Dugout 187
Tarasco, Tony 175, 176, 177, 189
Taylor, John I. 131
Taylor, Zack 47
Teammates 14
Tebbetts, Birdie 155
Tejada, Miguel 29, 31, 32, 36, 37, 38, 197, 198
Tenace, Gene 45, 108, 109
Tenney, Fred 23, 25, 148
Terry, Ralph 5, 85, 86, 87, *88*, 89, 99, 100, 167, 197, 199
Thayer, Ernest L. 5
Thevenow, Tommy 44, 151
$30,000 Muff 39, 41, 42, 43, 48, 52, 152, 191
Thompson, Hank 94
Thomson, Bobby 3, 5, 9, 71, 72, 73, 74, *75*, 76, 77, 85, 86, 92, 99, 100, 122, 159–161, 199
Thorn, John 144
Thorpe, Jim 145–147
Three Stooges 29, 31
Tinker, Joe 22, 23, 27, 124, 148–150
Tolan, Bobby 45, 49
Toney, Fred 145–147
Toronto Sun 79
Torre, Joe 81, 117, 175, 177
Torrez, Mike 100
Traynor, Pie 63
Tresh, Tom 87
Trillo, Manny 203
Troggs 78
Tyler, Lefty 42, 43

Ueberroth, Peter 180
Updike, John 50

Vander Meer, Johnny 139, 139
Van Slyke, Andy 164, 165
Varitek, Jason *30*, 31, 32
Vaughn, Jim 144–147
Vecsey, George 59
Verban, Emil 106, 114
Verlander, Justin 118
Vidmer, Richards 134
Viet Nam 201, 202
Virdon, Bill 85, 135
Vizquel, Omar 66, 67

Wagner, Honus 5, 7, 63, 65, *66*, 134, 197
Wahl, Kermit 170
walk-off home runs 98, 99
walk-off piece 92
Walker, Dixie 120
Walker, Harry 11, 12, 13
Walker, Rube 74
Wall Street Journal 76
Wallace, Joseph 122
Walters, Bucky 6, 111, 140
Washburn, Jarrod 182
Washington Post 59, 63, 69, 70, 78,

79, 84, 90, 91, 94, 104, 108, 116, 158, 164, 165
Wayne County, WV 201
Weaver, Jeff 99
Weeghman, Charles 169
Weeghman Park 144
Wertz, Vic 93, 94
What Baseball Means to Me 50
White, Devon 79
White, Frank 56
White, Paul 182
Whiteman, George 42, 43
Whitson, Ed 69
Wiggins, Alan 70
wild pitches 129, 136
Wild Thing 78, 79
Wiles, Tim 169
Williams, Bernie 156, 175
Williams, Charlie 78
Williams, Cy 145–147
Williams, Davey 94
Williams, Dick 69, 108, 151
Williams, Jimmy 130
Williams, Mitch 3, 5, 8, 78, 79, **80**, 98, 99, 118, 138, 194, 199
Williams, Ted 14, 55, 56, 107, 195
Wilson, Art 144, 145, 146, 147, 197
Wilson, Chief 21
Wilson, Hack 45, **46**, 47, 197
Wilson, Jimmie 125, 126
Wilson, Jimmy 16, 197
Wilson, Mookie 3, 60, 61, 138, ***153***, 162, 163, 199
Wilson, Willie 56
Winningham, Herm 116
Witness Protection Program 171, 173
Witt, Mike 81, 161, 162
Wolfe, Edgar Forrest (Jim Nasium) 18
Womack, Tony 117
Wood, Smoky Joe 39, 40, 52
World Series: (1903) 5, 65; (1907) 123; (1911) 104, 105, 142; (1912) 3, 4, 5, 6, 52, 61, 191; (1914) 7, 19, 50, 112, 193; (1917) 6, 8, 101, 102; (1918) 4, 5, 113, 191; (1922) 34, 113; (1923) 113; (1924) 50; (1925) 7, 8, 63, 158; (1926) 6, 7, 33, 43; (1929) 46; (1931) 125; (1939) 3, 140; (1940) 14, 15, 17, 18; (1941) 3, 119; (1944) 106, 113, 198; (1946) 3, 11, 12, 15, 18; (1947) 61, 123, 165; (1948) 185; (1952) 186; (1954) 93; (1960) 5, 61, 85, 89, 199; (1964) 34; (1966) 47, 151; (1967) 34; (1968) 34, 152; (1970) 182; (1972) 45; (1973) 69; (1975) 61, 128; (1980) 56; (1985) 54, 188; (1986) 3, 59, 61, 114, 153, 178, 199; (1988) 89; (1989) 117; (1990) 115, 116; (1993) 3, 5, 8, 78; (1995) 66; (1997) 66; (2001) 7, 8, 96, 111, 117, 193; (2004) 49
The World Series 14
World Series Encyclopedia 12
The World Series, an Illustrated Encyclopedia of the Fall Classic 17
World Series: 100 Years, an Opinionated Chronicle 122
The World Series, a 75th Anniversary 47
World Trade Center 117
Worrell, Todd 54, 179
Wright, Jaret 67
Wynn, Early 93

Yerkes, Steve 40, 52
York, Rudy 18
Young, Cy 130, 203
Young, Dick 166
Yvars, Sal 76

Zachary, Tom 158
Zimmerman, Heinie 5, 6, 8, 101, 102, ***103***, 109, 194, 198, 199, 200
Zullo, Allan 33
Zumaya, Joel 118

www.ingramcontent.com/pod-product-compliance
Lightning Source LLC
Chambersburg PA
CBHW081159230426
43666CB00016B/2861